EARTH'S MIGHTIEST

THE AVENGERS

THE FINAL HOST

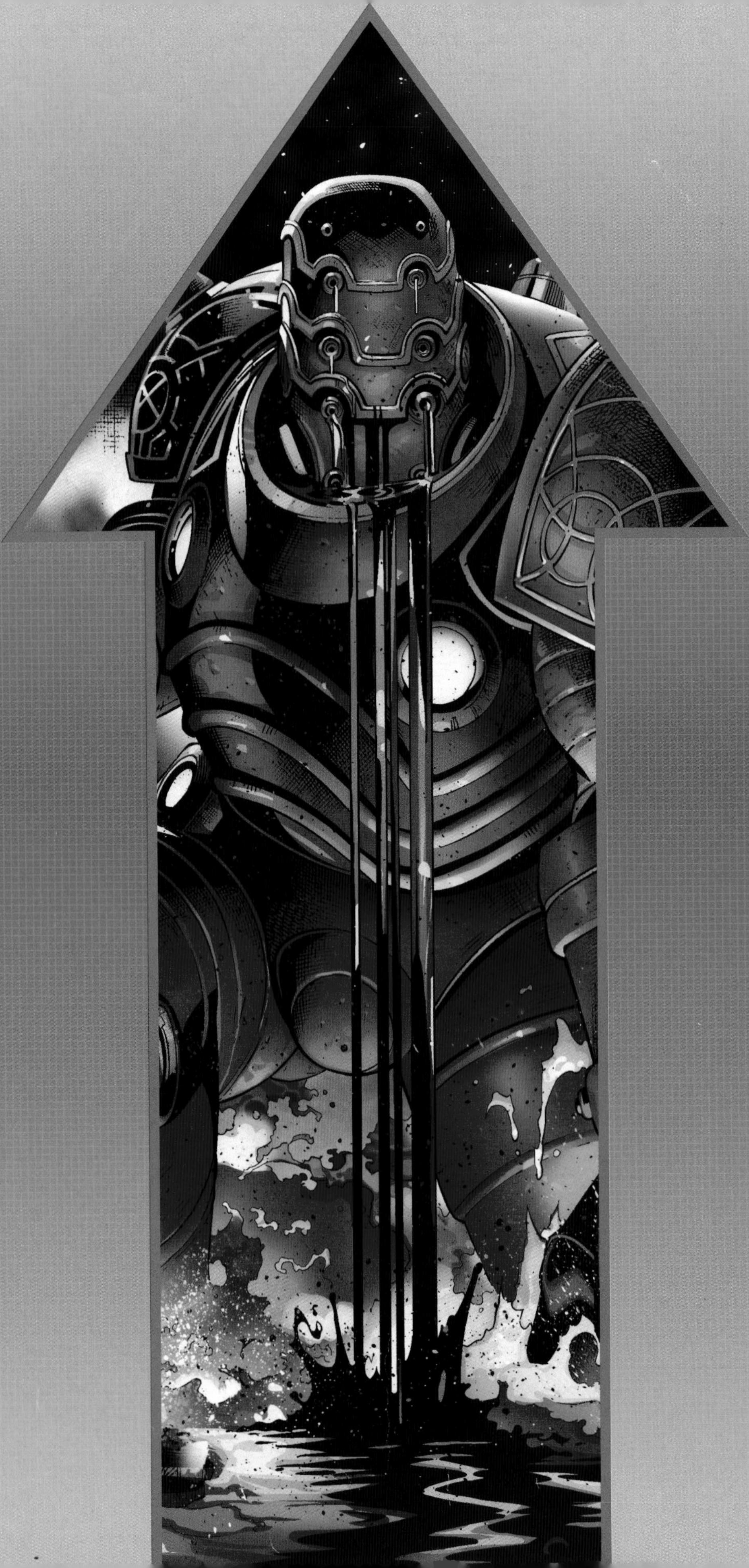

EARTH'S MIGHTIEST HEROES

THE AVENGERS

THE FINAL HOST

JASON AARON
WRITER

FREE COMIC BOOK DAY 2018 (AVENGERS/CAPTAIN AMERICA)

SARA PICHELLI
PENCILER

SARA PICHELLI WITH **ELISABETTA D'AMICO**
INKERS

JUSTIN PONSOR
COLOR ARTIST

SARA PICHELLI & **JUSTIN PONSOR**
COVER ART

AVENGERS #1-6

ED McGUINNESS [#1-6] & **PACO MEDINA** [#3-6]
PENCILERS

MARK MORALES [#1-6] & **JUAN VLASCO** [#3-6] WITH
JAY LEISTEN [#2-3] & **KARL STORY** [#5]
INKERS

DAVID CURIEL
COLOR ARTIST

ED McGUINNESS & **MARK MORALES** WITH
JUSTIN PONSOR [#1-3] & **JASON KEITH** [#4-6]
COVER ART

VC's CORY PETIT
LETTERER

ALANNA SMITH
ASSISTANT EDITOR

TOM BREVOORT
EDITOR

AVENGERS BY
STAN LEE & **JACK KIRBY**

COLLECTION EDITOR **JENNIFER GRÜNWALD**
ASSISTANT EDITOR **CAITLIN O'CONNELL**
ASSOCIATE MANAGING EDITOR **KATERI WOODY**
EDITOR, SPECIAL PROJECTS **MARK D. BEAZLEY**
VP PRODUCTION & SPECIAL PROJECTS **JEFF YOUNGQUIST**
SVP PRINT, SALES & MARKETING **DAVID GABRIEL**

BOOK DESIGNER **ADAM DEL RE**

EDITOR IN CHIEF **C.B. CEBULSKI**
CHIEF CREATIVE OFFICER **JOE QUESADA**
PRESIDENT **DAN BUCKLEY**
EXECUTIVE PRODUCER **ALAN FINE**

VENGERS BY JASON AARON VOL. 1: THE FINAL HOST. Contains material originally published in magazine form as AVENGERS #1-6 and FREE COMIC BOOK DAY 2018 (AVENGERS/CAPTAIN AMERICA) #1. First printing 2018. ISBN 978-302-91187-4. Published by MARVEL WORLDWIDE, INC., a subsidiary of MARVEL ENTERTAINMENT, LLC. OFFICE OF PUBLICATION: 135 West 50th Street, New York, NY 10020. **Printed in the U.S.A.** DAN BUCKLEY, esident, Marvel Entertainment; JOHN NEE, Publisher; JOE QUESADA, Chief Creative Officer; TOM BREVOORT, SVP of Publishing; DAVID BOGART, SVP of Business Affairs & Operations, Publishing & Partnership; DAVID GABRIEL, SVP of ales & Marketing, Publishing; JEFF YOUNGQUIST, VP of Production & Special Projects; DAN CARR, Executive Director of Publishing Technology; ALEX MORALES, Director of Publishing Operations; DAN EDINGTON, Managing Editor; SUSAN RESPI, Production Manager; STAN LEE, Chairman Emeritus. For information regarding advertising in Marvel Comics or on Marvel.com, please contact Vit DeBellis, Custom Solutions & Integrated Advertising Manager, at vdebellis@marvel.om. For Marvel subscription inquiries, please call 888-511-5480. **Manufactured between 8/10/2018 and 9/11/2018 by LSC COMMUNICATIONS INC., KENDALLVILLE, IN, USA.**

)987654321

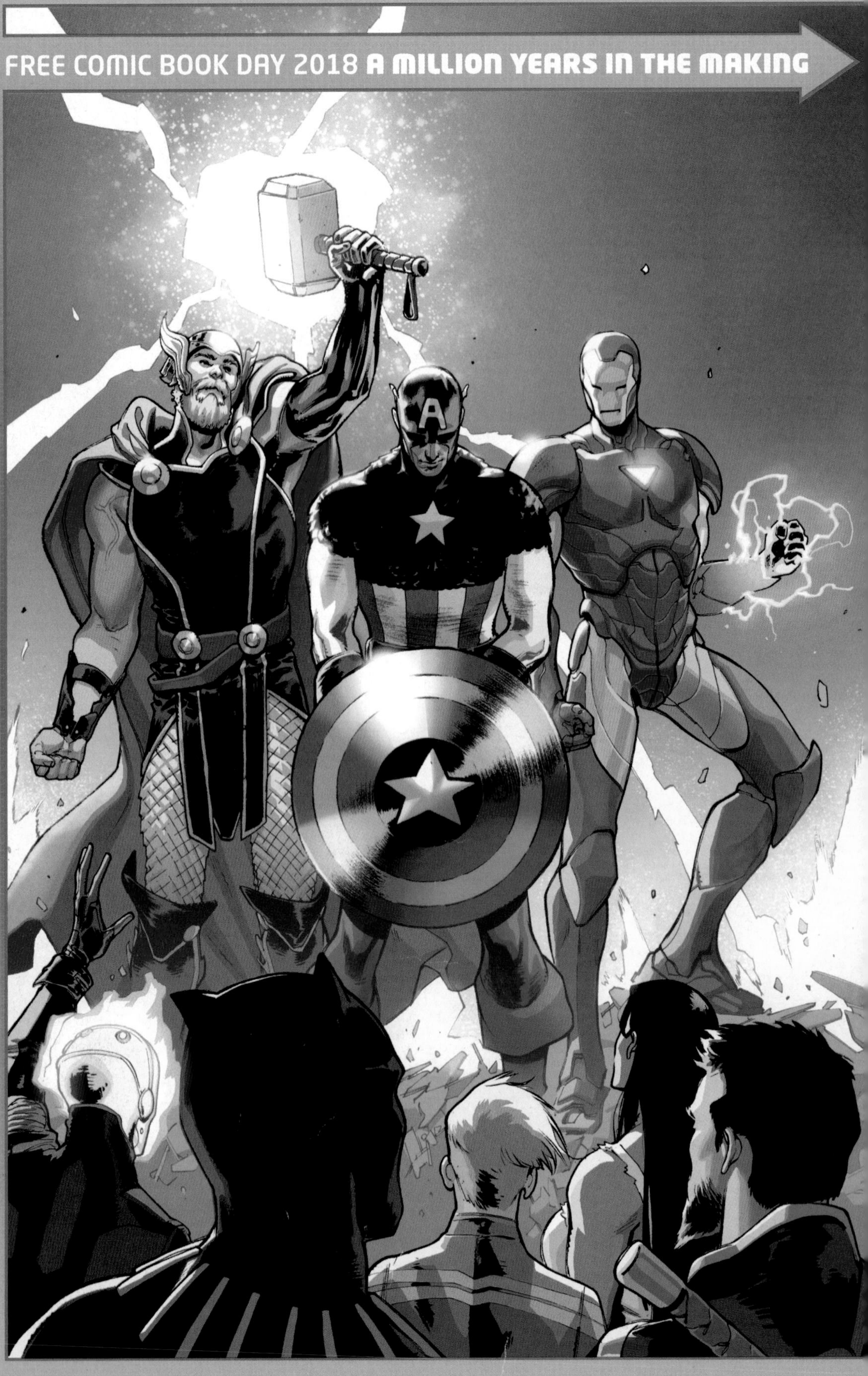
FREE COMIC BOOK DAY 2018 A MILLION YEARS IN THE MAKING

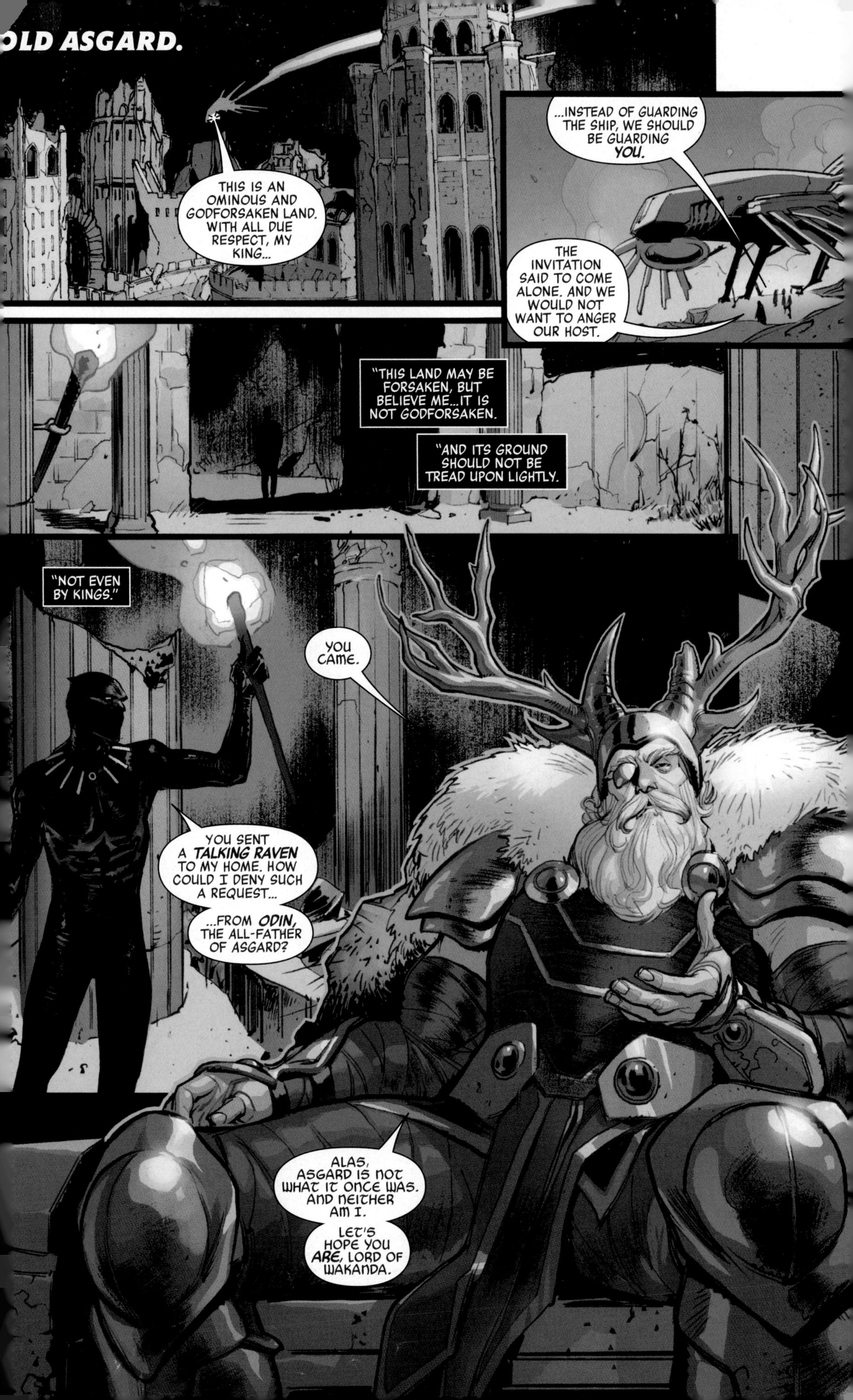
OLD ASGARD.
THIS IS AN OMINOUS AND GODFORSAKEN LAND. WITH ALL DUE RESPECT, MY KING...
...INSTEAD OF GUARDING THE SHIP, WE SHOULD BE GUARDING YOU.
THE INVITATION SAID TO COME ALONE. AND WE WOULD NOT WANT TO ANGER OUR HOST.
"THIS LAND MAY BE FORSAKEN, BUT BELIEVE ME...IT IS NOT GODFORSAKEN.
"AND ITS GROUND SHOULD NOT BE TREAD UPON LIGHTLY.
"NOT EVEN BY KINGS."
YOU CAME.
YOU SENT A TALKING RAVEN TO MY HOME. HOW COULD I DENY SUCH A REQUEST...
...FROM ODIN, THE ALL-FATHER OF ASGARD?
ALAS, ASGARD IS NOT WHAT IT ONCE WAS. AND NEITHER AM I.
LET'S HOPE YOU ARE, LORD OF WAKANDA.

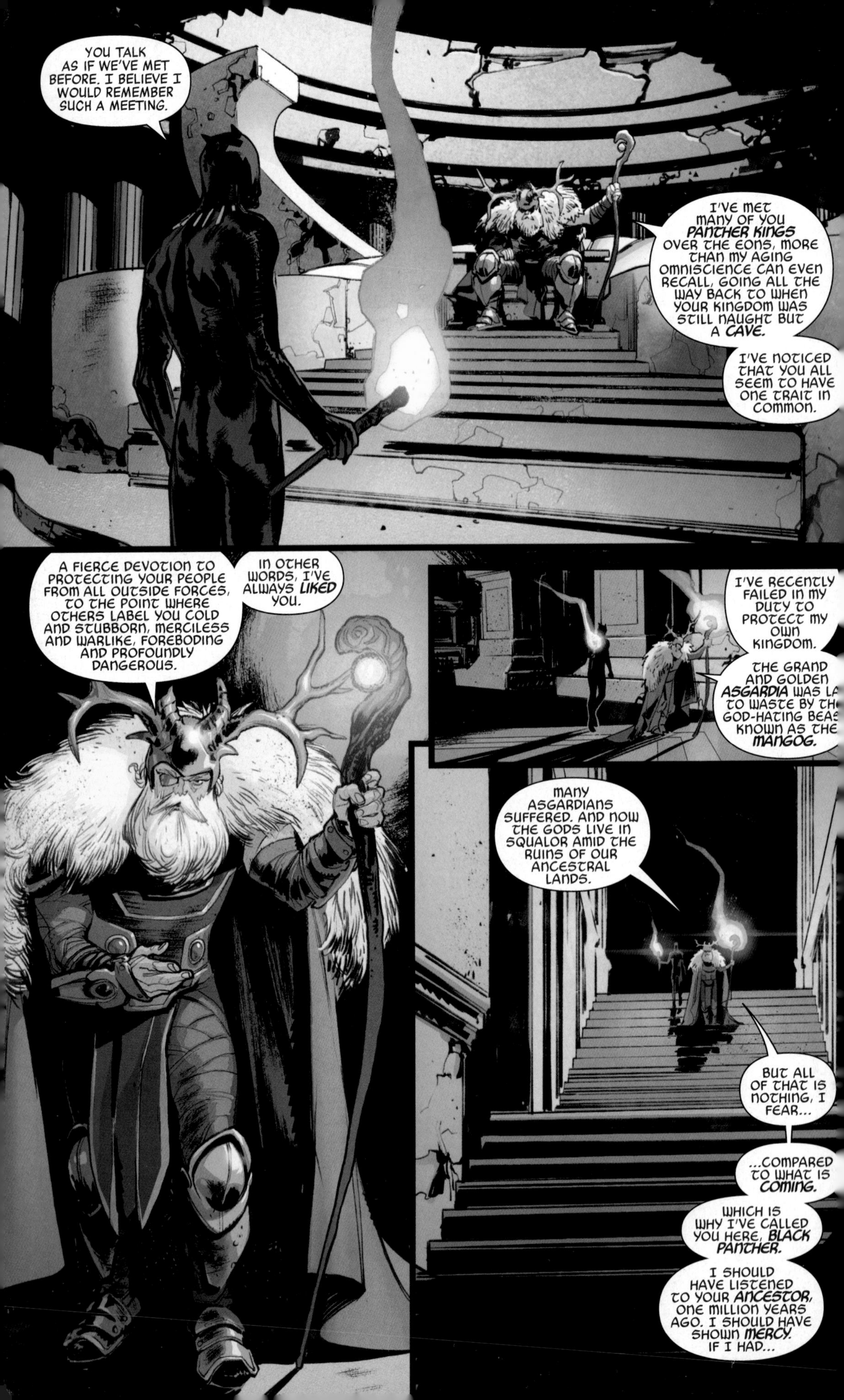
YOU TALK AS IF WE'VE MET BEFORE. I BELIEVE I WOULD REMEMBER SUCH A MEETING.
I'VE MET MANY OF YOU PANTHER KINGS OVER THE EONS, MORE THAN MY AGING OMNISCIENCE CAN EVEN RECALL, GOING ALL THE WAY BACK TO WHEN YOUR KINGDOM WAS STILL NAUGHT BUT A CAVE.
I'VE NOTICED THAT YOU ALL SEEM TO HAVE ONE TRAIT IN COMMON.
A FIERCE DEVOTION TO PROTECTING YOUR PEOPLE FROM ALL OUTSIDE FORCES, TO THE POINT WHERE OTHERS LABEL YOU COLD AND STUBBORN, MERCILESS AND WARLIKE, FOREBODING AND PROFOUNDLY DANGEROUS.
IN OTHER WORDS, I'VE ALWAYS LIKED YOU.
I'VE RECENTLY FAILED IN MY DUTY TO PROTECT MY OWN KINGDOM.
THE GRAND AND GOLDEN ASGARDIA WAS LA TO WASTE BY TH GOD-HATING BEAS KNOWN AS THE MANGOG.
MANY ASGARDIANS SUFFERED. AND NOW THE GODS LIVE IN SQUALOR AMID THE RUINS OF OUR ANCESTRAL LANDS.
BUT ALL OF THAT IS NOTHING, I FEAR...
...COMPARED TO WHAT IS COMING.
WHICH IS WHY I'VE CALLED YOU HERE, BLACK PANTHER.
I SHOULD HAVE LISTENED TO YOUR ANCESTOR, ONE MILLION YEARS AGO. I SHOULD HAVE SHOWN MERCY. IF I HAD...

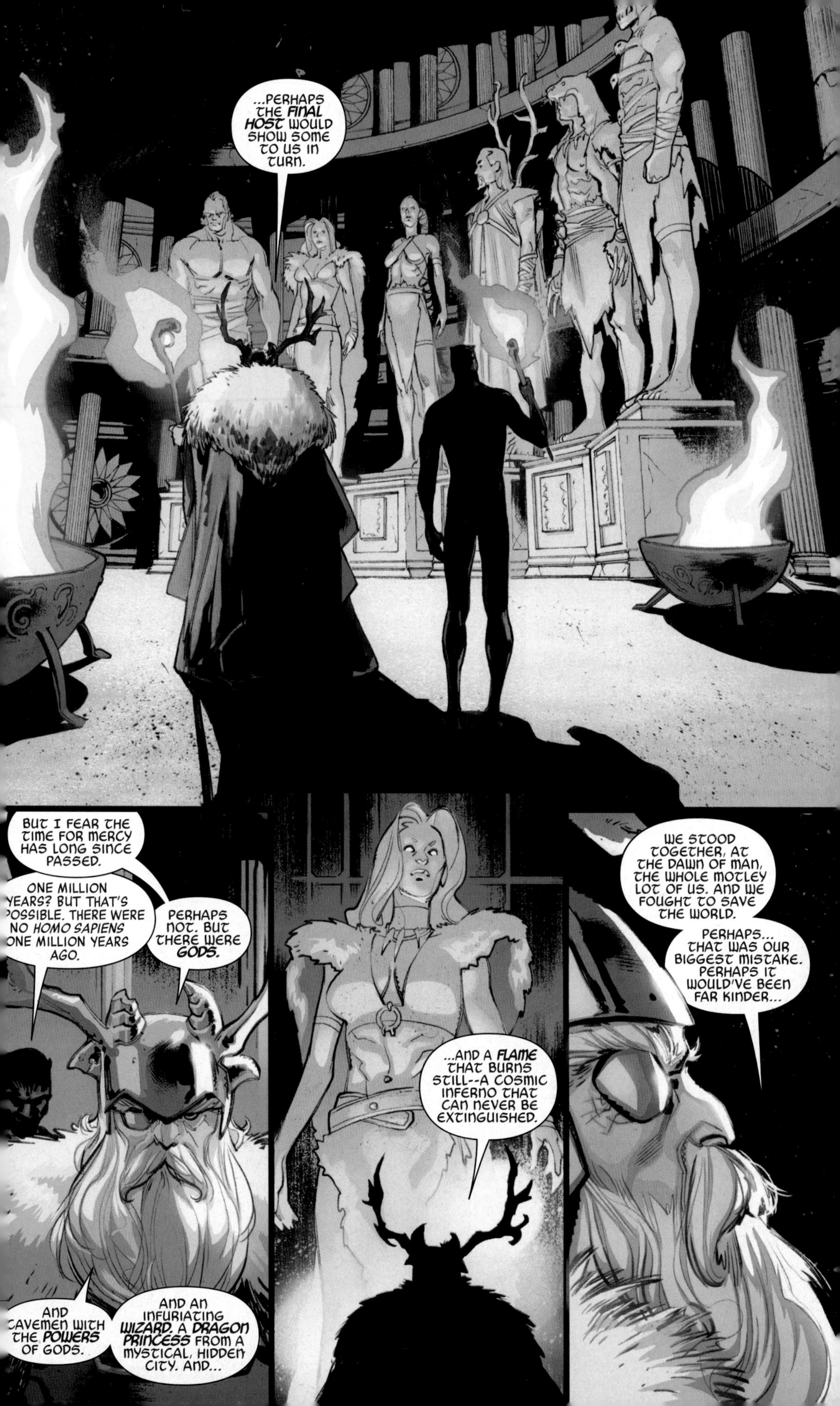
...PERHAPS THE FINAL HOST WOULD SHOW SOME TO US IN TURN.
BUT I FEAR THE TIME FOR MERCY HAS LONG SINCE PASSED.
ONE MILLION YEARS? BUT THAT'S POSSIBLE. THERE WERE NO HOMO SAPIENS ONE MILLION YEARS AGO.
PERHAPS NOT. BUT THERE WERE GODS.
AND CAVEMEN WITH THE POWERS OF GODS.
AND AN INFURIATING WIZARD, A DRAGON PRINCESS FROM A MYSTICAL, HIDDEN CITY. AND...
...AND A FLAME THAT BURNS STILL--A COSMIC INFERNO THAT CAN NEVER BE EXTINGUISHED.
WE STOOD TOGETHER, AT THE DAWN OF MAN, THE WHOLE MOTLEY LOT OF US. AND WE FOUGHT TO SAVE THE WORLD.
PERHAPS... THAT WAS OUR BIGGEST MISTAKE. PERHAPS IT WOULD'VE BEEN FAR KINDER...

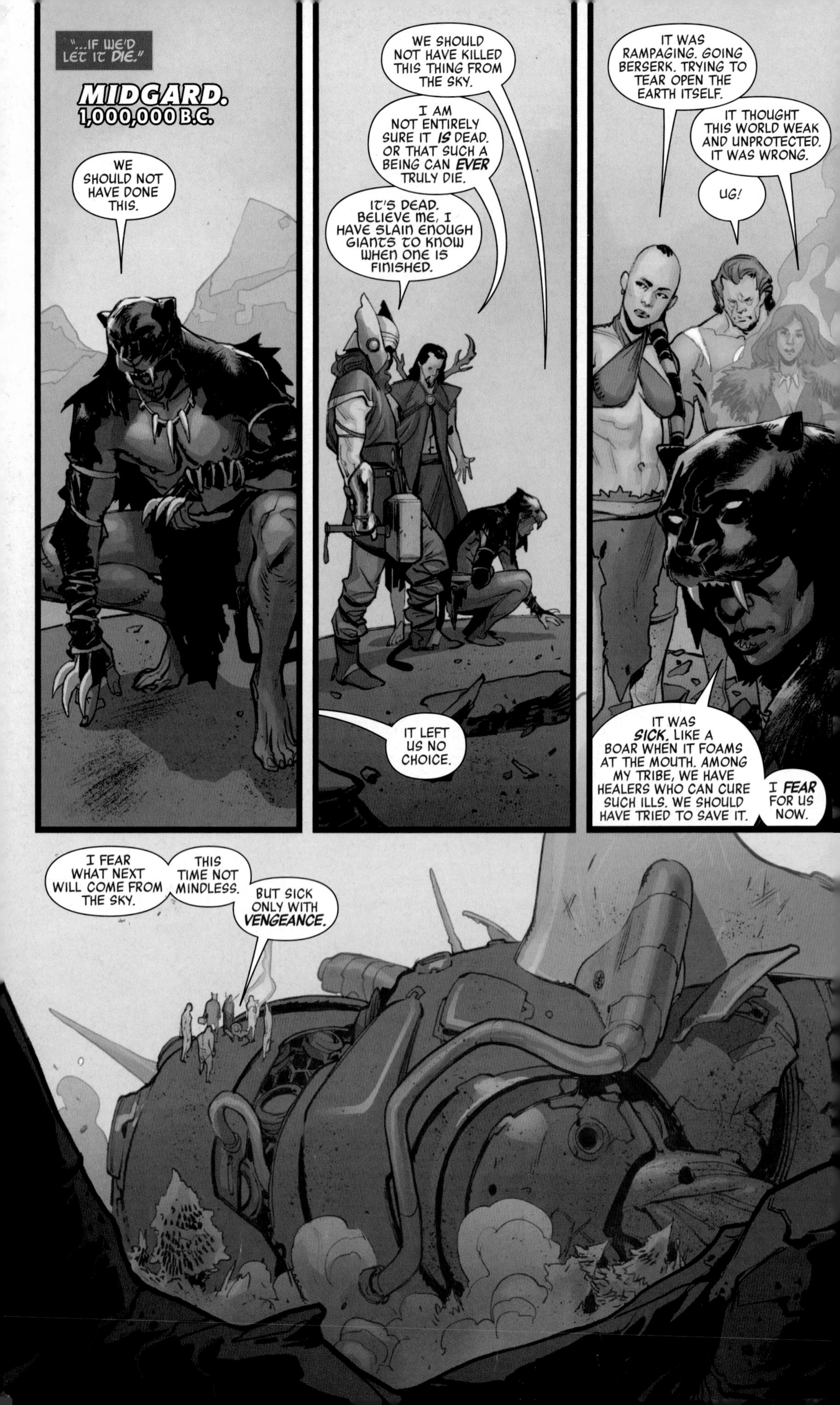

"...IF WE'D LET IT DIE."
MIDGARD. 1,000,000 B.C.
WE SHOULD NOT HAVE DONE THIS.
WE SHOULD NOT HAVE KILLED THIS THING FROM THE SKY.
I AM NOT ENTIRELY SURE IT IS DEAD. OR THAT SUCH A BEING CAN EVER TRULY DIE.
IT'S DEAD. BELIEVE ME, I HAVE SLAIN ENOUGH GIANTS TO KNOW WHEN ONE IS FINISHED.
IT LEFT US NO CHOICE.
IT WAS RAMPAGING. GOING BERSERK. TRYING TO TEAR OPEN THE EARTH ITSELF.
IT THOUGHT THIS WORLD WEAK AND UNPROTECTED. IT WAS WRONG.
UG!
IT WAS SICK. LIKE A BOAR WHEN IT FOAMS AT THE MOUTH. AMONG MY TRIBE, WE HAVE HEALERS WHO CAN CURE SUCH ILLS. WE SHOULD HAVE TRIED TO SAVE IT.
I FEAR FOR US NOW.
I FEAR WHAT NEXT WILL COME FROM THE SKY.
THIS TIME NOT MINDLESS.
BUT SICK ONLY WITH VENGEANCE.

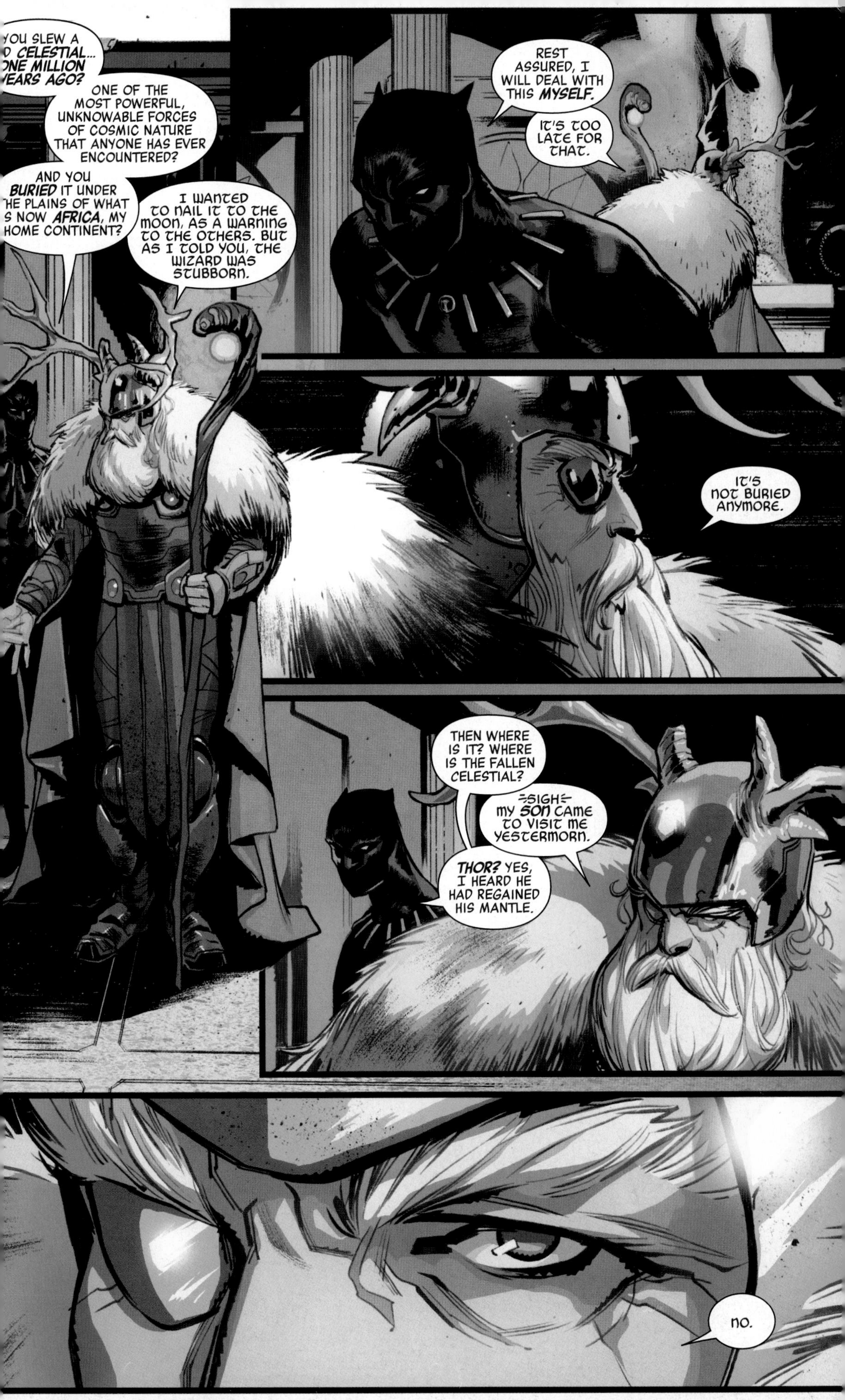
YOU SLEW A
D CELESTIAL...
ONE MILLION
YEARS AGO?
ONE OF THE MOST POWERFUL, UNKNOWABLE FORCES OF COSMIC NATURE THAT ANYONE HAS EVER ENCOUNTERED?
AND YOU BURIED IT UNDER THE PLAINS OF WHAT S NOW AFRICA, MY HOME CONTINENT?
I WANTED TO NAIL IT TO THE MOON, AS A WARNING TO THE OTHERS. BUT AS I TOLD YOU, THE WIZARD WAS STUBBORN.
REST ASSURED, I WILL DEAL WITH THIS MYSELF.
IT'S TOO LATE FOR THAT.
IT'S NOT BURIED ANYMORE.
THEN WHERE IS IT? WHERE IS THE FALLEN CELESTIAL?
=SIGH= my SON CAME TO VISIT ME YESTERMORN.
THOR? YES, I HEARD HE HAD REGAINED HIS MANTLE.
no.

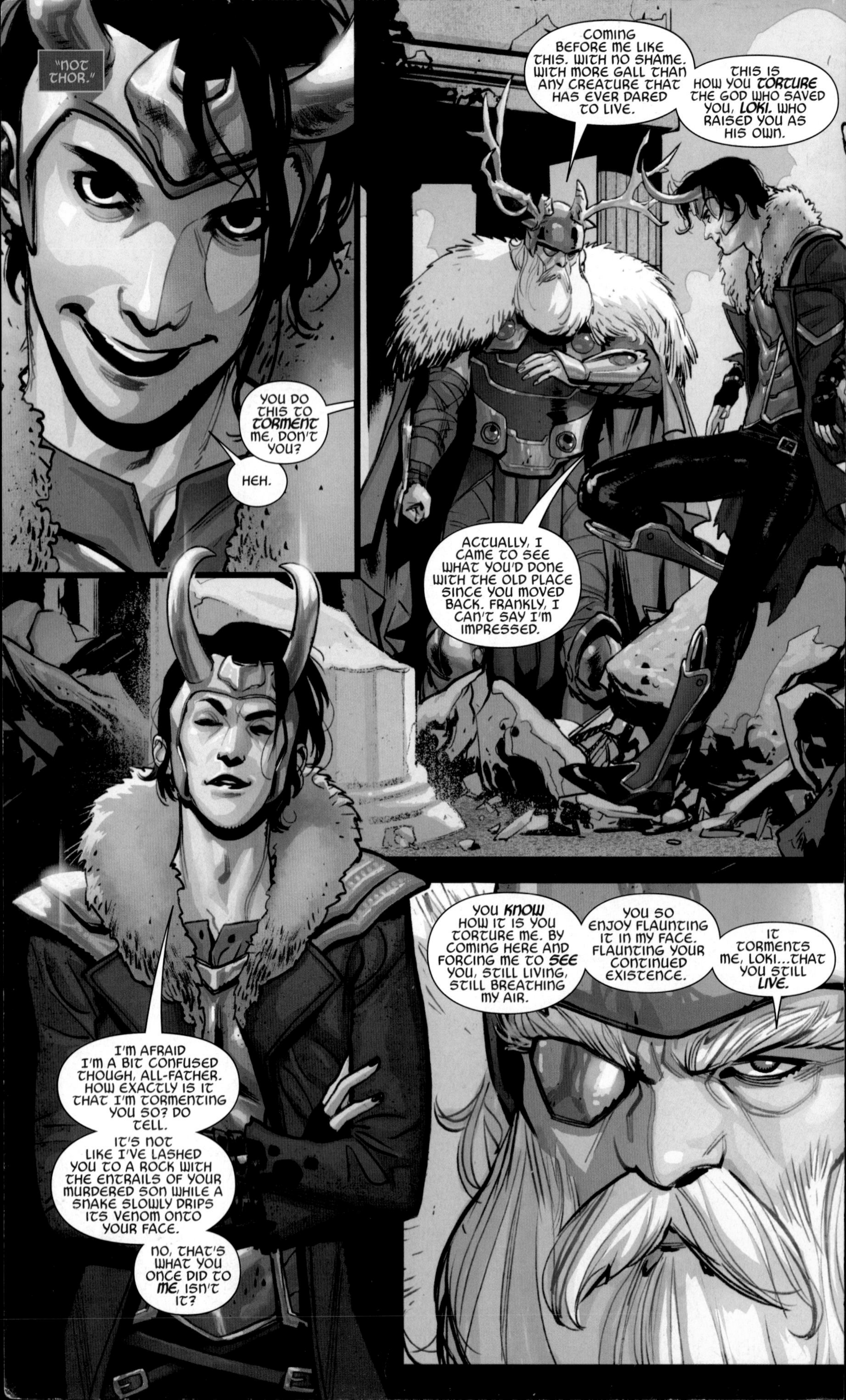
"NOT THOR."
YOU DO THIS TO TORMENT ME, DON'T YOU?
HEH.
COMING BEFORE ME LIKE THIS. WITH NO SHAME. WITH MORE GALL THAN ANY CREATURE THAT HAS EVER DARED TO LIVE.
THIS IS HOW YOU TORTURE THE GOD WHO SAVED YOU, LOKI. WHO RAISED YOU AS HIS OWN.
ACTUALLY, I CAME TO SEE WHAT YOU'D DONE WITH THE OLD PLACE SINCE YOU MOVED BACK. FRANKLY, I CAN'T SAY I'M IMPRESSED.
I'M AFRAID I'M A BIT CONFUSED THOUGH, ALL-FATHER. HOW EXACTLY IS IT THAT I'M TORMENTING YOU SO? DO TELL.
IT'S NOT LIKE I'VE LASHED YOU TO A ROCK WITH THE ENTRAILS OF YOUR MURDERED SON WHILE A SNAKE SLOWLY DRIPS ITS VENOM ONTO YOUR FACE.
NO, THAT'S WHAT YOU ONCE DID TO ME, ISN'T IT?
YOU KNOW HOW IT IS YOU TORTURE ME. BY COMING HERE AND FORCING ME TO SEE YOU, STILL LIVING, STILL BREATHING MY AIR.
YOU SO ENJOY FLAUNTING IT IN MY FACE. FLAUNTING YOUR CONTINUED EXISTENCE.
IT TORMENTS ME, LOKI...THAT YOU STILL LIVE.

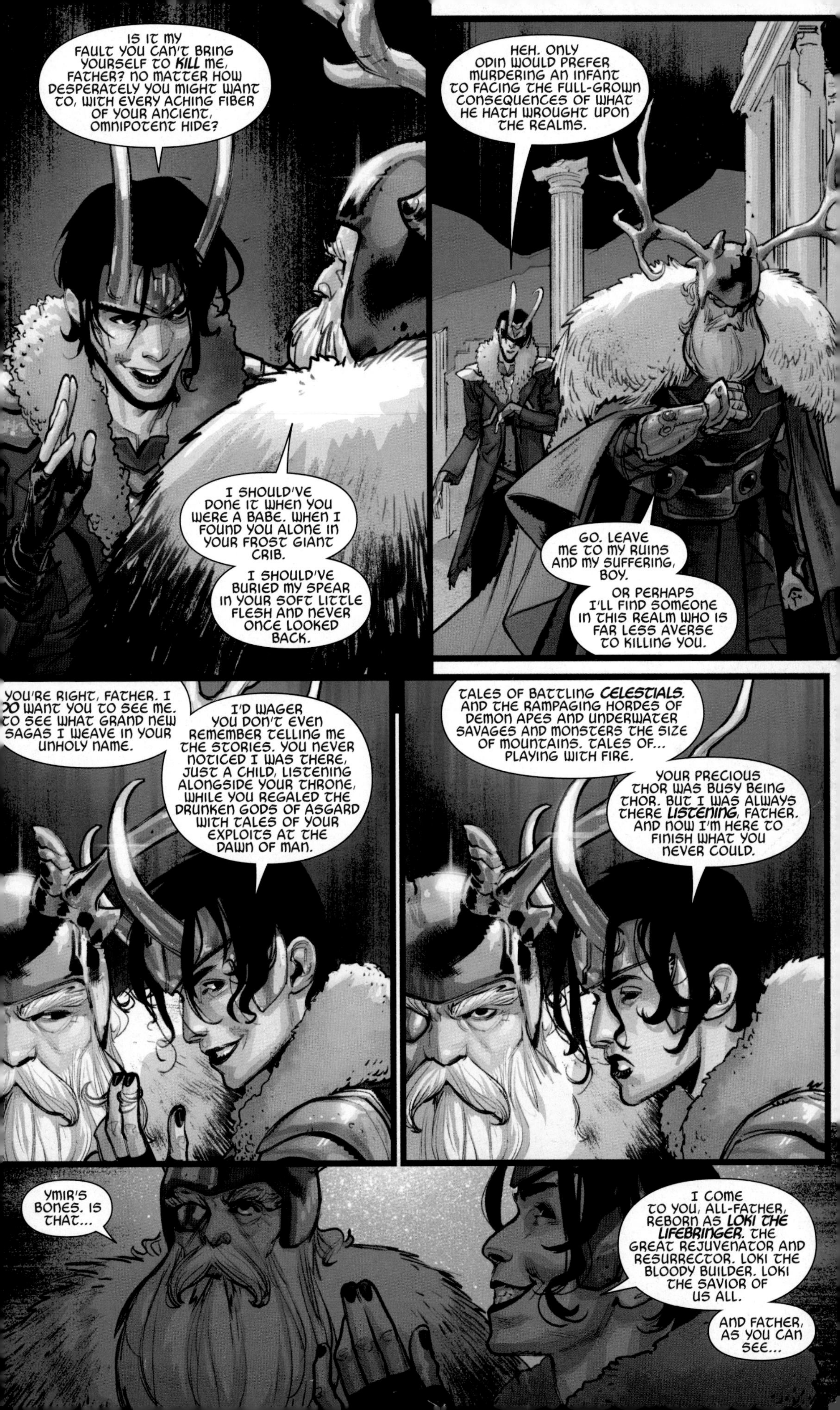
IS IT MY FAULT YOU CAN'T BRING YOURSELF TO KILL ME, FATHER? NO MATTER HOW DESPERATELY YOU MIGHT WANT TO, WITH EVERY ACHING FIBER OF YOUR ANCIENT, OMNIPOTENT HIDE?
I SHOULD'VE DONE IT WHEN YOU WERE A BABE. WHEN I FOUND YOU ALONE IN YOUR FROST GIANT CRIB.
I SHOULD'VE BURIED MY SPEAR IN YOUR SOFT LITTLE FLESH AND NEVER ONCE LOOKED BACK.
HEH. ONLY ODIN WOULD PREFER MURDERING AN INFANT TO FACING THE FULL-GROWN CONSEQUENCES OF WHAT HE HATH WROUGHT UPON THE REALMS.
GO. LEAVE ME TO MY RUINS AND MY SUFFERING, BOY.
OR PERHAPS I'LL FIND SOMEONE IN THIS REALM WHO IS FAR LESS AVERSE TO KILLING YOU.
YOU'RE RIGHT, FATHER. I DO WANT YOU TO SEE ME. TO SEE WHAT GRAND NEW SAGAS I WEAVE IN YOUR UNHOLY NAME.
I'D WAGER YOU DON'T EVEN REMEMBER TELLING ME THE STORIES. YOU NEVER NOTICED I WAS THERE, JUST A CHILD, LISTENING ALONGSIDE YOUR THRONE, WHILE YOU REGALED THE DRUNKEN GODS OF ASGARD WITH TALES OF YOUR EXPLOITS AT THE DAWN OF MAN.
TALES OF BATTLING CELESTIALS. AND THE RAMPAGING HORDES OF DEMON APES AND UNDERWATER SAVAGES AND MONSTERS THE SIZE OF MOUNTAINS. TALES OF... PLAYING WITH FIRE.
YOUR PRECIOUS THOR WAS BUSY BEING THOR. BUT I WAS ALWAYS THERE LISTENING, FATHER. AND NOW I'M HERE TO FINISH WHAT YOU NEVER COULD.
YMIR'S BONES. IS THAT...
I COME TO YOU, ALL-FATHER, REBORN AS LOKI THE LIFEBRINGER. THE GREAT REJUVENATOR AND RESURRECTOR. LOKI THE BLOODY BUILDER. LOKI THE SAVIOR OF US ALL.
AND FATHER, AS YOU CAN SEE...

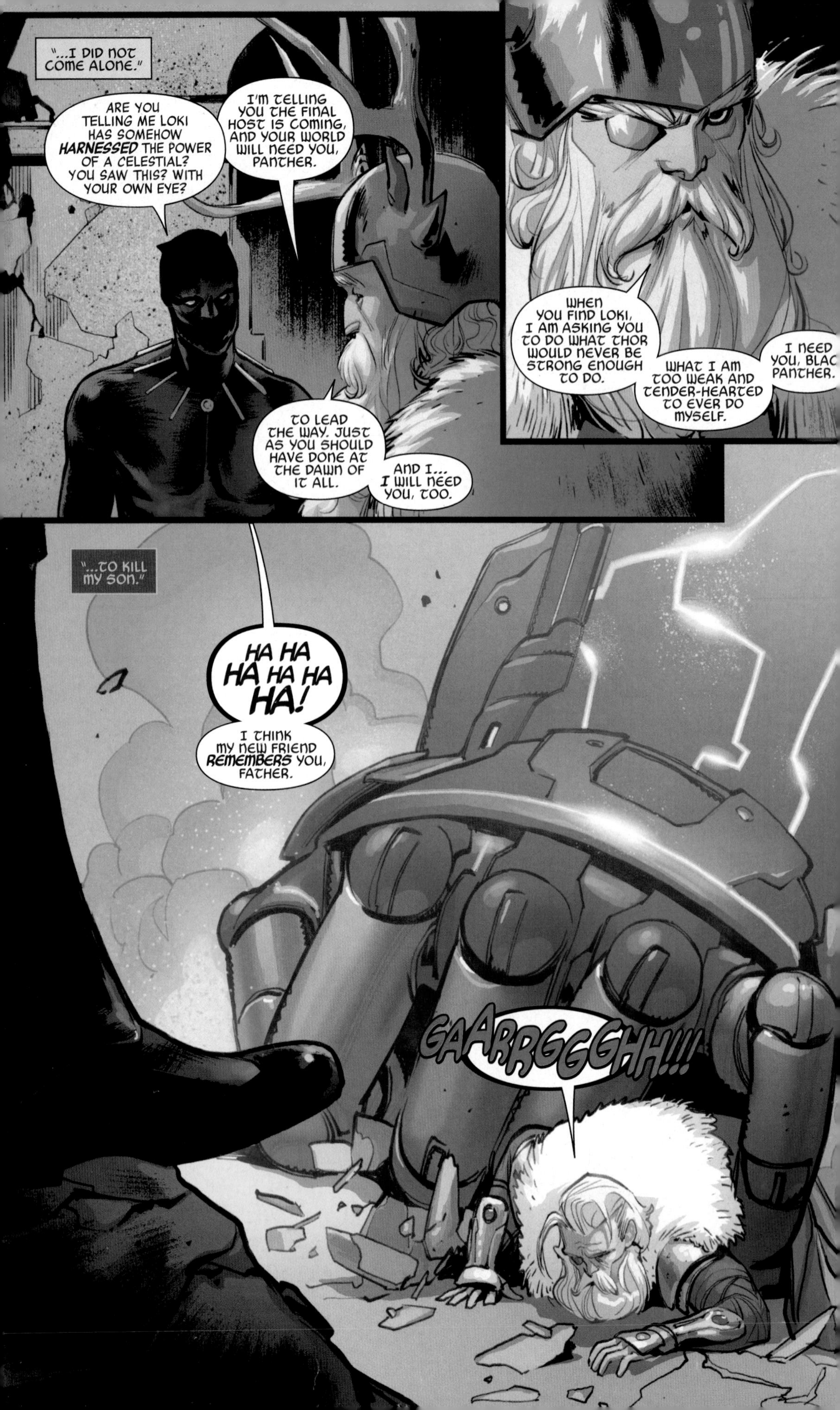
"...I DID NOT COME ALONE."
ARE YOU TELLING ME LOKI HAS SOMEHOW **HARNESSED** THE POWER OF A CELESTIAL? YOU SAW THIS? WITH YOUR OWN EYE?
I'M TELLING YOU THE FINAL HOST IS COMING, AND YOUR WORLD WILL NEED YOU, PANTHER.
TO LEAD THE WAY. JUST AS YOU SHOULD HAVE DONE AT THE DAWN OF IT ALL.
AND I... ***I*** WILL NEED YOU, TOO.
WHEN YOU FIND LOKI, I AM ASKING YOU TO DO WHAT THOR WOULD NEVER BE STRONG ENOUGH TO DO.
WHAT I AM TOO WEAK AND TENDER-HEARTED TO EVER DO MYSELF.
I NEED YOU, BLAC PANTHER.
"...TO KILL MY SON."
HA HA HA HA HA HA!
I THINK MY NEW FRIEND ***REMEMBERS*** YOU, FATHER.
GAARRGGGHH!!!

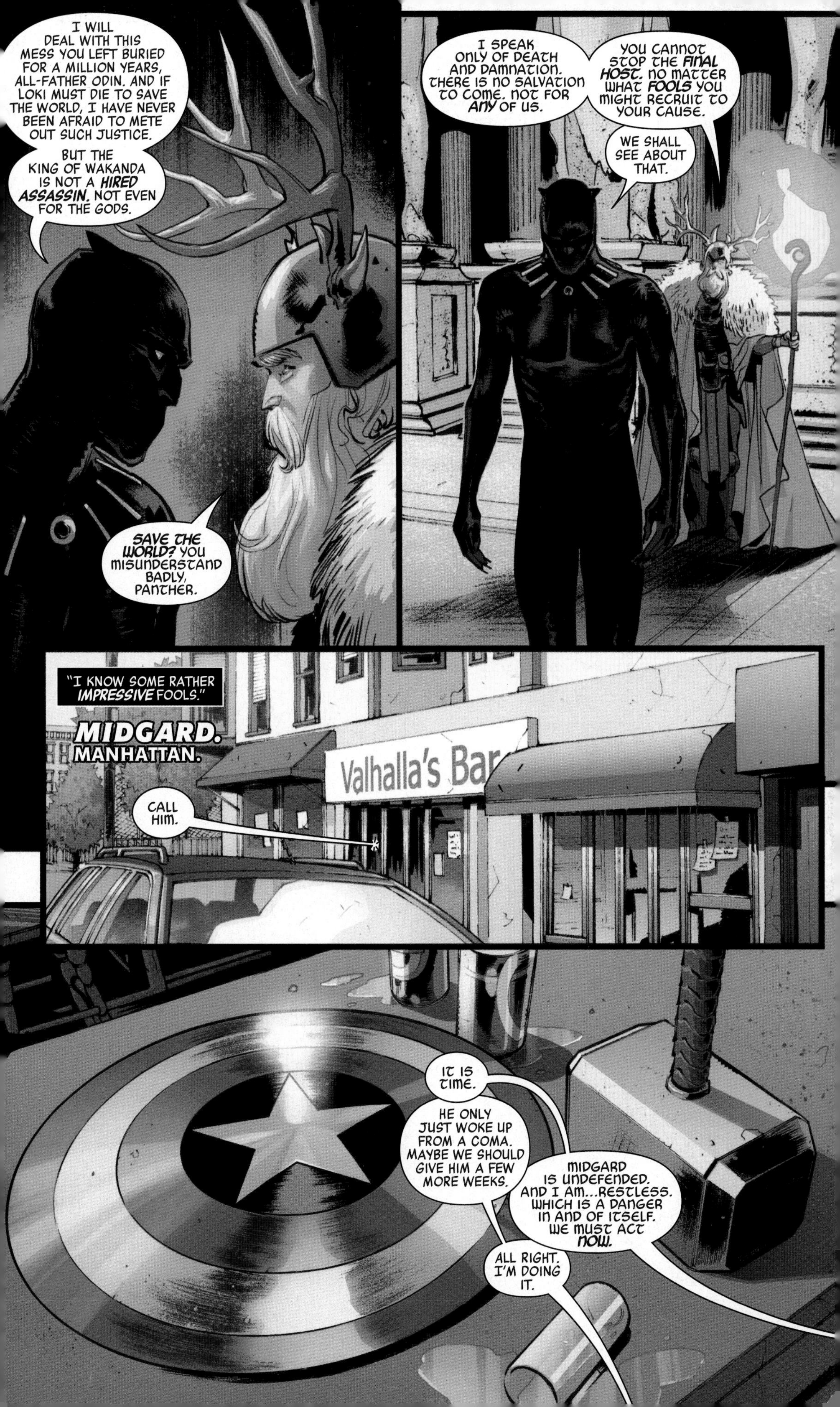
I WILL DEAL WITH THIS MESS YOU LEFT BURIED FOR A MILLION YEARS, ALL-FATHER ODIN. AND IF LOKI MUST DIE TO SAVE THE WORLD, I HAVE NEVER BEEN AFRAID TO METE OUT SUCH JUSTICE.
BUT THE KING OF WAKANDA IS NOT A HIRED ASSASSIN. NOT EVEN FOR THE GODS.
SAVE THE WORLD? YOU MISUNDERSTAND BADLY, PANTHER.
I SPEAK ONLY OF DEATH AND DAMNATION. THERE IS NO SALVATION TO COME. NOT FOR ANY OF US.
YOU CANNOT STOP THE FINAL HOST. NO MATTER WHAT FOOLS YOU MIGHT RECRUIT TO YOUR CAUSE.
WE SHALL SEE ABOUT THAT.
"I KNOW SOME RATHER IMPRESSIVE FOOLS."
MIDGARD.
MANHATTAN.
Valhalla's Bar
CALL HIM.
IT IS TIME.
HE ONLY JUST WOKE UP FROM A COMA. MAYBE WE SHOULD GIVE HIM A FEW MORE WEEKS.
MIDGARD IS UNDEFENDED. AND I AM...RESTLESS. WHICH IS A DANGER IN AND OF ITSELF. WE MUST ACT NOW.
ALL RIGHT. I'M DOING IT.

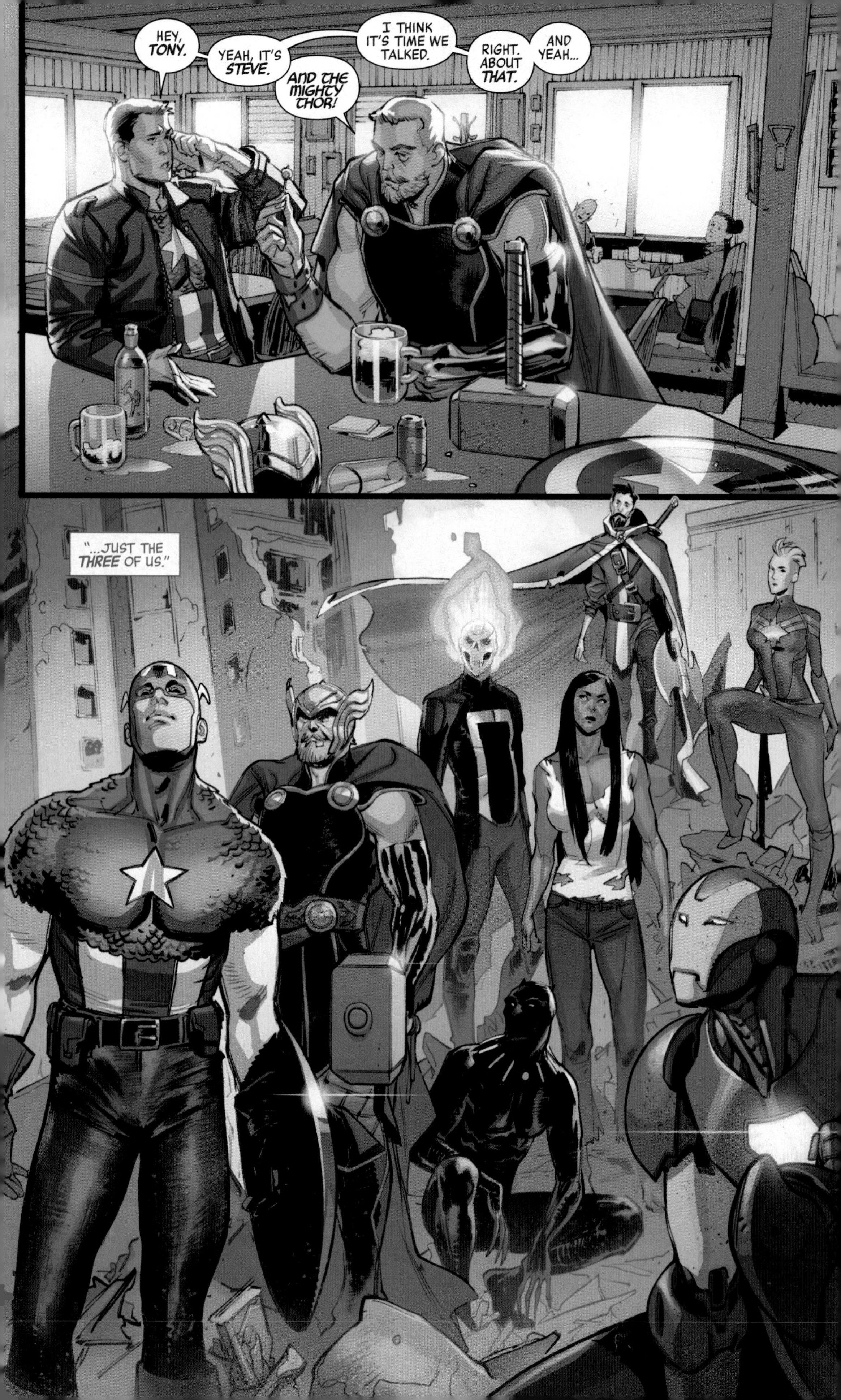
HEY, TONY.
YEAH, IT'S STEVE.
AND THE MIGHTY THOR!
I THINK IT'S TIME WE TALKED.
RIGHT. ABOUT THAT.
AND YEAH...
"...JUST THE THREE OF US."

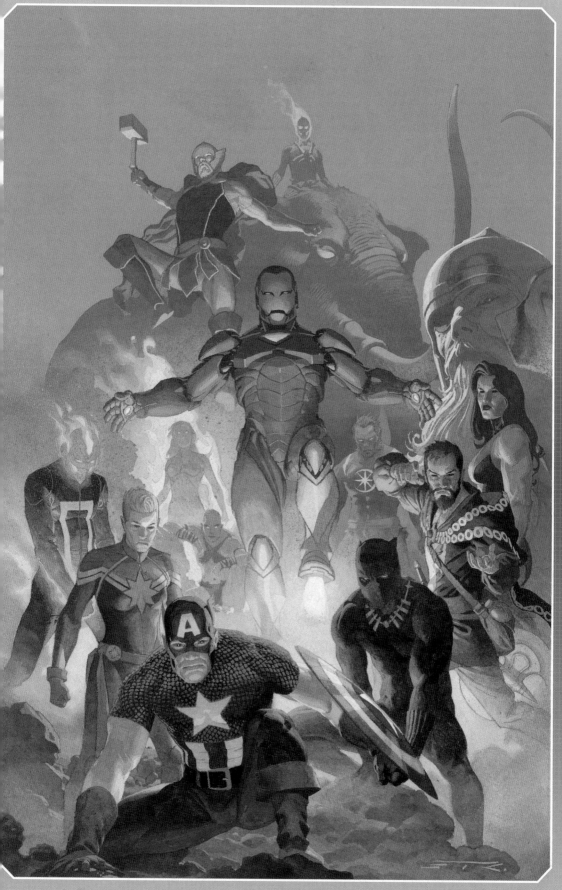

ESAD RIBIĆ
1 VARIANT COVER

1 THE FINAL HOST

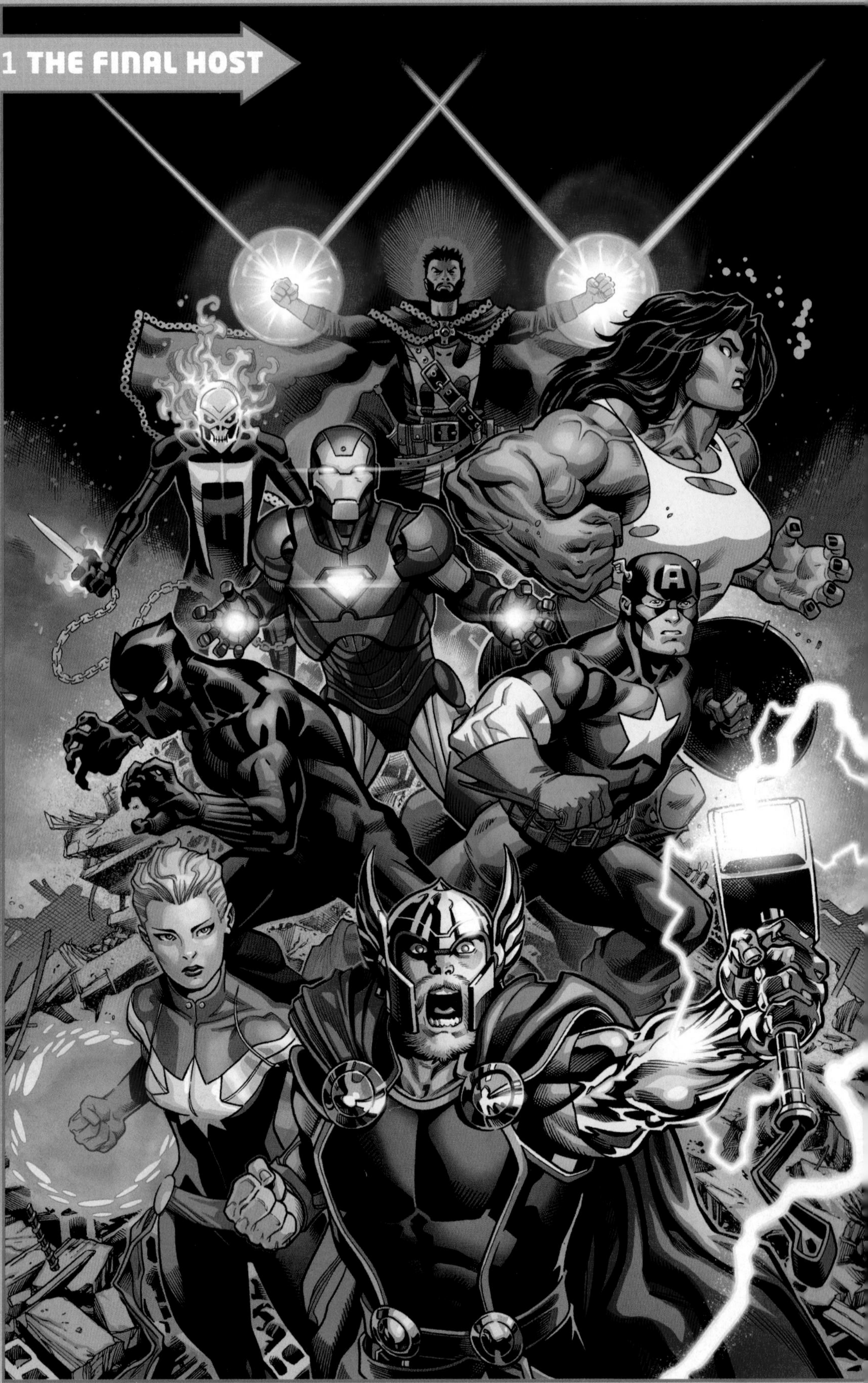

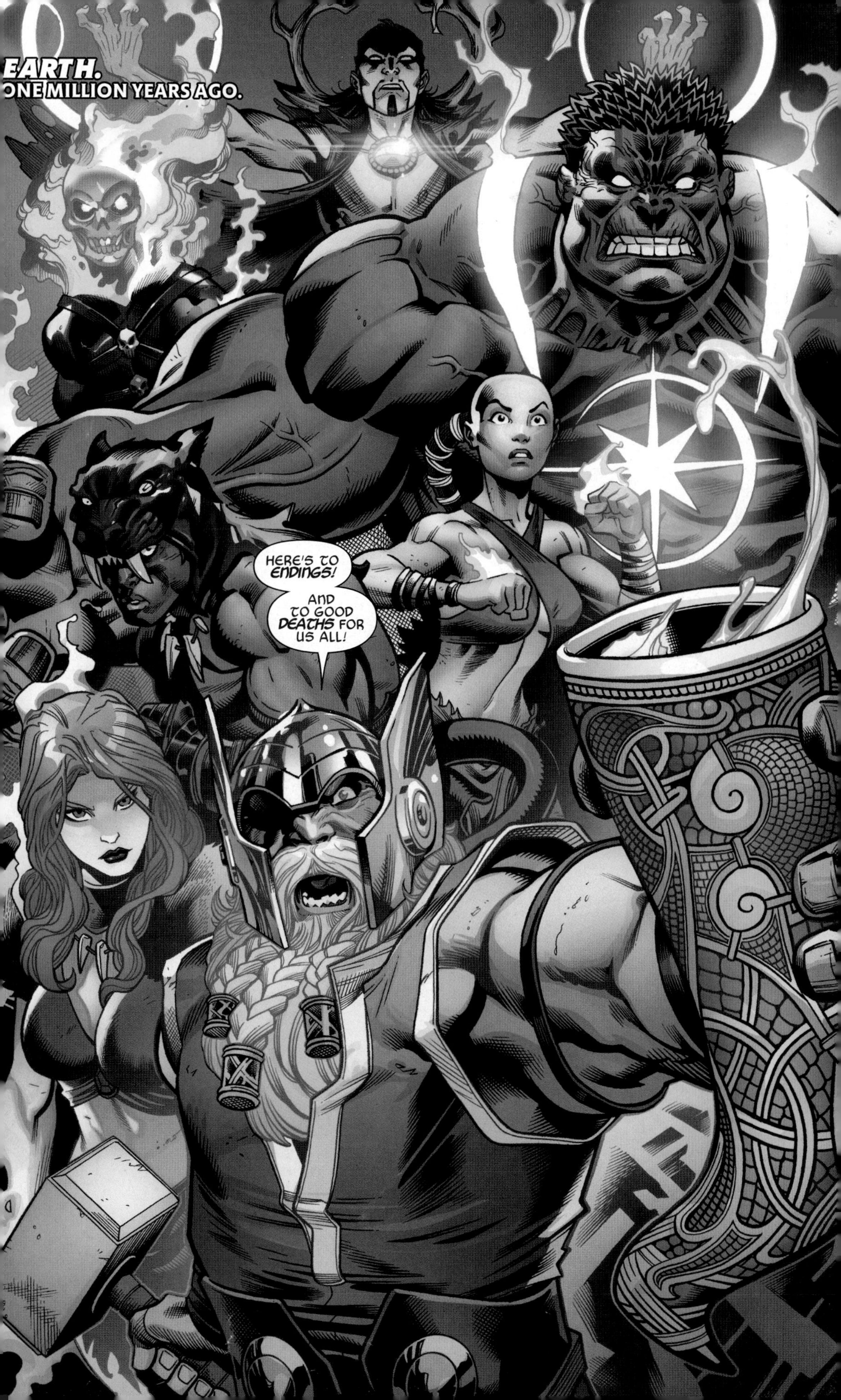
EARTH.
ONE MILLION YEARS AGO.
HERE'S TO ENDINGS!
AND TO GOOD DEATHS FOR US ALL!

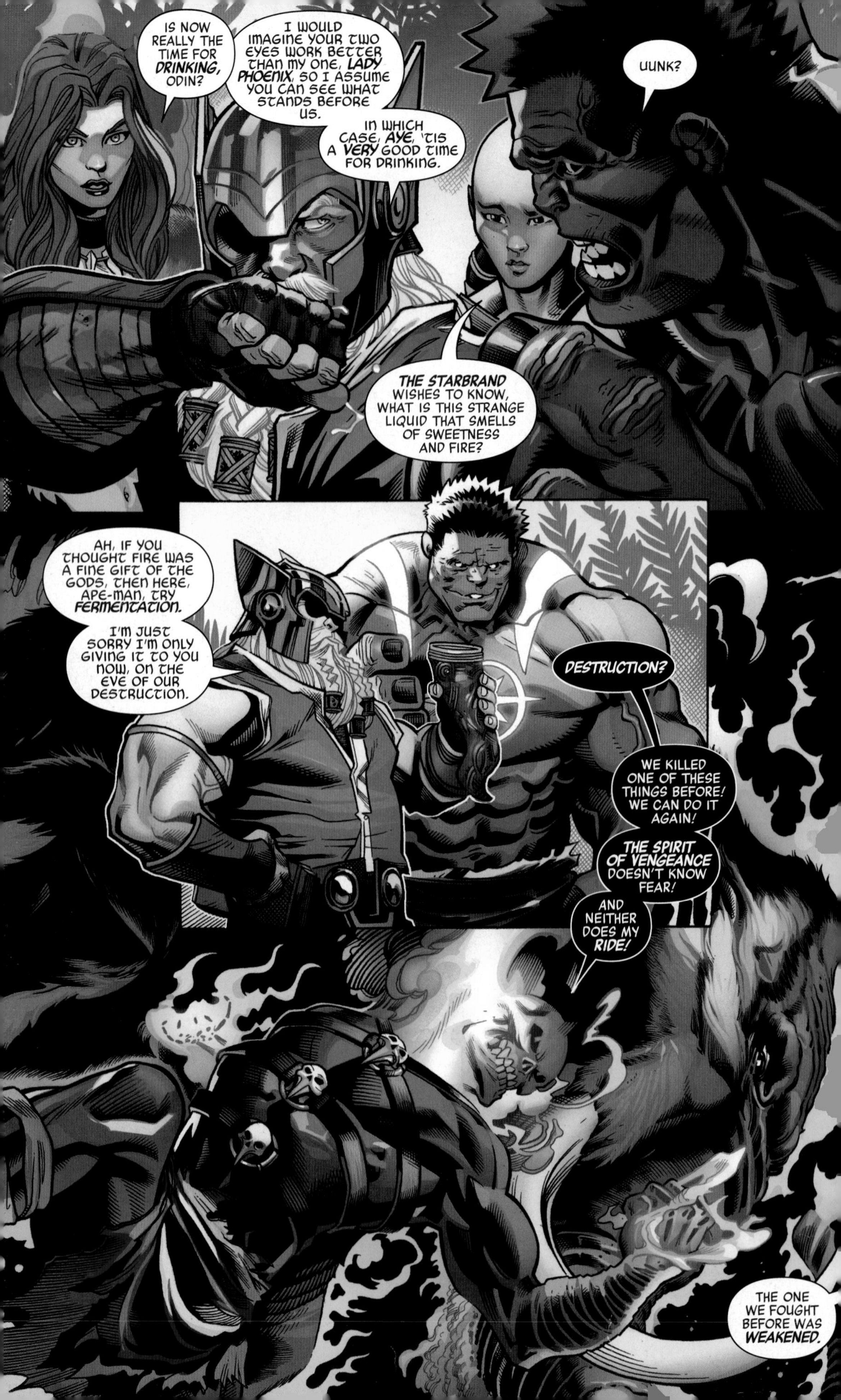
IS NOW REALLY THE TIME FOR DRINKING, ODIN?
I WOULD IMAGINE YOUR TWO EYES WORK BETTER THAN MY ONE, LADY PHOENIX, SO I ASSUME YOU CAN SEE WHAT STANDS BEFORE US.
IN WHICH CASE, AYE, 'TIS A VERY GOOD TIME FOR DRINKING.
UUNK?
THE STARBRAND WISHES TO KNOW, WHAT IS THIS STRANGE LIQUID THAT SMELLS OF SWEETNESS AND FIRE?
AH, IF YOU THOUGHT FIRE WAS A FINE GIFT OF THE GODS, THEN HERE, APE-MAN, TRY FERMENTATION.
I'M JUST SORRY I'M ONLY GIVING IT TO YOU NOW, ON THE EVE OF OUR DESTRUCTION.
DESTRUCTION?
WE KILLED ONE OF THESE THINGS BEFORE! WE CAN DO IT AGAIN!
THE SPIRIT OF VENGEANCE DOESN'T KNOW FEAR!
AND NEITHER DOES MY RIDE!
THE ONE WE FOUGHT BEFORE WAS WEAKENED.

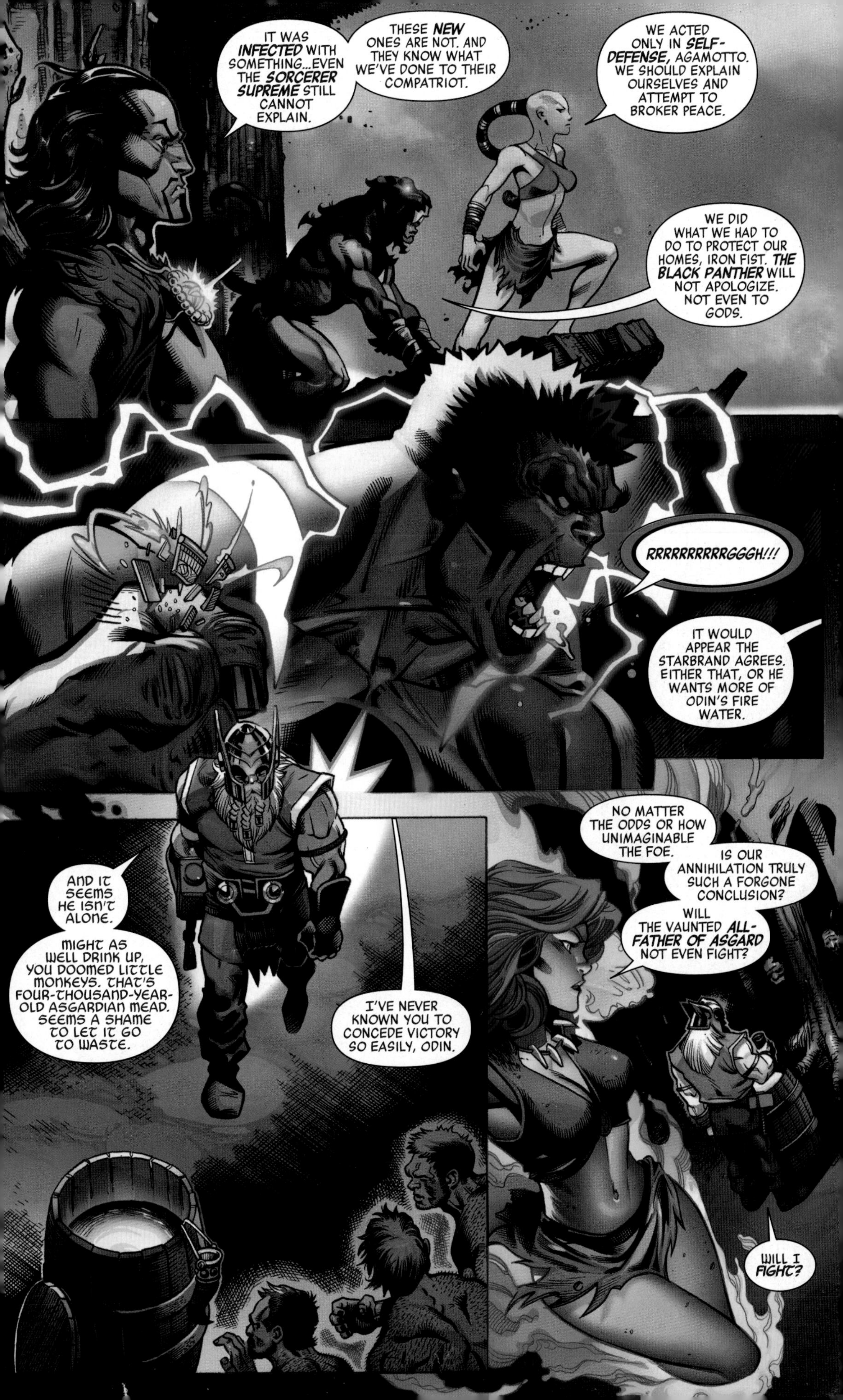
IT WAS INFECTED WITH SOMETHING...EVEN THE SORCERER SUPREME STILL CANNOT EXPLAIN.
THESE NEW ONES ARE NOT. AND THEY KNOW WHAT WE'VE DONE TO THEIR COMPATRIOT.
WE ACTED ONLY IN SELF-DEFENSE, AGAMOTTO. WE SHOULD EXPLAIN OURSELVES AND ATTEMPT TO BROKER PEACE.
WE DID WHAT WE HAD TO DO TO PROTECT OUR HOMES, IRON FIST. THE BLACK PANTHER WILL NOT APOLOGIZE. NOT EVEN TO GODS.
RRRRRRRRRRGGGH!!!
IT WOULD APPEAR THE STARBRAND AGREES. EITHER THAT, OR HE WANTS MORE OF ODIN'S FIRE WATER.
AND IT SEEMS HE ISN'T ALONE.
MIGHT AS WELL DRINK UP, YOU DOOMED LITTLE MONKEYS. THAT'S FOUR-THOUSAND-YEAR-OLD ASGARDIAN MEAD. SEEMS A SHAME TO LET IT GO TO WASTE.
I'VE NEVER KNOWN YOU TO CONCEDE VICTORY SO EASILY, ODIN.
NO MATTER THE ODDS OR HOW UNIMAGINABLE THE FOE.
IS OUR ANNIHILATION TRULY SUCH A FORGONE CONCLUSION?
WILL THE VAUNTED ALL-FATHER OF ASGARD NOT EVEN FIGHT?
WILL I FIGHT?

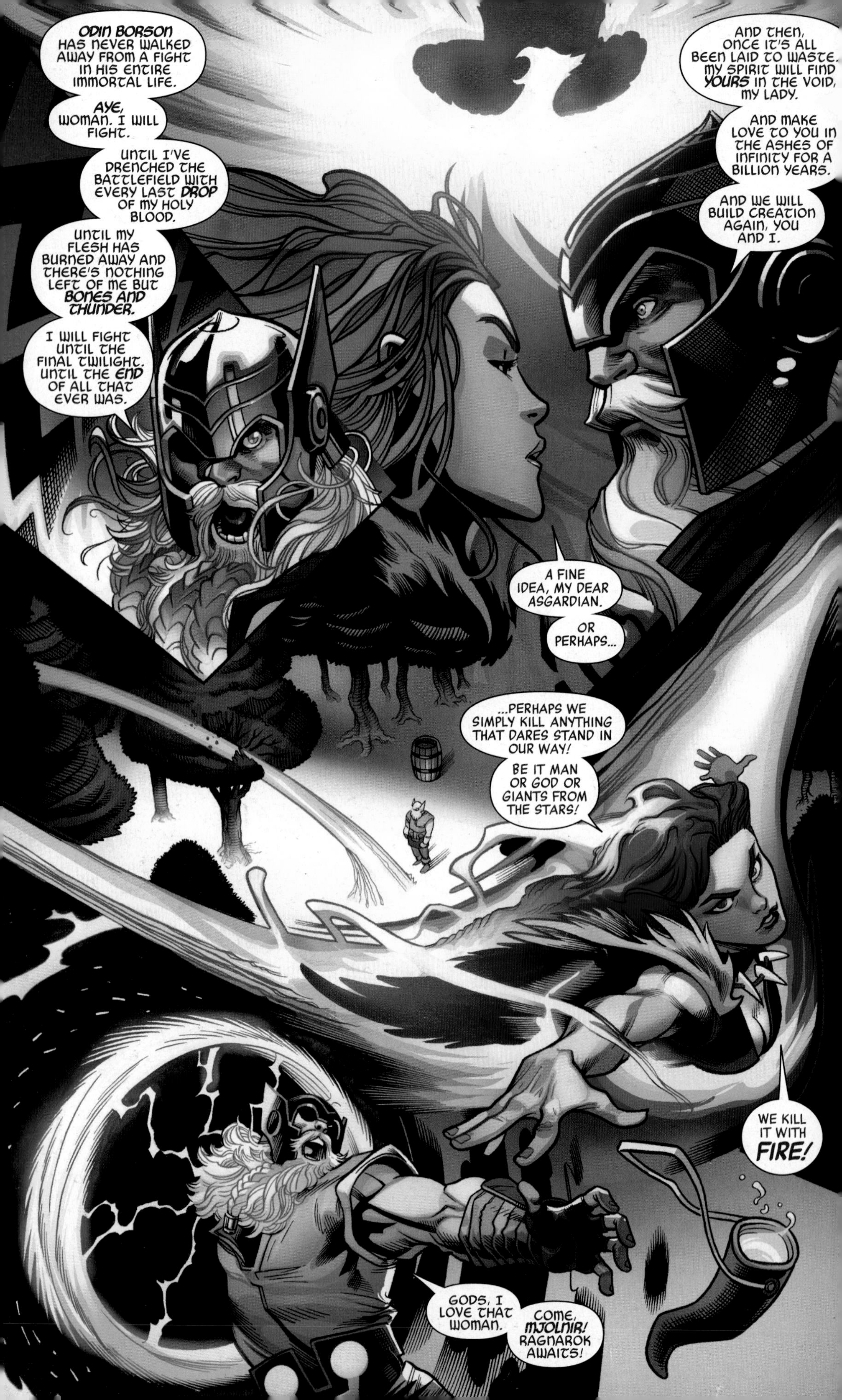

ODIN BORSON HAS NEVER WALKED AWAY FROM A FIGHT IN HIS ENTIRE IMMORTAL LIFE.
AYE, WOMAN. I WILL FIGHT.
UNTIL I'VE DRENCHED THE BATTLEFIELD WITH EVERY LAST DROP OF MY HOLY BLOOD.
UNTIL MY FLESH HAS BURNED AWAY AND THERE'S NOTHING LEFT OF ME BUT BONES AND THUNDER.
I WILL FIGHT UNTIL THE FINAL TWILIGHT. UNTIL THE END OF ALL THAT EVER WAS.
AND THEN, ONCE IT'S ALL BEEN LAID TO WASTE. MY SPIRIT WILL FIND YOURS IN THE VOID, MY LADY.
AND MAKE LOVE TO YOU IN THE ASHES OF INFINITY FOR A BILLION YEARS.
AND WE WILL BUILD CREATION AGAIN, YOU AND I.
A FINE IDEA, MY DEAR ASGARDIAN.
OR PERHAPS...
...PERHAPS WE SIMPLY KILL ANYTHING THAT DARES STAND IN OUR WAY!
BE IT MAN OR GOD OR GIANTS FROM THE STARS!
WE KILL IT WITH FIRE!
GODS, I LOVE THAT WOMAN.
COME, MJOLNIR! RAGNAROK AWAITS!

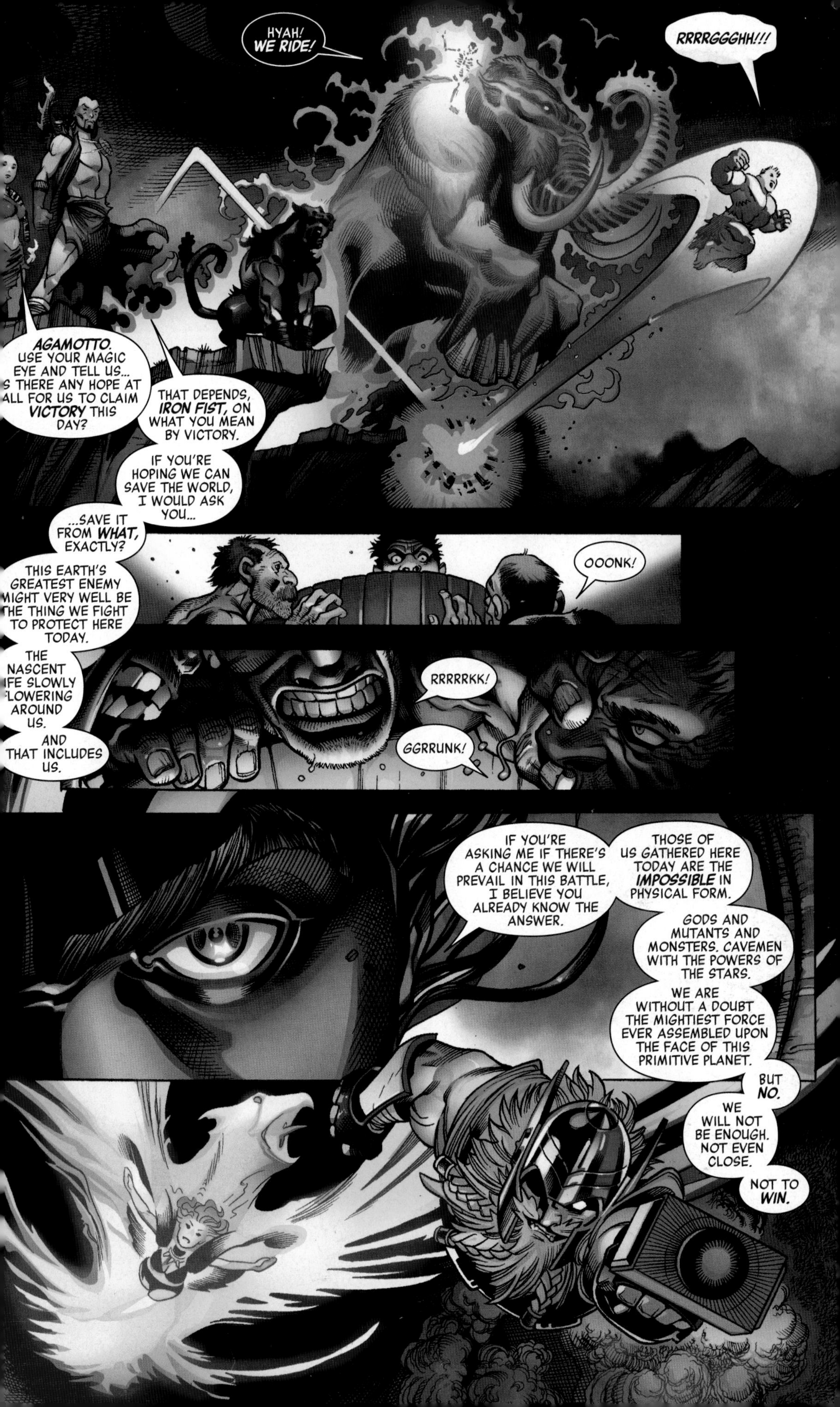
HYAH! WE RIDE!
RRRRGGGHH!!!
AGAMOTTO. USE YOUR MAGIC EYE AND TELL US... S THERE ANY HOPE AT ALL FOR US TO CLAIM VICTORY THIS DAY?
THAT DEPENDS, IRON FIST, ON WHAT YOU MEAN BY VICTORY.
IF YOU'RE HOPING WE CAN SAVE THE WORLD, I WOULD ASK YOU...
...SAVE IT FROM WHAT, EXACTLY?
THIS EARTH'S GREATEST ENEMY MIGHT VERY WELL BE THE THING WE FIGHT TO PROTECT HERE TODAY.
OOONK!
THE NASCENT IFE SLOWLY LOWERING AROUND US.
AND THAT INCLUDES US.
RRRRRKK!
GGRRUNK!
IF YOU'RE ASKING ME IF THERE'S A CHANCE WE WILL PREVAIL IN THIS BATTLE, I BELIEVE YOU ALREADY KNOW THE ANSWER.
THOSE OF US GATHERED HERE TODAY ARE THE IMPOSSIBLE IN PHYSICAL FORM.
GODS AND MUTANTS AND MONSTERS. CAVEMEN WITH THE POWERS OF THE STARS.
WE ARE WITHOUT A DOUBT THE MIGHTIEST FORCE EVER ASSEMBLED UPON THE FACE OF THIS PRIMITIVE PLANET.
BUT NO.
WE WILL NOT BE ENOUGH. NOT EVEN CLOSE.
NOT TO WIN.

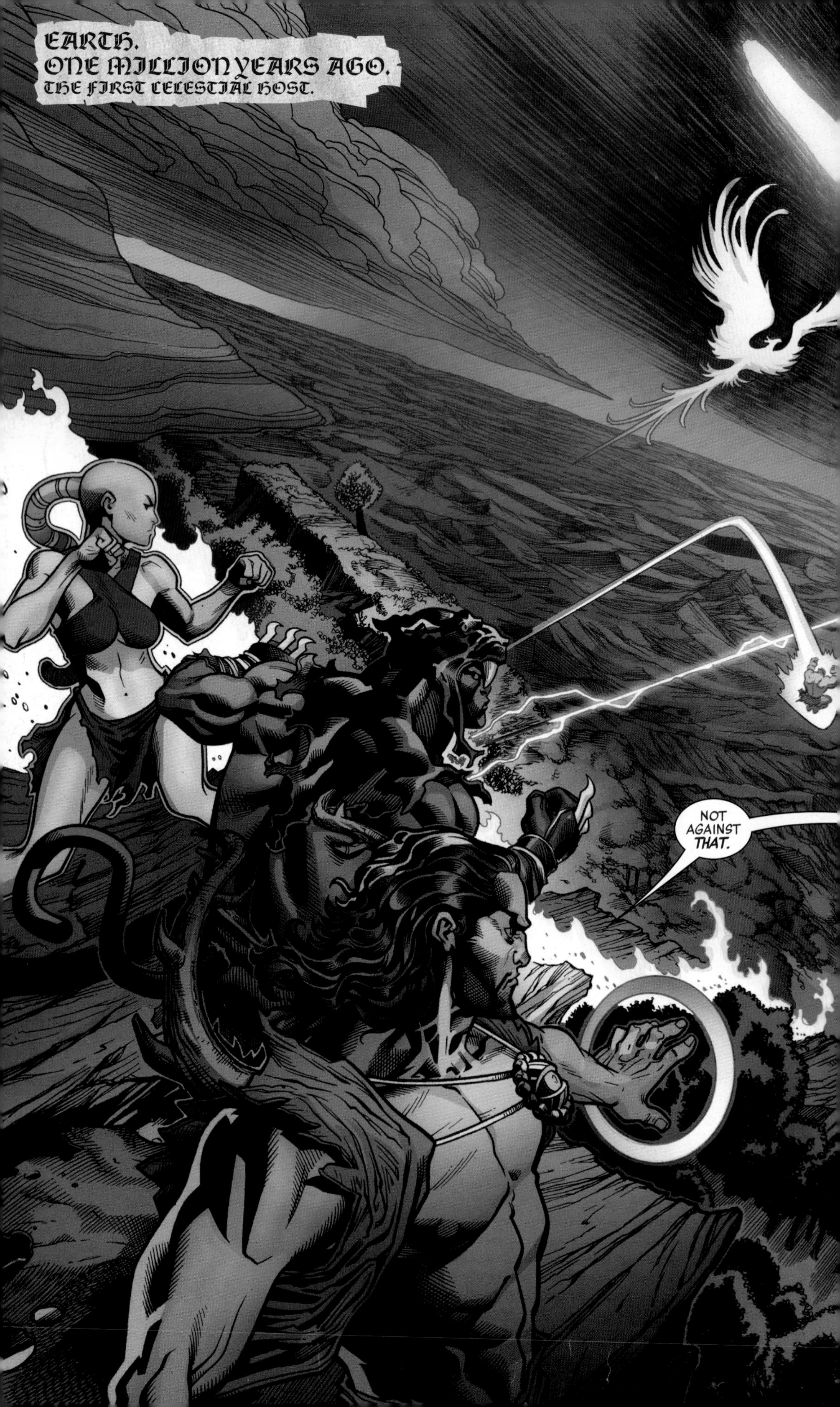
EARTH.
ONE MILLION YEARS AGO.
THE FIRST CELESTIAL HOST.
NOT AGAINST THAT.

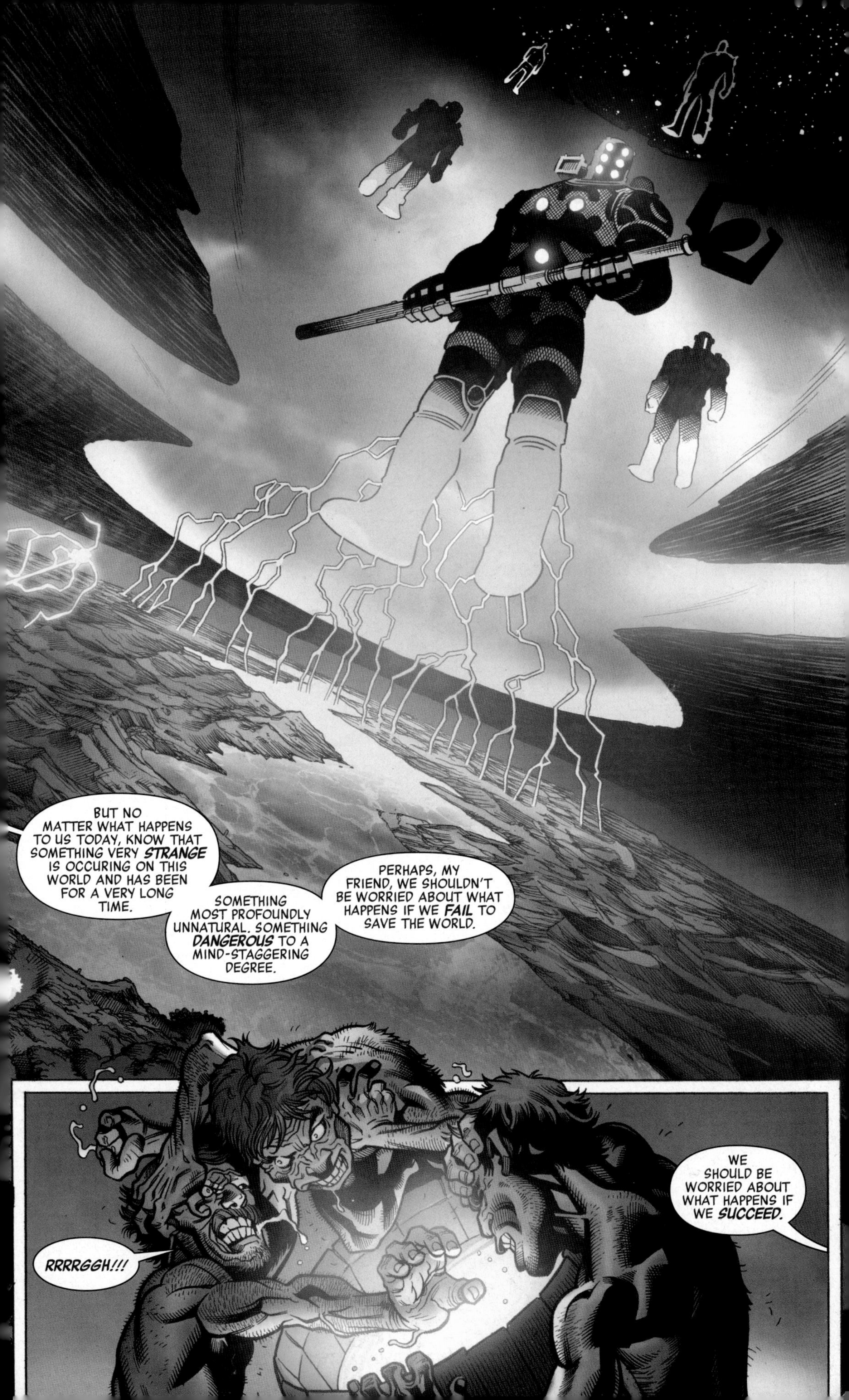
BUT NO MATTER WHAT HAPPENS TO US TODAY, KNOW THAT SOMETHING VERY STRANGE IS OCCURING ON THIS WORLD AND HAS BEEN FOR A VERY LONG TIME.
SOMETHING MOST PROFOUNDLY UNNATURAL. SOMETHING DANGEROUS TO A MIND-STAGGERING DEGREE.
PERHAPS, MY FRIEND, WE SHOULDN'T BE WORRIED ABOUT WHAT HAPPENS IF WE FAIL TO SAVE THE WORLD.
RRRRGGH!!!
WE SHOULD BE WORRIED ABOUT WHAT HAPPENS IF WE SUCCEED.

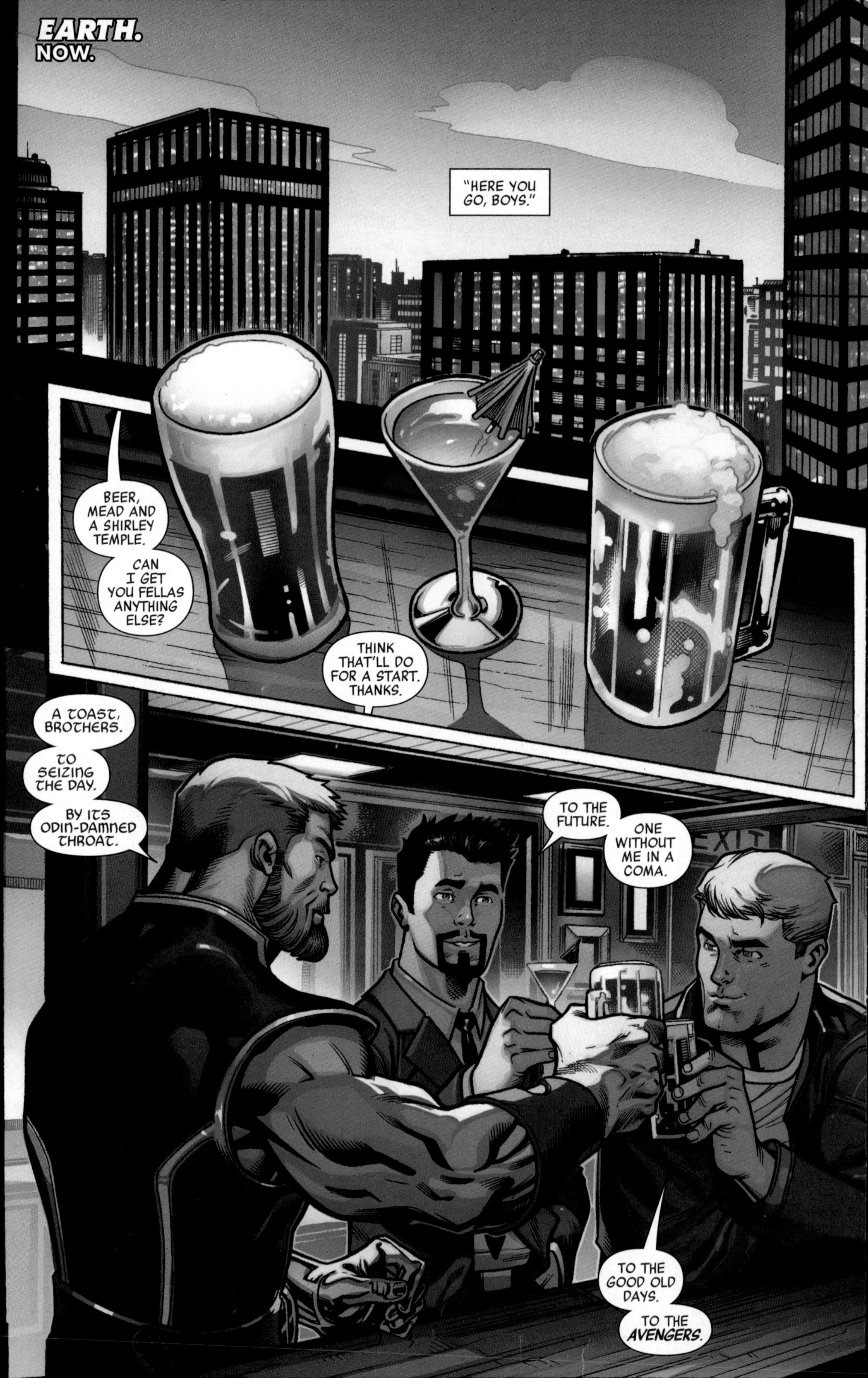
EARTH.
NOW.
"HERE YOU GO, BOYS."
BEER, MEAD AND A SHIRLEY TEMPLE.
CAN I GET YOU FELLAS ANYTHING ELSE?
THINK THAT'LL DO FOR A START. THANKS.
A TOAST, BROTHERS.
TO SEIZING THE DAY.
BY ITS ODIN-DAMNED THROAT.
TO THE FUTURE.
ONE WITHOUT ME IN A COMA.
TO THE GOOD OLD DAYS.
TO THE AVENGERS.
EXIT

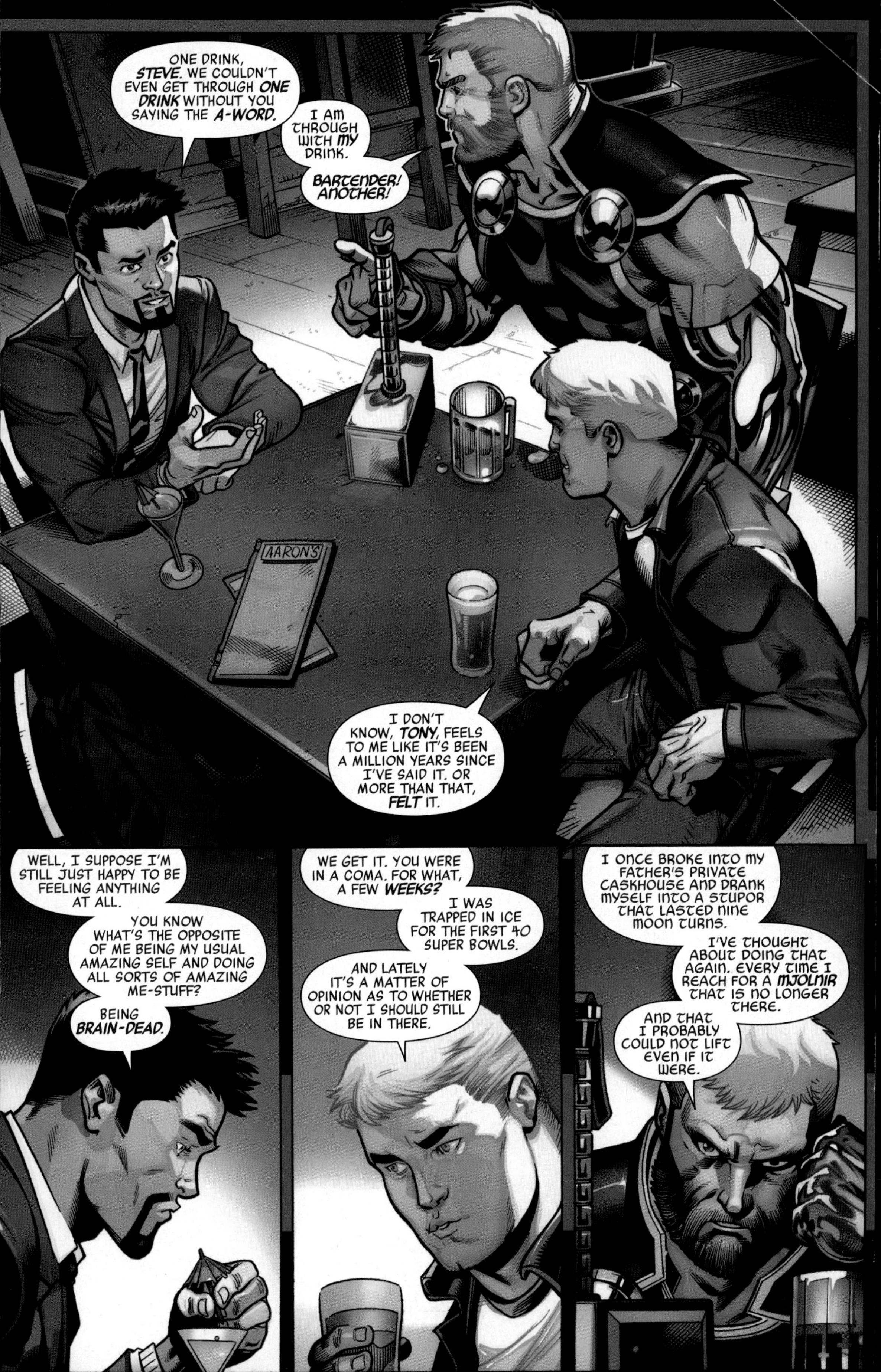
ONE DRINK, STEVE. WE COULDN'T EVEN GET THROUGH ONE DRINK WITHOUT YOU SAYING THE A-WORD.
I AM THROUGH WITH MY DRINK.
BARTENDER! ANOTHER!
AARON'S
I DON'T KNOW, TONY, FEELS TO ME LIKE IT'S BEEN A MILLION YEARS SINCE I'VE SAID IT. OR MORE THAN THAT, FELT IT.
WELL, I SUPPOSE I'M STILL JUST HAPPY TO BE FEELING ANYTHING AT ALL.
YOU KNOW WHAT'S THE OPPOSITE OF ME BEING MY USUAL AMAZING SELF AND DOING ALL SORTS OF AMAZING ME-STUFF?
BEING BRAIN-DEAD.
WE GET IT. YOU WERE IN A COMA. FOR WHAT, A FEW WEEKS?
I WAS TRAPPED IN ICE FOR THE FIRST 40 SUPER BOWLS.
AND LATELY IT'S A MATTER OF OPINION AS TO WHETHER OR NOT I SHOULD STILL BE IN THERE.
I ONCE BROKE INTO MY FATHER'S PRIVATE CASKHOUSE AND DRANK MYSELF INTO A STUPOR THAT LASTED NINE MOON TURNS.
I'VE THOUGHT ABOUT DOING THAT AGAIN. EVERY TIME I REACH FOR A MJOLNIR THAT IS NO LONGER THERE.
AND THAT I PROBABLY COULD NOT LIFT EVEN IF IT WERE.

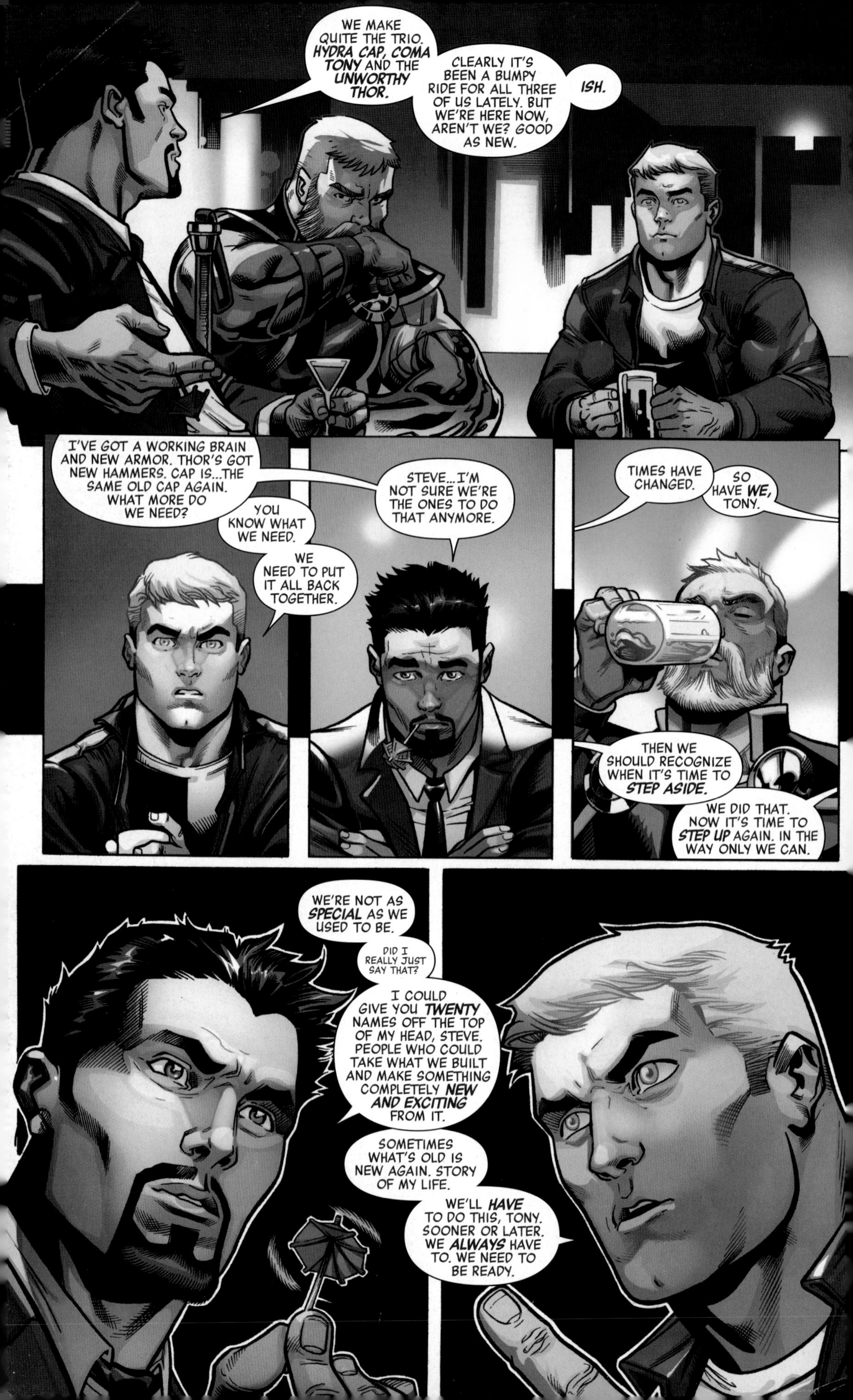
WE MAKE QUITE THE TRIO. HYDRA CAP, COMA TONY AND THE UNWORTHY THOR.
CLEARLY IT'S BEEN A BUMPY RIDE FOR ALL THREE OF US LATELY. BUT WE'RE HERE NOW, AREN'T WE? GOOD AS NEW.
ISH.
I'VE GOT A WORKING BRAIN AND NEW ARMOR. THOR'S GOT NEW HAMMERS. CAP IS...THE SAME OLD CAP AGAIN. WHAT MORE DO WE NEED?
YOU KNOW WHAT WE NEED.
WE NEED TO PUT IT ALL BACK TOGETHER.
STEVE...I'M NOT SURE WE'RE THE ONES TO DO THAT ANYMORE.
TIMES HAVE CHANGED.
SO HAVE WE, TONY.
THEN WE SHOULD RECOGNIZE WHEN IT'S TIME TO STEP ASIDE.
WE DID THAT. NOW IT'S TIME TO STEP UP AGAIN. IN THE WAY ONLY WE CAN.
WE'RE NOT AS SPECIAL AS WE USED TO BE.
DID I REALLY JUST SAY THAT?
I COULD GIVE YOU TWENTY NAMES OFF THE TOP OF MY HEAD, STEVE. PEOPLE WHO COULD TAKE WHAT WE BUILT AND MAKE SOMETHING COMPLETELY NEW AND EXCITING FROM IT.
SOMETIMES WHAT'S OLD IS NEW AGAIN. STORY OF MY LIFE.
WE'LL HAVE TO DO THIS, TONY. SOONER OR LATER. WE ALWAYS HAVE TO. WE NEED TO BE READY.

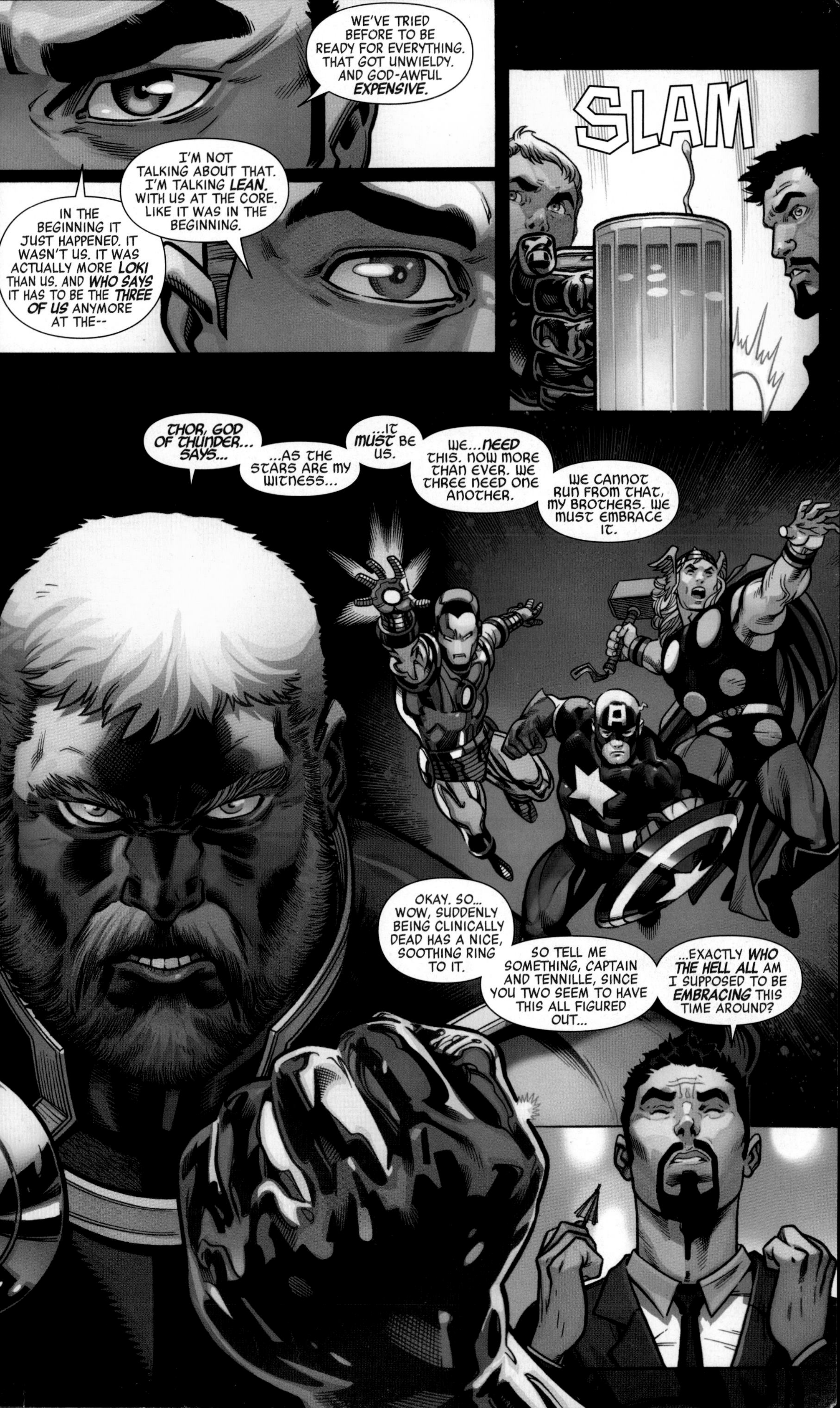
WE'VE TRIED BEFORE TO BE READY FOR EVERYTHING. THAT GOT UNWIELDY. AND GOD-AWFUL EXPENSIVE.
SLAM
I'M NOT TALKING ABOUT THAT. I'M TALKING LEAN. WITH US AT THE CORE. LIKE IT WAS IN THE BEGINNING.
IN THE BEGINNING IT JUST HAPPENED. IT WASN'T US. IT WAS ACTUALLY MORE LOKI THAN US. AND WHO SAYS IT HAS TO BE THE THREE OF US ANYMORE AT THE--
THOR, GOD OF THUNDER... SAYS...
...AS THE STARS ARE MY WITNESS...
...IT MUST BE US.
WE...NEED THIS. NOW MORE THAN EVER. WE THREE NEED ONE ANOTHER.
WE CANNOT RUN FROM THAT, MY BROTHERS. WE MUST EMBRACE IT.
OKAY. SO... WOW, SUDDENLY BEING CLINICALLY DEAD HAS A NICE, SOOTHING RING TO IT.
SO TELL ME SOMETHING, CAPTAIN AND TENNILLE, SINCE YOU TWO SEEM TO HAVE THIS ALL FIGURED OUT...
...EXACTLY WHO THE HELL ALL AM I SUPPOSED TO BE EMBRACING THIS TIME AROUND?

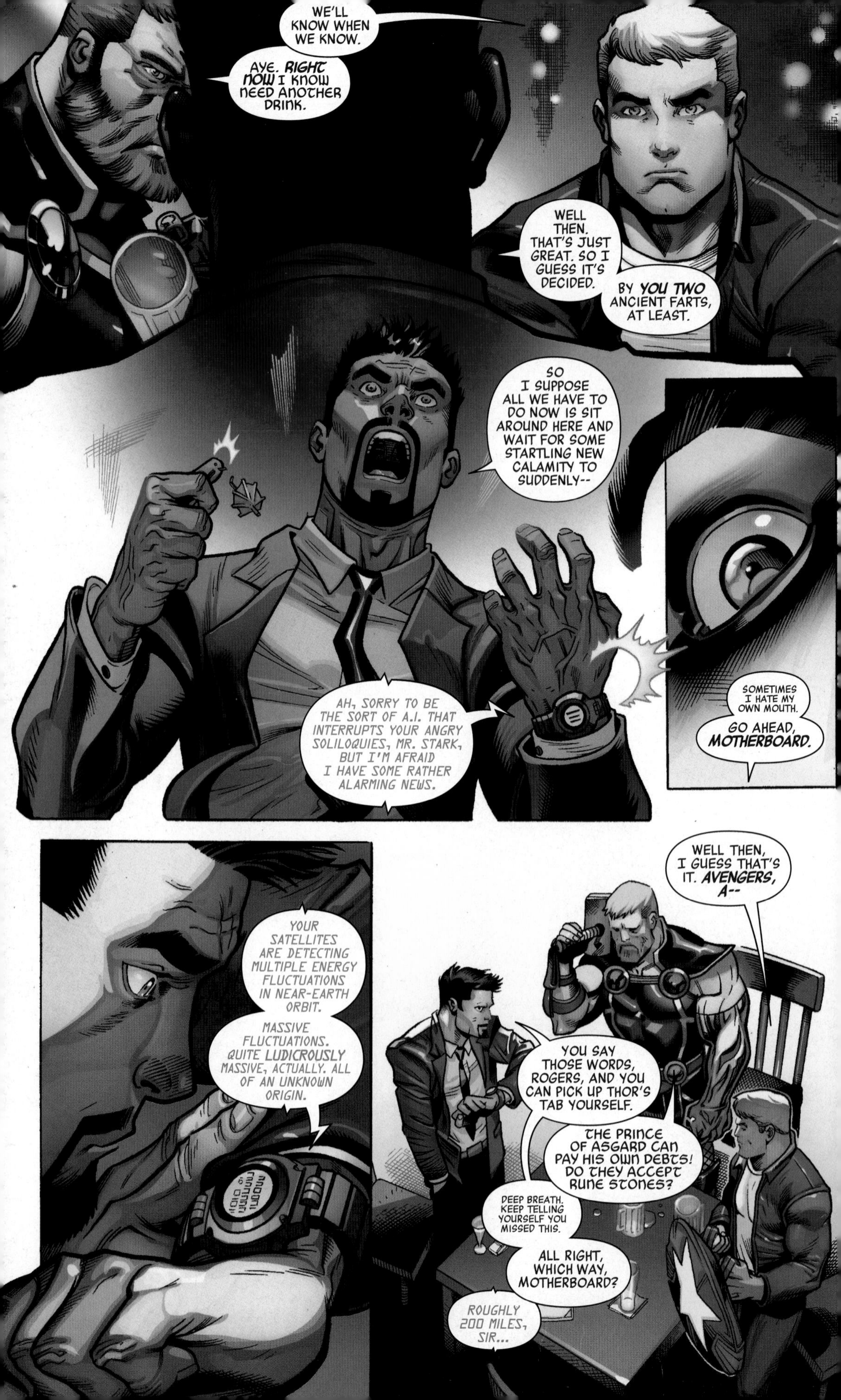

WE'LL KNOW WHEN WE KNOW.
AYE. RIGHT NOW I KNOW NEED ANOTHER DRINK.
WELL THEN. THAT'S JUST GREAT. SO I GUESS IT'S DECIDED.
BY YOU TWO ANCIENT FARTS, AT LEAST.
SO I SUPPOSE ALL WE HAVE TO DO NOW IS SIT AROUND HERE AND WAIT FOR SOME STARTLING NEW CALAMITY TO SUDDENLY--
AH, SORRY TO BE THE SORT OF A.I. THAT INTERRUPTS YOUR ANGRY SOLILOQUIES, MR. STARK, BUT I'M AFRAID I HAVE SOME RATHER ALARMING NEWS.
SOMETIMES I HATE MY OWN MOUTH.
GO AHEAD, MOTHERBOARD.
YOUR SATELLITES ARE DETECTING MULTIPLE ENERGY FLUCTUATIONS IN NEAR-EARTH ORBIT.
MASSIVE FLUCTUATIONS. QUITE LUDICROUSLY MASSIVE, ACTUALLY. ALL OF AN UNKNOWN ORIGIN.
WELL THEN, I GUESS THAT'S IT. AVENGERS, A--
YOU SAY THOSE WORDS, ROGERS, AND YOU CAN PICK UP THOR'S TAB YOURSELF.
THE PRINCE OF ASGARD CAN PAY HIS OWN DEBTS! DO THEY ACCEPT RUNE STONES?
DEEP BREATH. KEEP TELLING YOURSELF YOU MISSED THIS.
ALL RIGHT, WHICH WAY, MOTHERBOARD?
ROUGHLY 200 MILES, SIR...

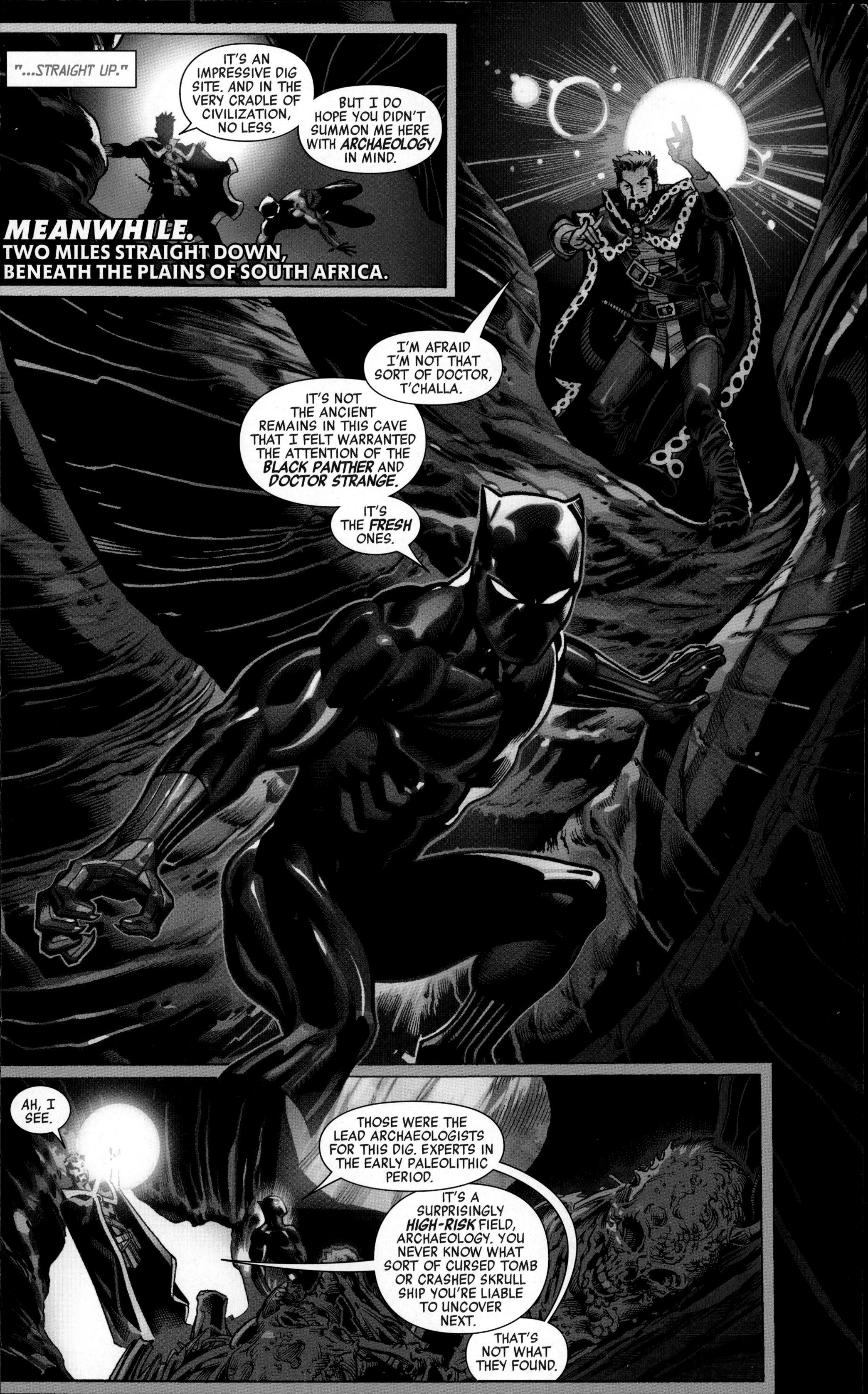
"...STRAIGHT UP."
IT'S AN IMPRESSIVE DIG SITE. AND IN THE VERY CRADLE OF CIVILIZATION, NO LESS.
BUT I DO HOPE YOU DIDN'T SUMMON ME HERE WITH ARCHAEOLOGY IN MIND.
MEANWHILE.
TWO MILES STRAIGHT DOWN, BENEATH THE PLAINS OF SOUTH AFRICA.
I'M AFRAID I'M NOT THAT SORT OF DOCTOR, T'CHALLA.
IT'S NOT THE ANCIENT REMAINS IN THIS CAVE THAT I FELT WARRANTED THE ATTENTION OF THE BLACK PANTHER AND DOCTOR STRANGE.
IT'S THE FRESH ONES.
AH, I SEE.
THOSE WERE THE LEAD ARCHAEOLOGISTS FOR THIS DIG. EXPERTS IN THE EARLY PALEOLITHIC PERIOD.
IT'S A SURPRISINGLY HIGH-RISK FIELD, ARCHAEOLOGY. YOU NEVER KNOW WHAT SORT OF CURSED TOMB OR CRASHED SKRULL SHIP YOU'RE LIABLE TO UNCOVER NEXT.
THAT'S NOT WHAT THEY FOUND.

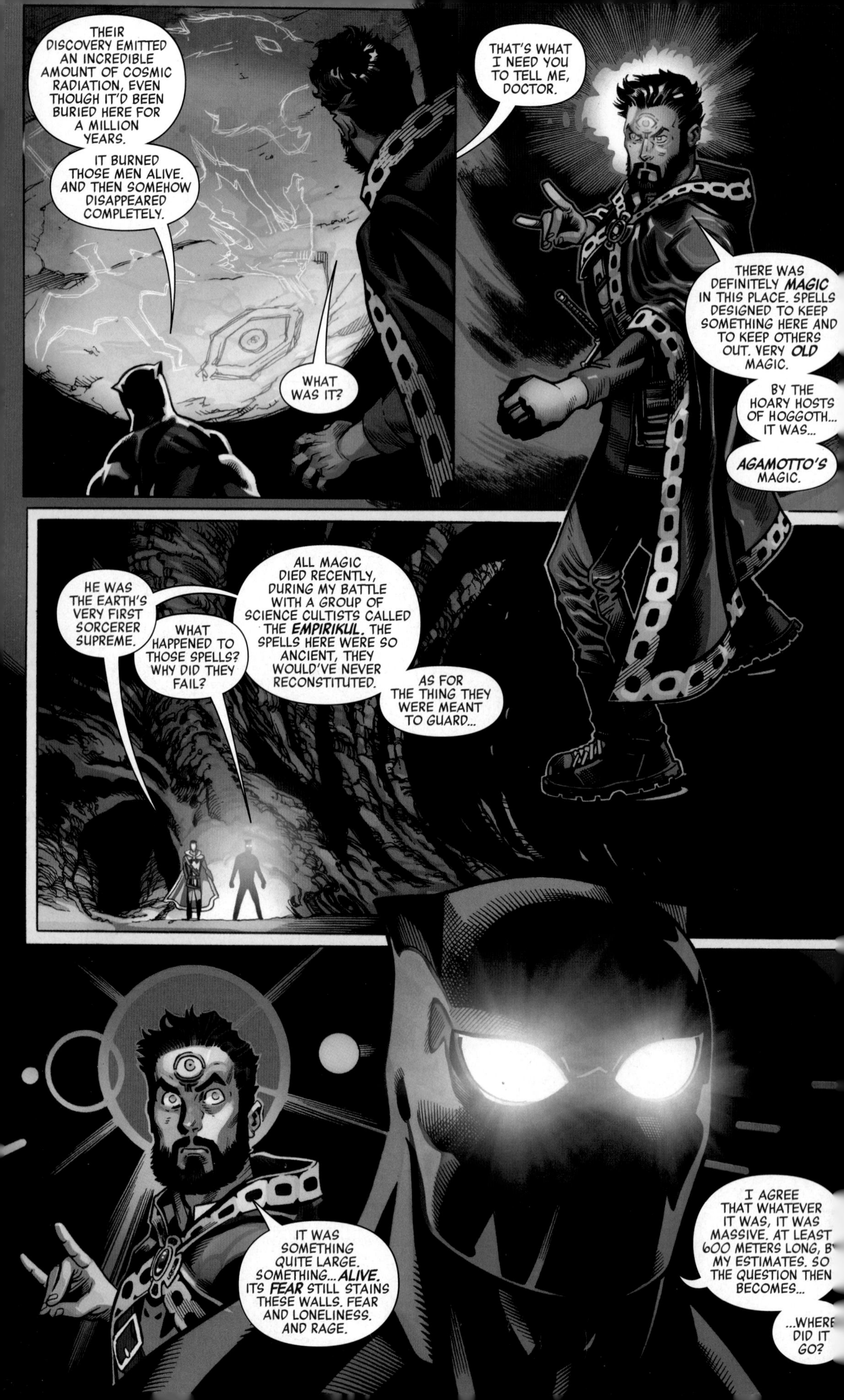
THEIR DISCOVERY EMITTED AN INCREDIBLE AMOUNT OF COSMIC RADIATION, EVEN THOUGH IT'D BEEN BURIED HERE FOR A MILLION YEARS.
IT BURNED THOSE MEN ALIVE. AND THEN SOMEHOW DISAPPEARED COMPLETELY.
WHAT WAS IT?
THAT'S WHAT I NEED YOU TO TELL ME, DOCTOR.
THERE WAS DEFINITELY MAGIC IN THIS PLACE. SPELLS DESIGNED TO KEEP SOMETHING HERE AND TO KEEP OTHERS OUT. VERY OLD MAGIC.
BY THE HOARY HOSTS OF HOGGOTH... IT WAS...
AGAMOTTO'S MAGIC.
HE WAS THE EARTH'S VERY FIRST SORCERER SUPREME.
WHAT HAPPENED TO THOSE SPELLS? WHY DID THEY FAIL?
ALL MAGIC DIED RECENTLY, DURING MY BATTLE WITH A GROUP OF SCIENCE CULTISTS CALLED THE EMPIRIKUL. THE SPELLS HERE WERE SO ANCIENT, THEY WOULD'VE NEVER RECONSTITUTED.
AS FOR THE THING THEY WERE MEANT TO GUARD...
IT WAS SOMETHING QUITE LARGE. SOMETHING... ALIVE. ITS FEAR STILL STAINS THESE WALLS. FEAR AND LONELINESS. AND RAGE.
I AGREE THAT WHATEVER IT WAS, IT WAS MASSIVE. AT LEAST 600 METERS LONG, BY MY ESTIMATES. SO THE QUESTION THEN BECOMES...
...WHERE DID IT GO?

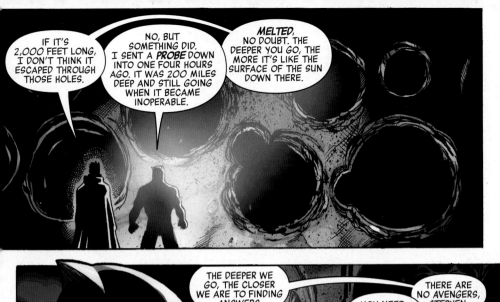

IF IT'S 2,000 FEET LONG, I DON'T THINK IT ESCAPED THROUGH THOSE HOLES.

NO, BUT SOMETHING DID. I SENT A *PROBE* DOWN INTO ONE FOUR HOURS AGO. IT WAS 200 MILES DEEP AND STILL GOING WHEN IT BECAME INOPERABLE.

MELTED, NO DOUBT. THE DEEPER YOU GO, THE MORE IT'S LIKE THE SURFACE OF THE SUN DOWN THERE.

THE DEEPER WE GO, THE CLOSER WE ARE TO FINDING ANSWERS.

YOU NEED THE *AVENGERS* ON THIS, T'CHALLA.

THERE ARE NO AVENGERS, STEPHEN.

I'VE SEEN THIS MOVIE BEFORE, YOU KNOW. THIS IS ONE OF THOSE THINGS THAT BLOWS UP IN OUR FACES IF WE GO BLUNDERING IN. AND MAYBE BLOWS UP THE EARTH ALONG WITH IT.

THE SYMBOLS ON THAT CAVE WALL DATE BACK TO THE *STONE AGE.* MINE IS AMONG THEM. AND SO IS YOURS.

WHATEVER IS HAPPENING HERE, DOCTOR, WE ARE ALREADY INVOLVED.

AND HAVE BEEN FOR A VERY LONG TIME.

I WILL SEE YOU BELOW.

GREAT. SO IF ANYBODY NEEDS ME...

...I SUPPOSE I'LL BE AT THE *CENTER OF THE EARTH.*

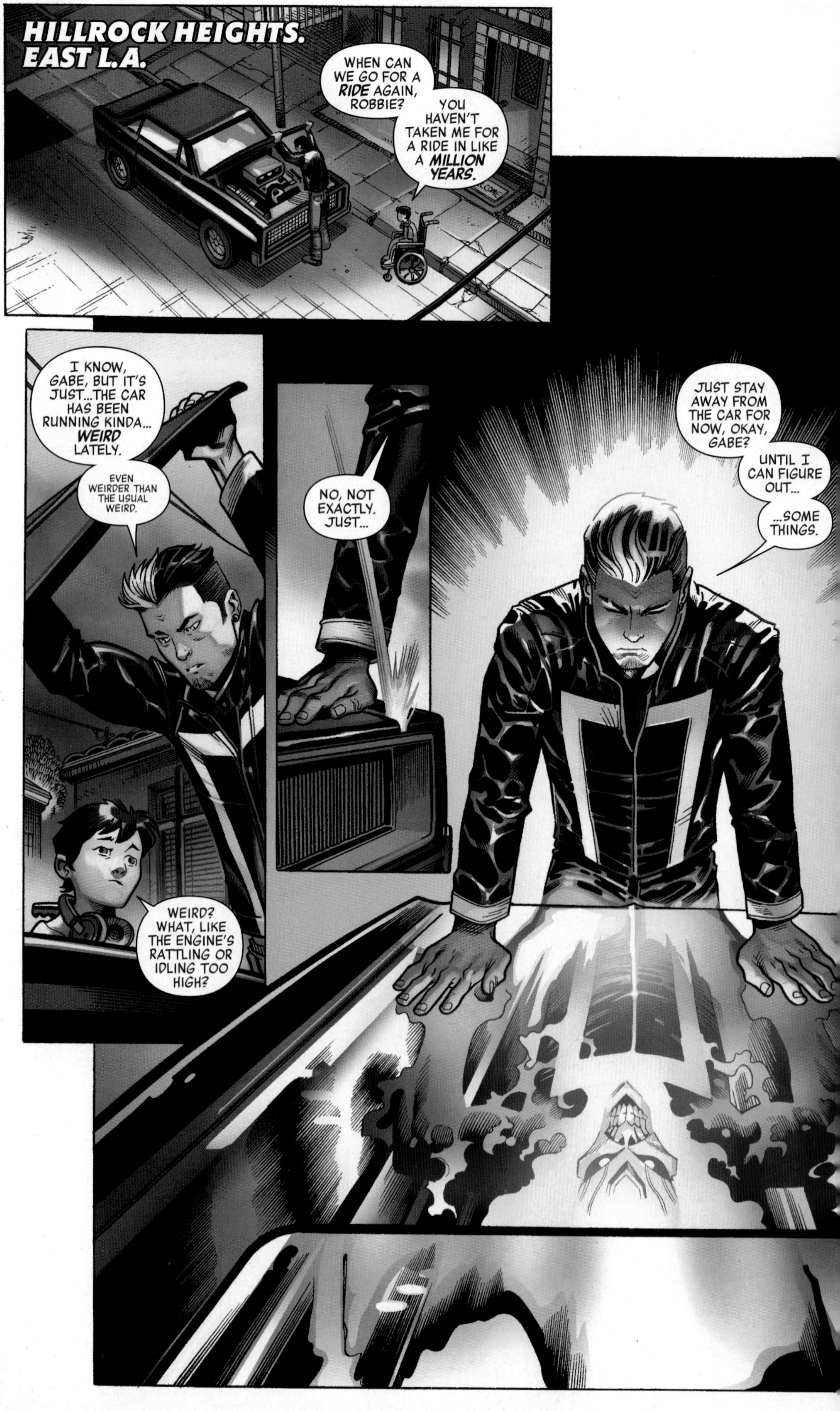
HILLROCK HEIGHTS. EAST L.A.
WHEN CAN WE GO FOR A RIDE AGAIN, ROBBIE?
YOU HAVEN'T TAKEN ME FOR A RIDE IN LIKE A MILLION YEARS.
I KNOW, GABE, BUT IT'S JUST...THE CAR HAS BEEN RUNNING KINDA... WEIRD LATELY.
EVEN WEIRDER THAN THE USUAL WEIRD.
WEIRD? WHAT, LIKE THE ENGINE'S RATTLING OR IDLING TOO HIGH?
NO, NOT EXACTLY. JUST...
JUST STAY AWAY FROM THE CAR FOR NOW, OKAY, GABE?
UNTIL I CAN FIGURE OUT...
...SOME THINGS.

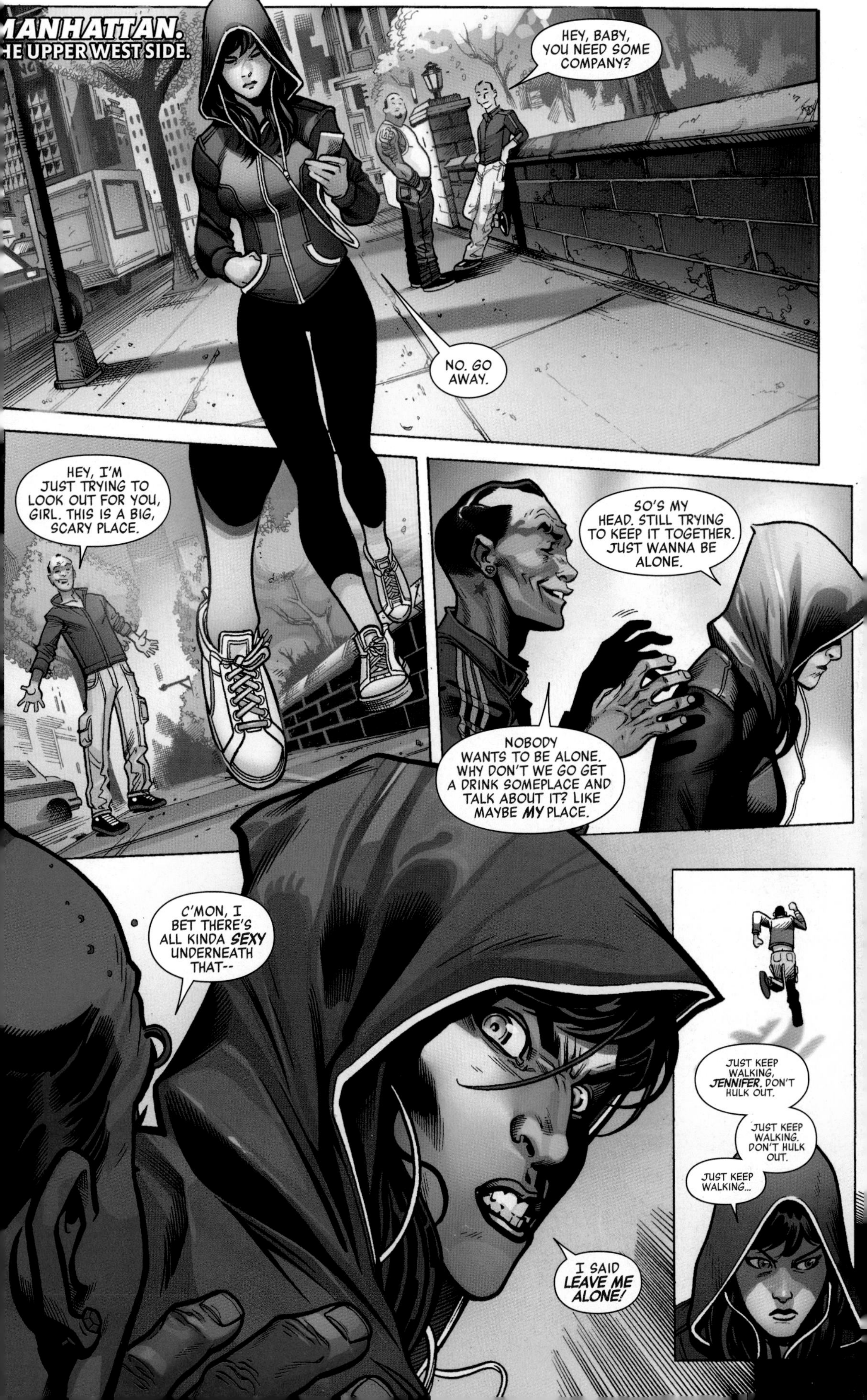
MANHATTAN.
HE UPPER WEST SIDE.
HEY, BABY, YOU NEED SOME COMPANY?
NO. GO AWAY.
HEY, I'M JUST TRYING TO LOOK OUT FOR YOU, GIRL. THIS IS A BIG, SCARY PLACE.
SO'S MY HEAD. STILL TRYING TO KEEP IT TOGETHER. JUST WANNA BE ALONE.
NOBODY WANTS TO BE ALONE. WHY DON'T WE GO GET A DRINK SOMEPLACE AND TALK ABOUT IT? LIKE MAYBE MY PLACE.
C'MON, I BET THERE'S ALL KINDA SEXY UNDERNEATH THAT--
I SAID LEAVE ME ALONE!
JUST KEEP WALKING, JENNIFER. DON'T HULK OUT.
JUST KEEP WALKING. DON'T HULK OUT.
JUST KEEP WALKING...

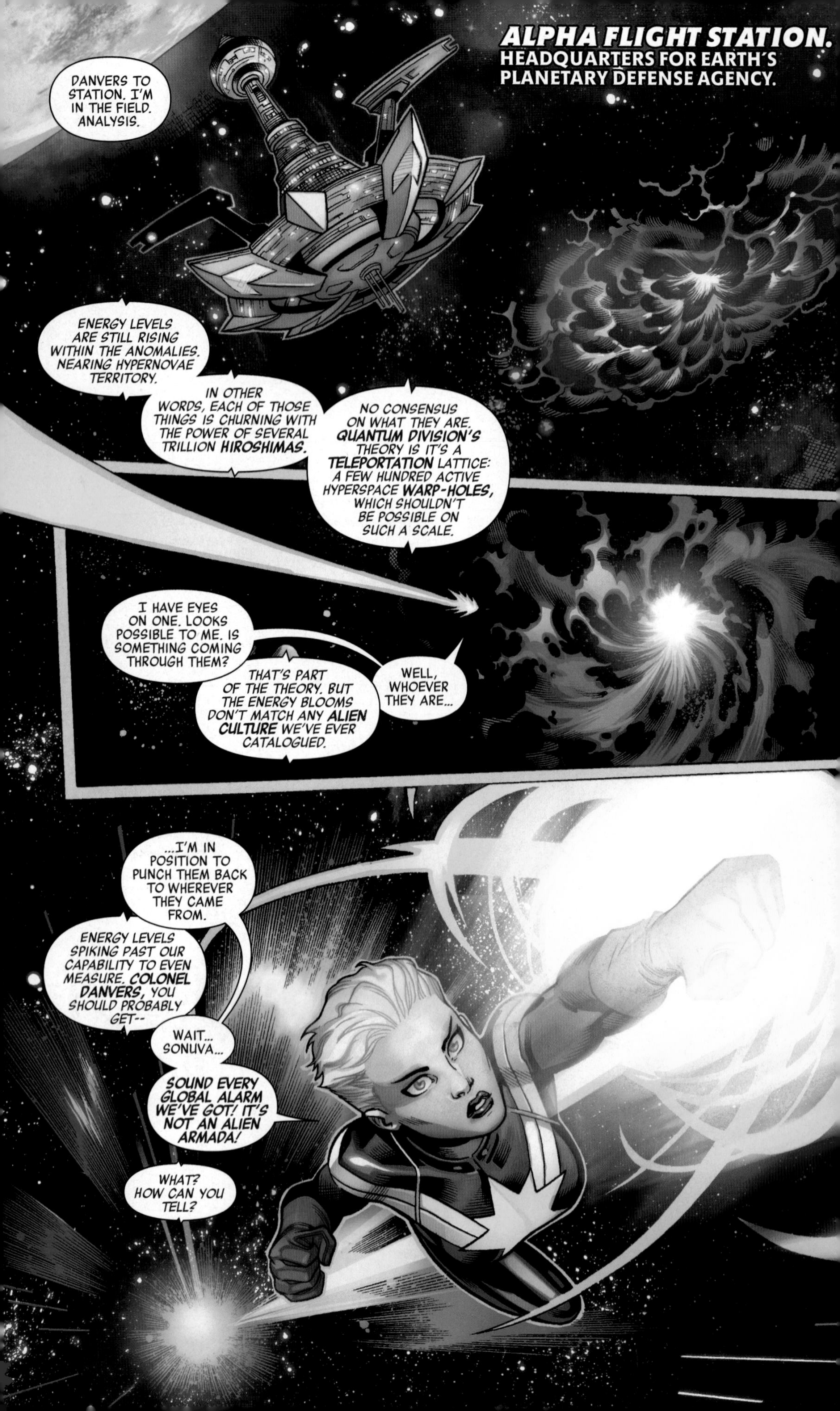
ALPHA FLIGHT STATION.
HEADQUARTERS FOR EARTH'S PLANETARY DEFENSE AGENCY.
DANVERS TO STATION. I'M IN THE FIELD. ANALYSIS.
ENERGY LEVELS ARE STILL RISING WITHIN THE ANOMALIES. NEARING HYPERNOVAE TERRITORY.
IN OTHER WORDS, EACH OF THOSE THINGS IS CHURNING WITH THE POWER OF SEVERAL TRILLION HIROSHIMAS.
NO CONSENSUS ON WHAT THEY ARE. QUANTUM DIVISION'S THEORY IS IT'S A TELEPORTATION LATTICE: A FEW HUNDRED ACTIVE HYPERSPACE WARP-HOLES, WHICH SHOULDN'T BE POSSIBLE ON SUCH A SCALE.
I HAVE EYES ON ONE. LOOKS POSSIBLE TO ME. IS SOMETHING COMING THROUGH THEM?
THAT'S PART OF THE THEORY. BUT THE ENERGY BLOOMS DON'T MATCH ANY ALIEN CULTURE WE'VE EVER CATALOGUED.
WELL, WHOEVER THEY ARE...
...I'M IN POSITION TO PUNCH THEM BACK TO WHEREVER THEY CAME FROM.
ENERGY LEVELS SPIKING PAST OUR CAPABILITY TO EVEN MEASURE. COLONEL DANVERS, YOU SHOULD PROBABLY GET--
WAIT... SONUVA...
SOUND EVERY GLOBAL ALARM WE'VE GOT! IT'S NOT AN ALIEN ARMADA!
WHAT? HOW CAN YOU TELL?

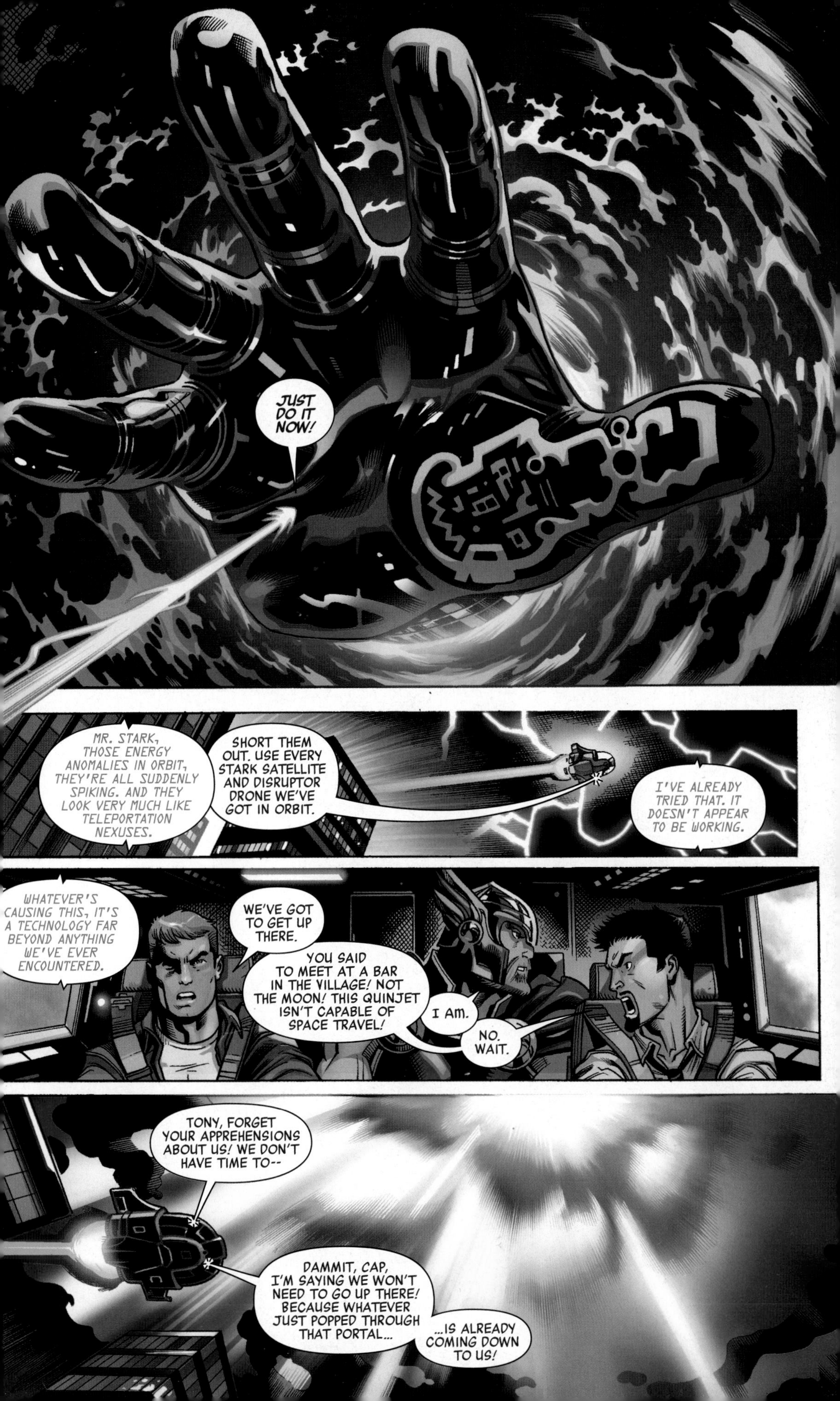
JUST DO IT NOW!
MR. STARK, THOSE ENERGY ANOMALIES IN ORBIT, THEY'RE ALL SUDDENLY SPIKING. AND THEY LOOK VERY MUCH LIKE TELEPORTATION NEXUSES.
SHORT THEM OUT. USE EVERY STARK SATELLITE AND DISRUPTOR DRONE WE'VE GOT IN ORBIT.
I'VE ALREADY TRIED THAT. IT DOESN'T APPEAR TO BE WORKING.
WHATEVER'S CAUSING THIS, IT'S A TECHNOLOGY FAR BEYOND ANYTHING WE'VE EVER ENCOUNTERED.
WE'VE GOT TO GET UP THERE.
YOU SAID TO MEET AT A BAR IN THE VILLAGE! NOT THE MOON! THIS QUINJET ISN'T CAPABLE OF SPACE TRAVEL!
I AM.
NO. WAIT.
TONY, FORGET YOUR APPREHENSIONS ABOUT US! WE DON'T HAVE TIME TO--
DAMMIT, CAP, I'M SAYING WE WON'T NEED TO GO UP THERE! BECAUSE WHATEVER JUST POPPED THROUGH THAT PORTAL...
...IS ALREADY COMING DOWN TO US!

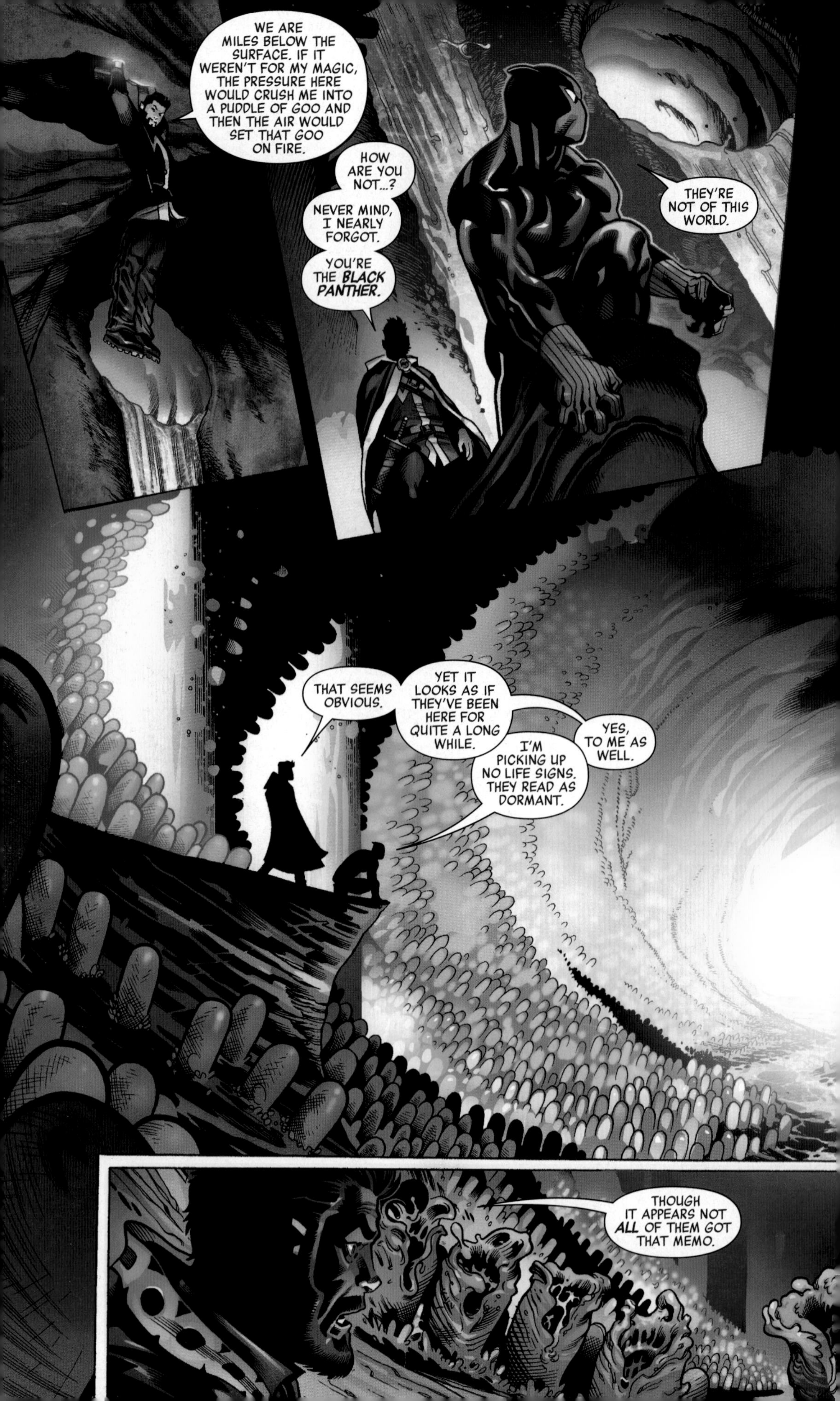
WE ARE MILES BELOW THE SURFACE. IF IT WEREN'T FOR MY MAGIC, THE PRESSURE HERE WOULD CRUSH ME INTO A PUDDLE OF GOO AND THEN THE AIR WOULD SET THAT GOO ON FIRE.
HOW ARE YOU NOT...?
NEVER MIND, I NEARLY FORGOT.
YOU'RE THE BLACK PANTHER.
THEY'RE NOT OF THIS WORLD.
THAT SEEMS OBVIOUS.
YET IT LOOKS AS IF THEY'VE BEEN HERE FOR QUITE A LONG WHILE.
YES, TO ME AS WELL.
I'M PICKING UP NO LIFE SIGNS. THEY READ AS DORMANT.
THOUGH IT APPEARS NOT ALL OF THEM GOT THAT MEMO.

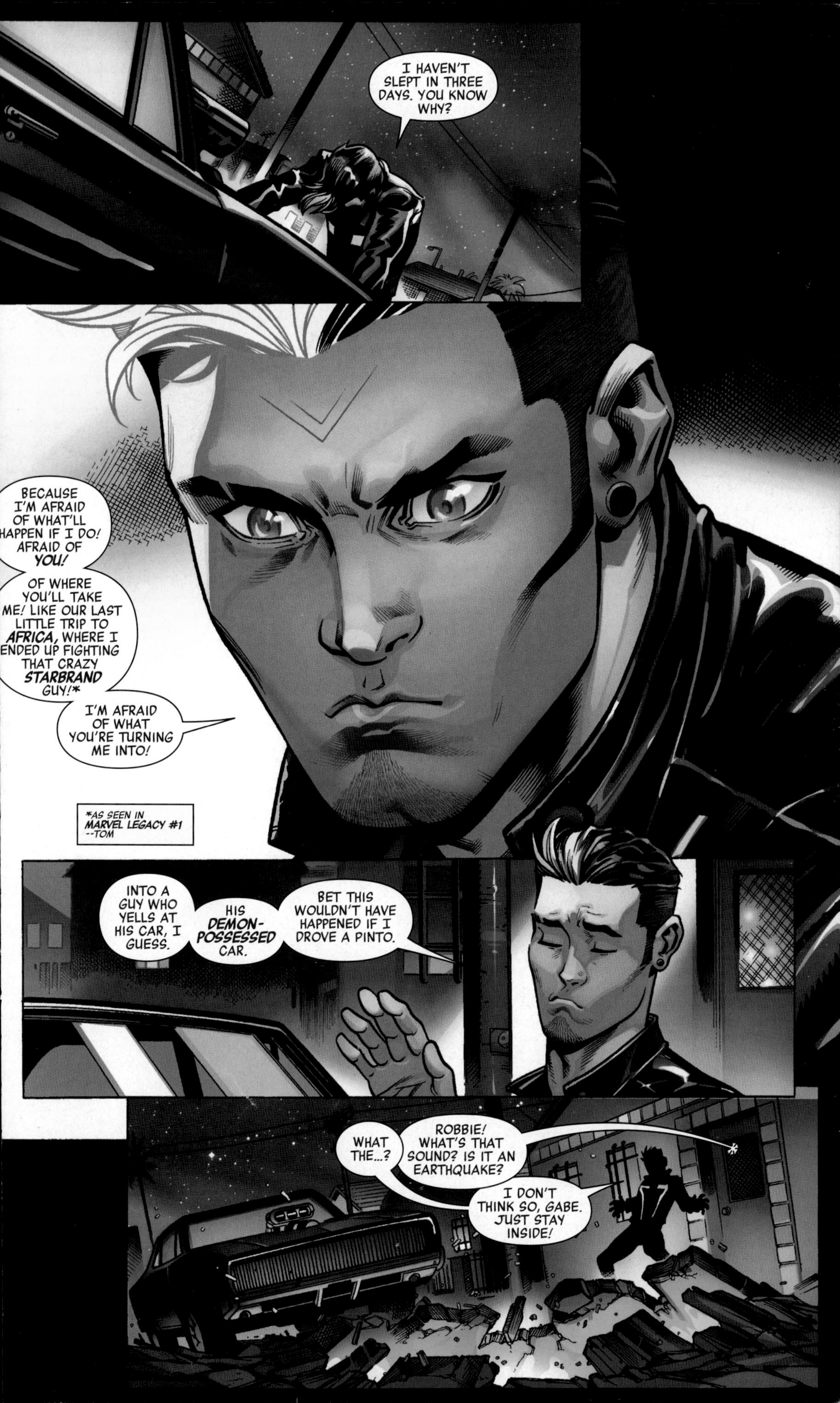
I HAVEN'T SLEPT IN THREE DAYS. YOU KNOW WHY?
BECAUSE I'M AFRAID OF WHAT'LL HAPPEN IF I DO! AFRAID OF YOU!
OF WHERE YOU'LL TAKE ME! LIKE OUR LAST LITTLE TRIP TO AFRICA, WHERE I ENDED UP FIGHTING THAT CRAZY STARBRAND GUY!*
I'M AFRAID OF WHAT YOU'RE TURNING ME INTO!
*AS SEEN IN MARVEL LEGACY #1 --TOM
INTO A GUY WHO YELLS AT HIS CAR, I GUESS.
HIS DEMON-POSSESSED CAR.
BET THIS WOULDN'T HAVE HAPPENED IF I DROVE A PINTO.
WHAT THE...?
ROBBIE! WHAT'S THAT SOUND? IS IT AN EARTHQUAKE?
I DON'T THINK SO, GABE. JUST STAY INSIDE!

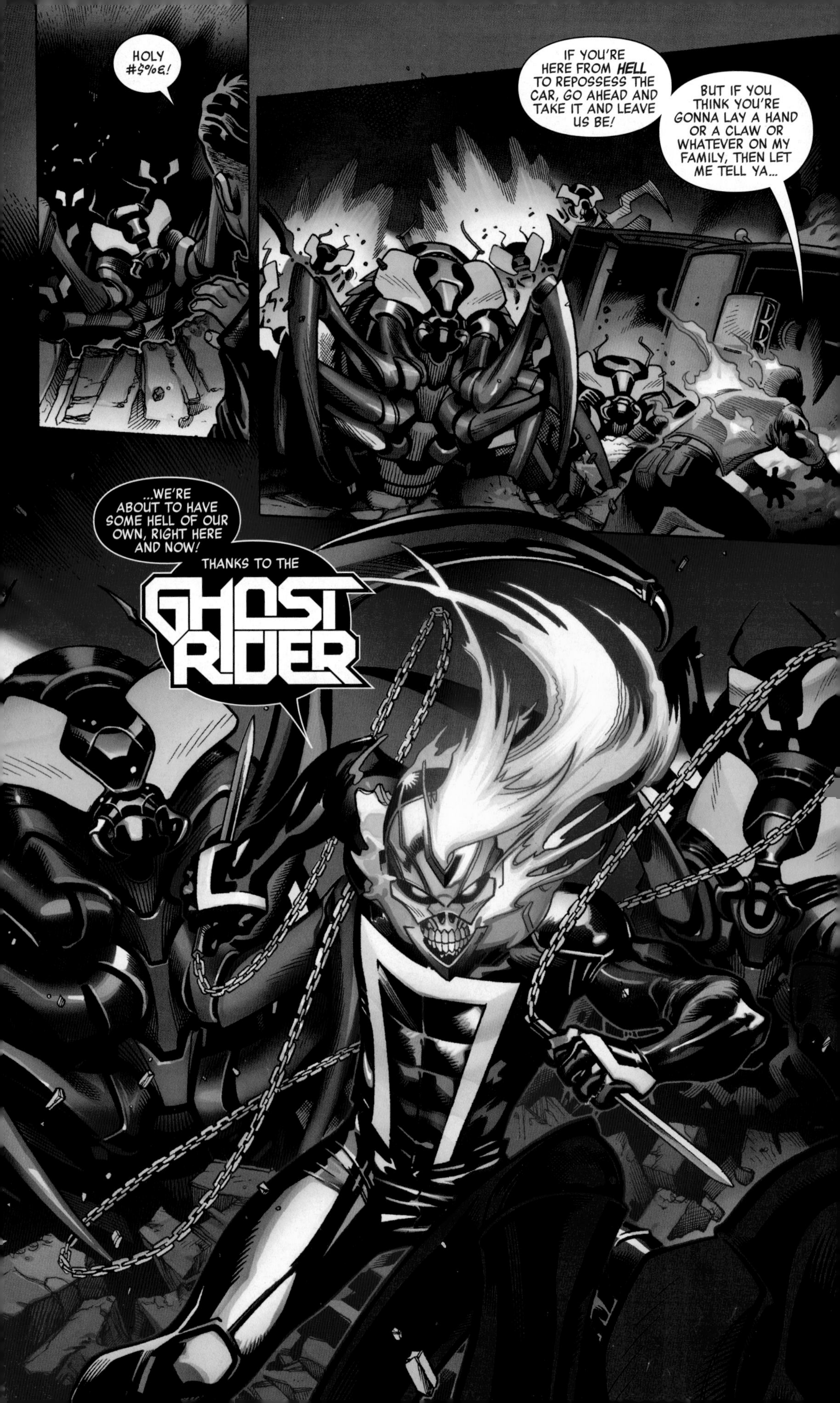
HOLY #$%&!
IF YOU'RE HERE FROM HELL TO REPOSSESS THE CAR, GO AHEAD AND TAKE IT AND LEAVE US BE!
BUT IF YOU THINK YOU'RE GONNA LAY A HAND OR A CLAW OR WHATEVER ON MY FAMILY, THEN LET ME TELL YA...
...WE'RE ABOUT TO HAVE SOME HELL OF OUR OWN, RIGHT HERE AND NOW!
THANKS TO THE
GHOST RIDER

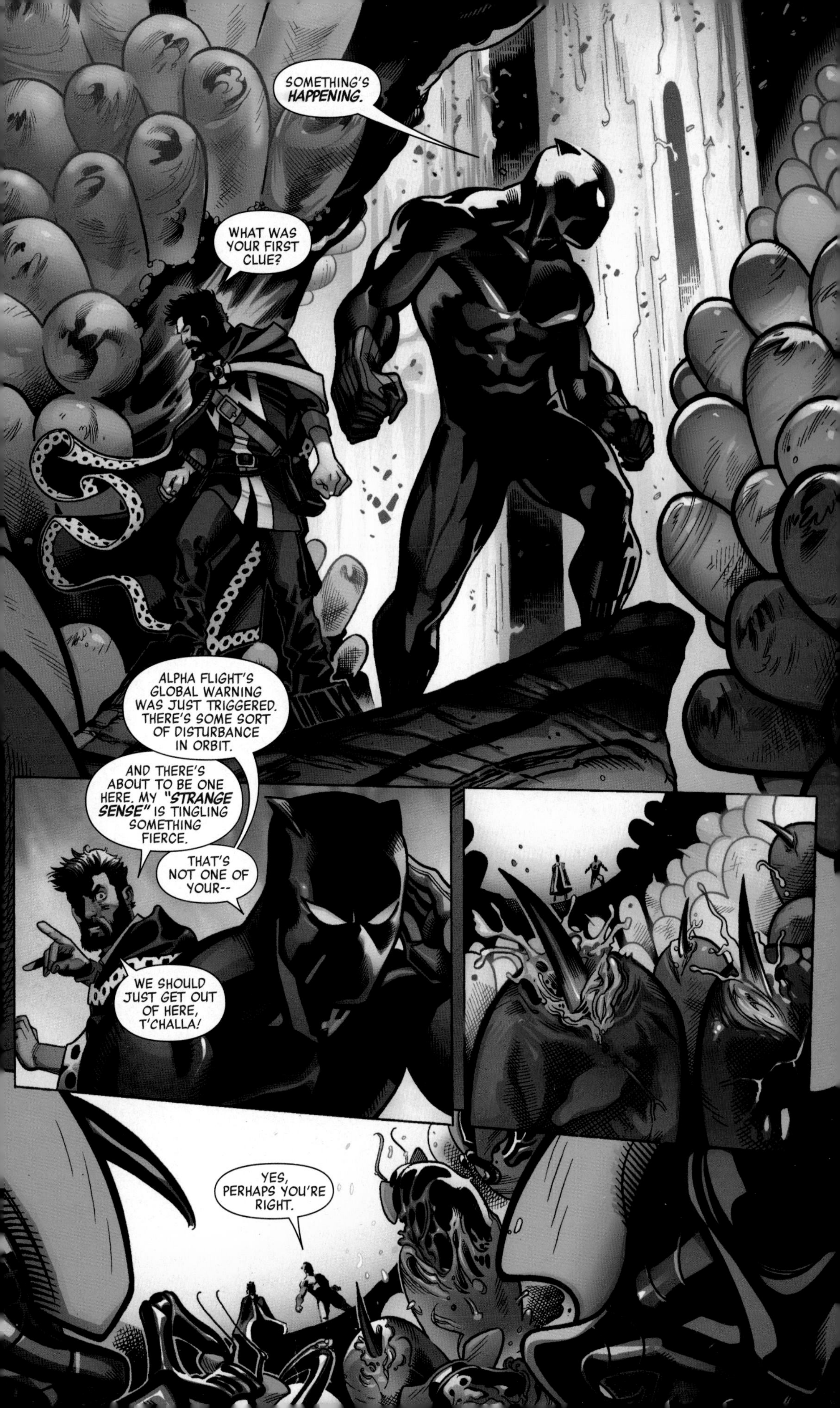
SOMETHING'S HAPPENING.
WHAT WAS YOUR FIRST CLUE?
ALPHA FLIGHT'S GLOBAL WARNING WAS JUST TRIGGERED. THERE'S SOME SORT OF DISTURBANCE IN ORBIT.
AND THERE'S ABOUT TO BE ONE HERE. MY "STRANGE SENSE" IS TINGLING SOMETHING FIERCE.
THAT'S NOT ONE OF YOUR--
WE SHOULD JUST GET OUT OF HERE, T'CHALLA!
YES, PERHAPS YOU'RE RIGHT.

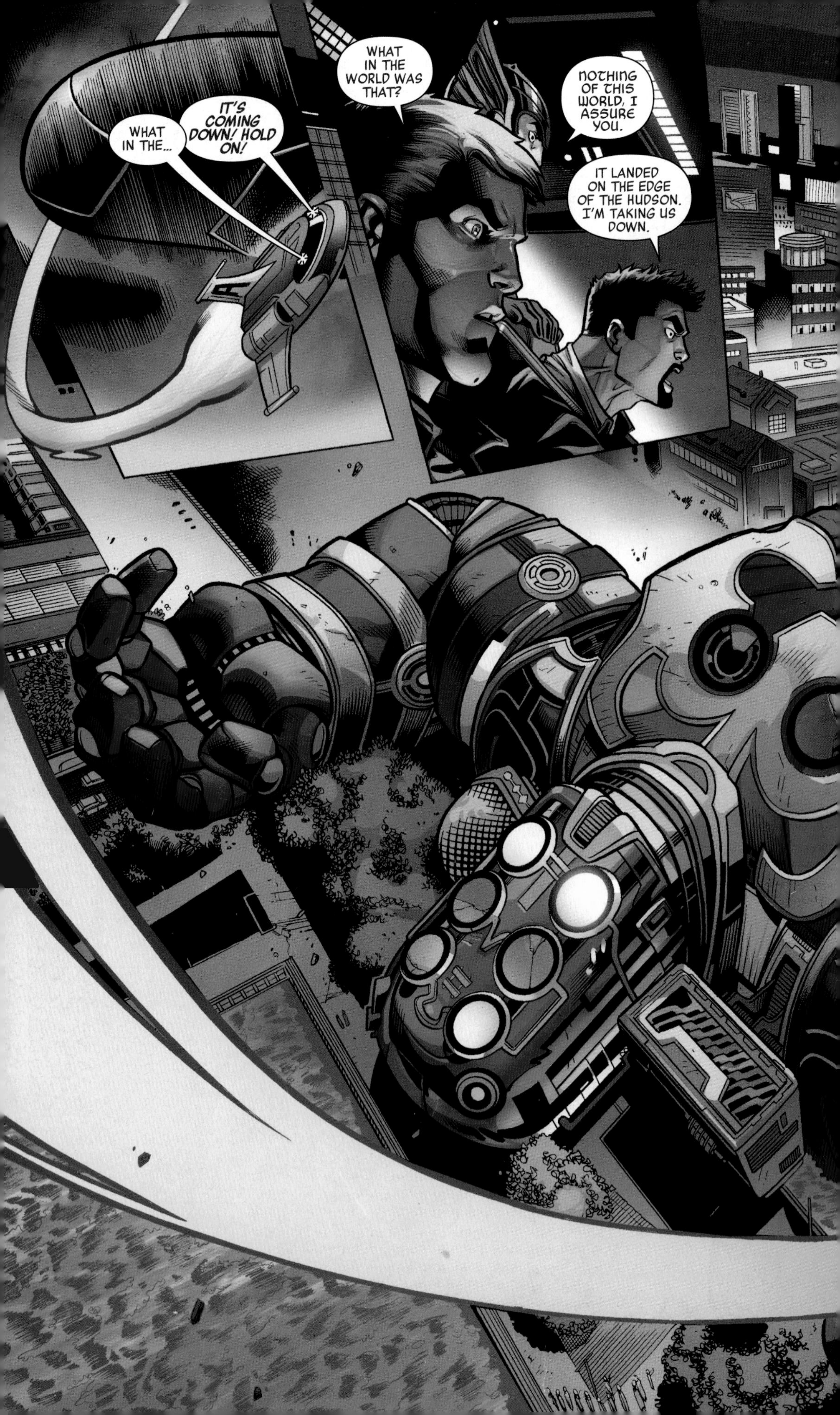
WHAT IN THE...
IT'S COMING DOWN! HOLD ON!
WHAT IN THE WORLD WAS THAT?
NOTHING OF THIS WORLD, I ASSURE YOU.
IT LANDED ON THE EDGE OF THE HUDSON. I'M TAKING US DOWN.

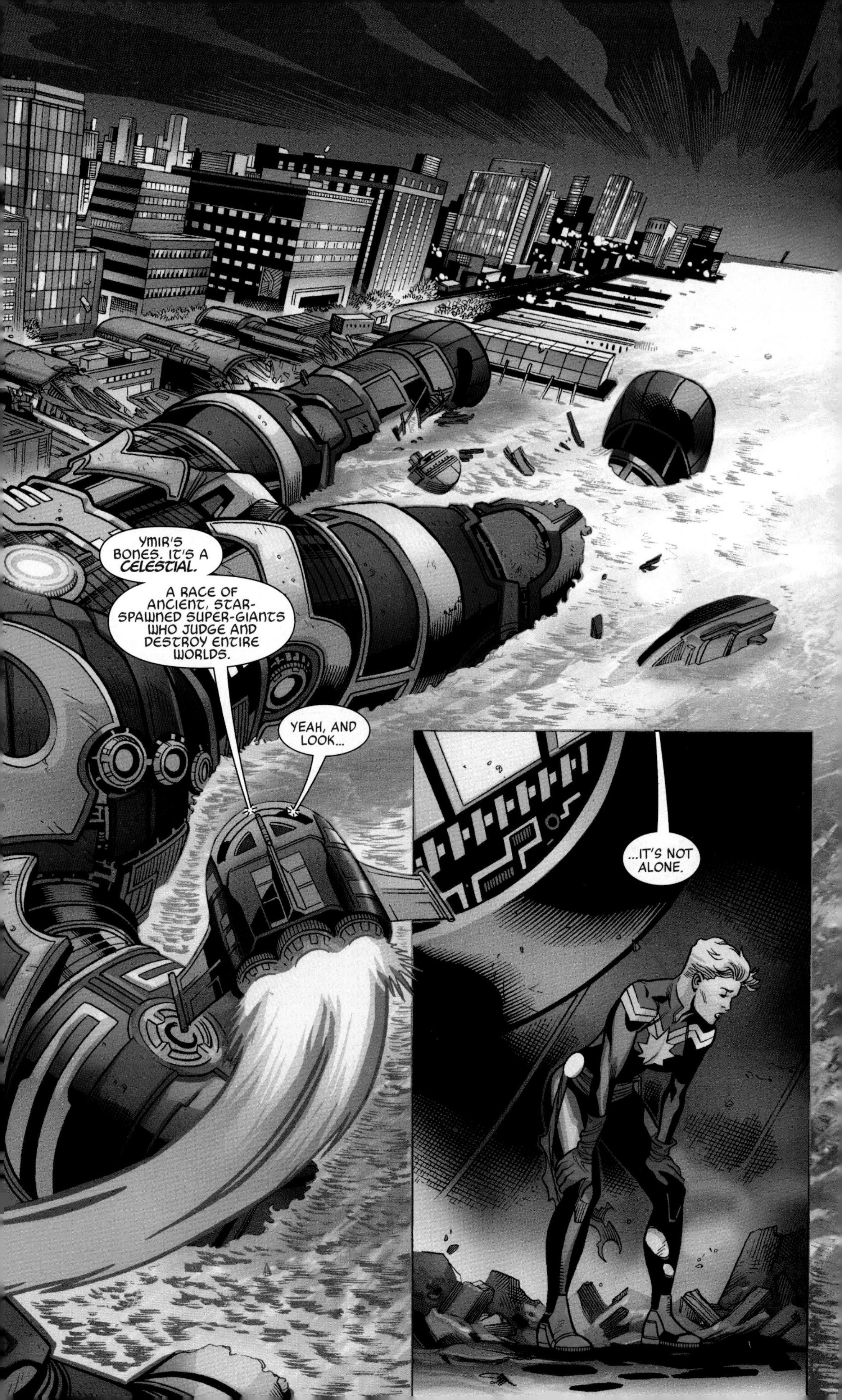
YMIR'S BONES. IT'S A CELESTIAL.
A RACE OF ANCIENT, STAR-SPAWNED SUPER-GIANTS WHO JUDGE AND DESTROY ENTIRE WORLDS.
YEAH, AND LOOK...
...IT'S NOT ALONE.

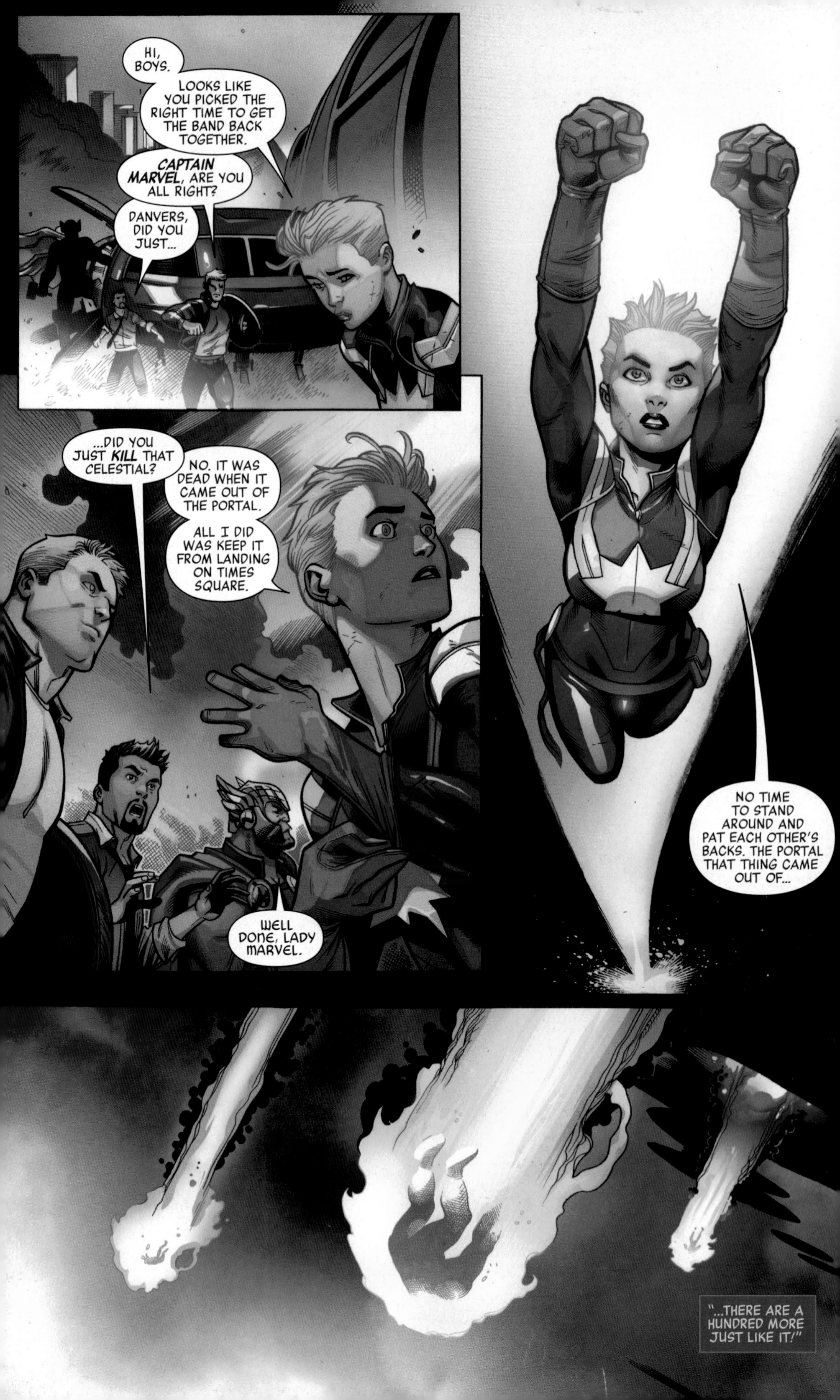

HI, BOYS.
LOOKS LIKE YOU PICKED THE RIGHT TIME TO GET THE BAND BACK TOGETHER.
CAPTAIN MARVEL, ARE YOU ALL RIGHT?
DANVERS, DID YOU JUST...
...DID YOU JUST KILL THAT CELESTIAL?
NO. IT WAS DEAD WHEN IT CAME OUT OF THE PORTAL.
ALL I DID WAS KEEP IT FROM LANDING ON TIMES SQUARE.
WELL DONE, LADY MARVEL.
NO TIME TO STAND AROUND AND PAT EACH OTHER'S BACKS. THE PORTAL THAT THING CAME OUT OF...
"...THERE ARE A HUNDRED MORE JUST LIKE IT!"

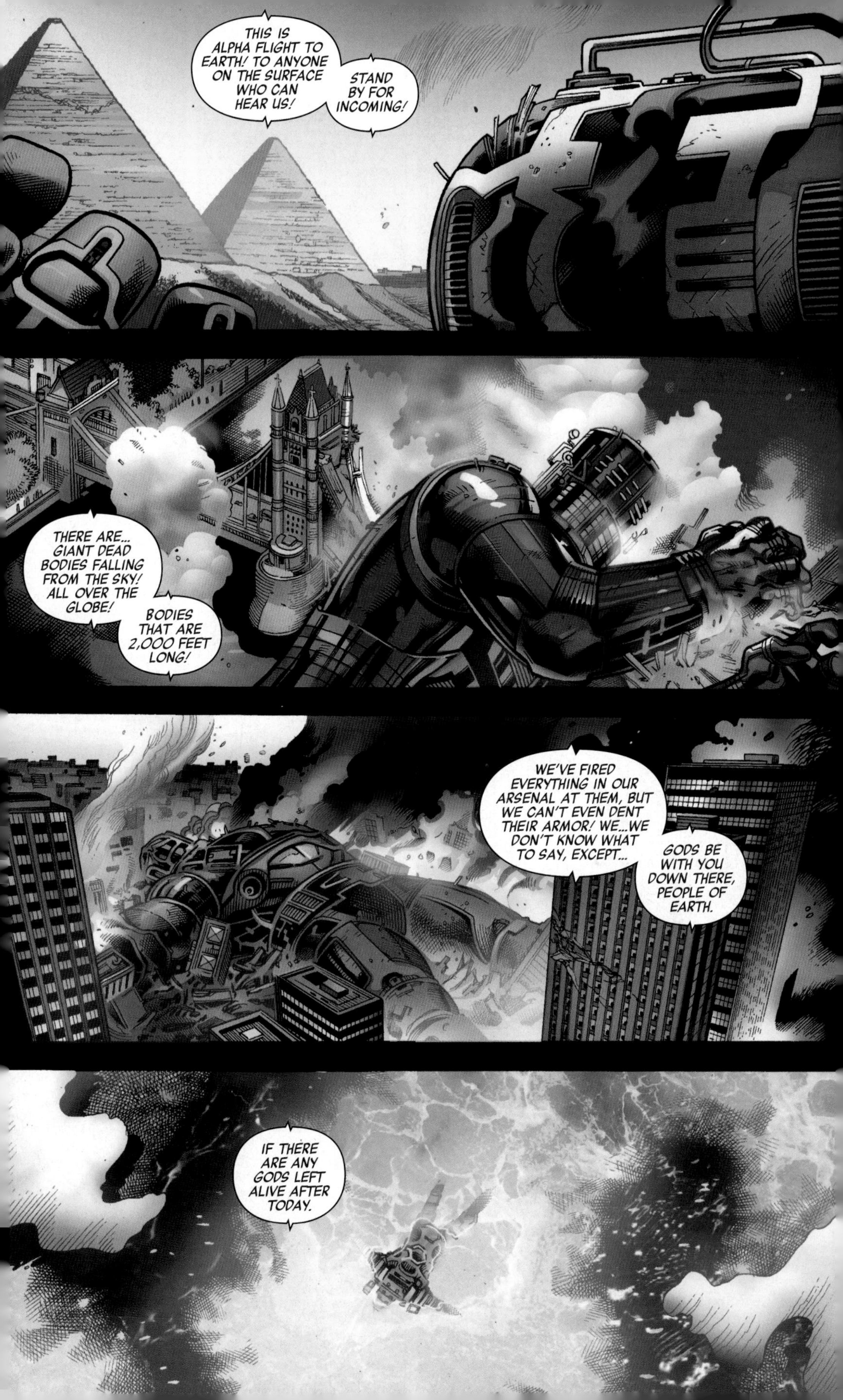
THIS IS ALPHA FLIGHT TO EARTH! TO ANYONE ON THE SURFACE WHO CAN HEAR US!
STAND BY FOR INCOMING!
THERE ARE... GIANT DEAD BODIES FALLING FROM THE SKY! ALL OVER THE GLOBE!
BODIES THAT ARE 2,000 FEET LONG!
WE'VE FIRED EVERYTHING IN OUR ARSENAL AT THEM, BUT WE CAN'T EVEN DENT THEIR ARMOR! WE...WE DON'T KNOW WHAT TO SAY, EXCEPT...
GODS BE WITH YOU DOWN THERE, PEOPLE OF EARTH.
IF THERE ARE ANY GODS LEFT ALIVE AFTER TODAY.

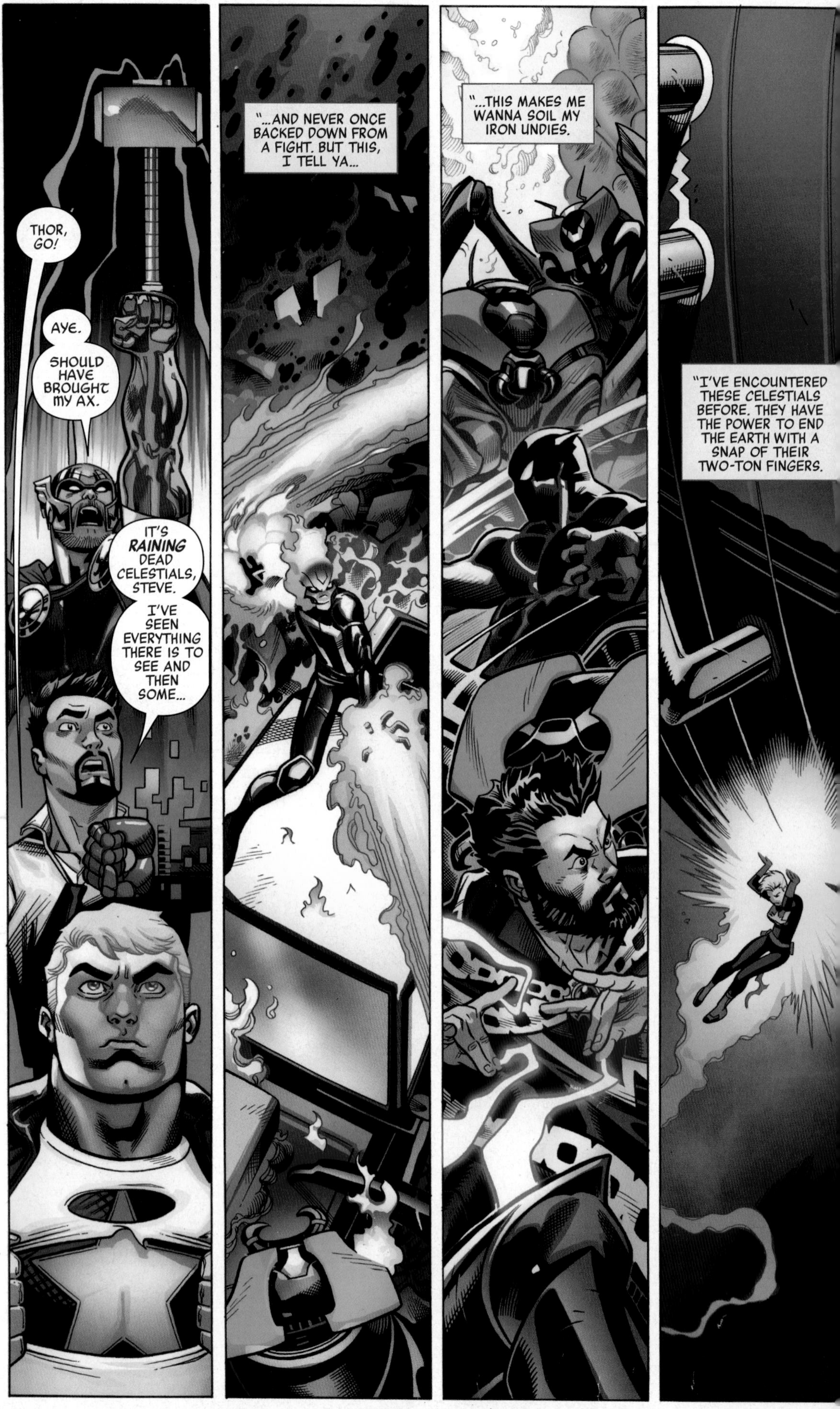

THOR, GO!
AYE.
SHOULD HAVE BROUGHT MY AX.
IT'S **RAINING** DEAD CELESTIALS, STEVE.
I'VE SEEN EVERYTHING THERE IS TO SEE AND THEN SOME...
"...AND NEVER ONCE BACKED DOWN FROM A FIGHT. BUT THIS, I TELL YA...
"...THIS MAKES ME WANNA SOIL MY IRON UNDIES.
"I'VE ENCOUNTERED THESE CELESTIALS BEFORE. THEY HAVE THE POWER TO END THE EARTH WITH A SNAP OF THEIR TWO-TON FINGERS.

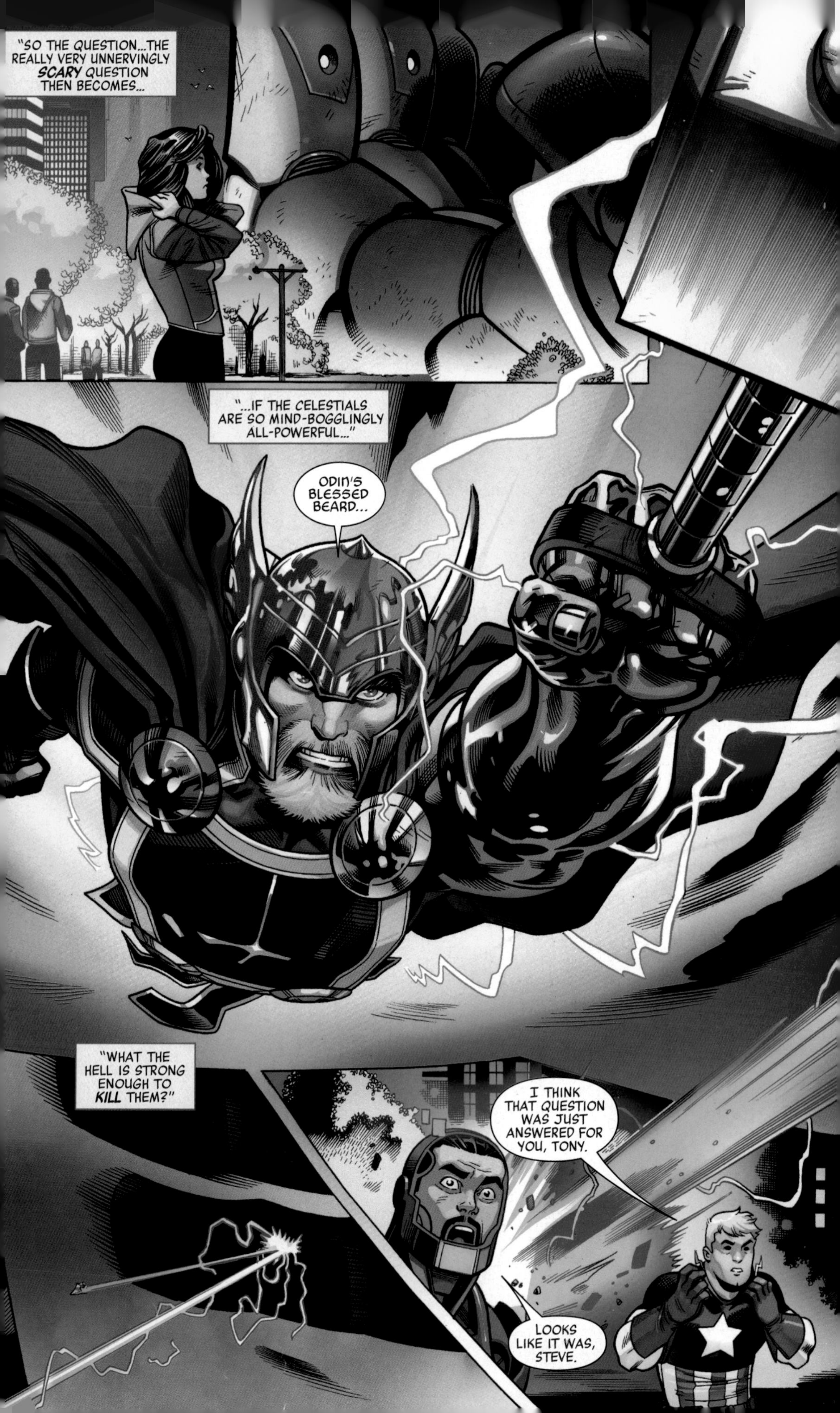
"SO THE QUESTION...THE REALLY VERY UNNERVINGLY SCARY QUESTION THEN BECOMES...
"...IF THE CELESTIALS ARE SO MIND-BOGGLINGLY ALL-POWERFUL..."
ODIN'S BLESSED BEARD...
"WHAT THE HELL IS STRONG ENOUGH TO KILL THEM?"
I THINK THAT QUESTION WAS JUST ANSWERED FOR YOU, TONY.
LOOKS LIKE IT WAS, STEVE.

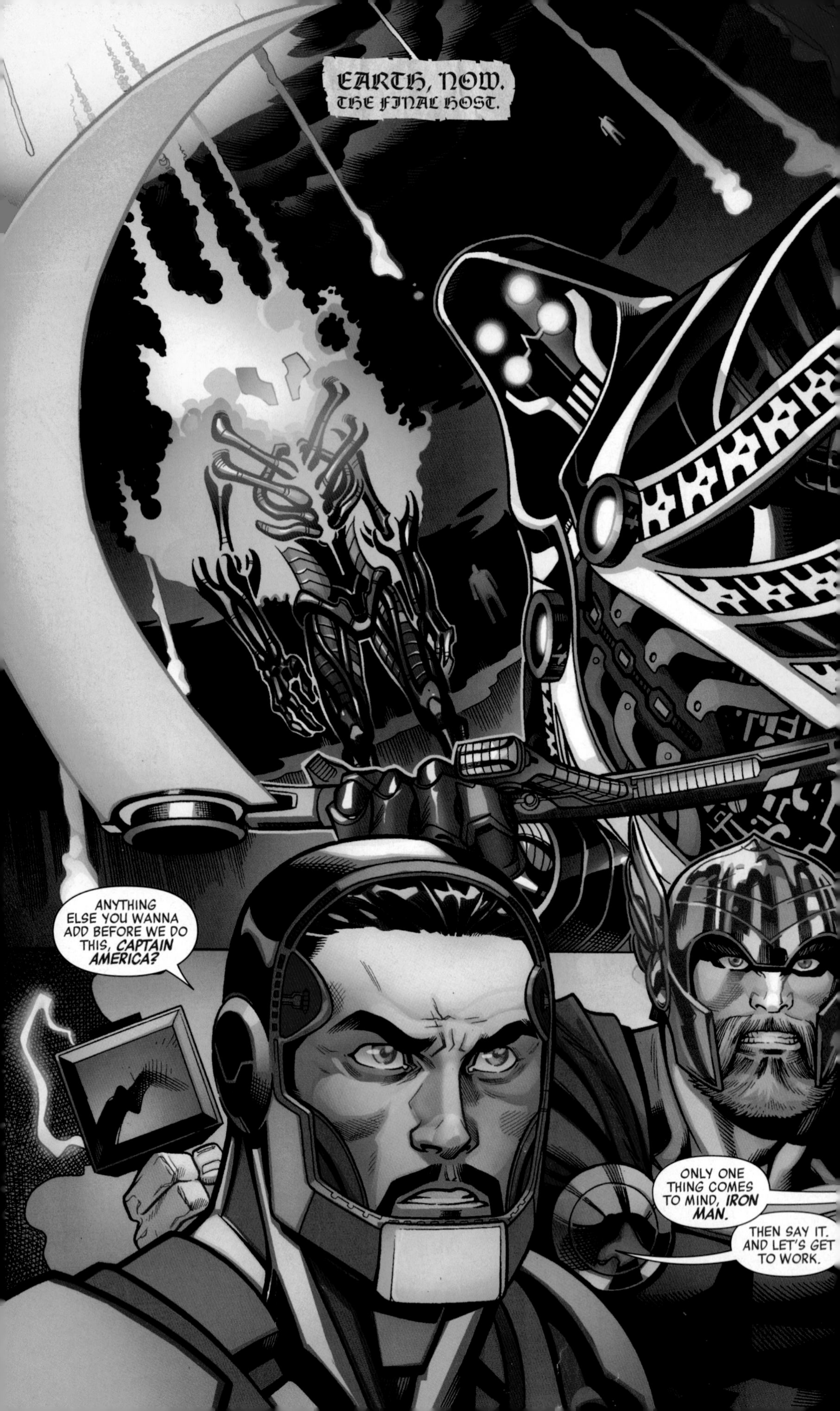
EARTH, NOW.
THE FINAL HOST.
ANYTHING ELSE YOU WANNA ADD BEFORE WE DO THIS, CAPTAIN AMERICA?
ONLY ONE THING COMES TO MIND, IRON MAN.
THEN SAY IT. AND LET'S GET TO WORK.

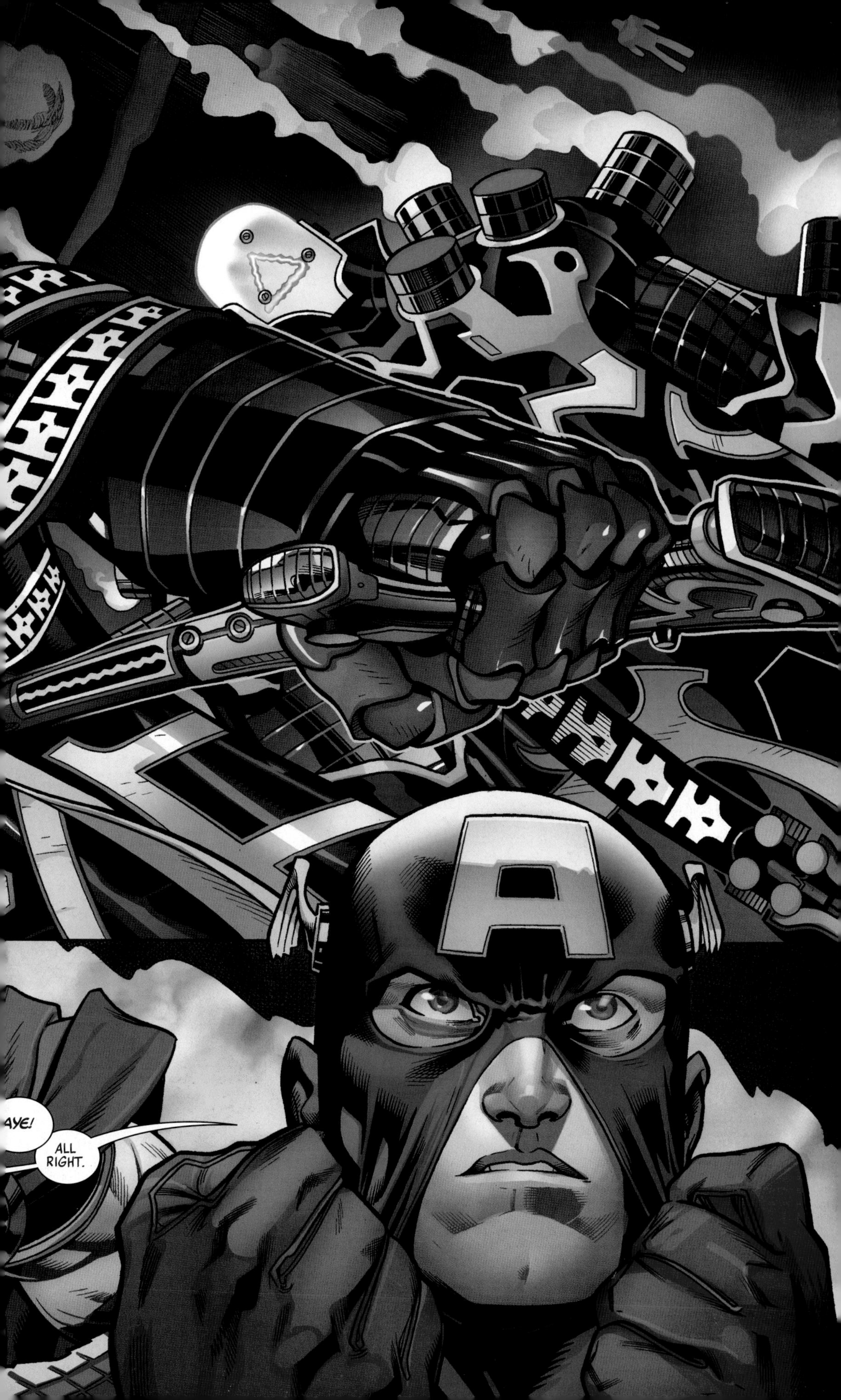

AYE!
ALL RIGHT.

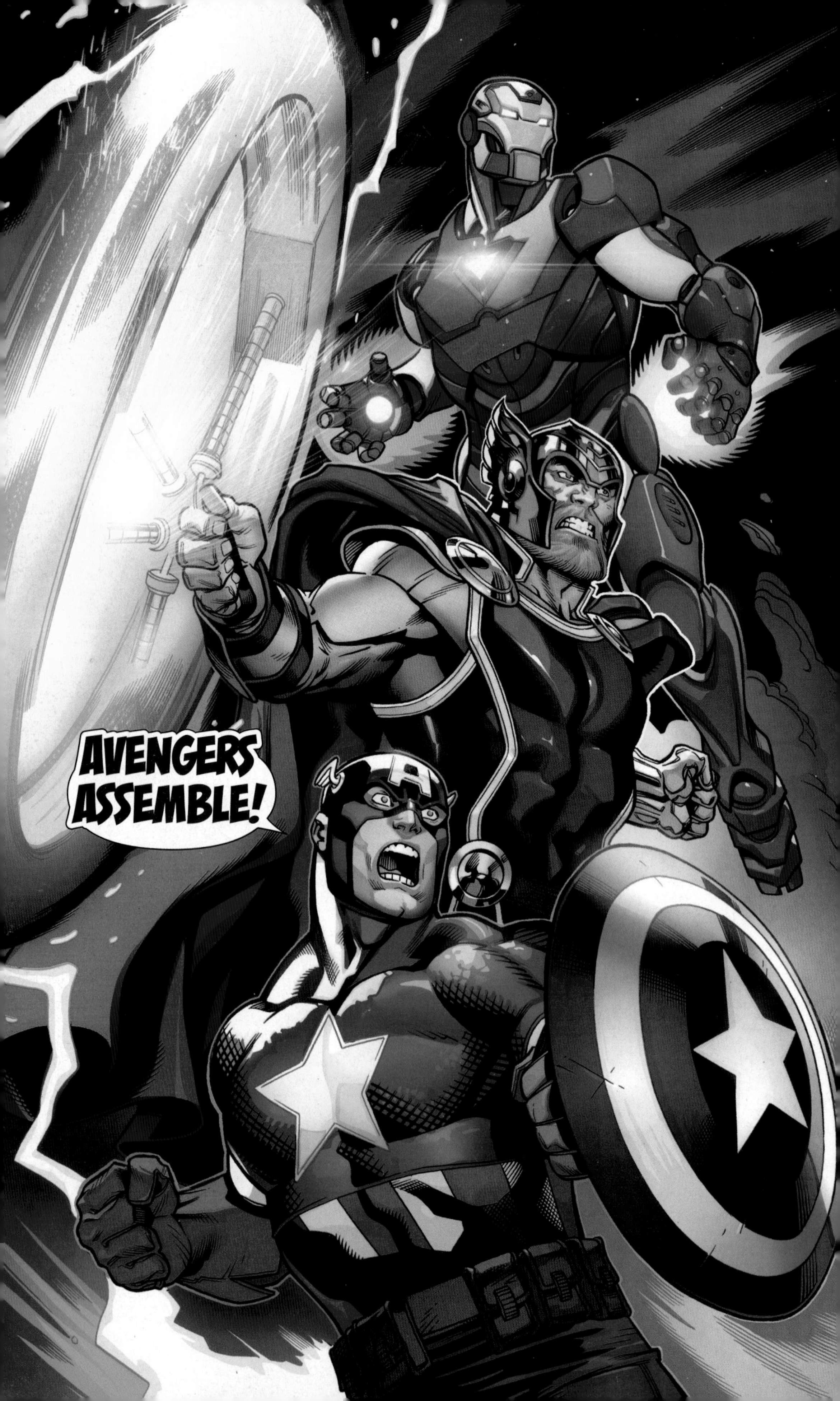
AVENGERS ASSEMBLE!

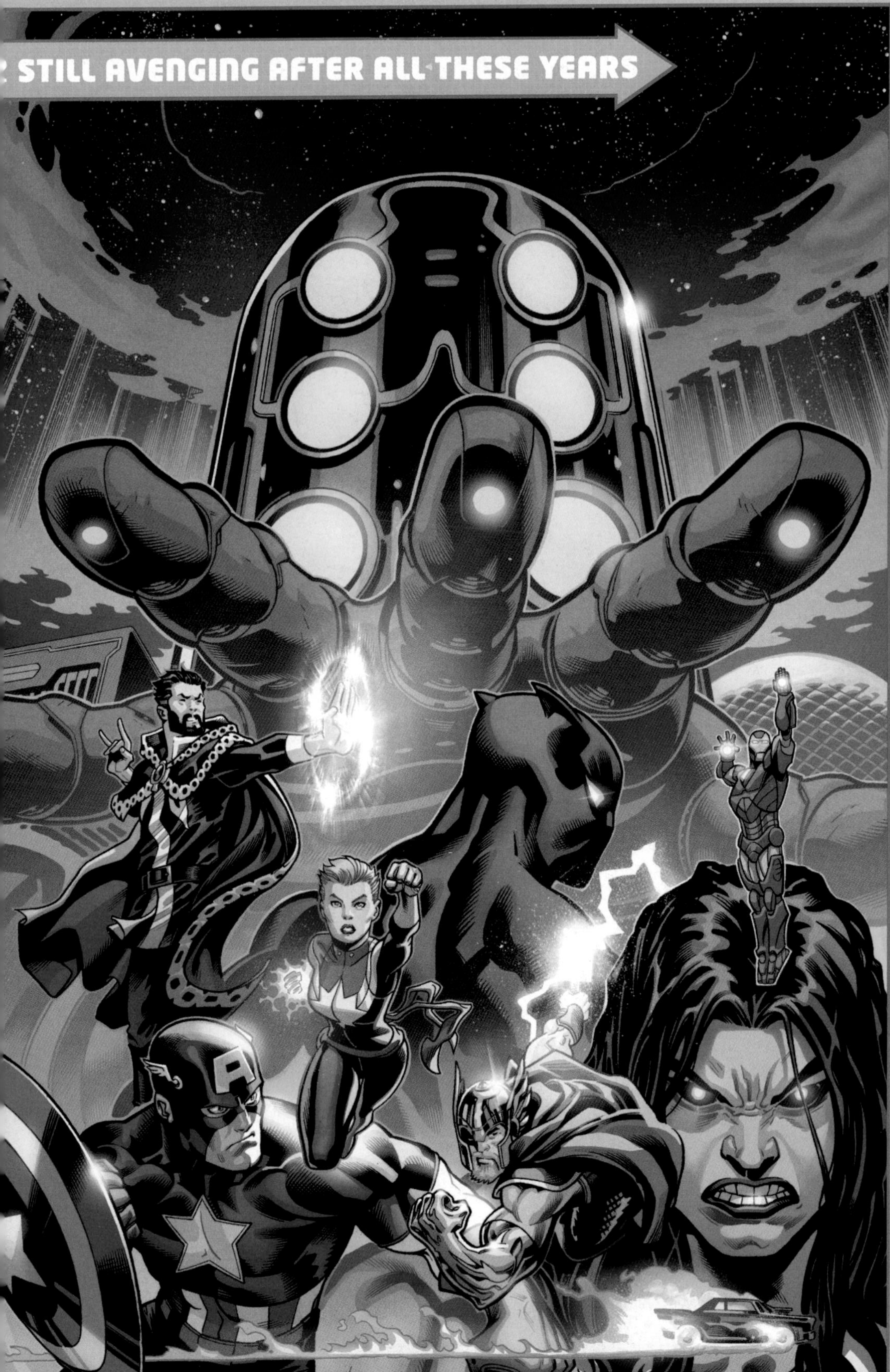
STILL AVENGING AFTER ALL THESE YEARS

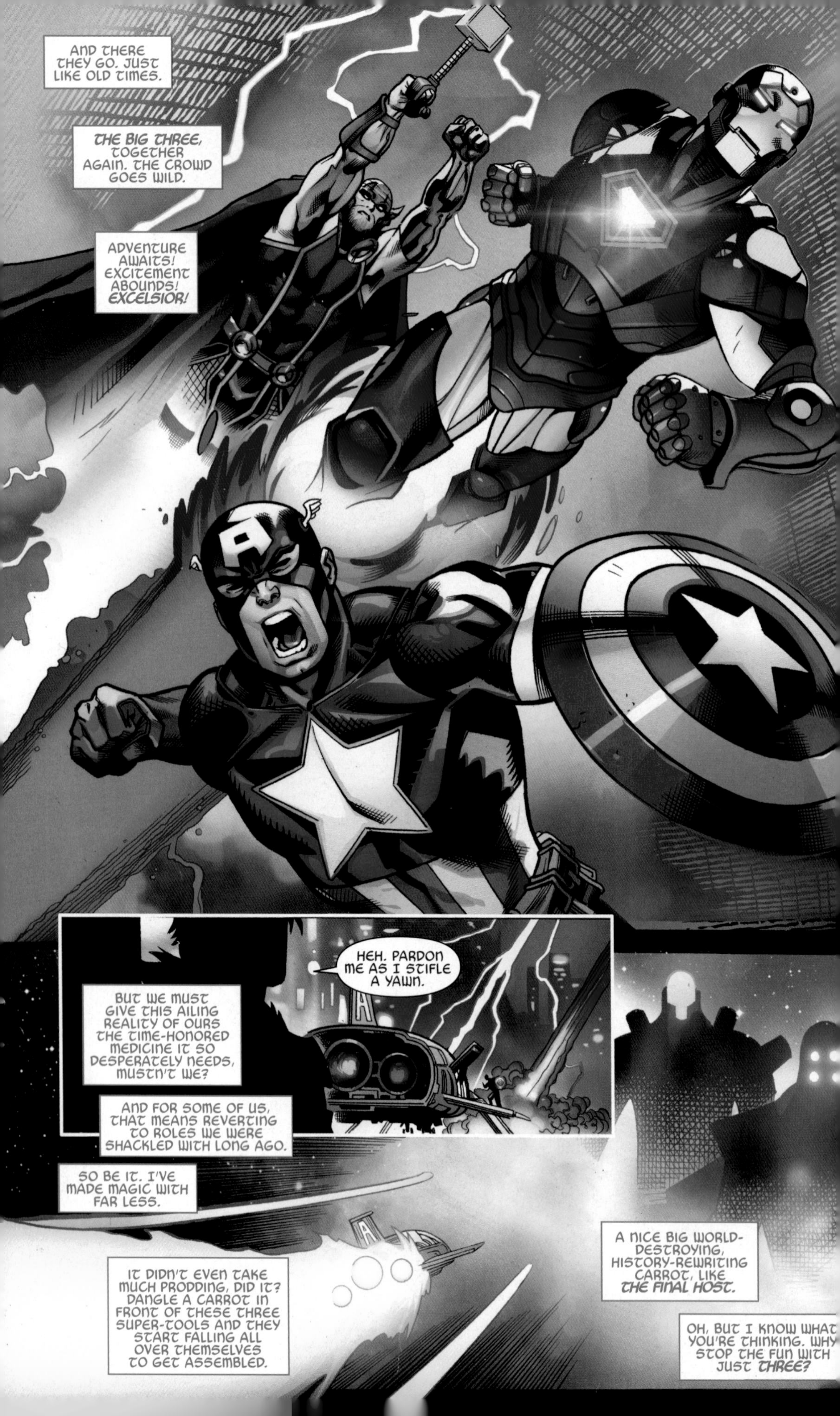
AND THERE THEY GO. JUST LIKE OLD TIMES.
THE BIG THREE, TOGETHER AGAIN. THE CROWD GOES WILD.
ADVENTURE AWAITS! EXCITEMENT ABOUNDS! EXCELSIOR!
HEH. PARDON ME AS I STIFLE A YAWN.
BUT WE MUST GIVE THIS AILING REALITY OF OURS THE TIME-HONORED MEDICINE IT SO DESPERATELY NEEDS, MUSTN'T WE?
AND FOR SOME OF US, THAT MEANS REVERTING TO ROLES WE WERE SHACKLED WITH LONG AGO.
SO BE IT. I'VE MADE MAGIC WITH FAR LESS.
IT DIDN'T EVEN TAKE MUCH PRODDING, DID IT? DANGLE A CARROT IN FRONT OF THESE THREE SUPER-TOOLS AND THEY START FALLING ALL OVER THEMSELVES TO GET ASSEMBLED.
A NICE BIG WORLD-DESTROYING, HISTORY-REWRITING CARROT, LIKE THE FINAL HOST.
OH, BUT I KNOW WHAT YOU'RE THINKING. WHY STOP THE FUN WITH JUST THREE?

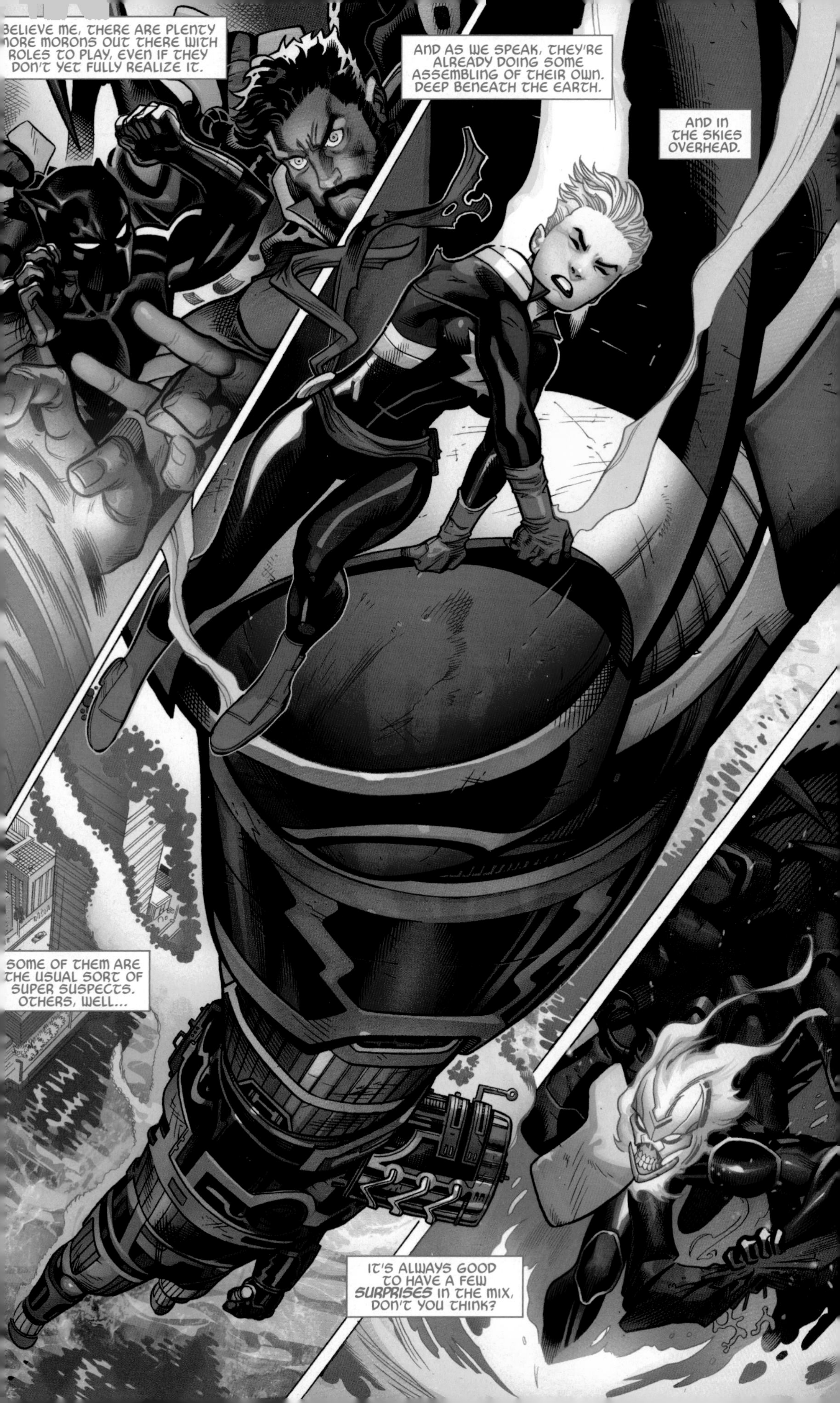
BELIEVE ME, THERE ARE PLENTY MORE MORONS OUT THERE WITH ROLES TO PLAY, EVEN IF THEY DON'T YET FULLY REALIZE IT.
AND AS WE SPEAK, THEY'RE ALREADY DOING SOME ASSEMBLING OF THEIR OWN. DEEP BENEATH THE EARTH.
AND IN THE SKIES OVERHEAD.
SOME OF THEM ARE THE USUAL SORT OF SUPER SUSPECTS. OTHERS, WELL...
IT'S ALWAYS GOOD TO HAVE A FEW SURPRISES IN THE MIX, DON'T YOU THINK?

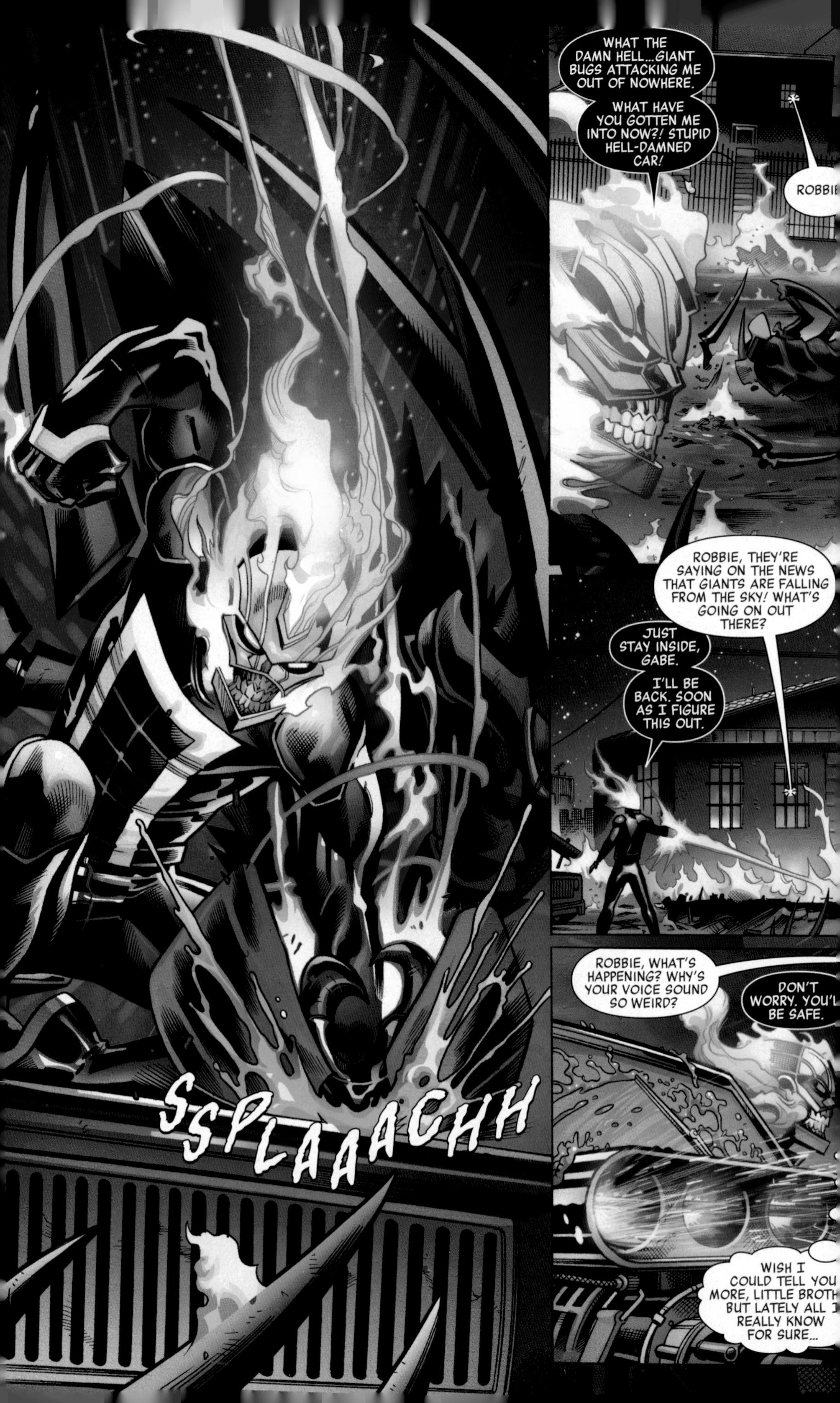
SSPLAAAACHH
WHAT THE DAMN HELL...GIANT BUGS ATTACKING ME OUT OF NOWHERE.
WHAT HAVE YOU GOTTEN ME INTO NOW?! STUPID HELL-DAMNED CAR!
ROBBIE
ROBBIE, THEY'RE SAYING ON THE NEWS THAT GIANTS ARE FALLING FROM THE SKY! WHAT'S GOING ON OUT THERE?
JUST STAY INSIDE, GABE.
I'LL BE BACK. SOON AS I FIGURE THIS OUT.
ROBBIE, WHAT'S HAPPENING? WHY'S YOUR VOICE SOUND SO WEIRD?
DON'T WORRY. YOU'L BE SAFE.
WISH I COULD TELL YOU MORE, LITTLE BROTH BUT LATELY ALL I REALLY KNOW FOR SURE...

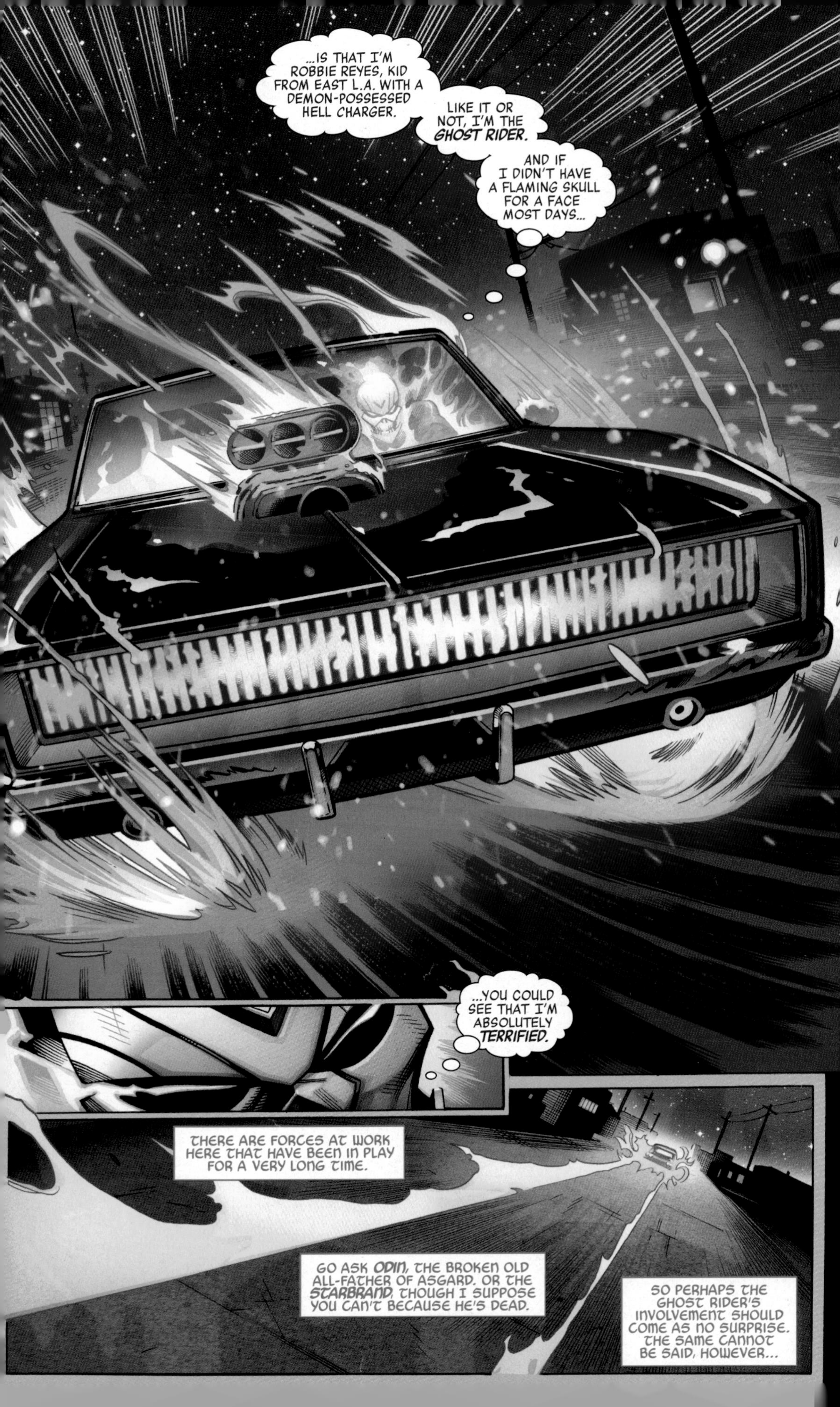
...IS THAT I'M ROBBIE REYES, KID FROM EAST L.A. WITH A DEMON-POSSESSED HELL CHARGER.
LIKE IT OR NOT, I'M THE GHOST RIDER.
AND IF I DIDN'T HAVE A FLAMING SKULL FOR A FACE MOST DAYS...
...YOU COULD SEE THAT I'M ABSOLUTELY TERRIFIED.
THERE ARE FORCES AT WORK HERE THAT HAVE BEEN IN PLAY FOR A VERY LONG TIME.
GO ASK ODIN, THE BROKEN OLD ALL-FATHER OF ASGARD. OR THE STARBRAND, THOUGH I SUPPOSE YOU CAN'T BECAUSE HE'S DEAD.
SO PERHAPS THE GHOST RIDER'S INVOLVEMENT SHOULD COME AS NO SURPRISE. THE SAME CANNOT BE SAID, HOWEVER...

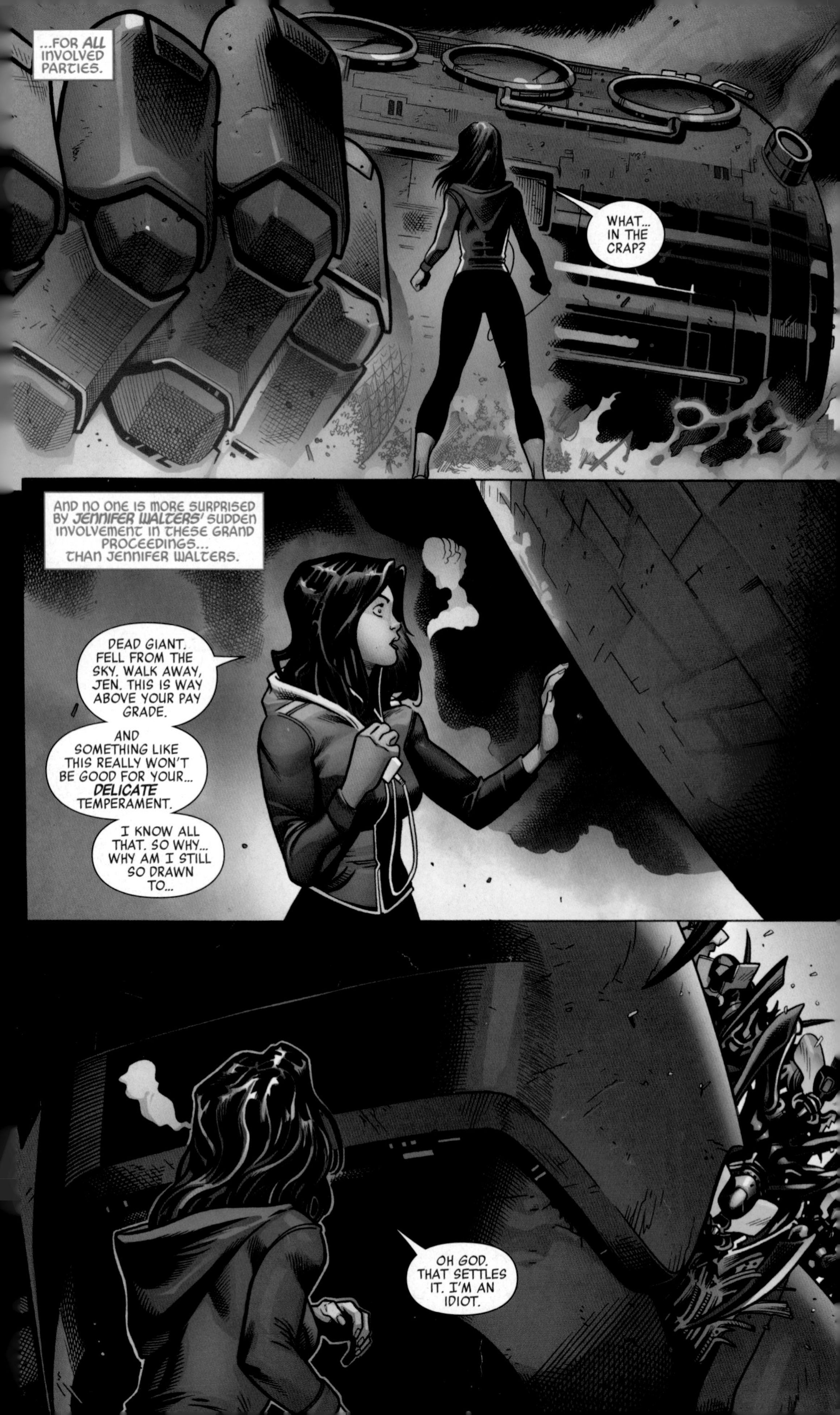
...FOR ALL INVOLVED PARTIES.
WHAT... IN THE CRAP?
AND NO ONE IS MORE SURPRISED BY JENNIFER WALTERS' SUDDEN INVOLVEMENT IN THESE GRAND PROCEEDINGS... THAN JENNIFER WALTERS.
DEAD GIANT. FELL FROM THE SKY. WALK AWAY, JEN. THIS IS WAY ABOVE YOUR PAY GRADE.
AND SOMETHING LIKE THIS REALLY WON'T BE GOOD FOR YOUR... DELICATE TEMPERAMENT.
I KNOW ALL THAT. SO WHY... WHY AM I STILL SO DRAWN TO...
OH GOD. THAT SETTLES IT. I'M AN IDIOT.

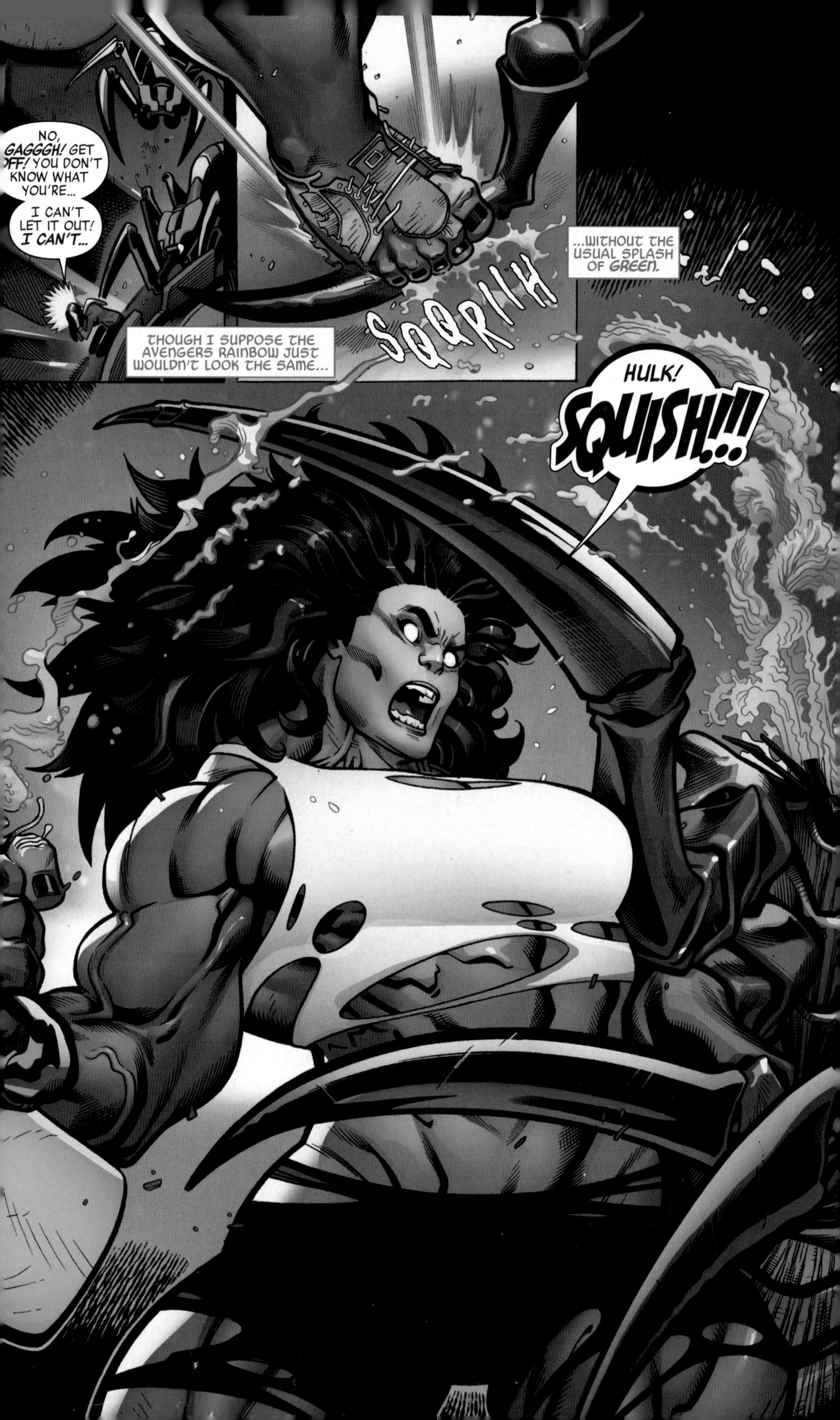

NO, GAGGGH! GET OFF! YOU DON'T KNOW WHAT YOU'RE...
I CAN'T LET IT OUT! I CAN'T...
THOUGH I SUPPOSE THE AVENGERS RAINBOW JUST WOULDN'T LOOK THE SAME...
SQQRLLH
...WITHOUT THE USUAL SPLASH OF GREEN.
HULK! SQUISH!!!

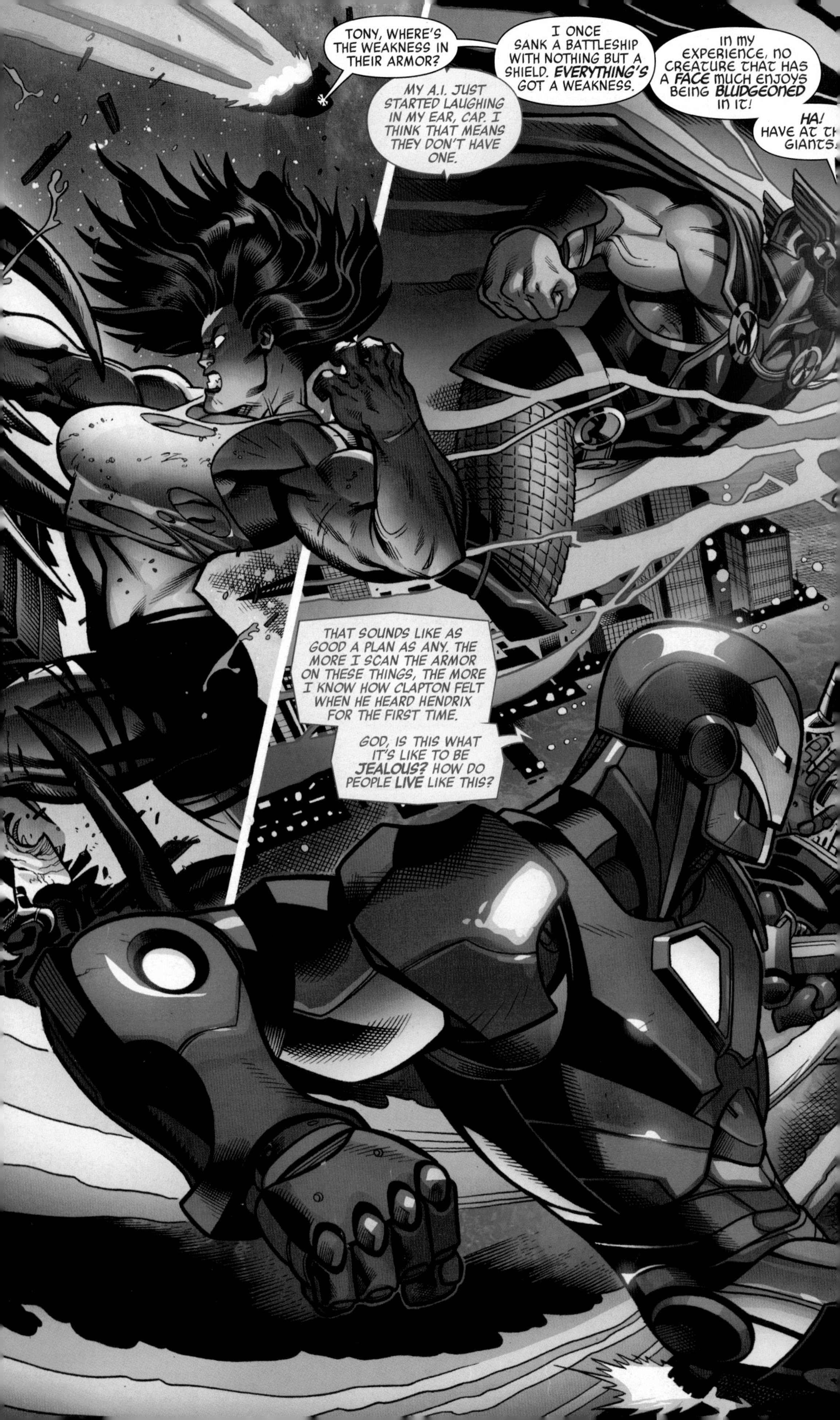

TONY, WHERE'S THE WEAKNESS IN THEIR ARMOR?
I ONCE SANK A BATTLESHIP WITH NOTHING BUT A SHIELD. EVERYTHING'S GOT A WEAKNESS.
MY A.I. JUST STARTED LAUGHING IN MY EAR, CAP. I THINK THAT MEANS THEY DON'T HAVE ONE.
IN MY EXPERIENCE, NO CREATURE THAT HAS A FACE MUCH ENJOYS BEING BLUDGEONED IN IT!
HA!
THAT SOUNDS LIKE AS GOOD A PLAN AS ANY. THE MORE I SCAN THE ARMOR ON THESE THINGS, THE MORE I KNOW HOW CLAPTON FELT WHEN HE HEARD HENDRIX FOR THE FIRST TIME.
GOD, IS THIS WHAT IT'S LIKE TO BE JEALOUS? HOW DO PEOPLE LIVE LIKE THIS?

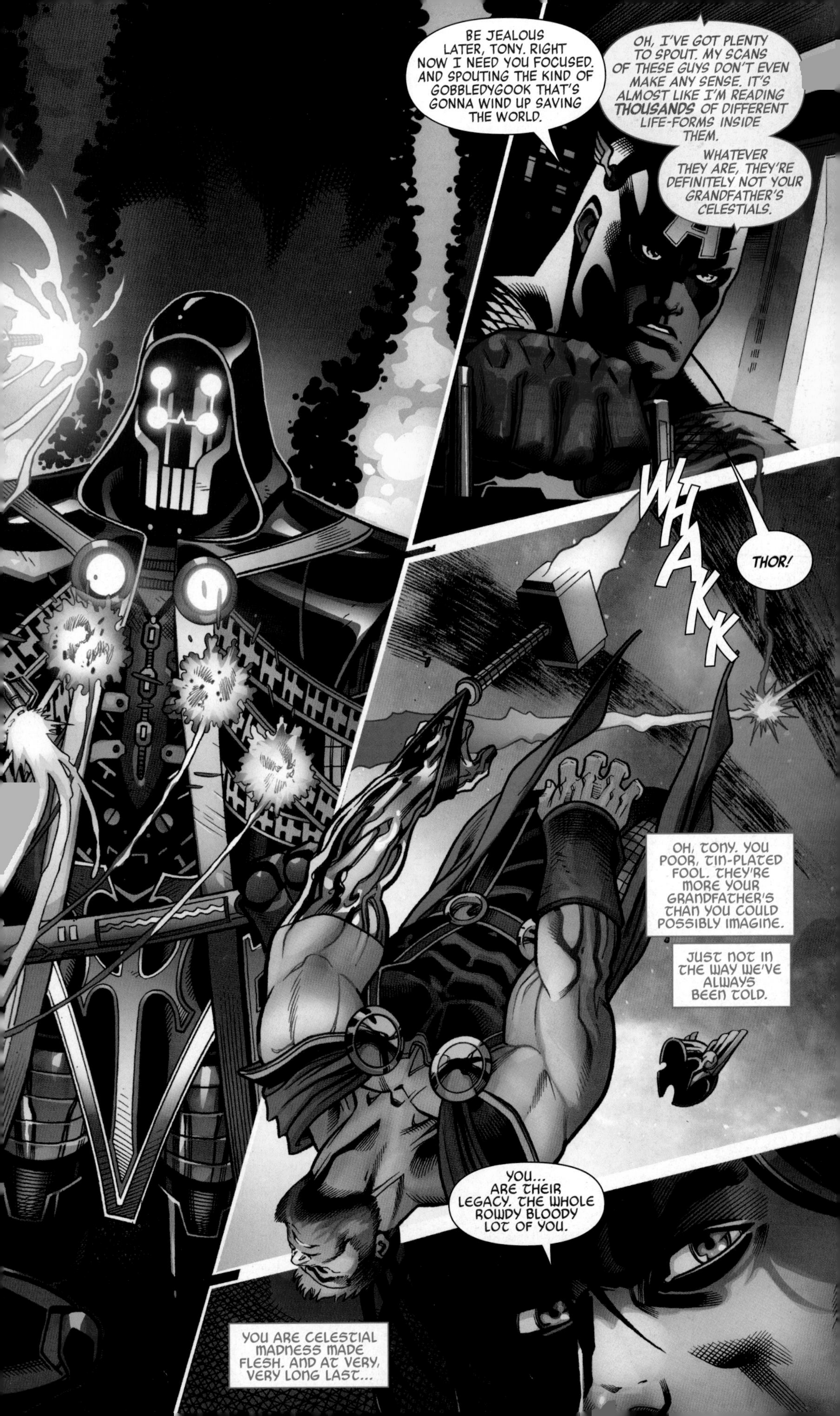
BE JEALOUS LATER, TONY. RIGHT NOW I NEED YOU FOCUSED. AND SPOUTING THE KIND OF GOBBLEDYGOOK THAT'S GONNA WIND UP SAVING THE WORLD.
OH, I'VE GOT PLENTY TO SPOUT. MY SCANS OF THESE GUYS DON'T EVEN MAKE ANY SENSE. IT'S ALMOST LIKE I'M READING THOUSANDS OF DIFFERENT LIFE-FORMS INSIDE THEM.
WHATEVER THEY ARE, THEY'RE DEFINITELY NOT YOUR GRANDFATHER'S CELESTIALS.
WHAKK
THOR!
OH, TONY. YOU POOR, TIN-PLATED FOOL. THEY'RE MORE YOUR GRANDFATHER'S THAN YOU COULD POSSIBLY IMAGINE.
JUST NOT IN THE WAY WE'VE ALWAYS BEEN TOLD.
YOU... ARE THEIR LEGACY. THE WHOLE ROWDY BLOODY LOT OF YOU.
YOU ARE CELESTIAL MADNESS MADE FLESH. AND AT VERY, VERY LONG LAST...

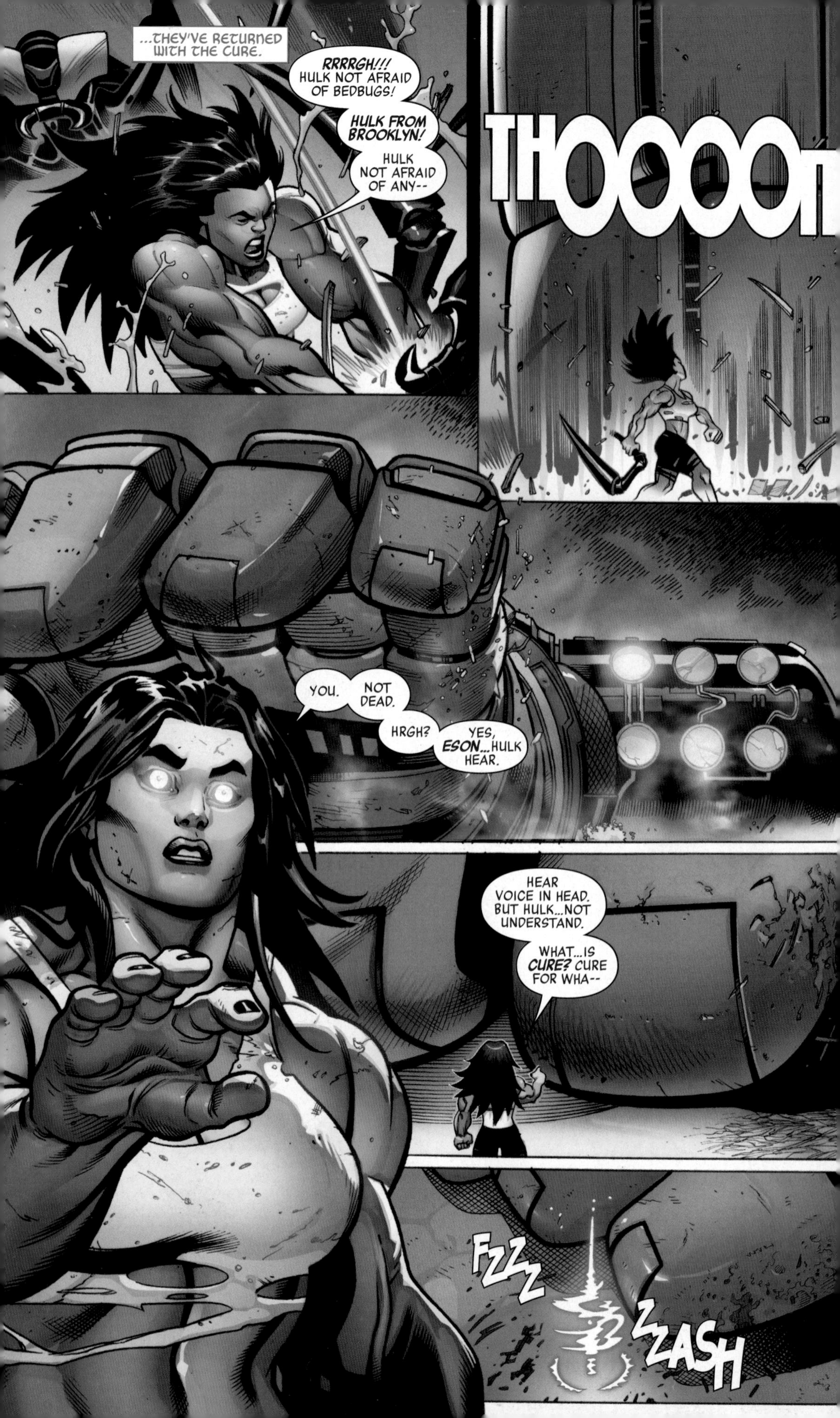
...THEY'VE RETURNED WITH THE CURE.
RRRRGH!!! HULK NOT AFRAID OF BEDBUGS!
HULK FROM BROOKLYN!
HULK NOT AFRAID OF ANY--
THOOOOM
YOU.
NOT DEAD.
HRGH?
YES, ESON...HULK HEAR.
HEAR VOICE IN HEAD. BUT HULK...NOT UNDERSTAND.
WHAT...IS CURE? CURE FOR WHA--
FZZZ
ZZASH

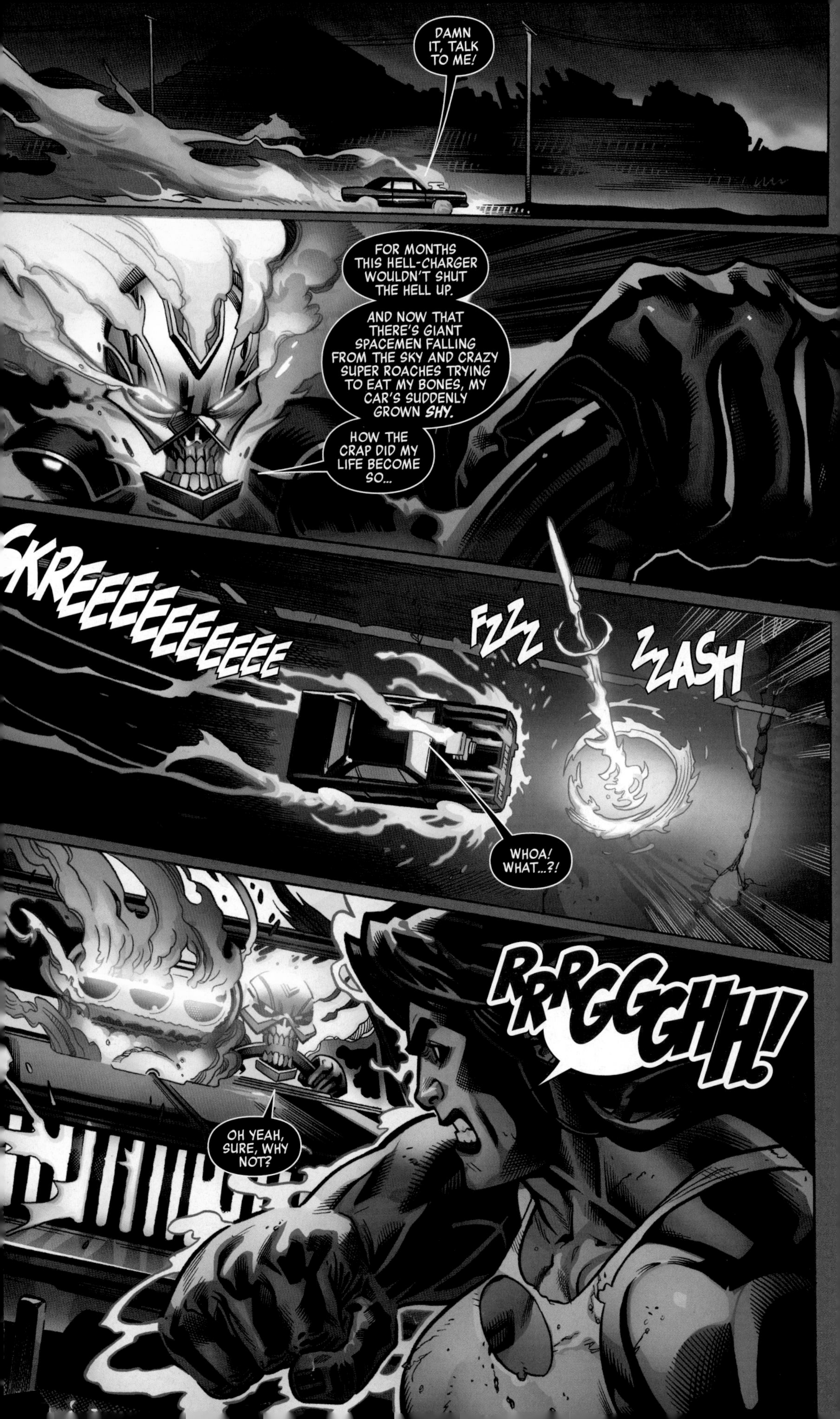
DAMN IT, TALK TO ME!
FOR MONTHS THIS HELL-CHARGER WOULDN'T SHUT THE HELL UP.
AND NOW THAT THERE'S GIANT SPACEMEN FALLING FROM THE SKY AND CRAZY SUPER ROACHES TRYING TO EAT MY BONES, MY CAR'S SUDDENLY GROWN SHY.
HOW THE CRAP DID MY LIFE BECOME SO...
SKREEEEEEEEEEE
FZZZ
ZZASH
WHOA! WHAT...?!
RRRGGGHH!
OH YEAH, SURE, WHY NOT?

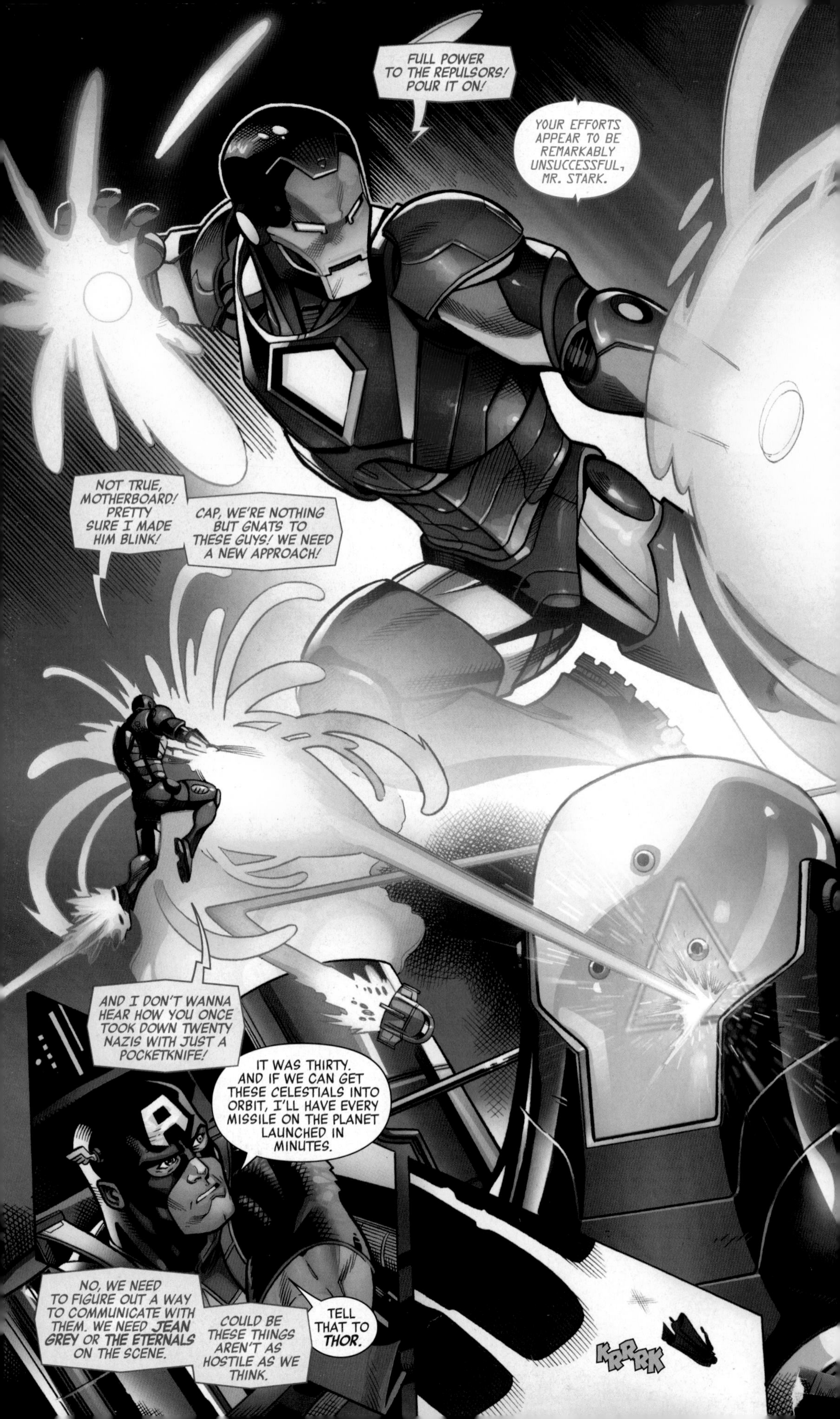

FULL POWER TO THE REPULSORS! POUR IT ON!
YOUR EFFORTS APPEAR TO BE REMARKABLY UNSUCCESSFUL, MR. STARK.
NOT TRUE, MOTHERBOARD! PRETTY SURE I MADE HIM BLINK!
CAP, WE'RE NOTHING BUT GNATS TO THESE GUYS! WE NEED A NEW APPROACH!
AND I DON'T WANNA HEAR HOW YOU ONCE TOOK DOWN TWENTY NAZIS WITH JUST A POCKETKNIFE!
IT WAS THIRTY. AND IF WE CAN GET THESE CELESTIALS INTO ORBIT, I'LL HAVE EVERY MISSILE ON THE PLANET LAUNCHED IN MINUTES.
NO, WE NEED TO FIGURE OUT A WAY TO COMMUNICATE WITH THEM. WE NEED JEAN GREY OR THE ETERNALS ON THE SCENE.
COULD BE THESE THINGS AREN'T AS HOSTILE AS WE THINK.
TELL THAT TO THOR.
KRRRK

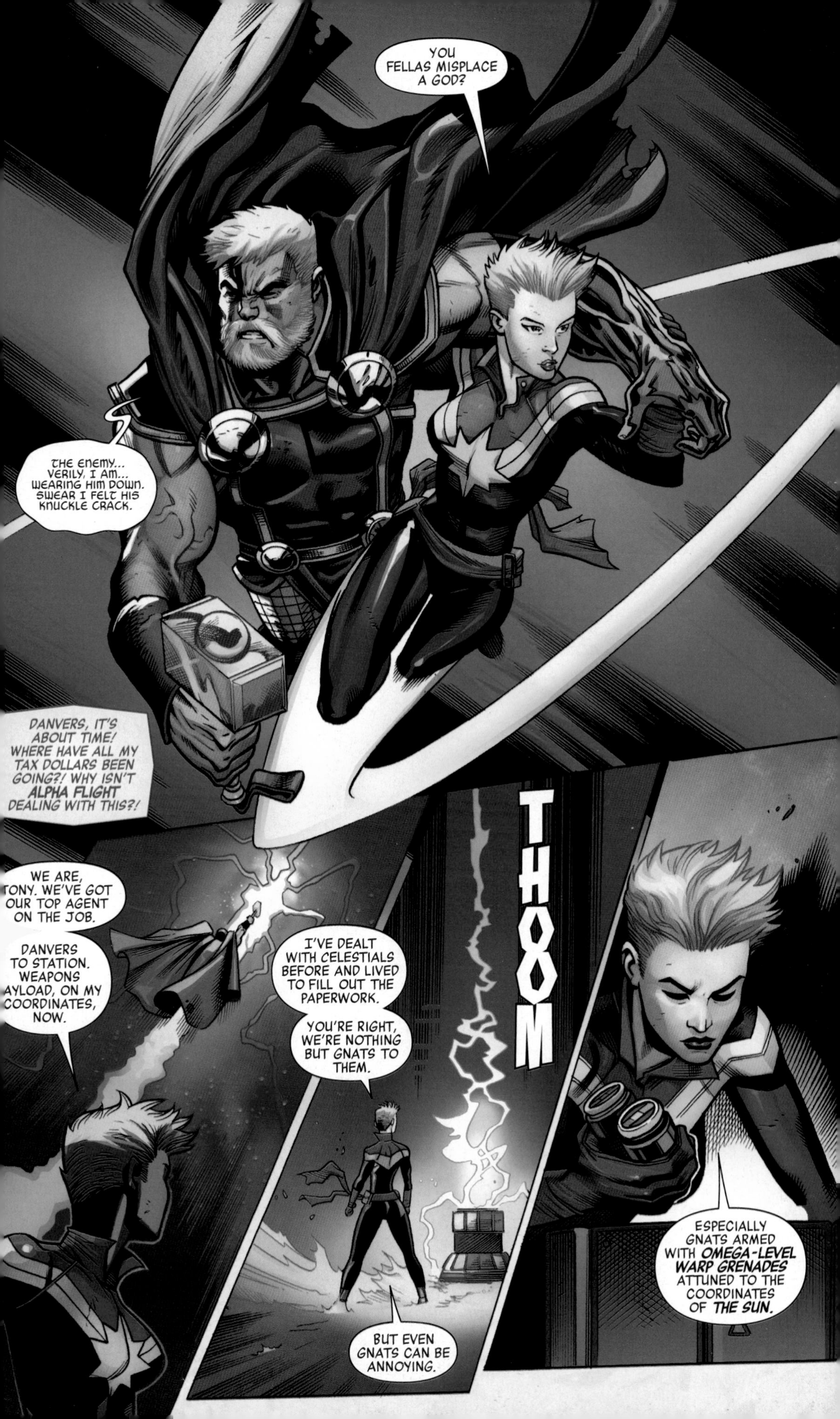
YOU FELLAS MISPLACE A GOD?
THE ENEMY... VERILY, I AM... WEARING HIM DOWN. SWEAR I FELT HIS KNUCKLE CRACK.
DANVERS, IT'S ABOUT TIME! WHERE HAVE ALL MY TAX DOLLARS BEEN GOING?! WHY ISN'T ALPHA FLIGHT DEALING WITH THIS?!
WE ARE, TONY. WE'VE GOT OUR TOP AGENT ON THE JOB.
DANVERS TO STATION. WEAPONS AYLOAD, ON MY COORDINATES, NOW.
I'VE DEALT WITH CELESTIALS BEFORE AND LIVED TO FILL OUT THE PAPERWORK.
YOU'RE RIGHT, WE'RE NOTHING BUT GNATS TO THEM.
BUT EVEN GNATS CAN BE ANNOYING.
THOOM
ESPECIALLY GNATS ARMED WITH OMEGA-LEVEL WARP GRENADES ATTUNED TO THE COORDINATES OF THE SUN.

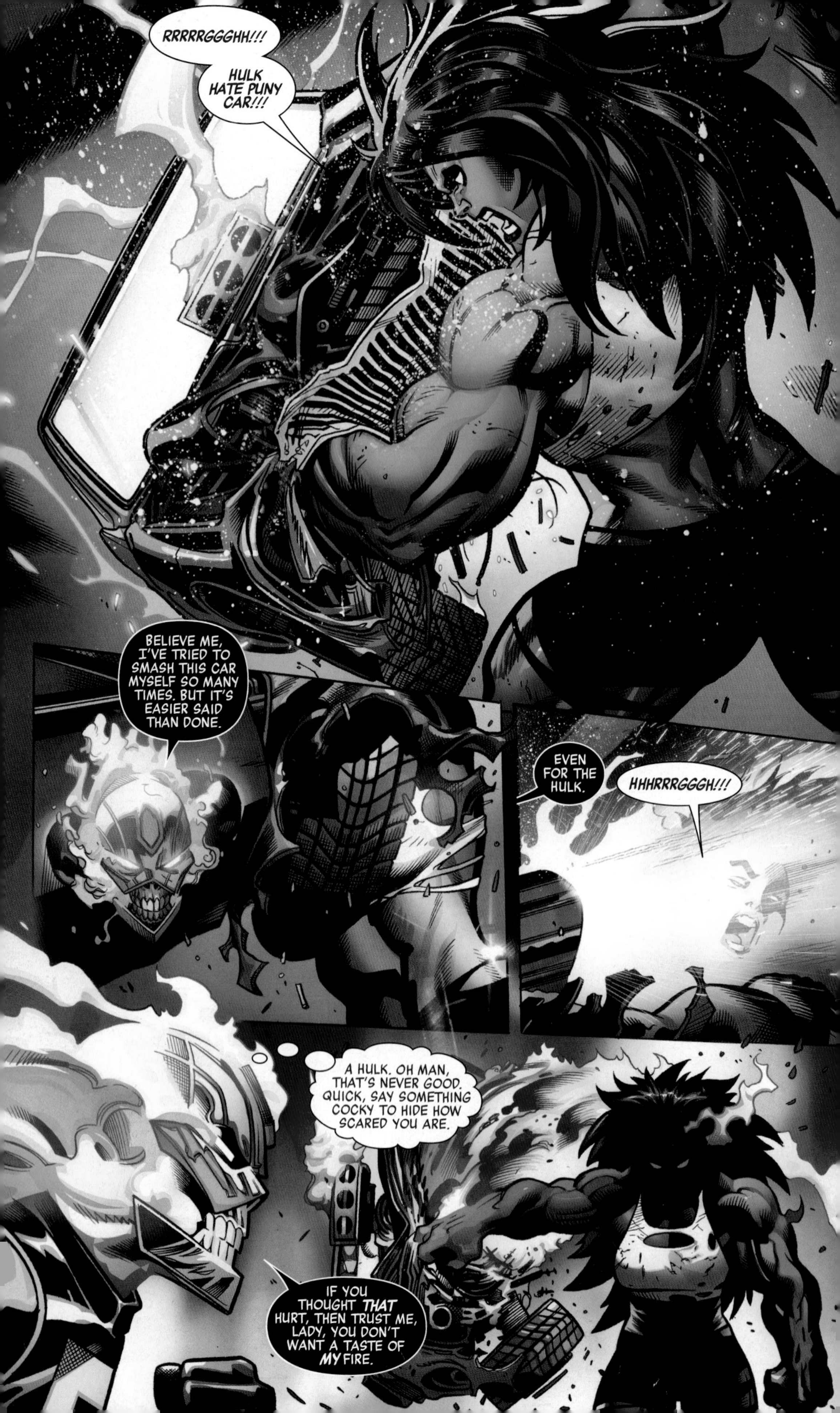
RRRRRGGGHH!!!
HULK HATE PUNY CAR!!!
BELIEVE ME, I'VE TRIED TO SMASH THIS CAR MYSELF SO MANY TIMES. BUT IT'S EASIER SAID THAN DONE.
EVEN FOR THE HULK.
HHHRRRGGGH!!!
A HULK. OH MAN, THAT'S NEVER GOOD. QUICK, SAY SOMETHING COCKY TO HIDE HOW SCARED YOU ARE.
IF YOU THOUGHT THAT HURT, THEN TRUST ME, LADY, YOU DON'T WANT A TASTE OF MY FIRE.

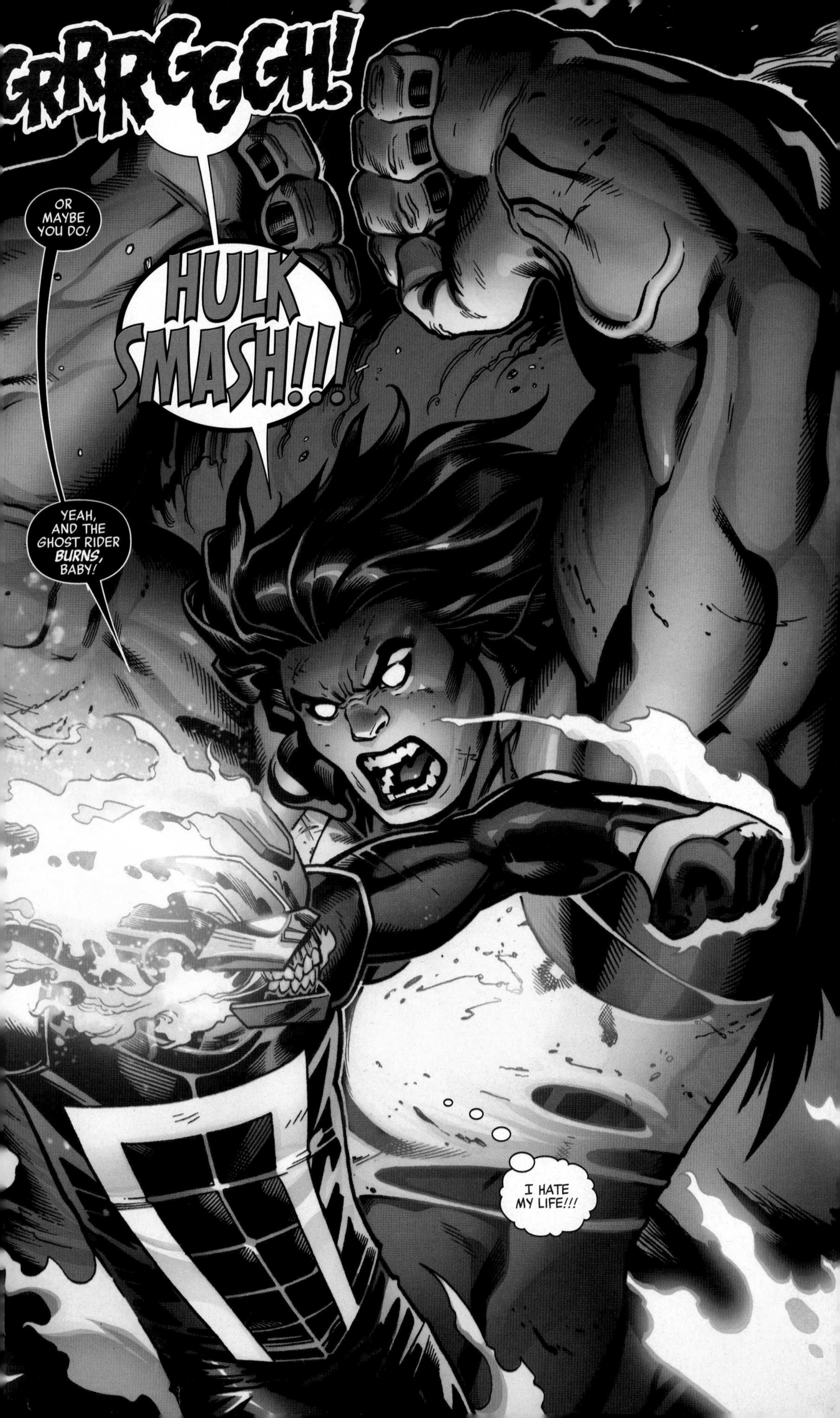
GRRRGGGH!
HULK SMASH!!!
OR MAYBE YOU DO!
YEAH, AND THE GHOST RIDER BURNS, BABY!
I HATE MY LIFE!!!

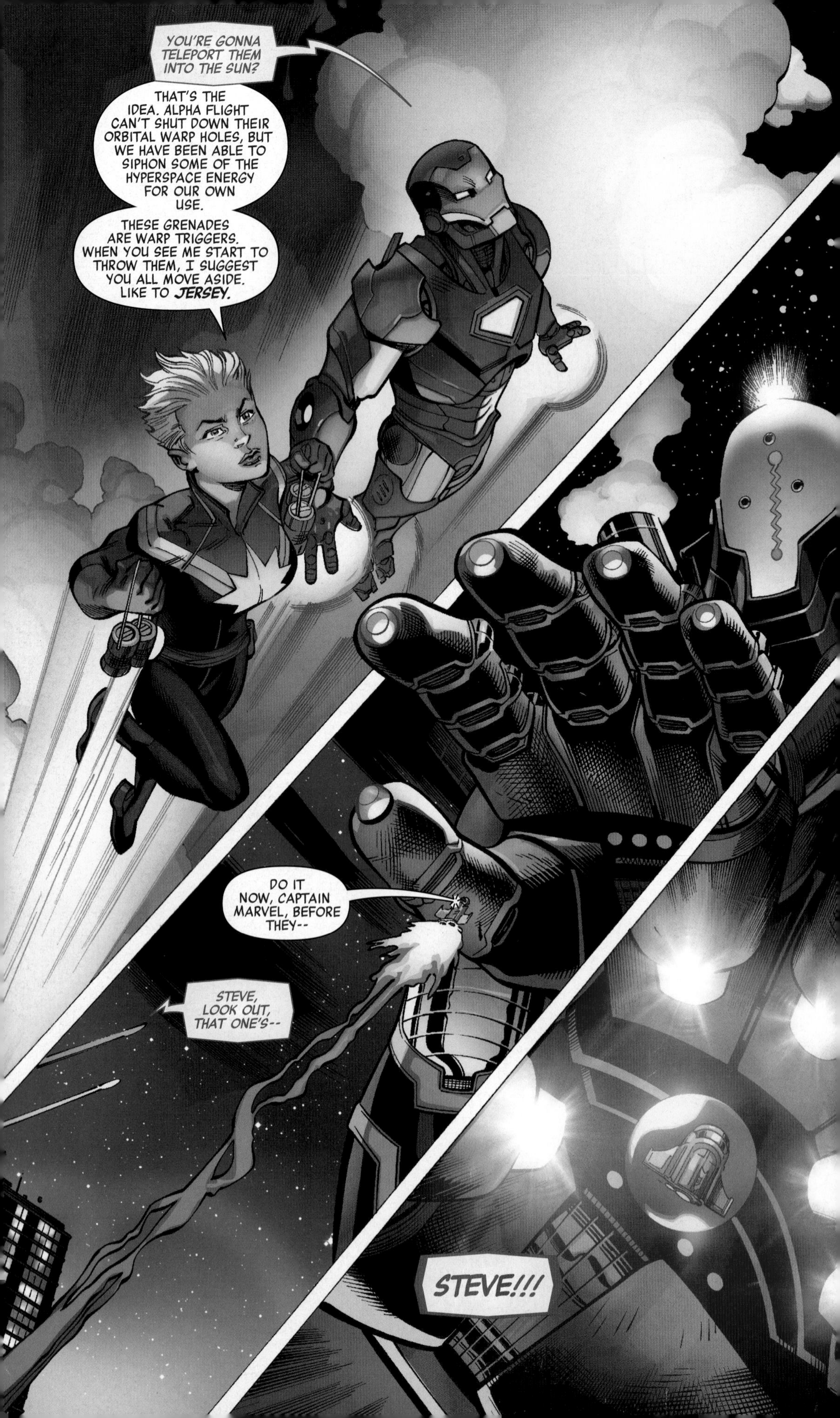
YOU'RE GONNA TELEPORT THEM INTO THE SUN?
THAT'S THE IDEA. ALPHA FLIGHT CAN'T SHUT DOWN THEIR ORBITAL WARP HOLES, BUT WE HAVE BEEN ABLE TO SIPHON SOME OF THE HYPERSPACE ENERGY FOR OUR OWN USE.
THESE GRENADES ARE WARP TRIGGERS. WHEN YOU SEE ME START TO THROW THEM, I SUGGEST YOU ALL MOVE ASIDE. LIKE TO JERSEY.
DO IT NOW, CAPTAIN MARVEL, BEFORE THEY--
STEVE, LOOK OUT, THAT ONE'S--
STEVE!!!

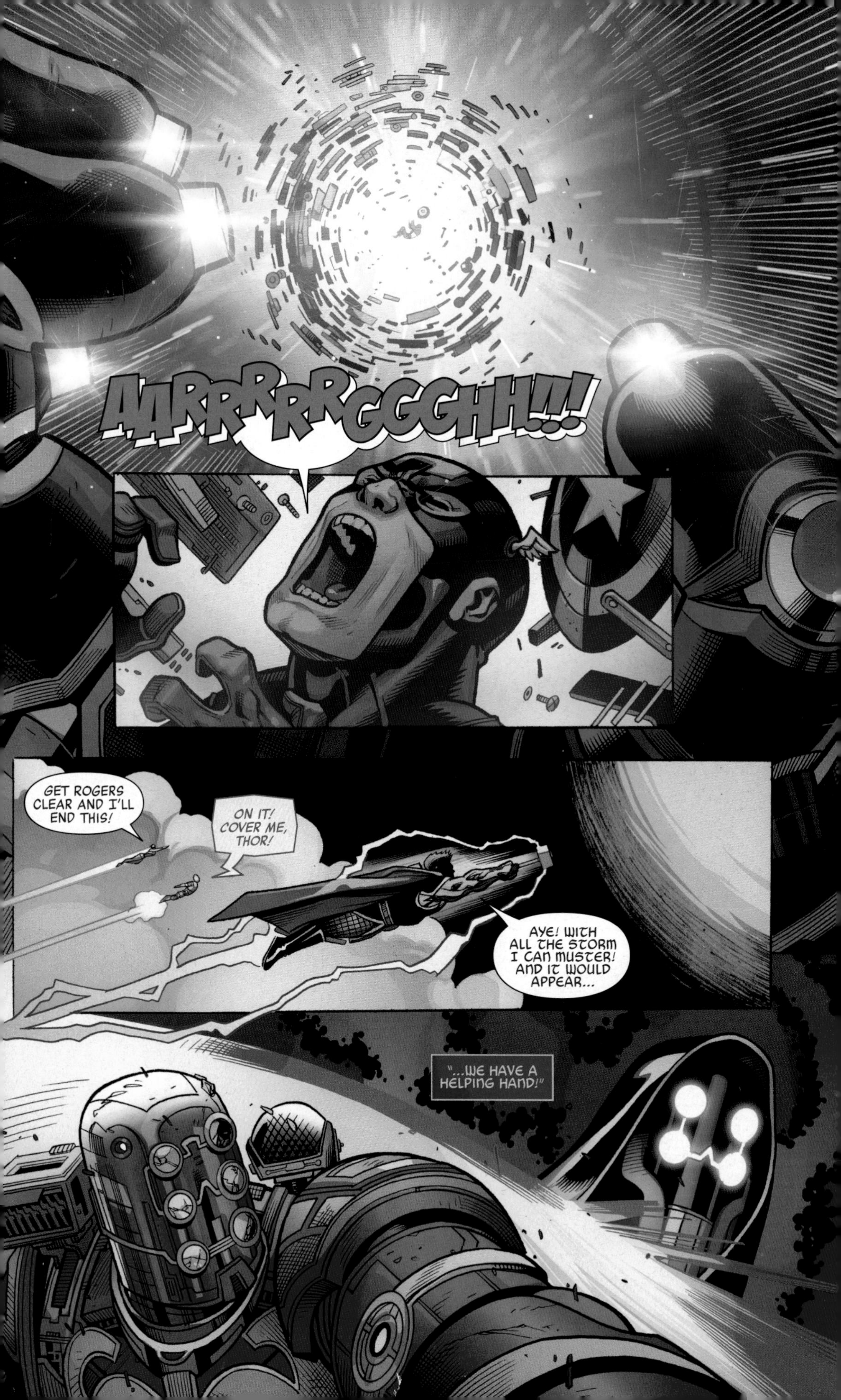
AARRRRRRGGGHH!!!
GET ROGERS CLEAR AND I'LL END THIS!
ON IT! COVER ME, THOR!
AYE! WITH ALL THE STORM I CAN MUSTER! AND IT WOULD APPEAR...
"...WE HAVE A HELPING HAND!"

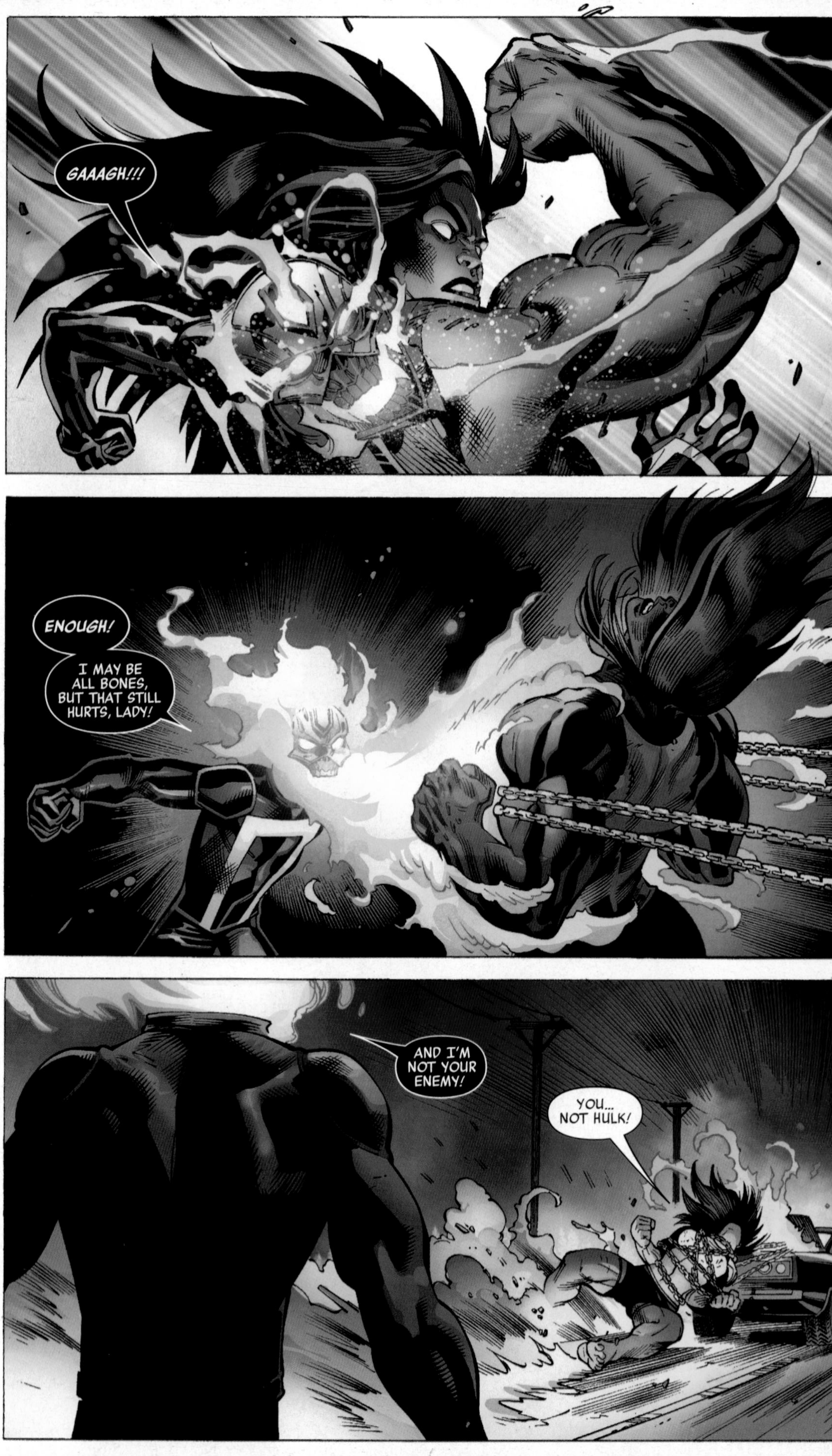
GAAAGH!!!
ENOUGH!
I MAY BE ALL BONES, BUT THAT STILL HURTS, LADY!
AND I'M NOT YOUR ENEMY!
YOU... NOT HULK!

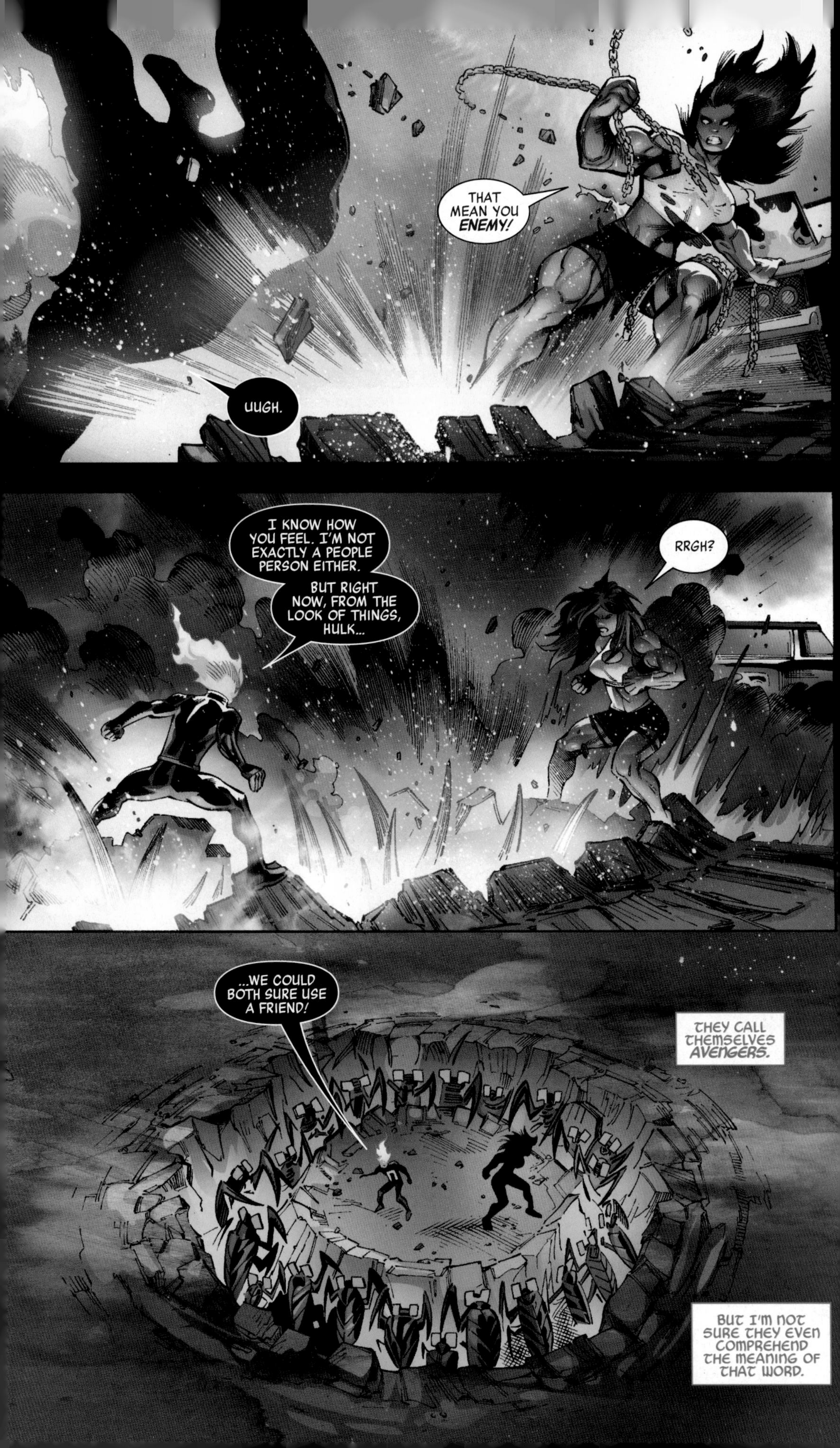
THAT MEAN YOU ENEMY!
UUGH.
I KNOW HOW YOU FEEL. I'M NOT EXACTLY A PEOPLE PERSON EITHER.
BUT RIGHT NOW, FROM THE LOOK OF THINGS, HULK...
RRGH?
...WE COULD BOTH SURE USE A FRIEND!
THEY CALL THEMSELVES AVENGERS.
BUT I'M NOT SURE THEY EVEN COMPREHEND THE MEANING OF THAT WORD.

WHAT DO THEY HAVE TO AVENGE?

HAVE THEY BEEN SCORNED AND REJECTED THEIR ENTIRE LIFE, EVEN BY THOSE THEY CALL FAMILY?

HAVE THEY BEEN HUNTED AND HOUNDED TO THE ENDS OF THE EARTH AND BEYOND?

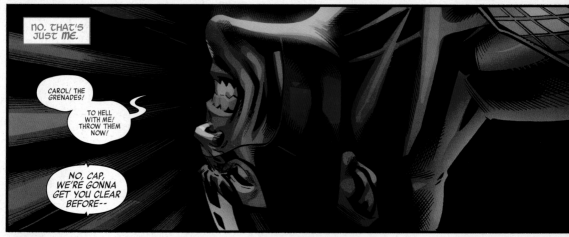

NO. THAT'S JUST ME.

CAROL! THE GRENADES!

TO HELL WITH ME! THROW THEM NOW!

NO, CAP, WE'RE GONNA GET YOU CLEAR BEFORE--

AAAAGGHH!!!

I'M THE ONLY ONE WHO EVER DOES ANY ACTUAL AVENGING AROUND HERE. THERE WOULDN'T EVEN BE AN AVENGERS IF IT WEREN'T FOR ME.

YOU MIGHT EVEN GO SO FAR AS TO SAY...

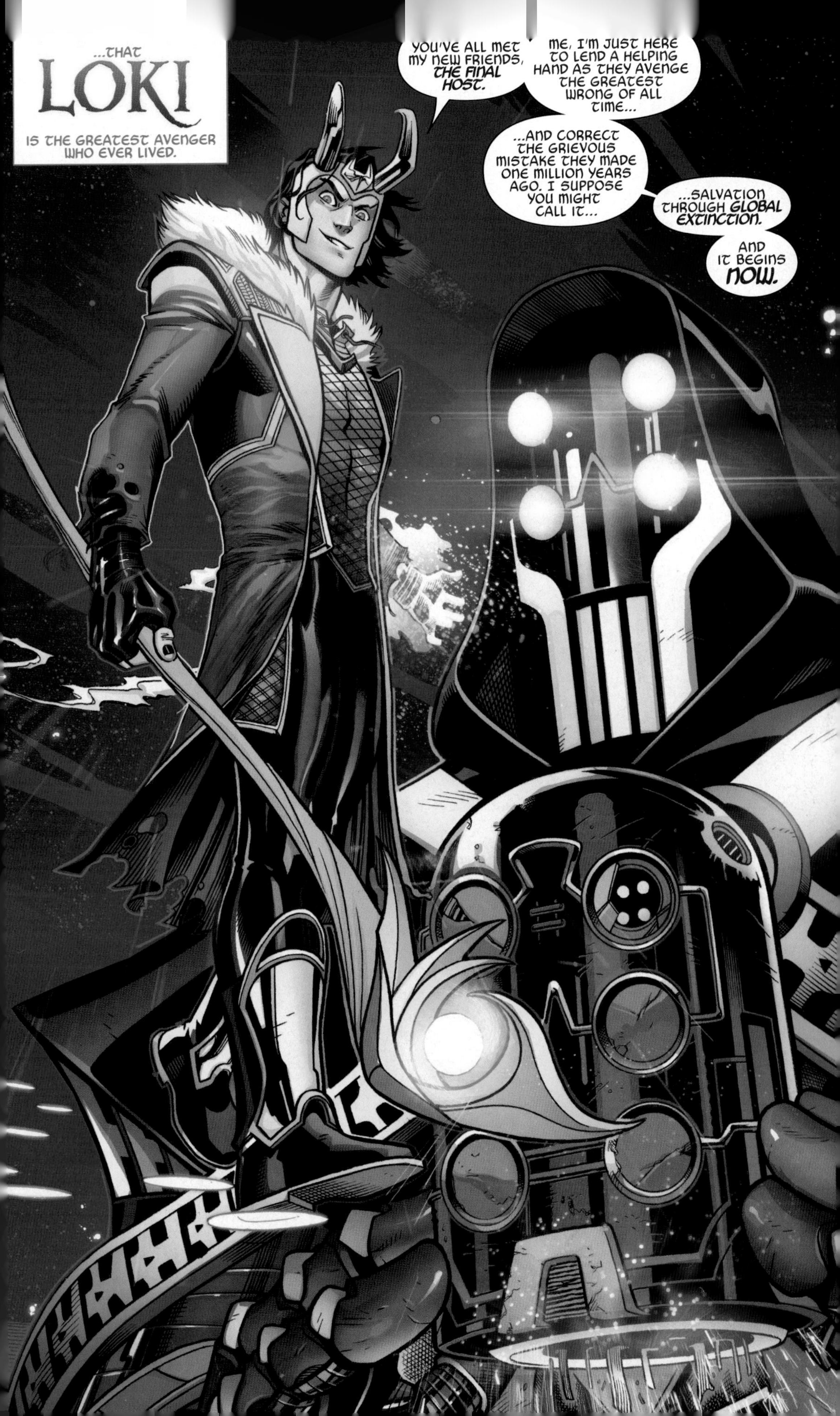
...THAT
LOKI
IS THE GREATEST AVENGER WHO EVER LIVED.
YOU'VE ALL MET MY NEW FRIENDS, THE FINAL HOST.
ME, I'M JUST HERE TO LEND A HELPING HAND AS THEY AVENGE THE GREATEST WRONG OF ALL TIME...
...AND CORRECT THE GRIEVOUS MISTAKE THEY MADE ONE MILLION YEARS AGO. I SUPPOSE YOU MIGHT CALL IT...
...SALVATION THROUGH GLOBAL EXTINCTION.
AND IT BEGINS NOW.

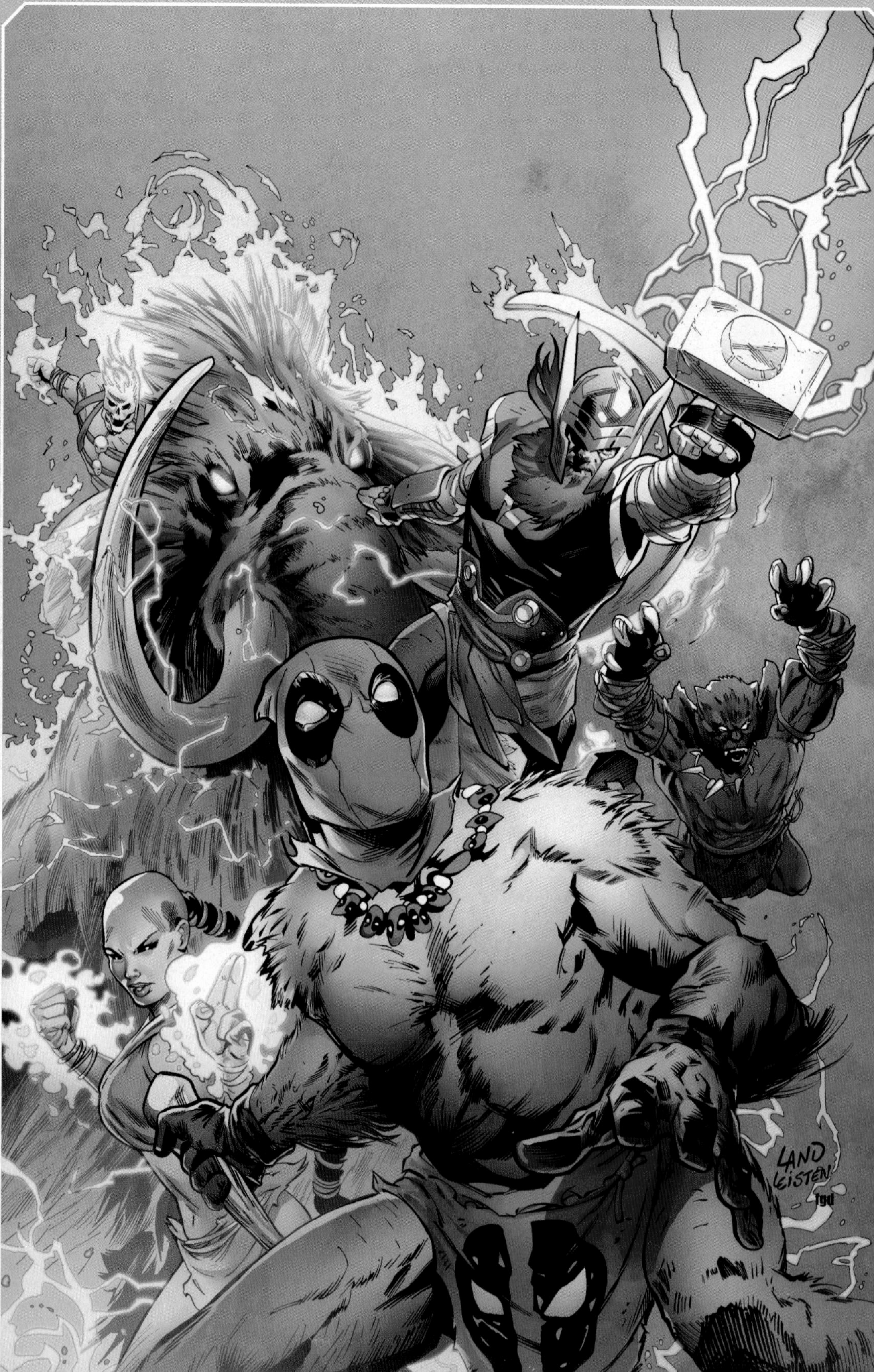

GREG LAND, JAY LEISTEN & FRANK D'ARMATA
1 PARTY VARIANT COVER

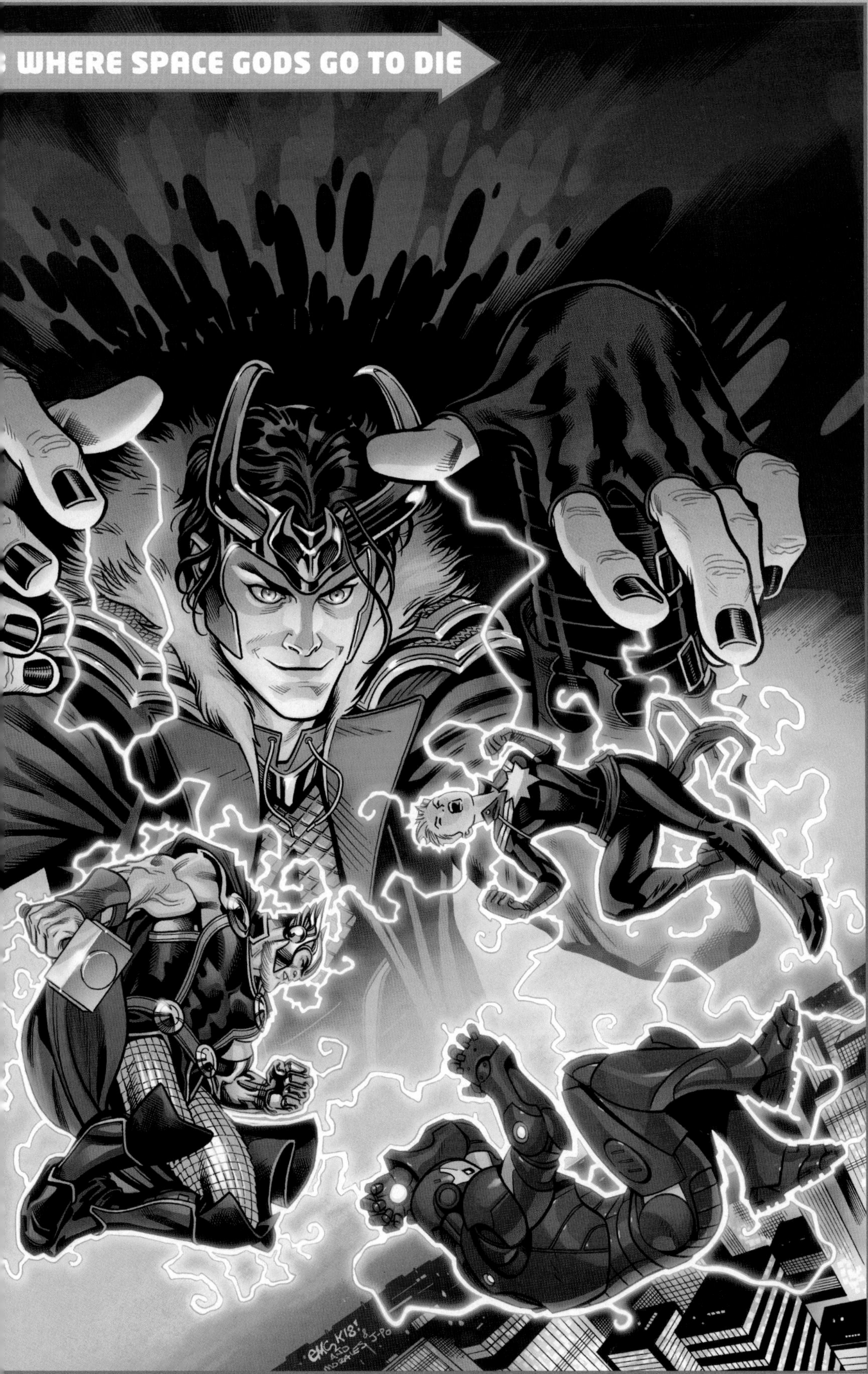
WHERE SPACE GODS GO TO DIE

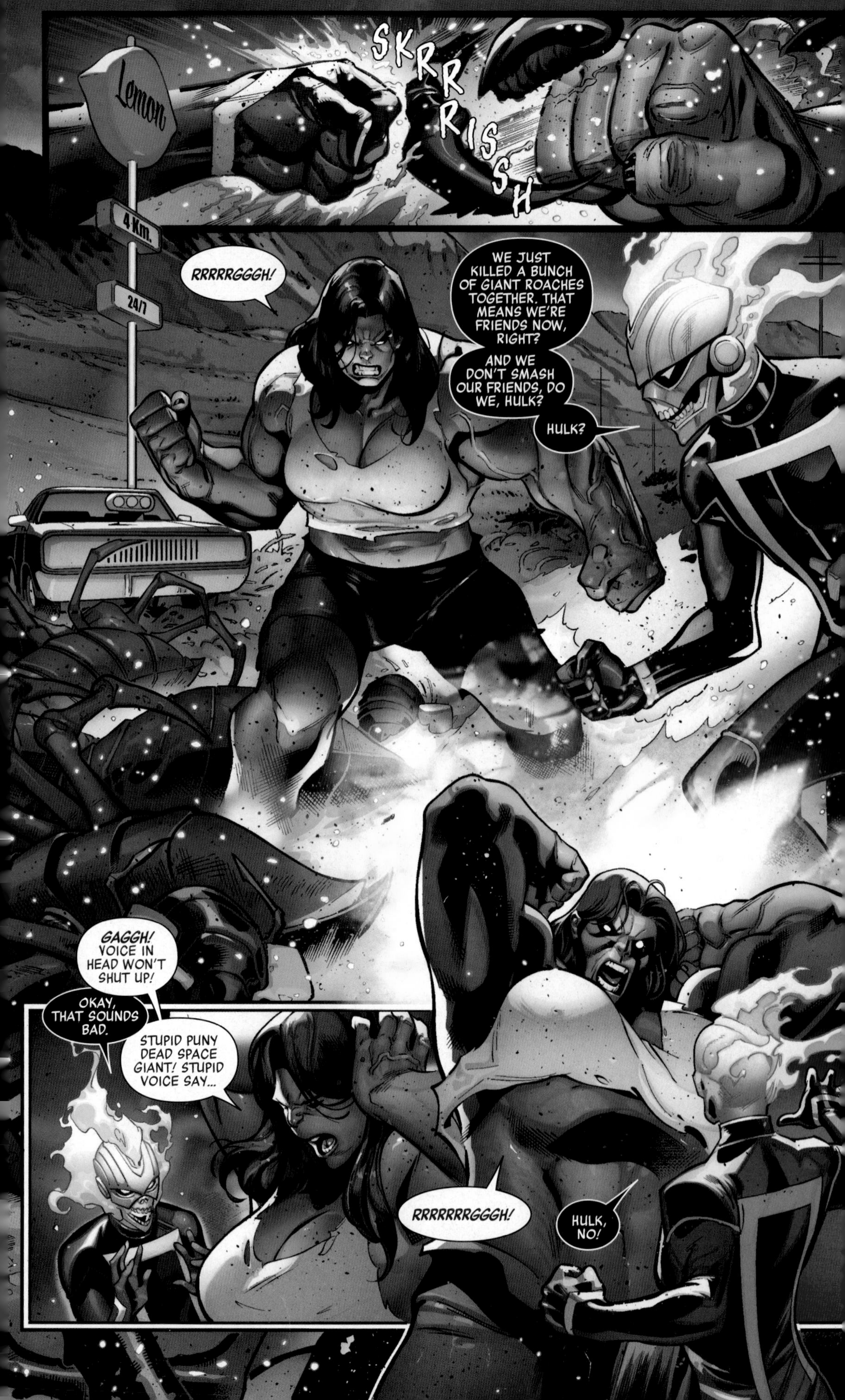
SKRRRISSH
Lemon
4 Km.
24/7
RRRRRGGGH!
WE JUST KILLED A BUNCH OF GIANT ROACHES TOGETHER. THAT MEANS WE'RE FRIENDS NOW, RIGHT?
AND WE DON'T SMASH OUR FRIENDS, DO WE, HULK?
HULK?
GAGGH! VOICE IN HEAD WON'T SHUT UP!
OKAY, THAT SOUNDS BAD.
STUPID PUNY DEAD SPACE GIANT! STUPID VOICE SAY...
RRRRRRRGGGH!
HULK, NO!

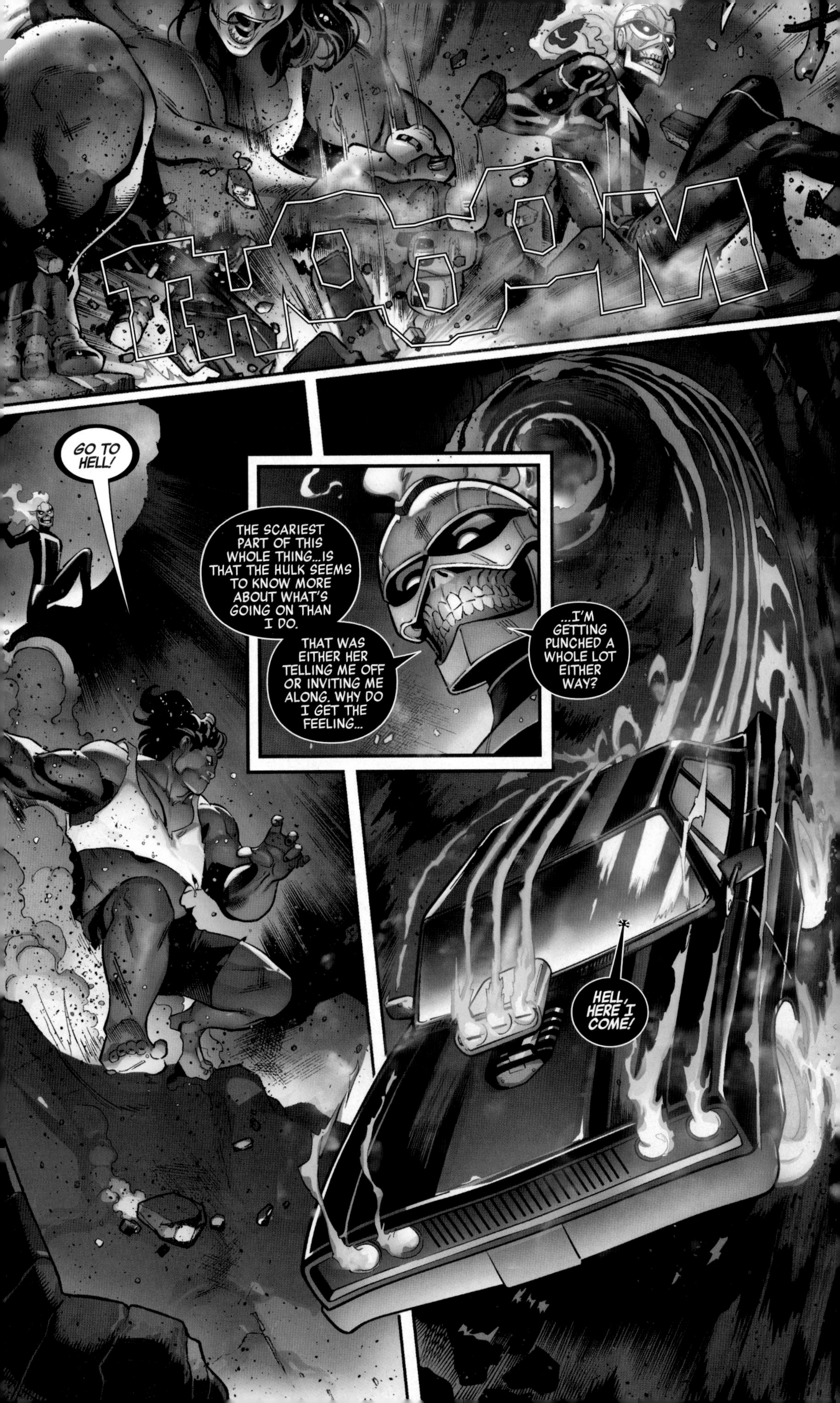
THOOOM
GO TO HELL!
THE SCARIEST PART OF THIS WHOLE THING...IS THAT THE HULK SEEMS TO KNOW MORE ABOUT WHAT'S GOING ON THAN I DO.
THAT WAS EITHER HER TELLING ME OFF OR INVITING ME ALONG. WHY DO I GET THE FEELING...
...I'M GETTING PUNCHED A WHOLE LOT EITHER WAY?
HELL, HERE I COME!

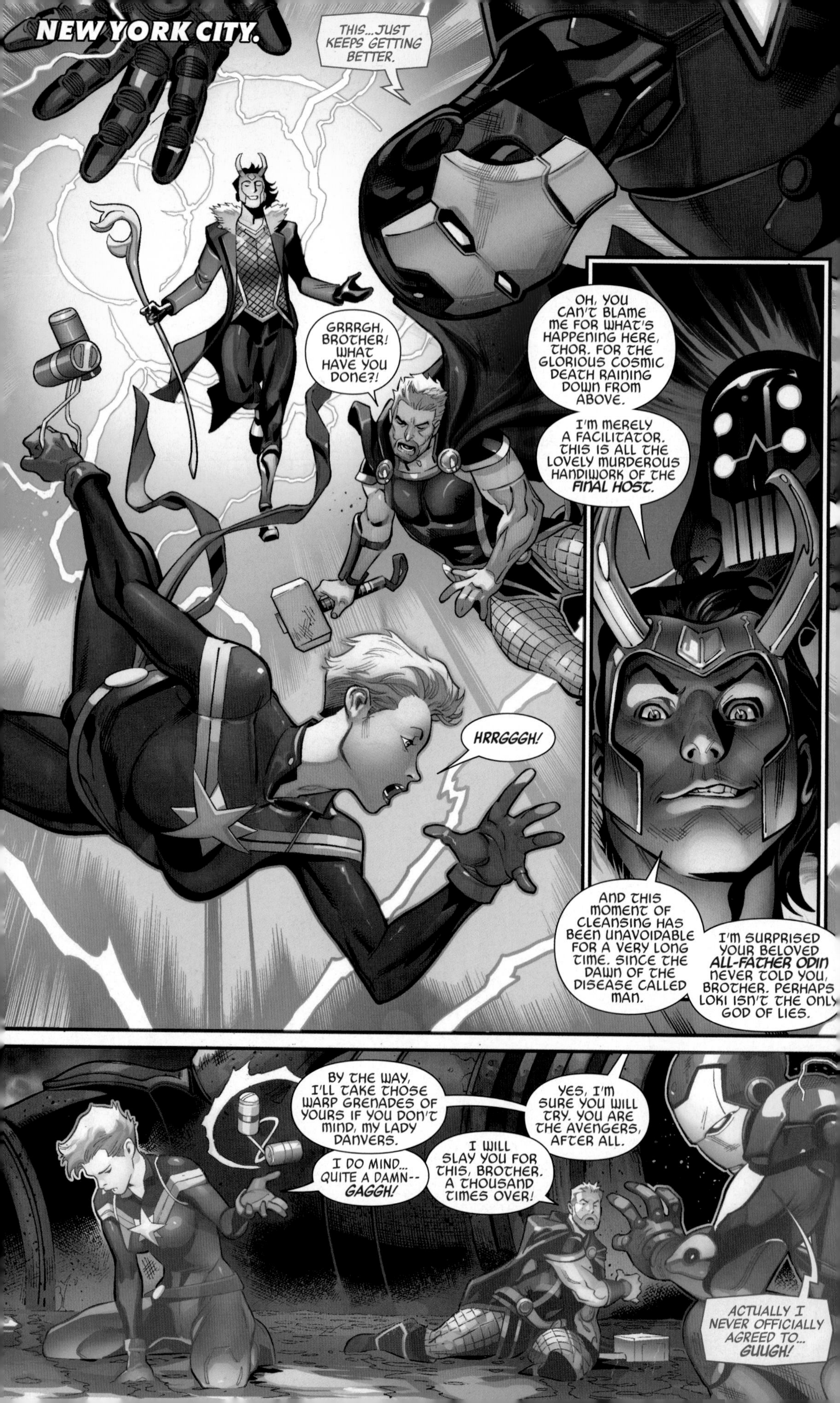
NEW YORK CITY.
THIS...JUST KEEPS GETTING BETTER.
GRRRGH, BROTHER! WHAT HAVE YOU DONE?!
OH, YOU CAN'T BLAME ME FOR WHAT'S HAPPENING HERE, THOR. FOR THE GLORIOUS COSMIC DEATH RAINING DOWN FROM ABOVE.
I'M MERELY A FACILITATOR. THIS IS ALL THE LOVELY MURDEROUS HANDIWORK OF THE FINAL HOST.
HRRGGGH!
AND THIS MOMENT OF CLEANSING HAS BEEN UNAVOIDABLE FOR A VERY LONG TIME. SINCE THE DAWN OF THE DISEASE CALLED MAN.
I'M SURPRISED YOUR BELOVED ALL-FATHER ODIN NEVER TOLD YOU, BROTHER. PERHAPS LOKI ISN'T THE ONLY GOD OF LIES.
BY THE WAY, I'LL TAKE THOSE WARP GRENADES OF YOURS IF YOU DON'T MIND, MY LADY DANVERS.
I DO MIND... QUITE A DAMN-- GAGGH!
YES, I'M SURE YOU WILL TRY. YOU ARE THE AVENGERS, AFTER ALL.
I WILL SLAY YOU FOR THIS, BROTHER. A THOUSAND TIMES OVER!
ACTUALLY I NEVER OFFICIALLY AGREED TO... GUUGH!

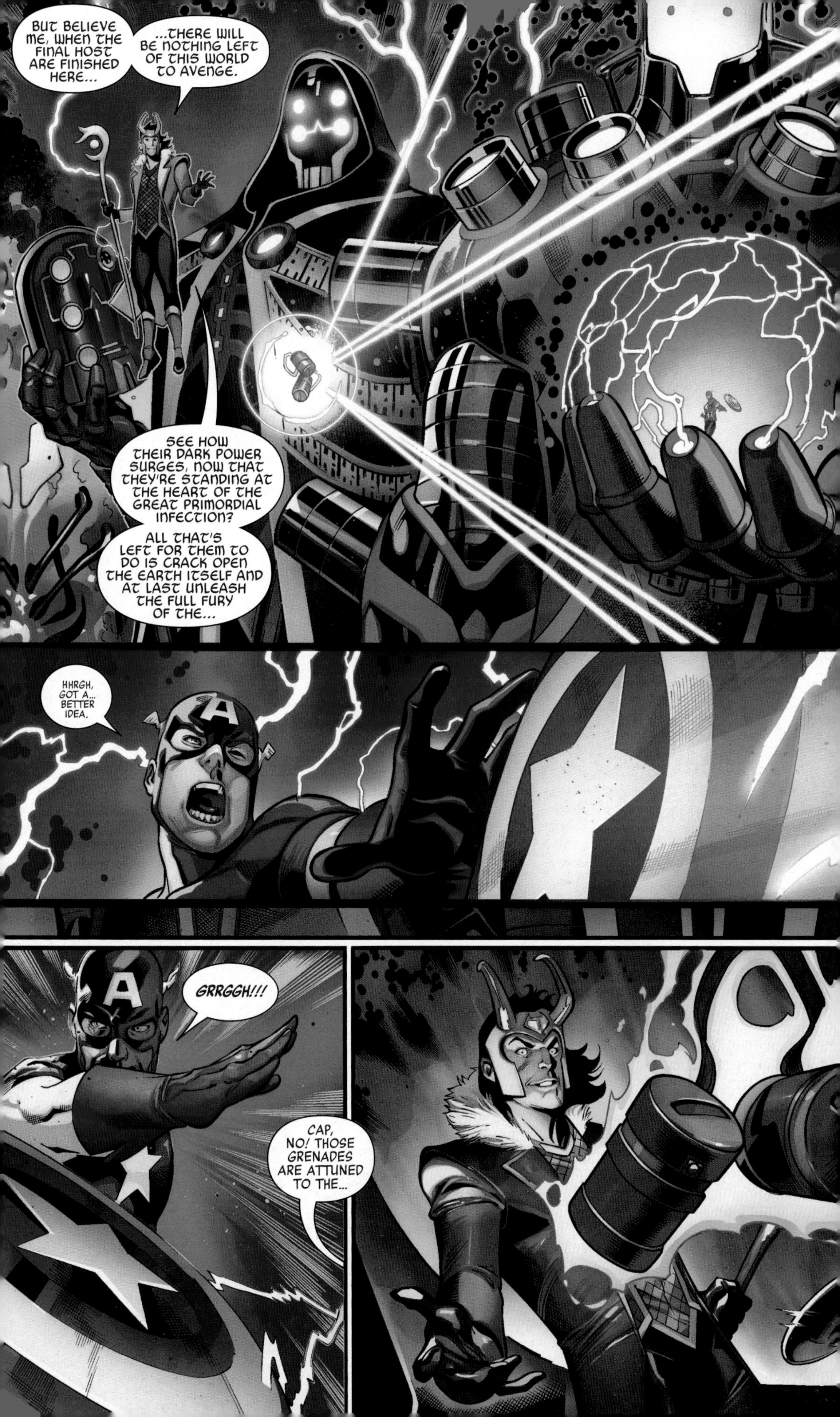
BUT BELIEVE ME, WHEN THE FINAL HOST ARE FINISHED HERE...
...THERE WILL BE NOTHING LEFT OF THIS WORLD TO AVENGE.
SEE HOW THEIR DARK POWER SURGES, NOW THAT THEY'RE STANDING AT THE HEART OF THE GREAT PRIMORDIAL INFECTION?
ALL THAT'S LEFT FOR THEM TO DO IS CRACK OPEN THE EARTH ITSELF AND AT LAST UNLEASH THE FULL FURY OF THE...
HHRGH, GOT A... BETTER IDEA.
GRRGGH!!!
CAP, NO! THOSE GRENADES ARE ATTUNED TO THE...

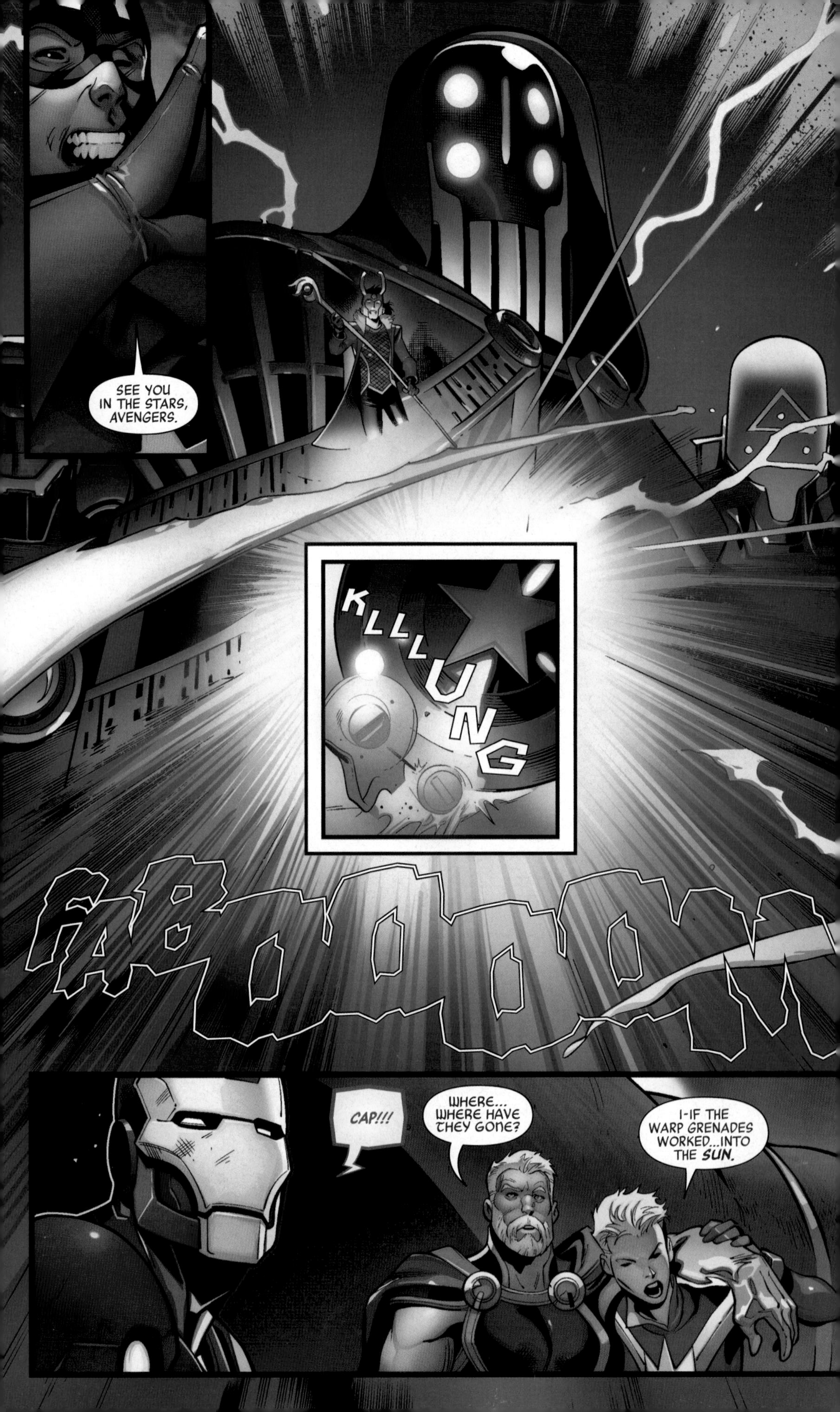
SEE YOU IN THE STARS, AVENGERS.
KLLLUNG
FABOOOOOM
CAP!!!
WHERE... WHERE HAVE THEY GONE?
I-IF THE WARP GRENADES WORKED...INTO THE SUN.

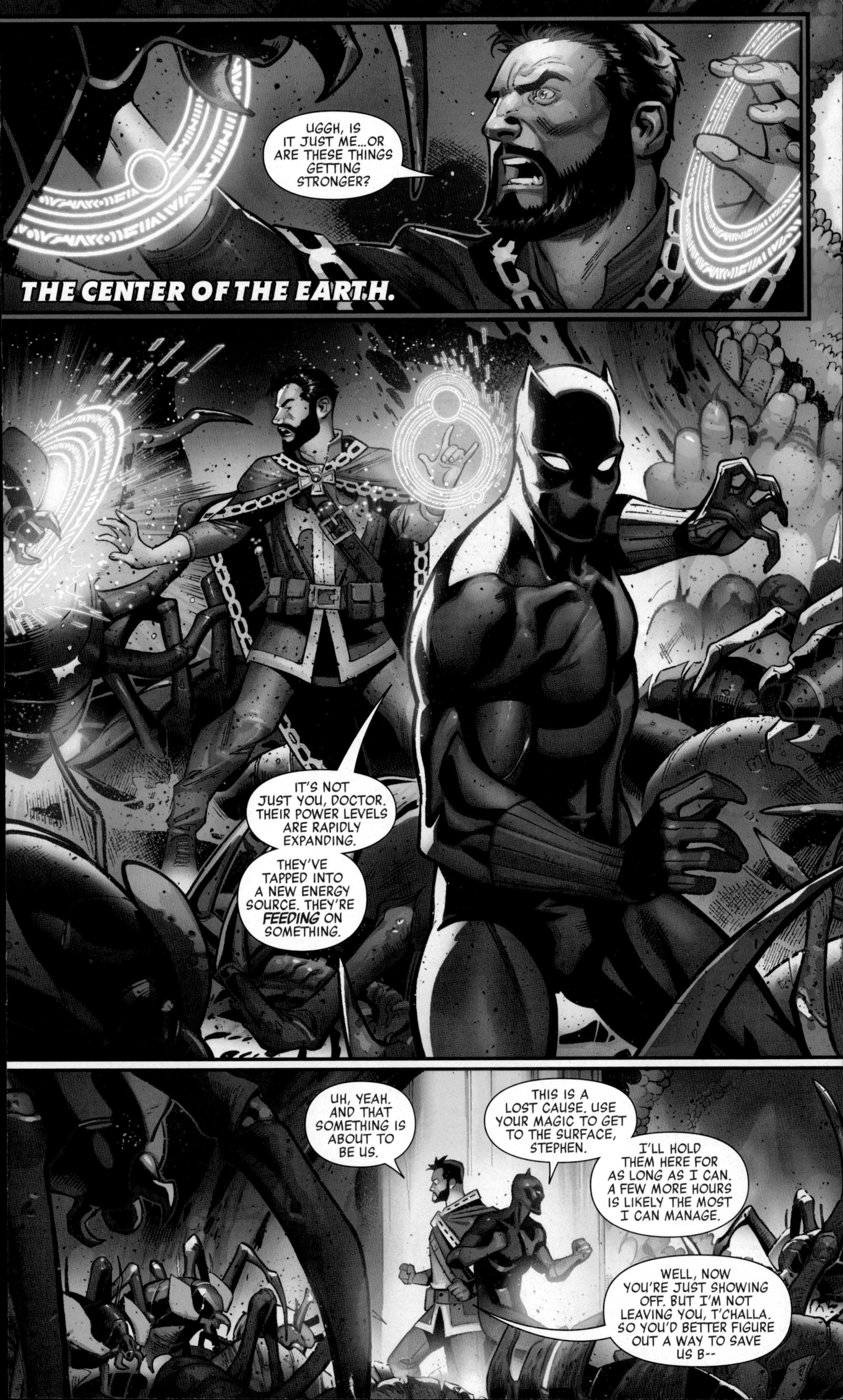
UGGH, IS IT JUST ME...OR ARE THESE THINGS GETTING STRONGER?
THE CENTER OF THE EARTH.
IT'S NOT JUST YOU, DOCTOR. THEIR POWER LEVELS ARE RAPIDLY EXPANDING.
THEY'VE TAPPED INTO A NEW ENERGY SOURCE. THEY'RE FEEDING ON SOMETHING.
UH, YEAH. AND THAT SOMETHING IS ABOUT TO BE US.
THIS IS A LOST CAUSE. USE YOUR MAGIC TO GET TO THE SURFACE, STEPHEN.
I'LL HOLD THEM HERE FOR AS LONG AS I CAN. A FEW MORE HOURS IS LIKELY THE MOST I CAN MANAGE.
WELL, NOW YOU'RE JUST SHOWING OFF. BUT I'M NOT LEAVING YOU, T'CHALLA. SO YOU'D BETTER FIGURE OUT A WAY TO SAVE US B--

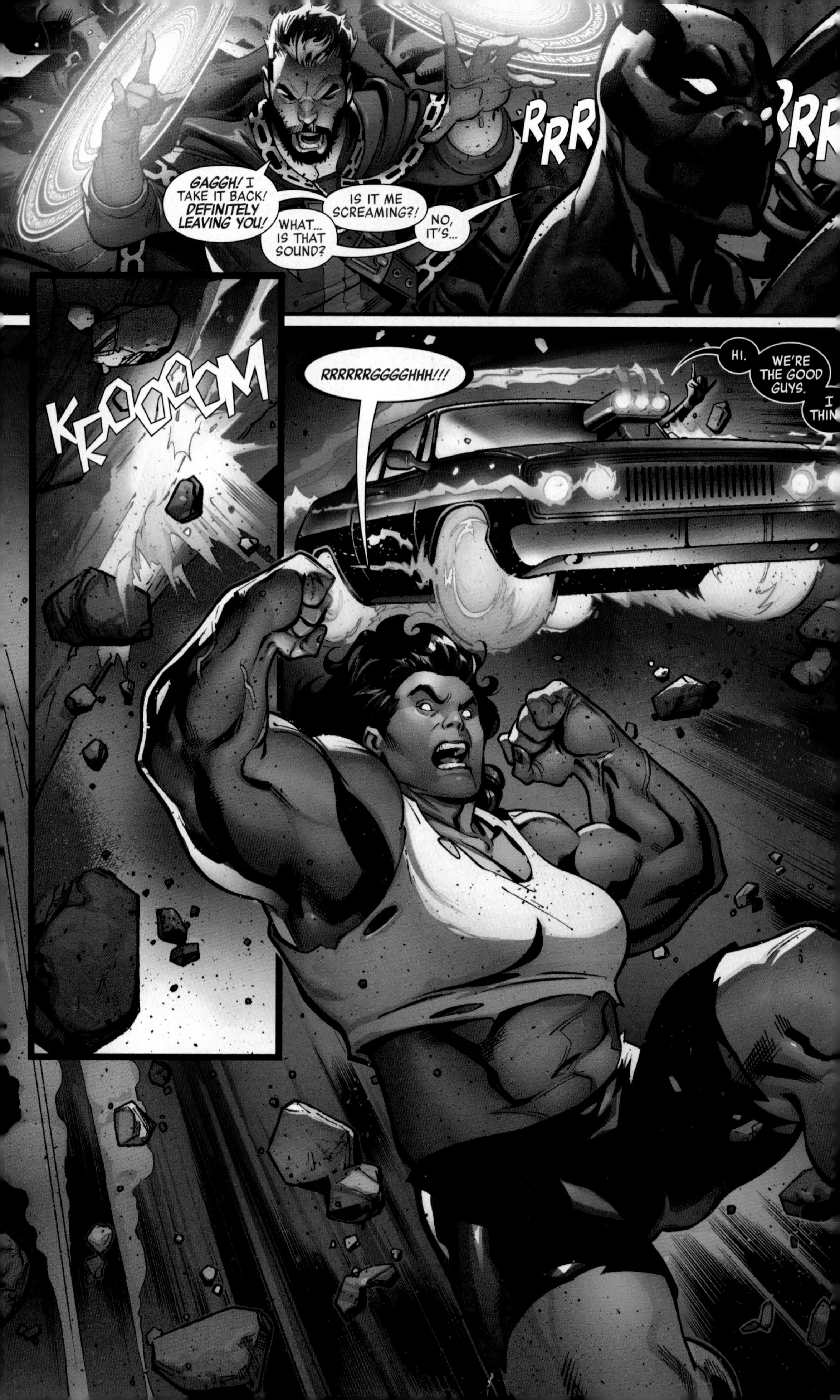
RRR
RRR
GAGGH! I TAKE IT BACK! DEFINITELY LEAVING YOU!
IS IT ME SCREAMING?!
WHAT... IS THAT SOUND?
NO, IT'S...
KROOOOM
RRRRRRGGGGHHH!!!
HI.
WE'RE THE GOOD GUYS.
I THIN

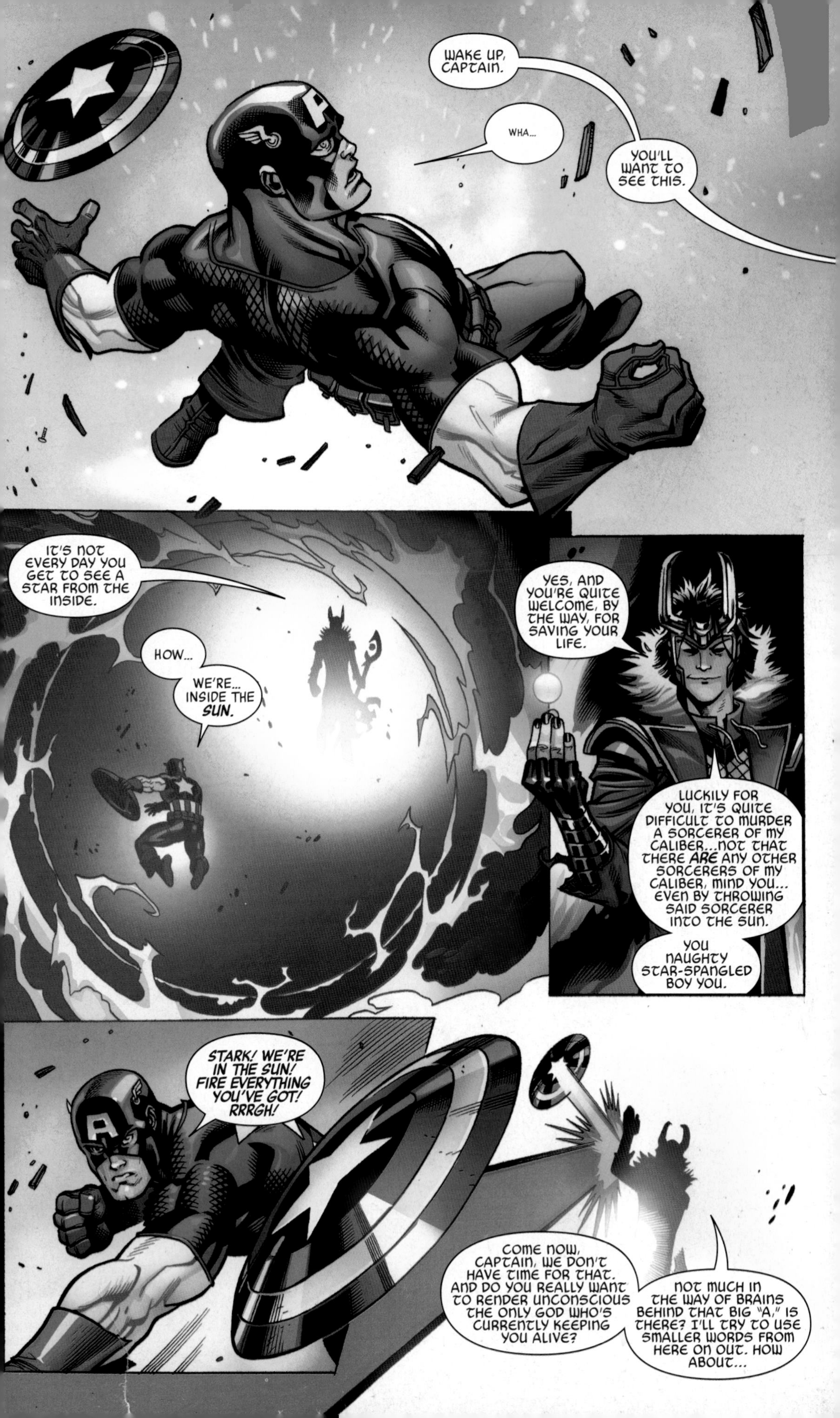
WAKE UP, CAPTAIN.
WHA...
YOU'LL WANT TO SEE THIS.
IT'S NOT EVERY DAY YOU GET TO SEE A STAR FROM THE INSIDE.
HOW...
WE'RE... INSIDE THE SUN.
YES, AND YOU'RE QUITE WELCOME, BY THE WAY, FOR SAVING YOUR LIFE.
LUCKILY FOR YOU, IT'S QUITE DIFFICULT TO MURDER A SORCERER OF MY CALIBER...NOT THAT THERE ARE ANY OTHER SORCERERS OF MY CALIBER, MIND YOU... EVEN BY THROWING SAID SORCERER INTO THE SUN.
YOU NAUGHTY STAR-SPANGLED BOY YOU.
STARK! WE'RE IN THE SUN! FIRE EVERYTHING YOU'VE GOT! RRRGH!
COME NOW, CAPTAIN, WE DON'T HAVE TIME FOR THAT. AND DO YOU REALLY WANT TO RENDER UNCONSCIOUS THE ONLY GOD WHO'S CURRENTLY KEEPING YOU ALIVE?
NOT MUCH IN THE WAY OF BRAINS BEHIND THAT BIG "A," IS THERE? I'LL TRY TO USE SMALLER WORDS FROM HERE ON OUT. HOW ABOUT...

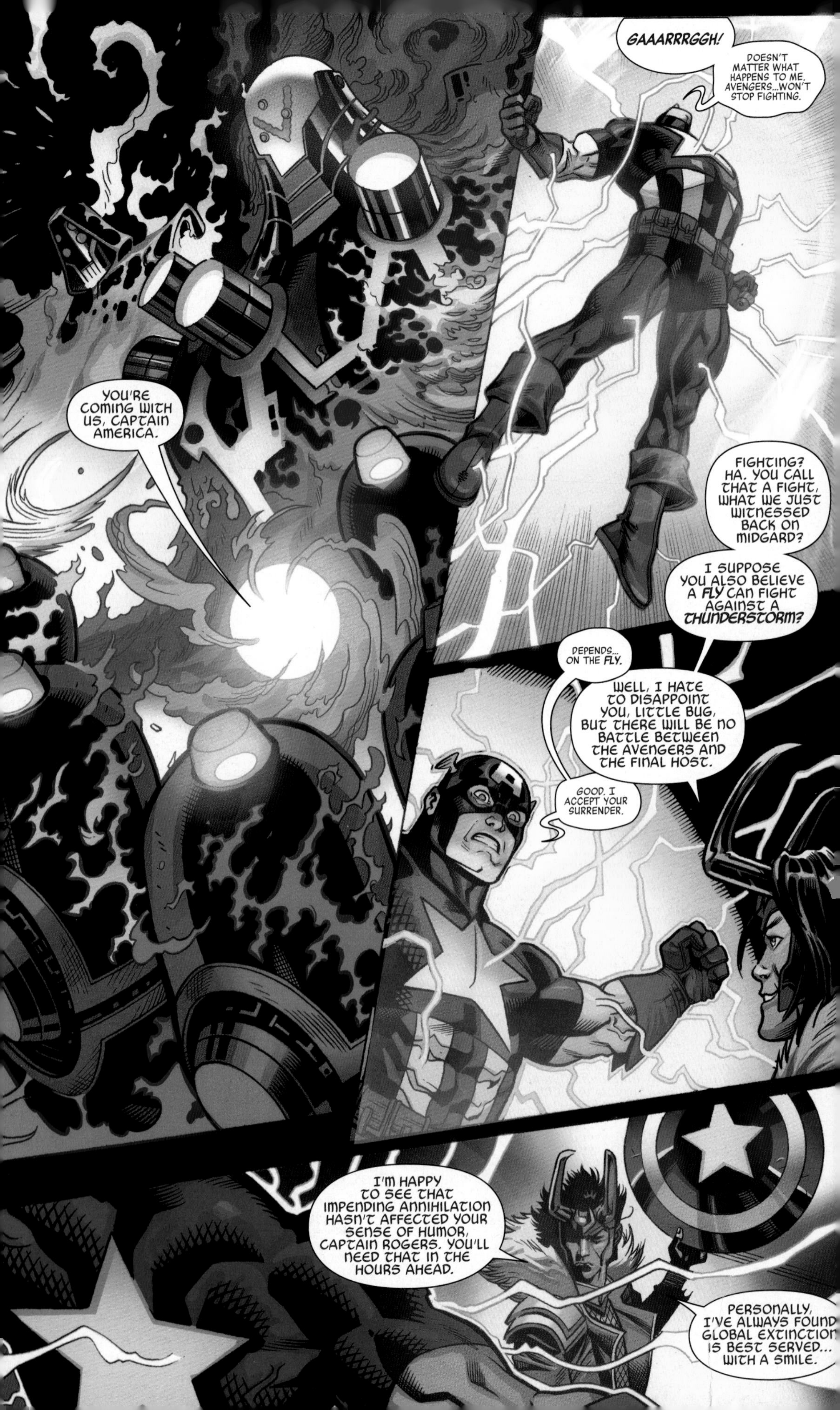
YOU'RE COMING WITH US, CAPTAIN AMERICA.
GAAARRRGGH!
DOESN'T MATTER WHAT HAPPENS TO ME. AVENGERS...WON'T STOP FIGHTING.
FIGHTING? HA. YOU CALL THAT A FIGHT, WHAT WE JUST WITNESSED BACK ON MIDGARD?
I SUPPOSE YOU ALSO BELIEVE A FLY CAN FIGHT AGAINST A THUNDERSTORM?
DEPENDS... ON THE FLY.
WELL, I HATE TO DISAPPOINT YOU, LITTLE BUG, BUT THERE WILL BE NO BATTLE BETWEEN THE AVENGERS AND THE FINAL HOST.
GOOD. I ACCEPT YOUR SURRENDER.
I'M HAPPY TO SEE THAT IMPENDING ANNIHILATION HASN'T AFFECTED YOUR SENSE OF HUMOR, CAPTAIN ROGERS. YOU'LL NEED THAT IN THE HOURS AHEAD.
PERSONALLY, I'VE ALWAYS FOUND GLOBAL EXTINCTION IS BEST SERVED... WITH A SMILE.

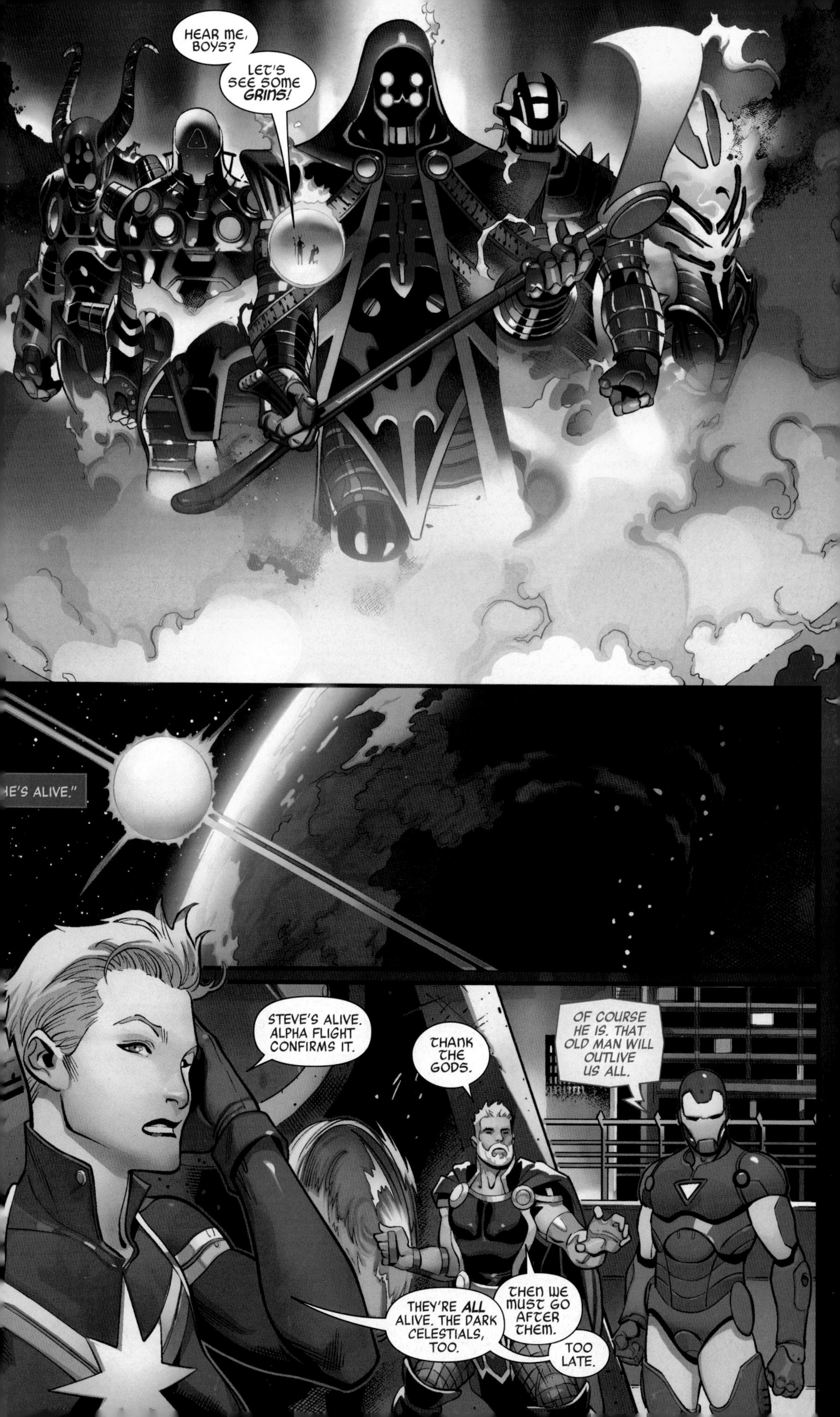
HEAR ME, BOYS?
LET'S SEE SOME GRINS!
...HE'S ALIVE."
STEVE'S ALIVE. ALPHA FLIGHT CONFIRMS IT.
THANK THE GODS.
OF COURSE HE IS. THAT OLD MAN WILL OUTLIVE US ALL.
THEY'RE ALL ALIVE. THE DARK CELESTIALS, TOO.
THEN WE MUST GO AFTER THEM.
TOO LATE.

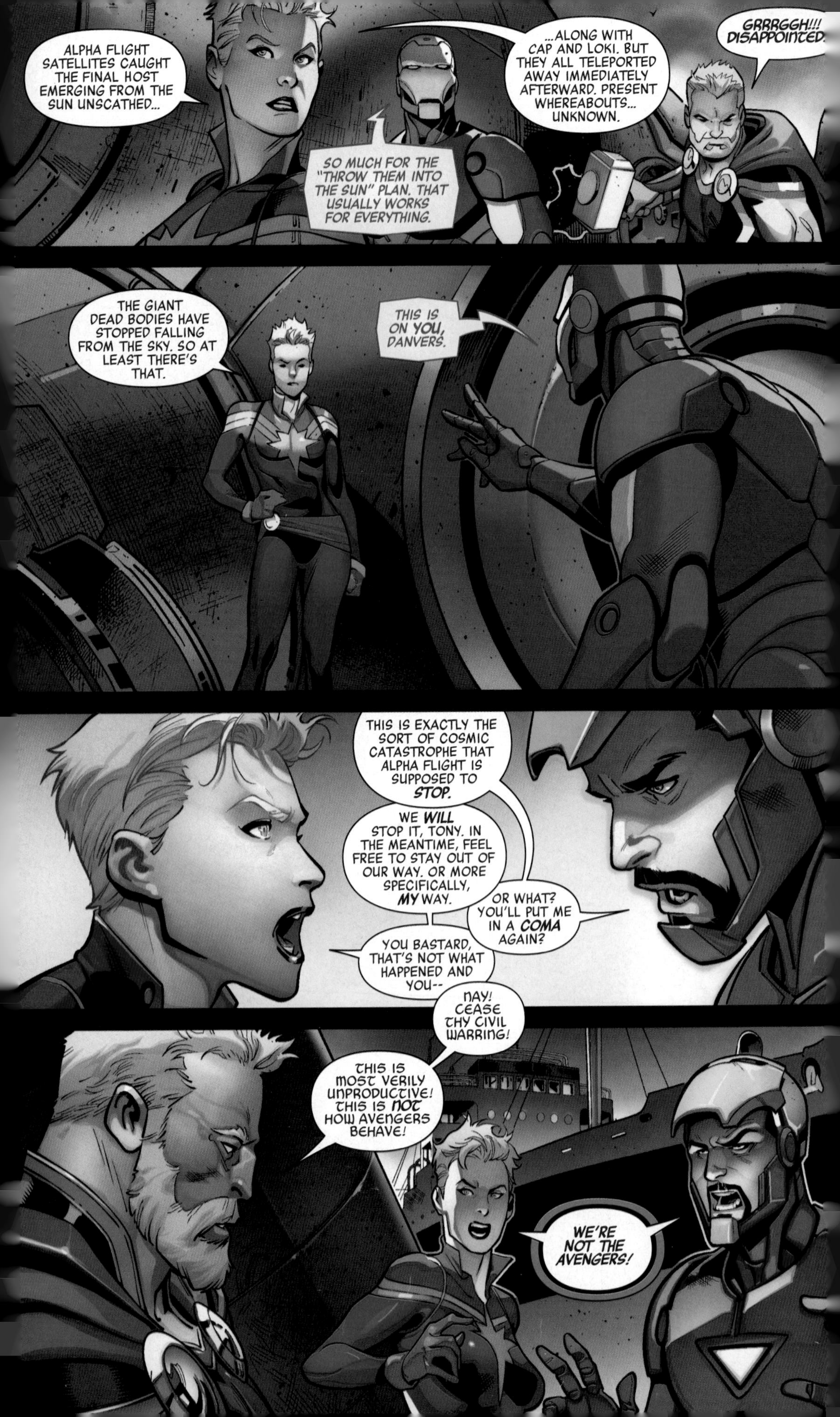
ALPHA FLIGHT SATELLITES CAUGHT THE FINAL HOST EMERGING FROM THE SUN UNSCATHED...
...ALONG WITH CAP AND LOKI. BUT THEY ALL TELEPORTED AWAY IMMEDIATELY AFTERWARD. PRESENT WHEREABOUTS... UNKNOWN.
GRRRGGH!!! DISAPPOINTED.
SO MUCH FOR THE "THROW THEM INTO THE SUN" PLAN. THAT USUALLY WORKS FOR EVERYTHING.
THE GIANT DEAD BODIES HAVE STOPPED FALLING FROM THE SKY. SO AT LEAST THERE'S THAT.
THIS IS ON YOU, DANVERS.
THIS IS EXACTLY THE SORT OF COSMIC CATASTROPHE THAT ALPHA FLIGHT IS SUPPOSED TO STOP.
WE WILL STOP IT, TONY. IN THE MEANTIME, FEEL FREE TO STAY OUT OF OUR WAY. OR MORE SPECIFICALLY, MY WAY.
OR WHAT? YOU'LL PUT ME IN A COMA AGAIN?
YOU BASTARD, THAT'S NOT WHAT HAPPENED AND YOU--
NAY! CEASE THY CIVIL WARRING!
THIS IS MOST VERILY UNPRODUCTIVE! THIS IS NOT HOW AVENGERS BEHAVE!
WE'RE NOT THE AVENGERS!

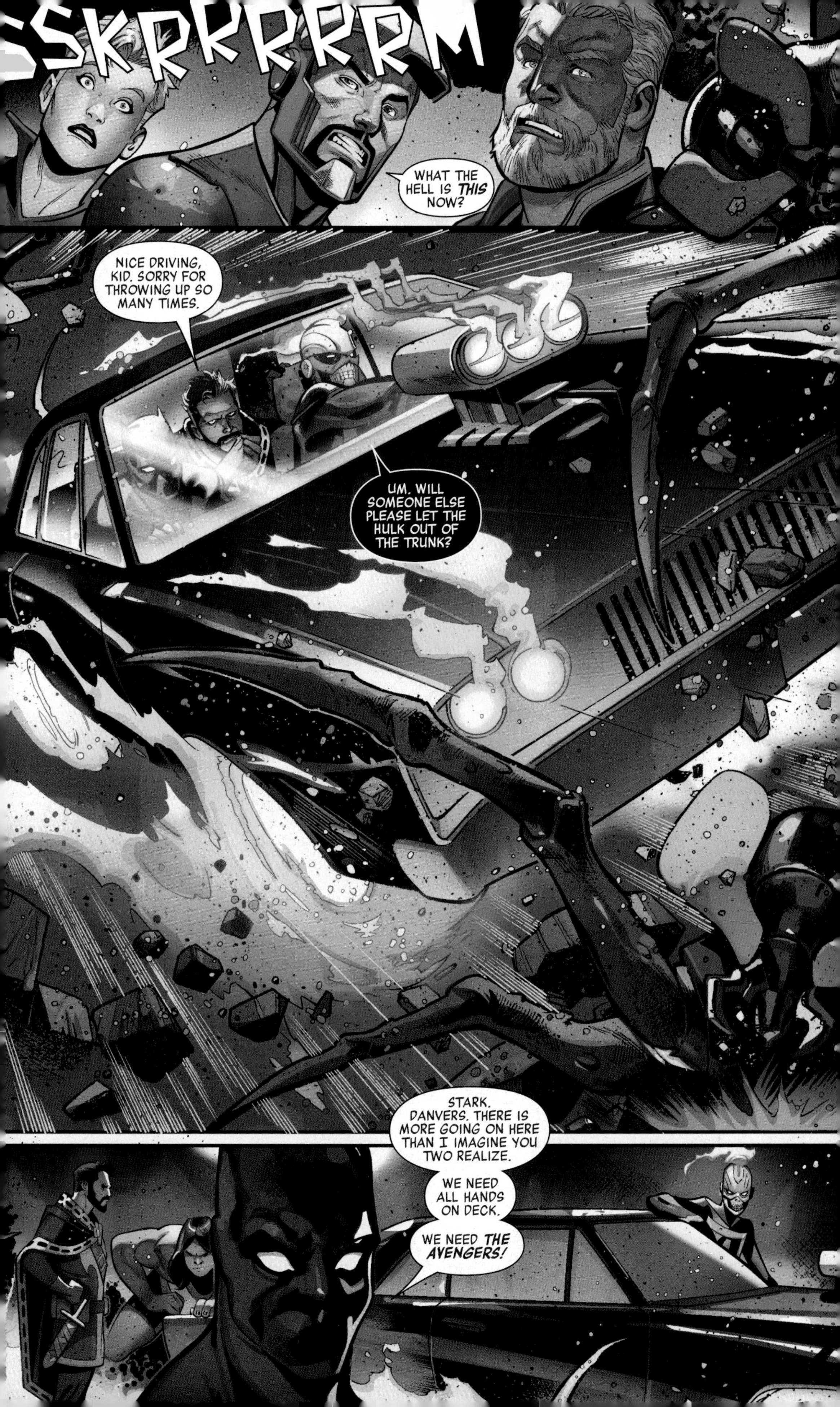
SKRRRRRM
WHAT THE HELL IS THIS NOW?
NICE DRIVING, KID. SORRY FOR THROWING UP SO MANY TIMES.
UM. WILL SOMEONE ELSE PLEASE LET THE HULK OUT OF THE TRUNK?
STARK. DANVERS. THERE IS MORE GOING ON HERE THAN I IMAGINE YOU TWO REALIZE.
WE NEED ALL HANDS ON DECK.
WE NEED THE AVENGERS!

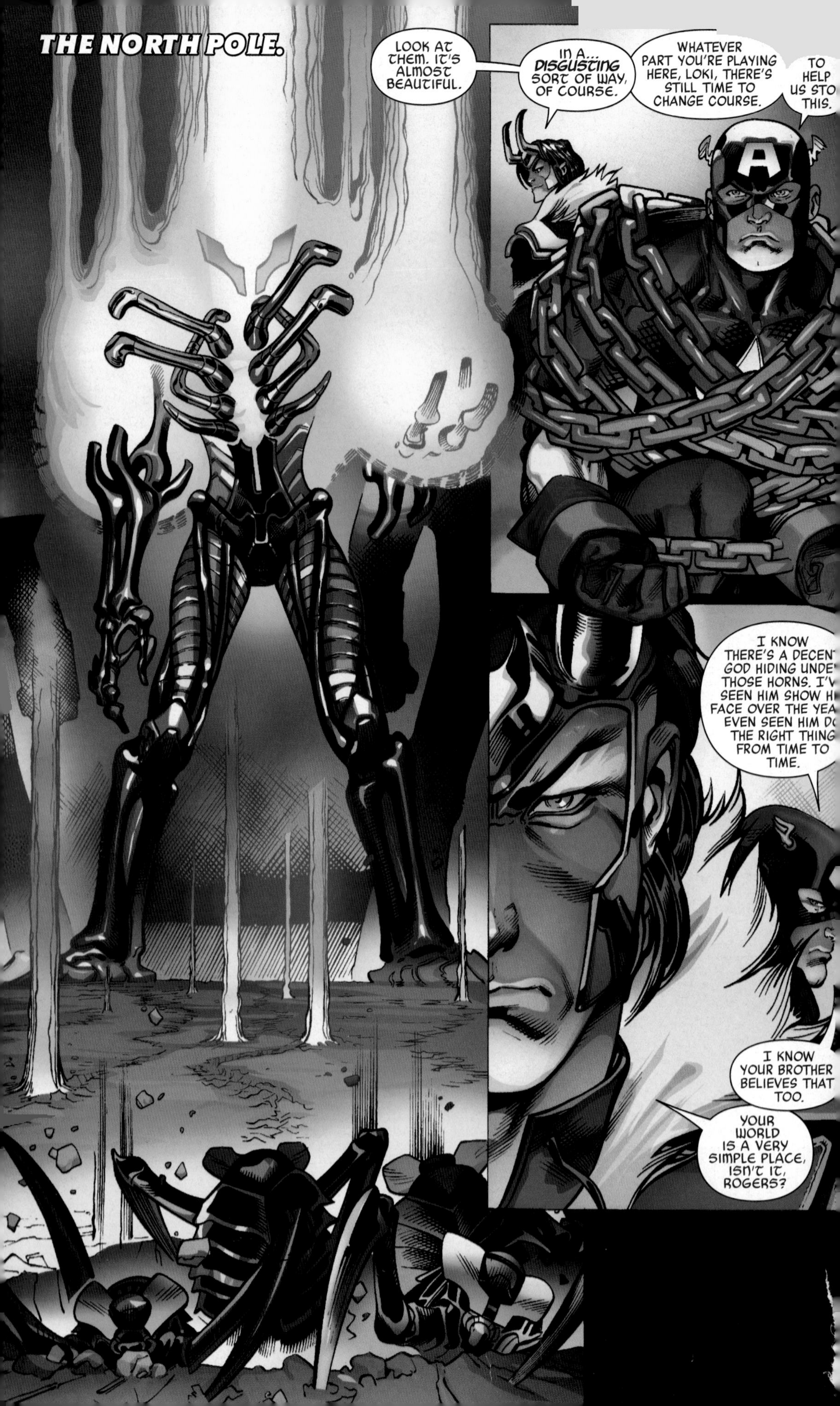
THE NORTH POLE.
LOOK AT THEM. IT'S ALMOST BEAUTIFUL.
IN A... DISGUSTING SORT OF WAY, OF COURSE.
WHATEVER PART YOU'RE PLAYING HERE, LOKI, THERE'S STILL TIME TO CHANGE COURSE.
TO HELP US STO THIS.
I KNOW THERE'S A DECEN GOD HIDING UNDE THOSE HORNS. I'V SEEN HIM SHOW H FACE OVER THE YEA EVEN SEEN HIM D THE RIGHT THING FROM TIME TO TIME.
I KNOW YOUR BROTHER BELIEVES THAT TOO.
YOUR WORLD IS A VERY SIMPLE PLACE, ISN'T IT, ROGERS?

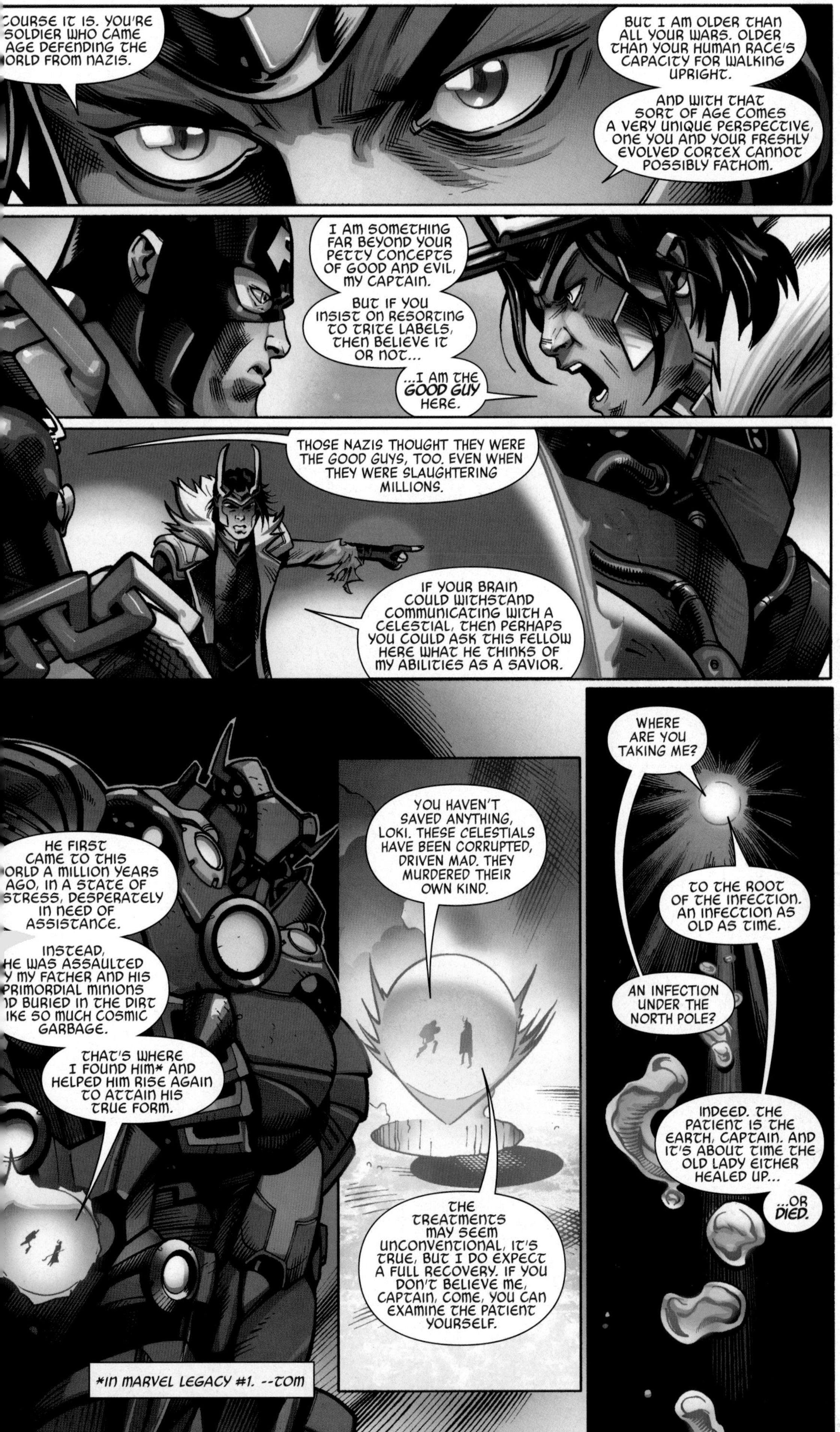
COURSE IT IS. YOU'RE SOLDIER WHO CAME AGE DEFENDING THE ORLD FROM NAZIS.
BUT I AM OLDER THAN ALL YOUR WARS. OLDER THAN YOUR HUMAN RACE'S CAPACITY FOR WALKING UPRIGHT.
AND WITH THAT SORT OF AGE COMES A VERY UNIQUE PERSPECTIVE, ONE YOU AND YOUR FRESHLY EVOLVED CORTEX CANNOT POSSIBLY FATHOM.
I AM SOMETHING FAR BEYOND YOUR PETTY CONCEPTS OF GOOD AND EVIL, MY CAPTAIN.
BUT IF YOU INSIST ON RESORTING TO TRITE LABELS, THEN BELIEVE IT OR NOT...
...I AM THE GOOD GUY HERE.
THOSE NAZIS THOUGHT THEY WERE THE GOOD GUYS, TOO. EVEN WHEN THEY WERE SLAUGHTERING MILLIONS.
IF YOUR BRAIN COULD WITHSTAND COMMUNICATING WITH A CELESTIAL, THEN PERHAPS YOU COULD ASK THIS FELLOW HERE WHAT HE THINKS OF MY ABILITIES AS A SAVIOR.
HE FIRST CAME TO THIS ORLD A MILLION YEARS AGO, IN A STATE OF STRESS, DESPERATELY IN NEED OF ASSISTANCE.
INSTEAD, HE WAS ASSAULTED Y MY FATHER AND HIS PRIMORDIAL MINIONS D BURIED IN THE DIRT IKE SO MUCH COSMIC GARBAGE.
THAT'S WHERE I FOUND HIM* AND HELPED HIM RISE AGAIN TO ATTAIN HIS TRUE FORM.
YOU HAVEN'T SAVED ANYTHING, LOKI. THESE CELESTIALS HAVE BEEN CORRUPTED, DRIVEN MAD. THEY MURDERED THEIR OWN KIND.
THE TREATMENTS MAY SEEM UNCONVENTIONAL, IT'S TRUE, BUT I DO EXPECT A FULL RECOVERY. IF YOU DON'T BELIEVE ME, CAPTAIN, COME, YOU CAN EXAMINE THE PATIENT YOURSELF.
*IN MARVEL LEGACY #1. --TOM
WHERE ARE YOU TAKING ME?
TO THE ROOT OF THE INFECTION. AN INFECTION AS OLD AS TIME.
AN INFECTION UNDER THE NORTH POLE?
INDEED. THE PATIENT IS THE EARTH, CAPTAIN. AND IT'S ABOUT TIME THE OLD LADY EITHER HEALED UP...
...OR DIED.

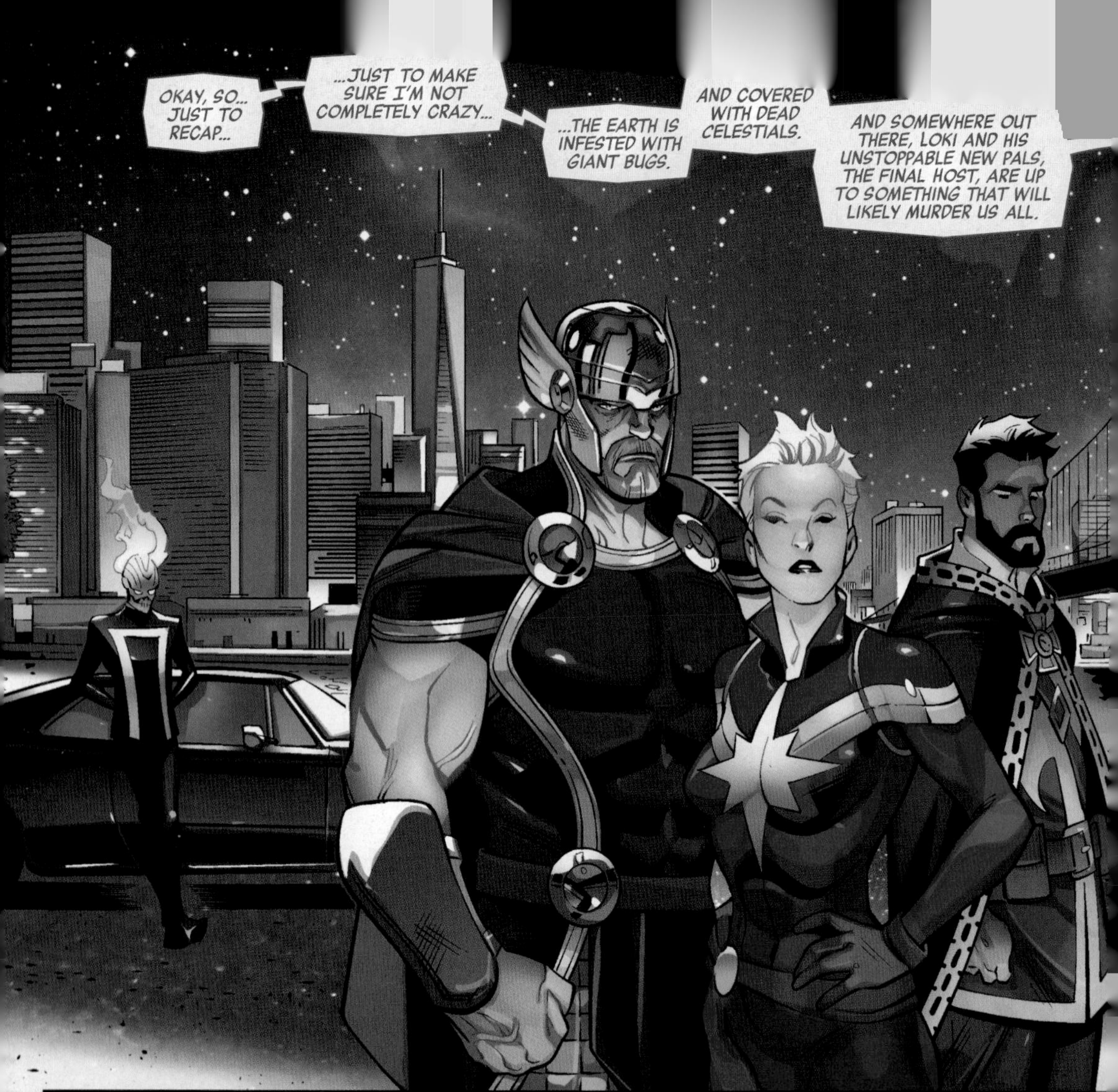
OKAY, SO... JUST TO RECAP...
...JUST TO MAKE SURE I'M NOT COMPLETELY CRAZY...
...THE EARTH IS INFESTED WITH GIANT BUGS.
AND COVERED WITH DEAD CELESTIALS.
AND SOMEWHERE OUT THERE, LOKI AND HIS UNSTOPPABLE NEW PALS, THE FINAL HOST, ARE UP TO SOMETHING THAT WILL LIKELY MURDER US ALL.
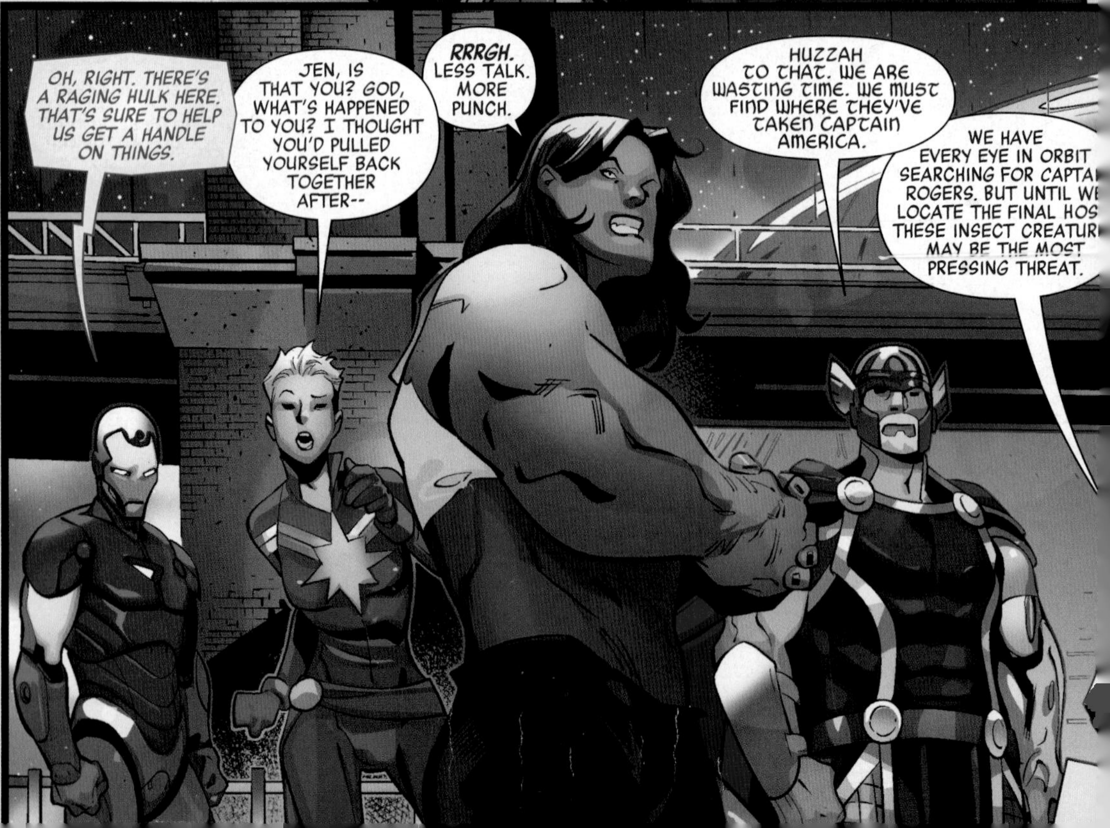
OH, RIGHT. THERE'S A RAGING HULK HERE. THAT'S SURE TO HELP US GET A HANDLE ON THINGS.
JEN, IS THAT YOU? GOD, WHAT'S HAPPENED TO YOU? I THOUGHT YOU'D PULLED YOURSELF BACK TOGETHER AFTER--
RRRGH. LESS TALK. MORE PUNCH.
HUZZAH TO THAT. WE ARE WASTING TIME. WE MUST FIND WHERE THEY'VE TAKEN CAPTAIN AMERICA.
WE HAVE EVERY EYE IN ORBIT SEARCHING FOR CAPTAI ROGERS. BUT UNTIL WE LOCATE THE FINAL HOS THESE INSECT CREATUR MAY BE THE MOST PRESSING THREAT.

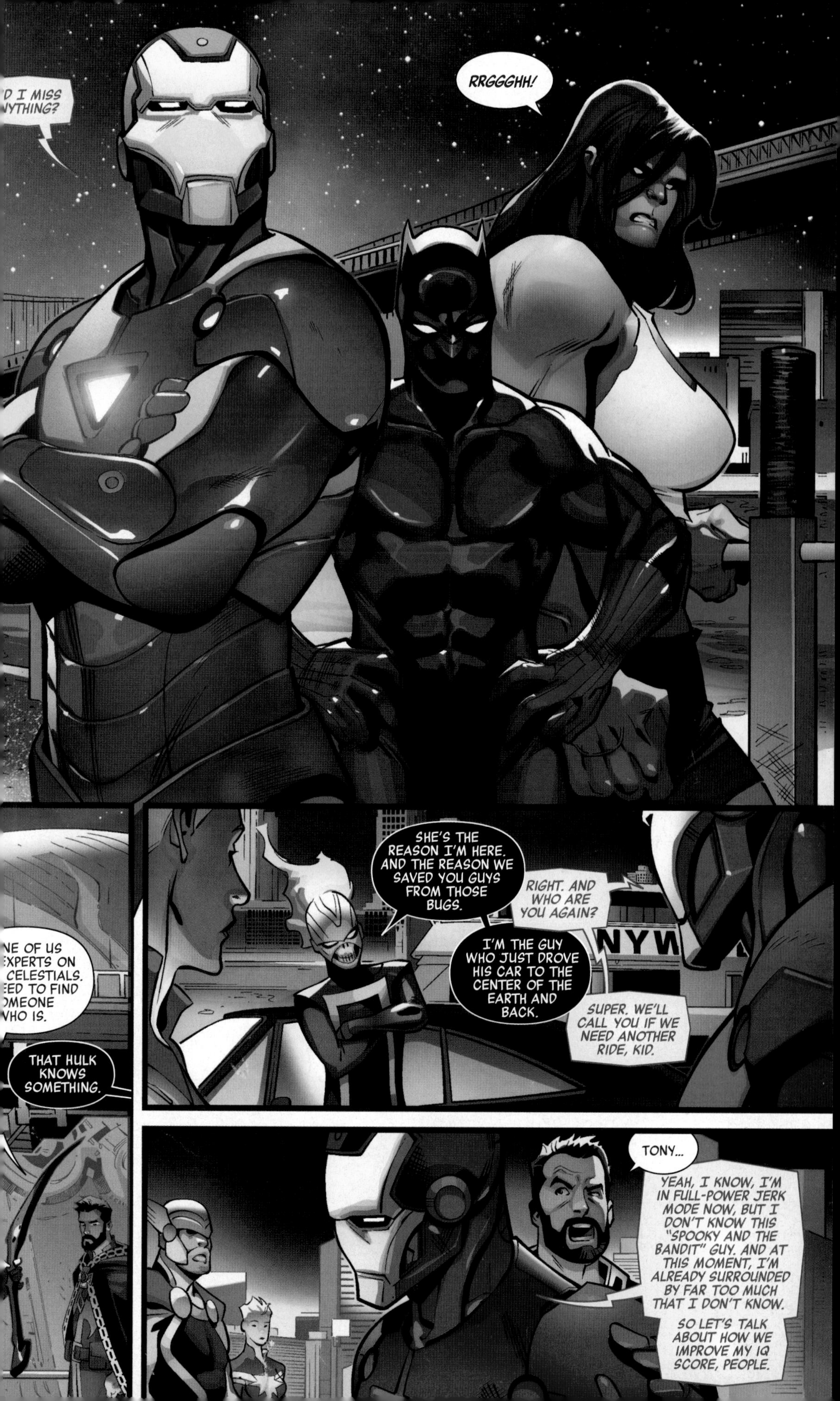

D I MISS
NYTHING?
RRGGGHH!
NE OF US
EXPERTS ON
CELESTIALS.
EED TO FIND
OMEONE
WHO IS.
THAT HULK
KNOWS
SOMETHING.
SHE'S THE REASON I'M HERE. AND THE REASON WE SAVED YOU GUYS FROM THOSE BUGS.
RIGHT. AND WHO ARE YOU AGAIN?
I'M THE GUY WHO JUST DROVE HIS CAR TO THE CENTER OF THE EARTH AND BACK.
SUPER. WE'LL CALL YOU IF WE NEED ANOTHER RIDE, KID.
NYW
TONY...
YEAH, I KNOW, I'M IN FULL-POWER JERK MODE NOW, BUT I DON'T KNOW THIS "SPOOKY AND THE BANDIT" GUY. AND AT THIS MOMENT, I'M ALREADY SURROUNDED BY FAR TOO MUCH THAT I DON'T KNOW.
SO LET'S TALK ABOUT HOW WE IMPROVE MY IQ SCORE, PEOPLE.

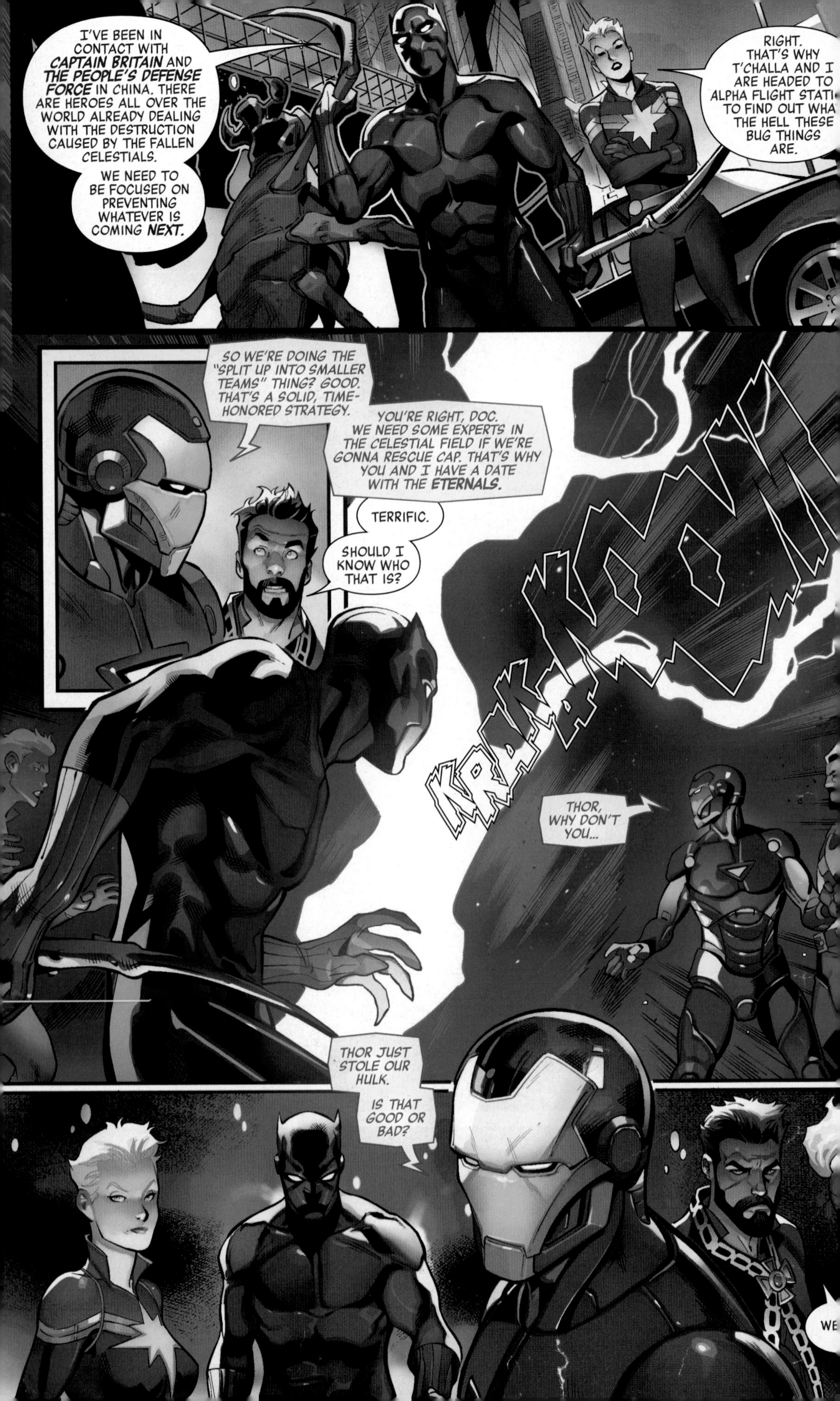

I'VE BEEN IN CONTACT WITH CAPTAIN BRITAIN AND THE PEOPLE'S DEFENSE FORCE IN CHINA. THERE ARE HEROES ALL OVER THE WORLD ALREADY DEALING WITH THE DESTRUCTION CAUSED BY THE FALLEN CELESTIALS.
WE NEED TO BE FOCUSED ON PREVENTING WHATEVER IS COMING NEXT.
RIGHT. THAT'S WHY T'CHALLA AND I ARE HEADED TO ALPHA FLIGHT STATI TO FIND OUT WHA THE HELL THESE BUG THINGS ARE.
SO WE'RE DOING THE "SPLIT UP INTO SMALLER TEAMS" THING? GOOD. THAT'S A SOLID, TIME-HONORED STRATEGY.
YOU'RE RIGHT, DOC. WE NEED SOME EXPERTS IN THE CELESTIAL FIELD IF WE'RE GONNA RESCUE CAP. THAT'S WHY YOU AND I HAVE A DATE WITH THE ETERNALS.
TERRIFIC.
SHOULD I KNOW WHO THAT IS?
KRAK-A-KOOM
THOR, WHY DON'T YOU...
THOR JUST STOLE OUR HULK.
IS THAT GOOD OR BAD?
WE

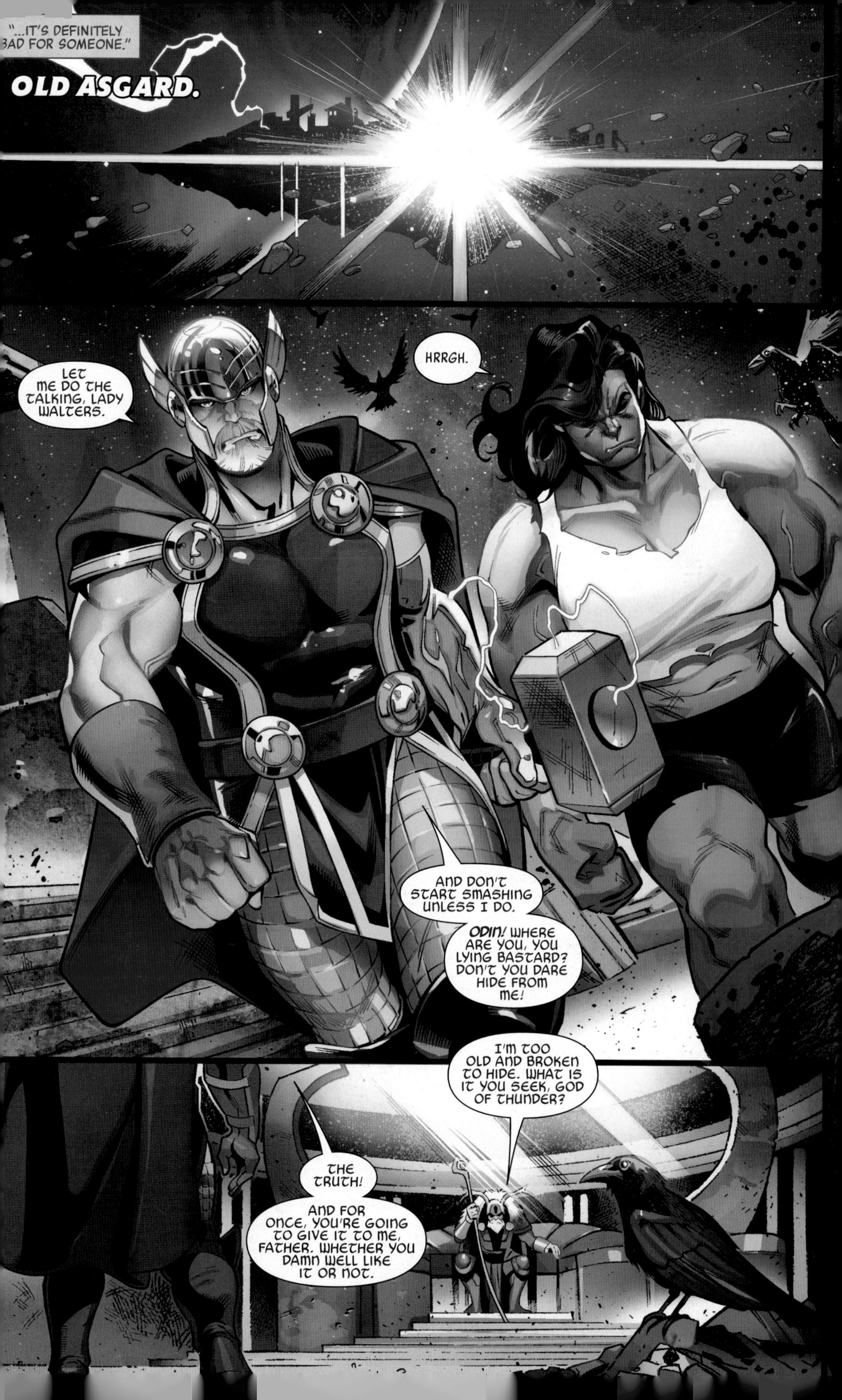
"...IT'S DEFINITELY
BAD FOR SOMEONE."
OLD ASGARD.
LET ME DO THE TALKING, LADY WALTERS.
HRRGH.
AND DON'T START SMASHING UNLESS I DO.
ODIN! WHERE ARE YOU, YOU LYING BASTARD? DON'T YOU DARE HIDE FROM ME!
I'M TOO OLD AND BROKEN TO HIDE. WHAT IS IT YOU SEEK, GOD OF THUNDER?
THE TRUTH!
AND FOR ONCE, YOU'RE GOING TO GIVE IT TO ME, FATHER. WHETHER YOU DAMN WELL LIKE IT OR NOT.

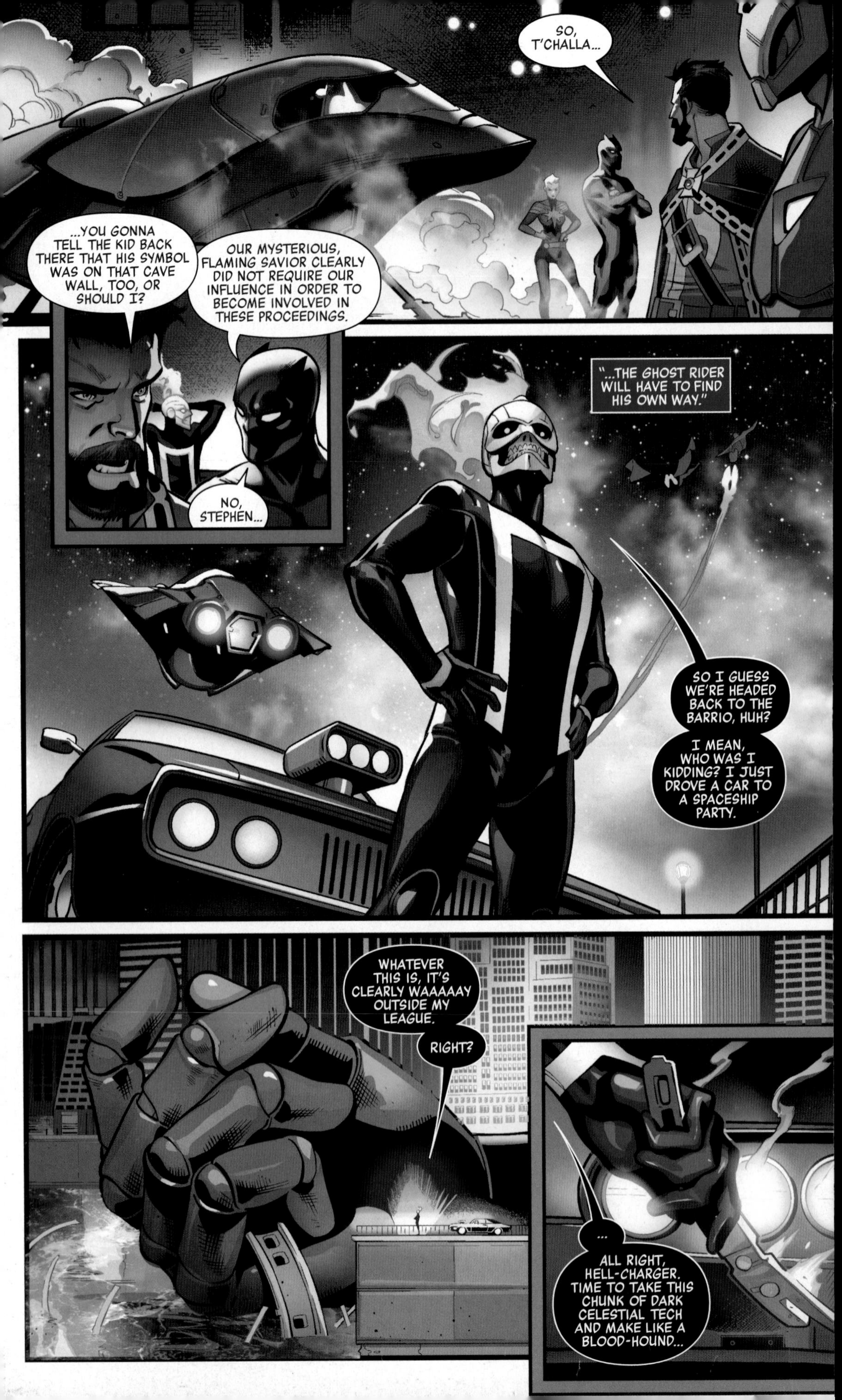

SO, T'CHALLA...
...YOU GONNA TELL THE KID BACK THERE THAT HIS SYMBOL WAS ON THAT CAVE WALL, TOO, OR SHOULD I?
NO, STEPHEN...
OUR MYSTERIOUS, FLAMING SAVIOR CLEARLY DID NOT REQUIRE OUR INFLUENCE IN ORDER TO BECOME INVOLVED IN THESE PROCEEDINGS.
"...THE GHOST RIDER WILL HAVE TO FIND HIS OWN WAY."
SO I GUESS WE'RE HEADED BACK TO THE BARRIO, HUH?
I MEAN, WHO WAS I KIDDING? I JUST DROVE A CAR TO A SPACESHIP PARTY.
WHATEVER THIS IS, IT'S CLEARLY WAAAAAY OUTSIDE MY LEAGUE.
RIGHT?
...
ALL RIGHT, HELL-CHARGER. TIME TO TAKE THIS CHUNK OF DARK CELESTIAL TECH AND MAKE LIKE A BLOOD-HOUND...

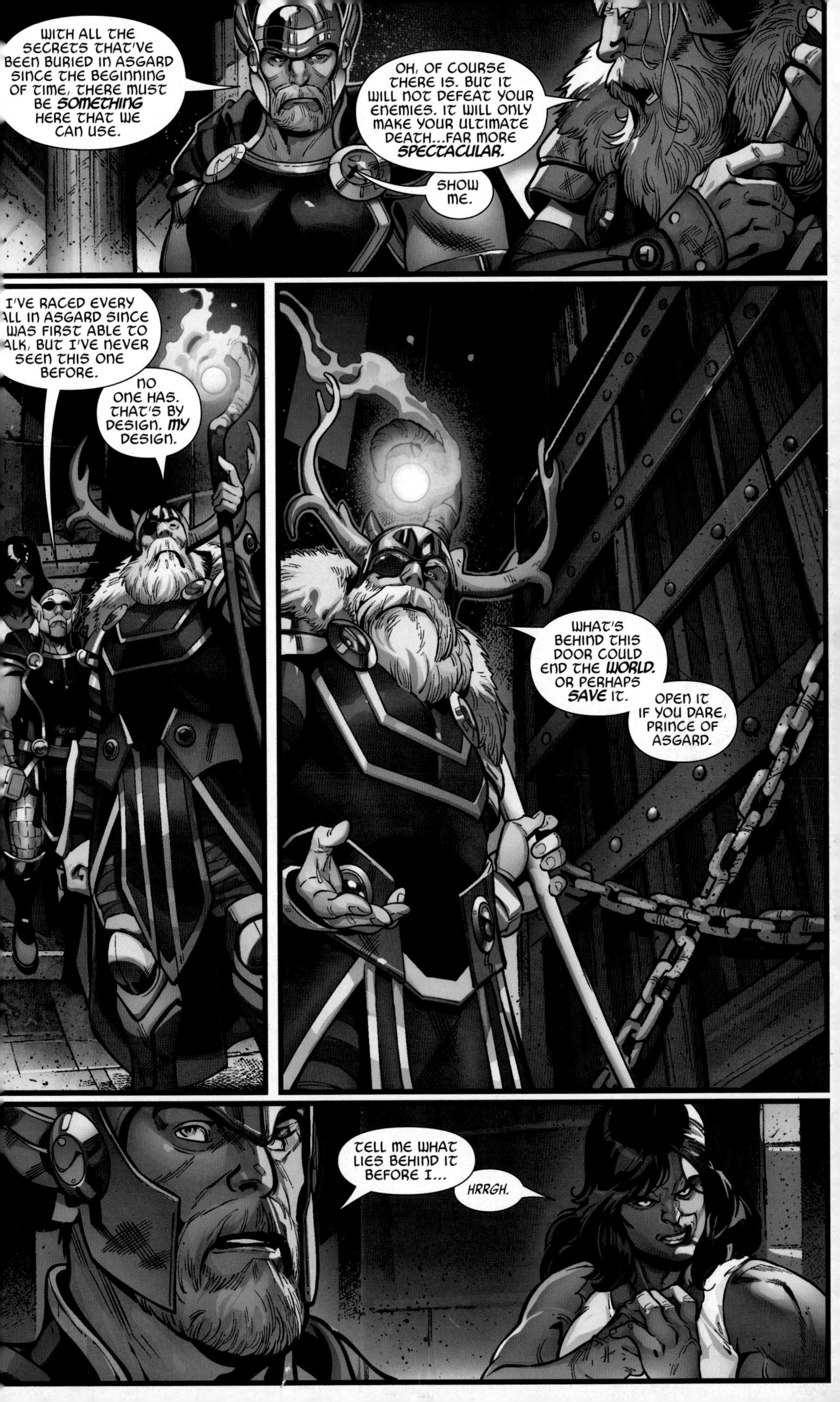
WITH ALL THE SECRETS THAT'VE BEEN BURIED IN ASGARD SINCE THE BEGINNING OF TIME, THERE MUST BE SOMETHING HERE THAT WE CAN USE.
OH, OF COURSE THERE IS. BUT IT WILL NOT DEFEAT YOUR ENEMIES. IT WILL ONLY MAKE YOUR ULTIMATE DEATH...FAR MORE SPECTACULAR.
SHOW ME.
I'VE RACED EVERY ALL IN ASGARD SINCE WAS FIRST ABLE TO ALK, BUT I'VE NEVER SEEN THIS ONE BEFORE.
NO ONE HAS. THAT'S BY DESIGN. MY DESIGN.
WHAT'S BEHIND THIS DOOR COULD END THE WORLD. OR PERHAPS SAVE IT.
OPEN IT IF YOU DARE, PRINCE OF ASGARD.
TELL ME WHAT LIES BEHIND IT BEFORE I...
HRRGH.

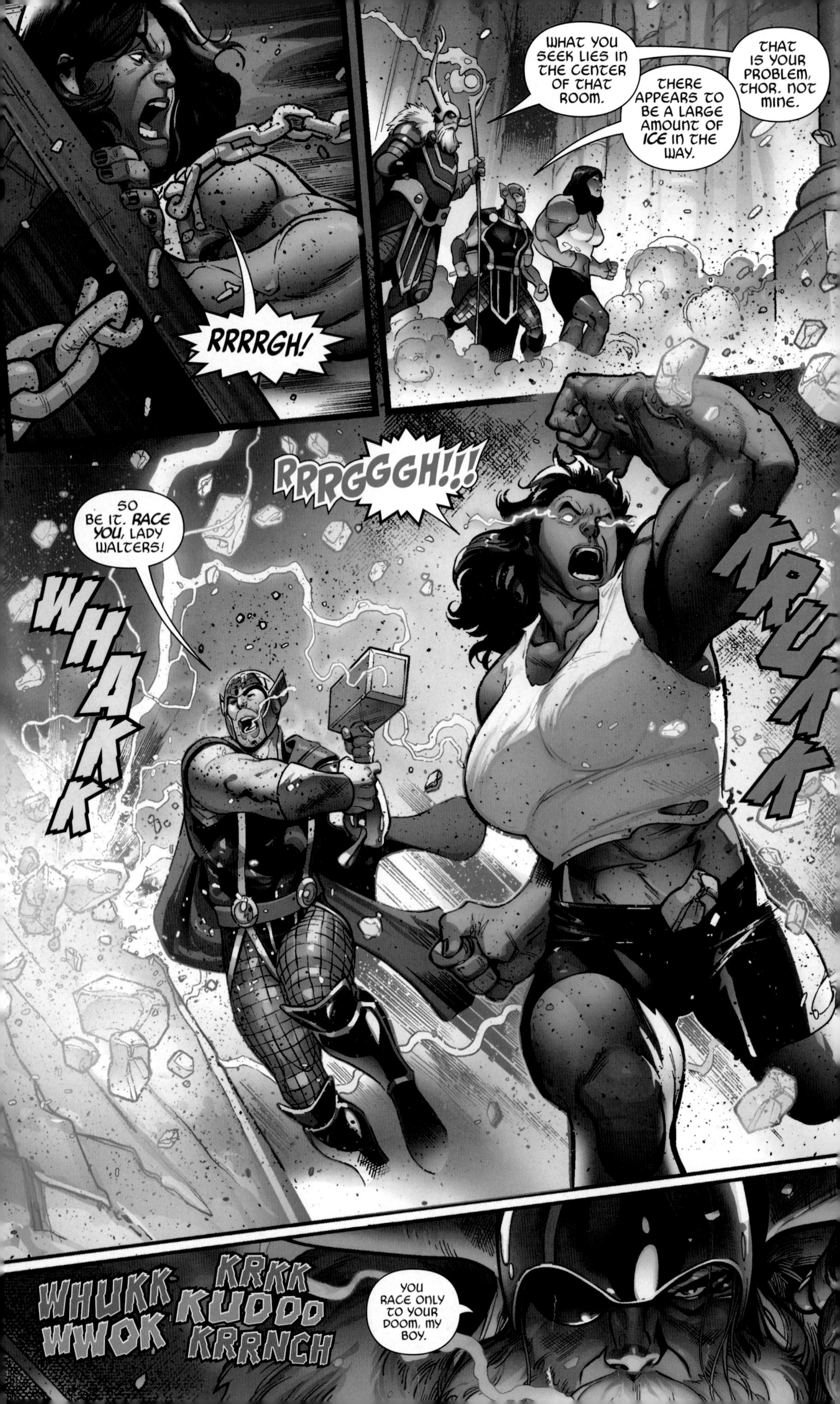

RRRRGH!
WHAT YOU SEEK LIES IN THE CENTER OF THAT ROOM.
THERE APPEARS TO BE A LARGE AMOUNT OF ICE IN THE WAY.
THAT IS YOUR PROBLEM, THOR. NOT MINE.
RRRGGGH!!!
SO BE IT. RACE YOU, LADY WALTERS!
WHAKK
KRUKKK
WHUKK WWOK
KRKK KUDDD KRRNCH
YOU RACE ONLY TO YOUR DOOM, MY BOY.

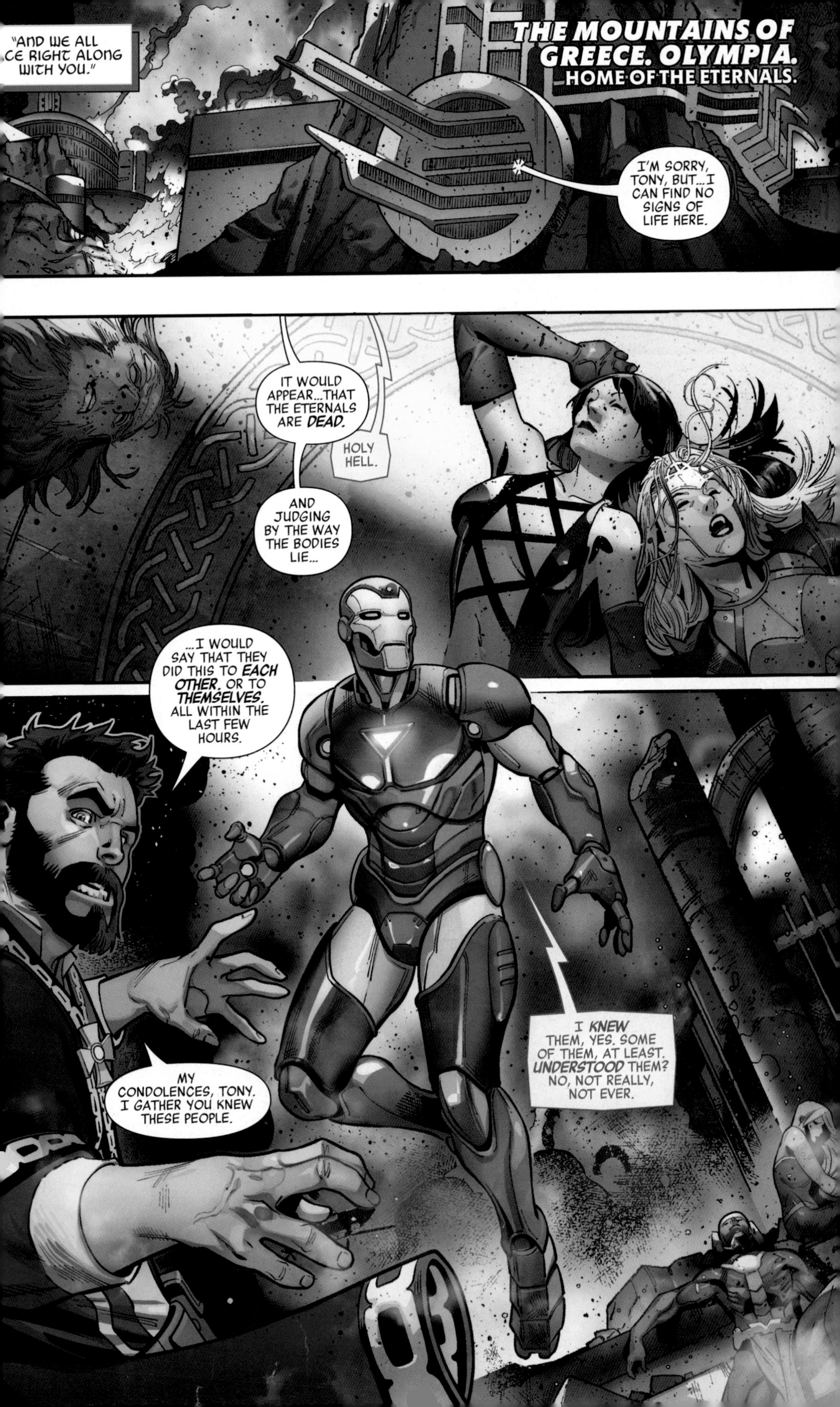
"AND WE ALL
CE RIGHT ALONG
WITH YOU."
THE MOUNTAINS OF GREECE. OLYMPIA.
HOME OF THE ETERNALS.
I'M SORRY, TONY, BUT...I CAN FIND NO SIGNS OF LIFE HERE.
IT WOULD APPEAR...THAT THE ETERNALS ARE DEAD.
HOLY HELL.
AND JUDGING BY THE WAY THE BODIES LIE...
...I WOULD SAY THAT THEY DID THIS TO EACH OTHER. OR TO THEMSELVES. ALL WITHIN THE LAST FEW HOURS.
MY CONDOLENCES, TONY. I GATHER YOU KNEW THESE PEOPLE.
I KNEW THEM, YES. SOME OF THEM, AT LEAST. UNDERSTOOD THEM? NO, NOT REALLY, NOT EVER.

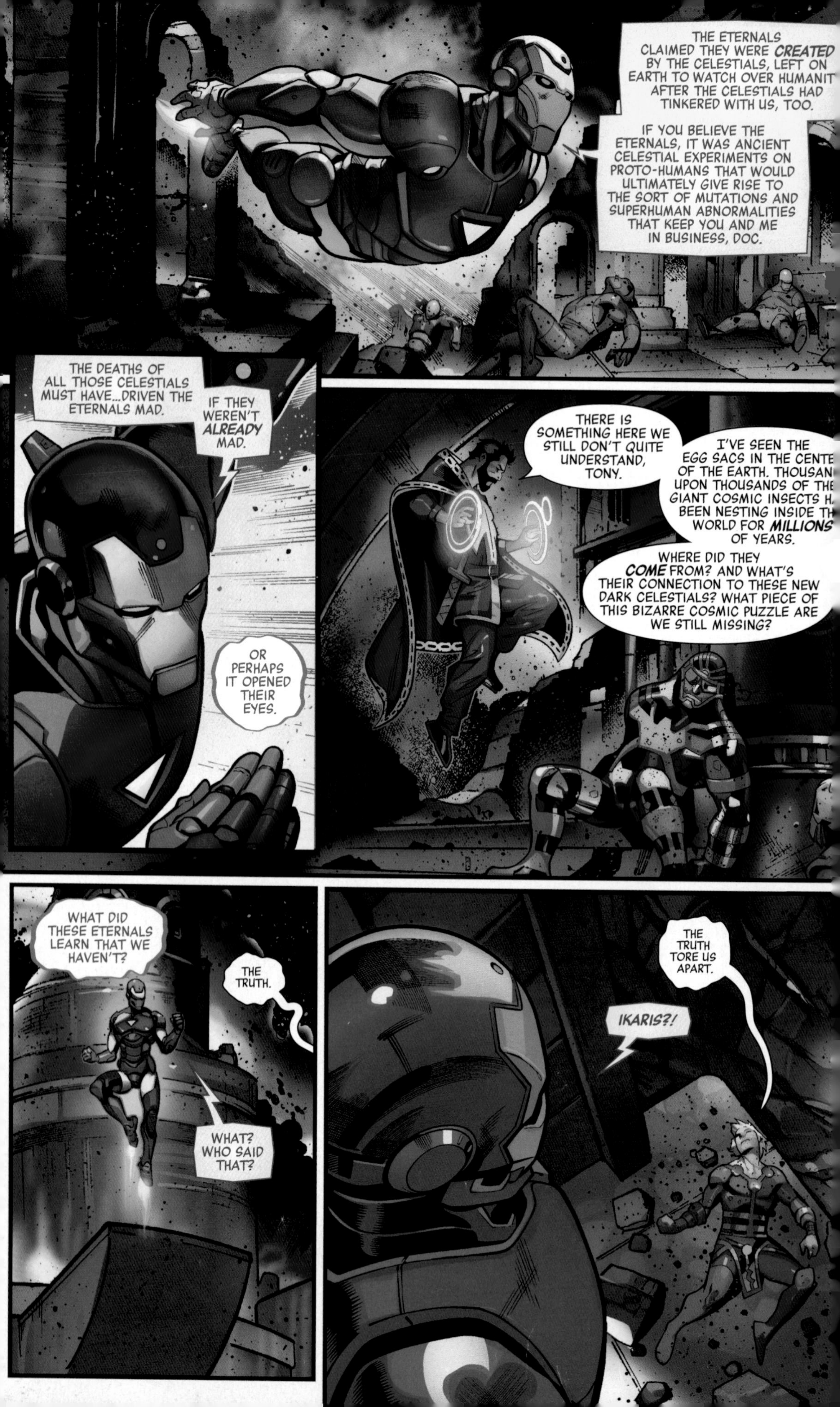
THE ETERNALS CLAIMED THEY WERE CREATED BY THE CELESTIALS, LEFT ON EARTH TO WATCH OVER HUMANIT AFTER THE CELESTIALS HAD TINKERED WITH US, TOO.
IF YOU BELIEVE THE ETERNALS, IT WAS ANCIENT CELESTIAL EXPERIMENTS ON PROTO-HUMANS THAT WOULD ULTIMATELY GIVE RISE TO THE SORT OF MUTATIONS AND SUPERHUMAN ABNORMALITIES THAT KEEP YOU AND ME IN BUSINESS, DOC.
THE DEATHS OF ALL THOSE CELESTIALS MUST HAVE...DRIVEN THE ETERNALS MAD.
IF THEY WEREN'T ALREADY MAD.
OR PERHAPS IT OPENED THEIR EYES.
THERE IS SOMETHING HERE WE STILL DON'T QUITE UNDERSTAND, TONY.
I'VE SEEN THE EGG SACS IN THE CENTE OF THE EARTH. THOUSAN UPON THOUSANDS OF THE GIANT COSMIC INSECTS H BEEN NESTING INSIDE TH WORLD FOR MILLIONS OF YEARS.
WHERE DID THEY COME FROM? AND WHAT'S THEIR CONNECTION TO THESE NEW DARK CELESTIALS? WHAT PIECE OF THIS BIZARRE COSMIC PUZZLE ARE WE STILL MISSING?
WHAT DID THESE ETERNALS LEARN THAT WE HAVEN'T?
THE TRUTH.
WHAT? WHO SAID THAT?
THE TRUTH TORE US APART.
IKARIS?!

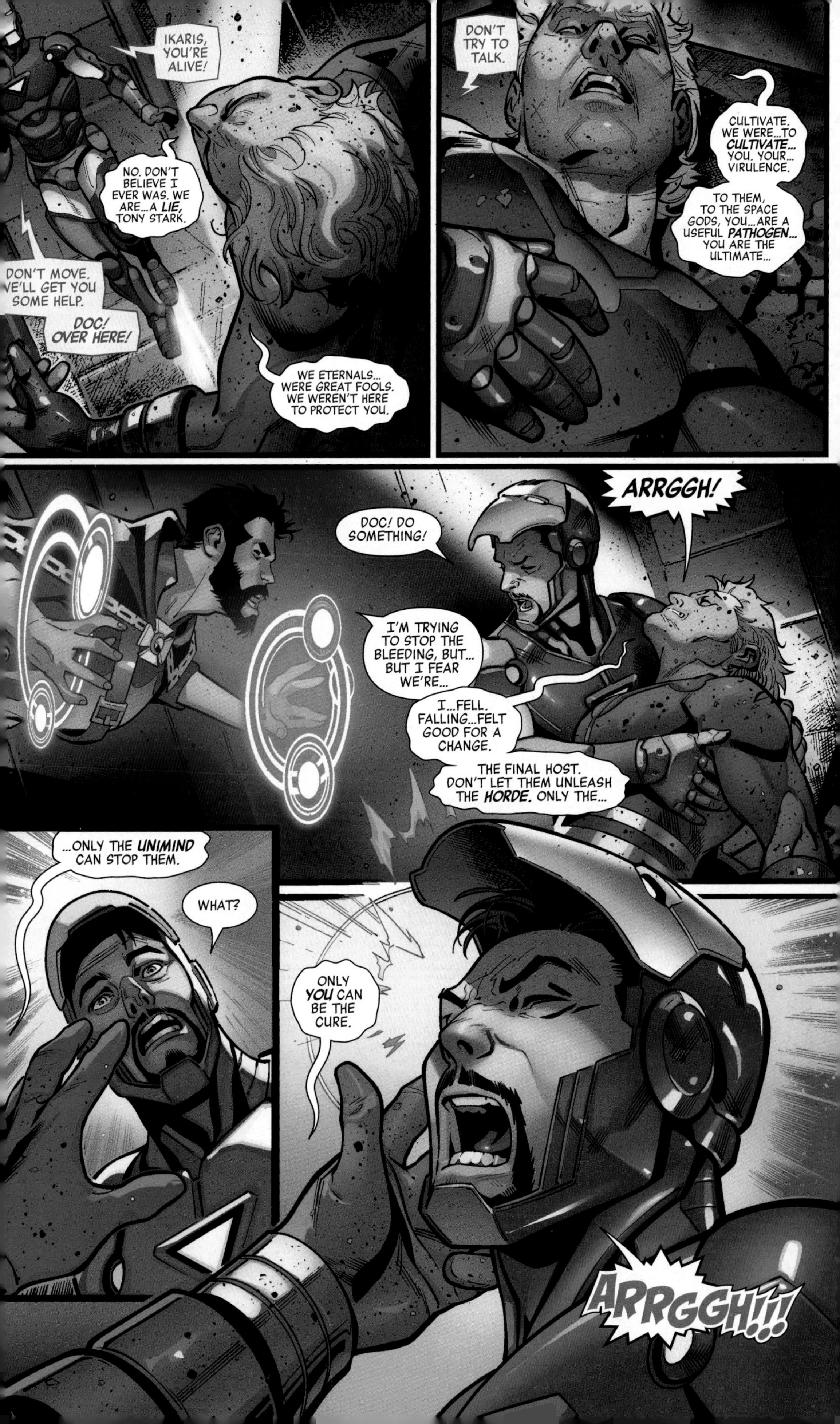

IKARIS, YOU'RE ALIVE!
NO. DON'T BELIEVE I EVER WAS. WE ARE...A LIE, TONY STARK.
DON'T MOVE. WE'LL GET YOU SOME HELP.
DOC! OVER HERE!
WE ETERNALS... WERE GREAT FOOLS. WE WEREN'T HERE TO PROTECT YOU.
DON'T TRY TO TALK.
CULTIVATE. WE WERE...TO CULTIVATE... YOU. YOUR... VIRULENCE.
TO THEM, TO THE SPACE GODS, YOU...ARE A USEFUL PATHOGEN... YOU ARE THE ULTIMATE...
ARRGGH!
DOC! DO SOMETHING!
I'M TRYING TO STOP THE BLEEDING, BUT... BUT I FEAR WE'RE...
I...FELL. FALLING...FELT GOOD FOR A CHANGE.
THE FINAL HOST. DON'T LET THEM UNLEASH THE HORDE. ONLY THE...
...ONLY THE UNIMIND CAN STOP THEM.
WHAT?
ONLY YOU CAN BE THE CURE.
ARRGGH!!!

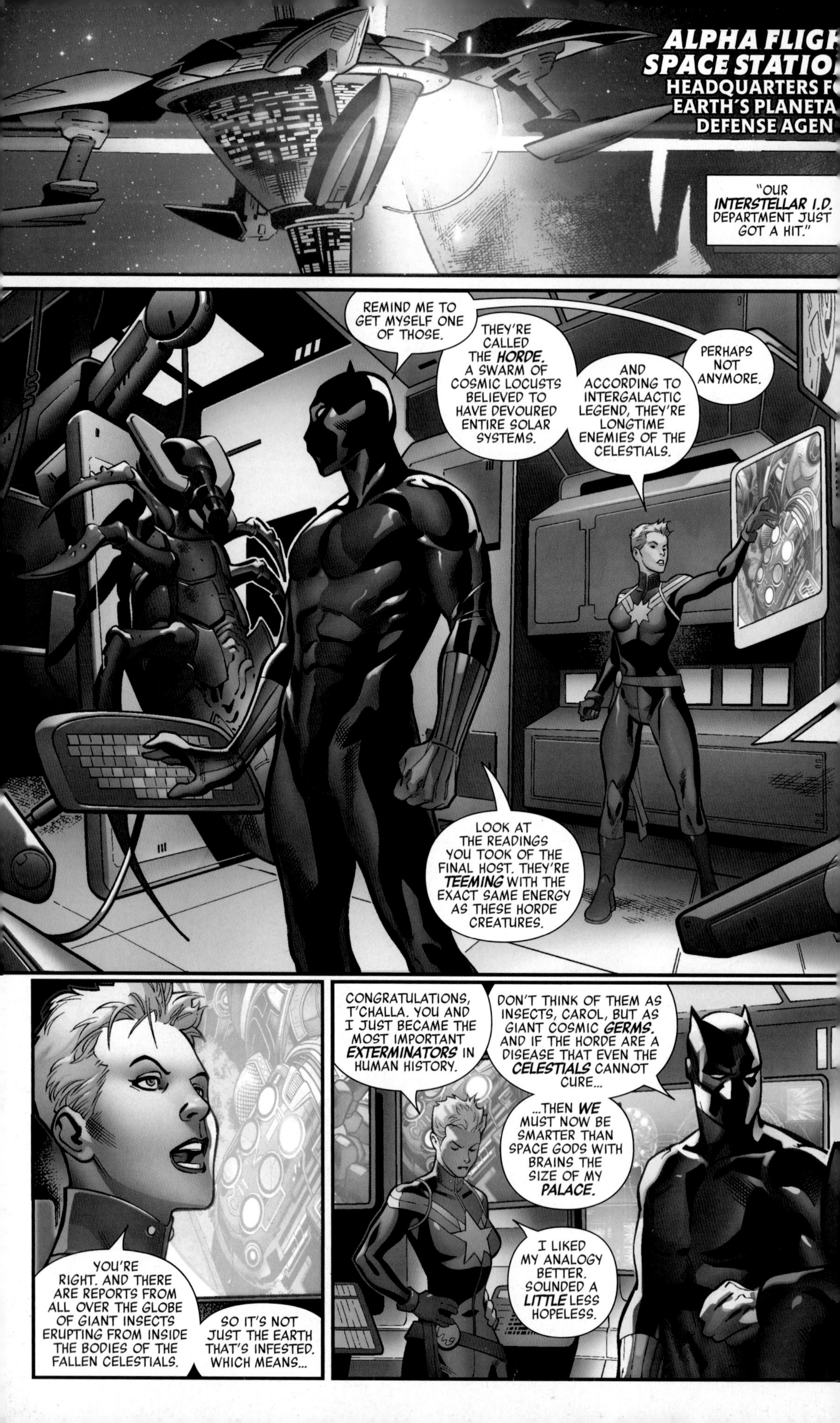

ALPHA FLIGH
SPACE STATIO
HEADQUARTERS F
EARTH'S PLANETA
DEFENSE AGEN
"OUR INTERSTELLAR I.D. DEPARTMENT JUST GOT A HIT."
REMIND ME TO GET MYSELF ONE OF THOSE.
THEY'RE CALLED THE HORDE. A SWARM OF COSMIC LOCUSTS BELIEVED TO HAVE DEVOURED ENTIRE SOLAR SYSTEMS.
AND ACCORDING TO INTERGALACTIC LEGEND, THEY'RE LONGTIME ENEMIES OF THE CELESTIALS.
PERHAPS NOT ANYMORE.
LOOK AT THE READINGS YOU TOOK OF THE FINAL HOST. THEY'RE TEEMING WITH THE EXACT SAME ENERGY AS THESE HORDE CREATURES.
YOU'RE RIGHT. AND THERE ARE REPORTS FROM ALL OVER THE GLOBE OF GIANT INSECTS ERUPTING FROM INSIDE THE BODIES OF THE FALLEN CELESTIALS.
SO IT'S NOT JUST THE EARTH THAT'S INFESTED. WHICH MEANS...
CONGRATULATIONS, T'CHALLA. YOU AND I JUST BECAME THE MOST IMPORTANT EXTERMINATORS IN HUMAN HISTORY.
DON'T THINK OF THEM AS INSECTS, CAROL, BUT AS GIANT COSMIC GERMS. AND IF THE HORDE ARE A DISEASE THAT EVEN THE CELESTIALS CANNOT CURE...
...THEN WE MUST NOW BE SMARTER THAN SPACE GODS WITH BRAINS THE SIZE OF MY PALACE.
I LIKED MY ANALOGY BETTER. SOUNDED A LITTLE LESS HOPELESS.

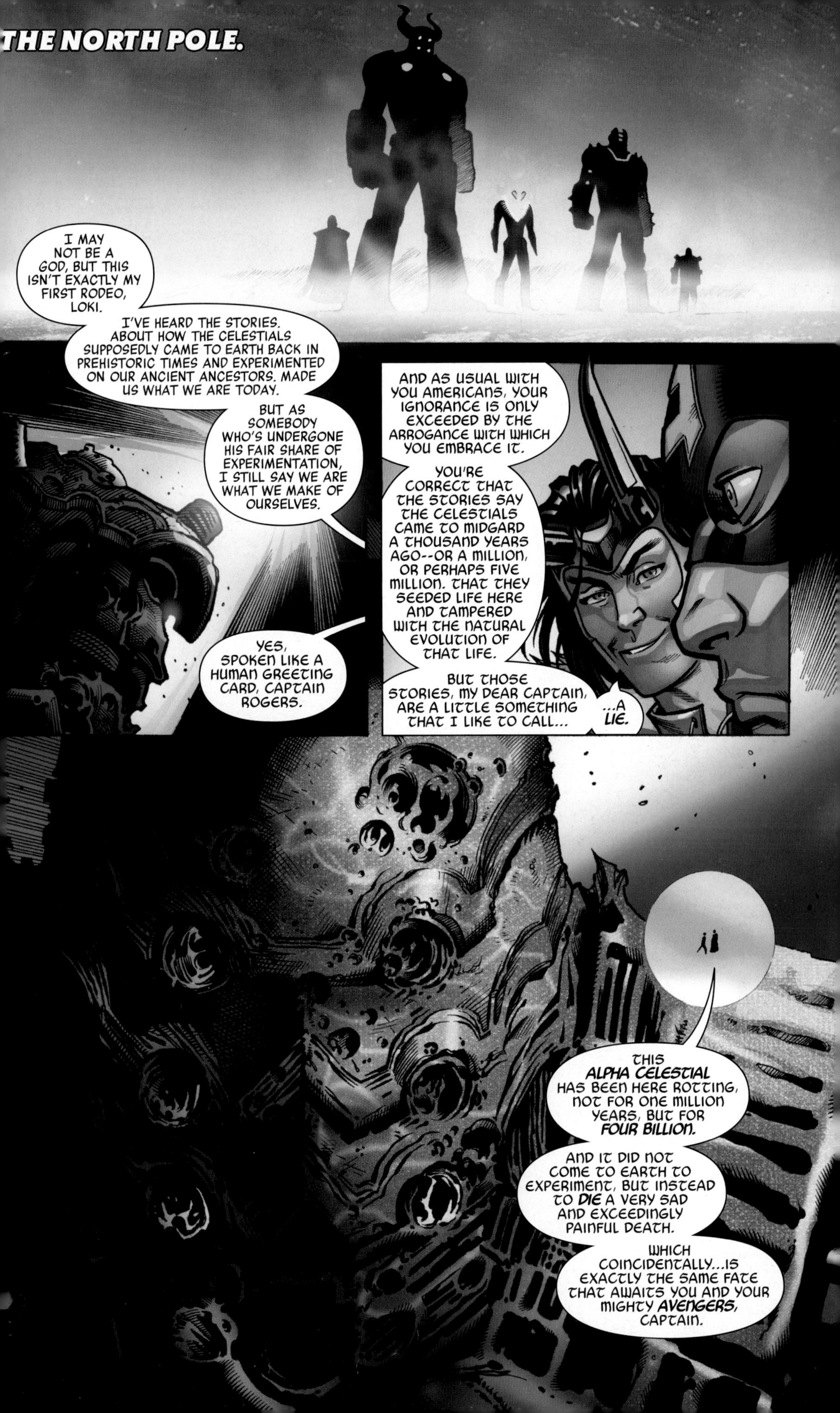
THE NORTH POLE.
I MAY NOT BE A GOD, BUT THIS ISN'T EXACTLY MY FIRST RODEO, LOKI.
I'VE HEARD THE STORIES. ABOUT HOW THE CELESTIALS SUPPOSEDLY CAME TO EARTH BACK IN PREHISTORIC TIMES AND EXPERIMENTED ON OUR ANCIENT ANCESTORS. MADE US WHAT WE ARE TODAY.
BUT AS SOMEBODY WHO'S UNDERGONE HIS FAIR SHARE OF EXPERIMENTATION, I STILL SAY WE ARE WHAT WE MAKE OF OURSELVES.
YES, SPOKEN LIKE A HUMAN GREETING CARD, CAPTAIN ROGERS.
AND AS USUAL WITH YOU AMERICANS, YOUR IGNORANCE IS ONLY EXCEEDED BY THE ARROGANCE WITH WHICH YOU EMBRACE IT.
YOU'RE CORRECT THAT THE STORIES SAY THE CELESTIALS CAME TO MIDGARD A THOUSAND YEARS AGO--OR A MILLION, OR PERHAPS FIVE MILLION. THAT THEY SEEDED LIFE HERE AND TAMPERED WITH THE NATURAL EVOLUTION OF THAT LIFE.
BUT THOSE STORIES, MY DEAR CAPTAIN, ARE A LITTLE SOMETHING THAT I LIKE TO CALL...
...A LIE.
THIS ALPHA CELESTIAL HAS BEEN HERE ROTTING, NOT FOR ONE MILLION YEARS, BUT FOR FOUR BILLION.
AND IT DID NOT COME TO EARTH TO EXPERIMENT, BUT INSTEAD TO DIE A VERY SAD AND EXCEEDINGLY PAINFUL DEATH.
WHICH COINCIDENTALLY...IS EXACTLY THE SAME FATE THAT AWAITS YOU AND YOUR MIGHTY AVENGERS, CAPTAIN.

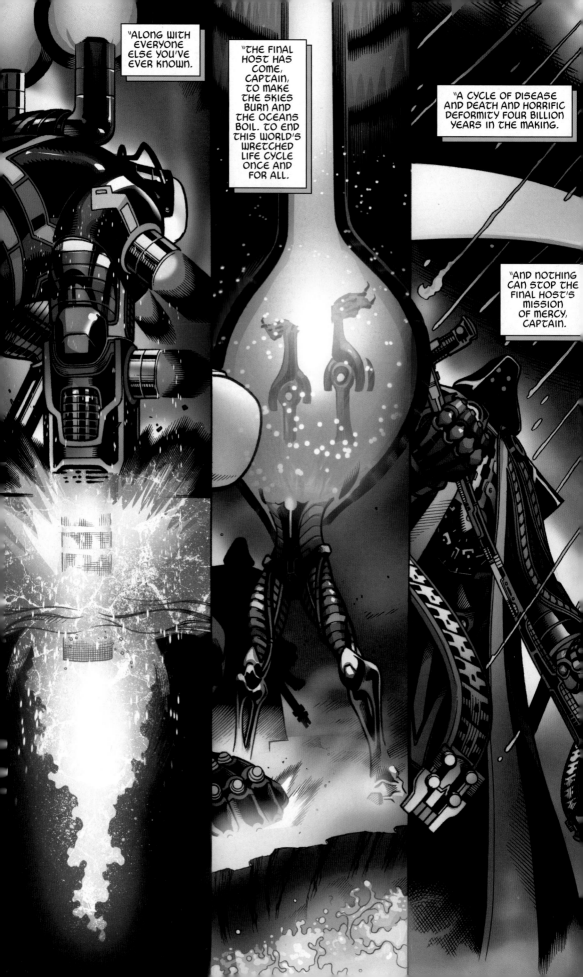

"ALONG WITH EVERYONE ELSE YOU'VE EVER KNOWN.

"THE FINAL HOST HAS COME, CAPTAIN, TO MAKE THE SKIES BURN AND THE OCEANS BOIL. TO END THIS WORLD'S WRETCHED LIFE CYCLE ONCE AND FOR ALL.

"A CYCLE OF DISEASE AND DEATH AND HORRIFIC DEFORMITY FOUR BILLION YEARS IN THE MAKING.

"AND NOTHING CAN STOP THE FINAL HOST'S MISSION OF MERCY, CAPTAIN.

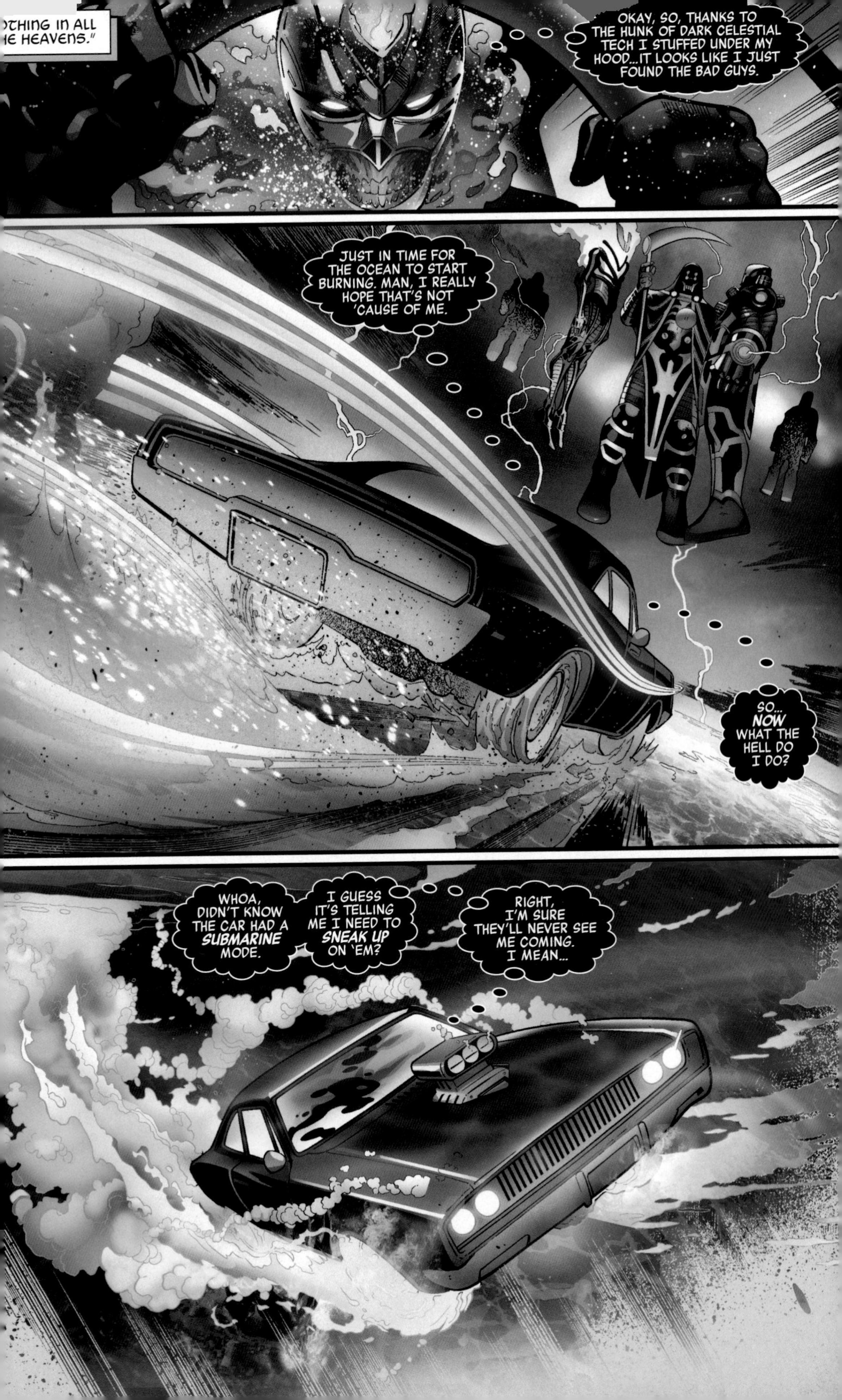

...OTHING IN ALL ...E HEAVENS."
OKAY, SO, THANKS TO THE HUNK OF DARK CELESTIAL TECH I STUFFED UNDER MY HOOD...IT LOOKS LIKE I JUST FOUND THE BAD GUYS.
JUST IN TIME FOR THE OCEAN TO START BURNING. MAN, I REALLY HOPE THAT'S NOT 'CAUSE OF ME.
SO... NOW WHAT THE HELL DO I DO?
WHOA, DIDN'T KNOW THE CAR HAD A SUBMARINE MODE.
I GUESS IT'S TELLING ME I NEED TO SNEAK UP ON 'EM?
RIGHT, I'M SURE THEY'LL NEVER SEE ME COMING. I MEAN...

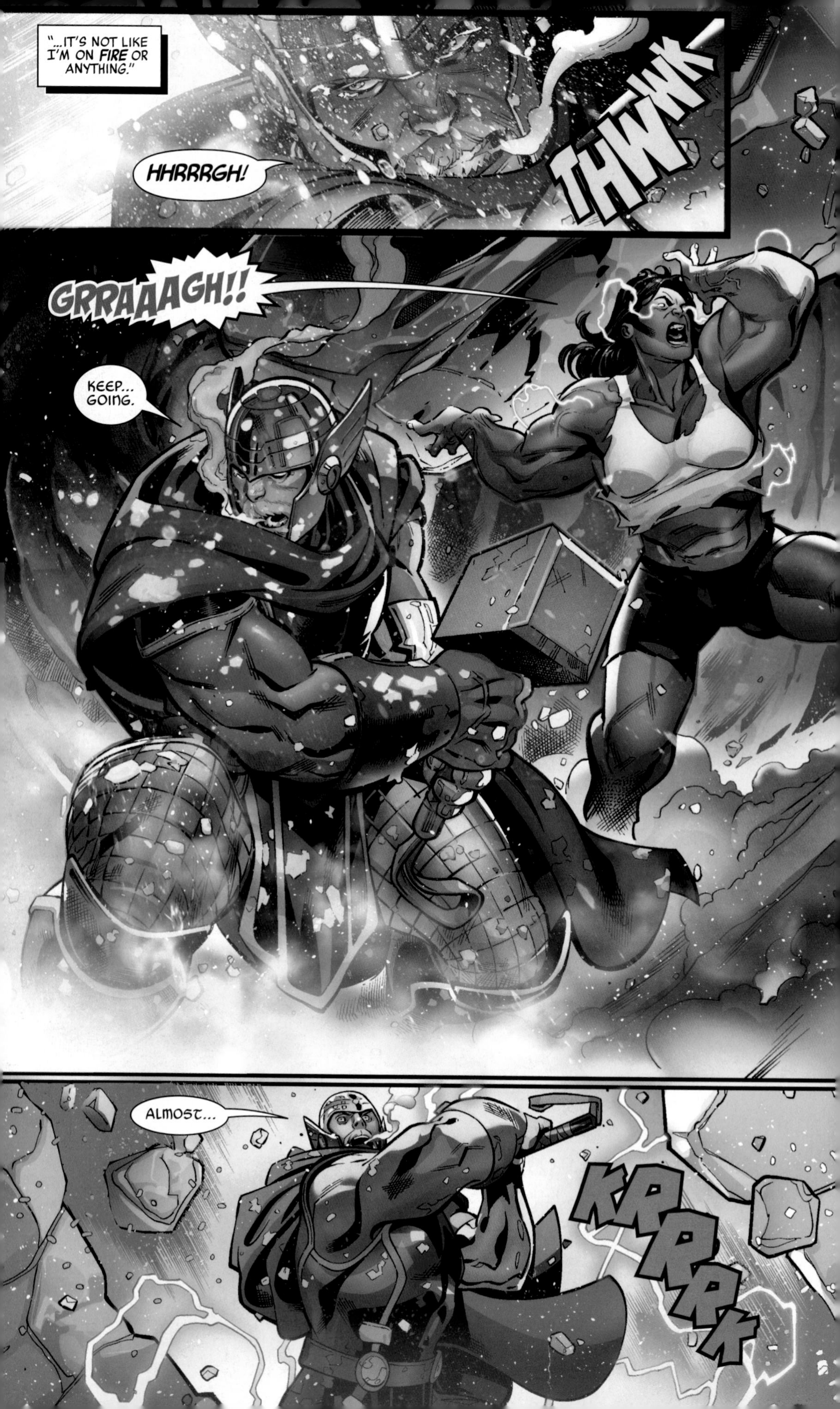
"...IT'S NOT LIKE I'M ON FIRE OR ANYTHING."
THWK
HHRRRGH!
GRRAAAGH!!
KEEP... GOING.
ALMOST...
TKRRRRK

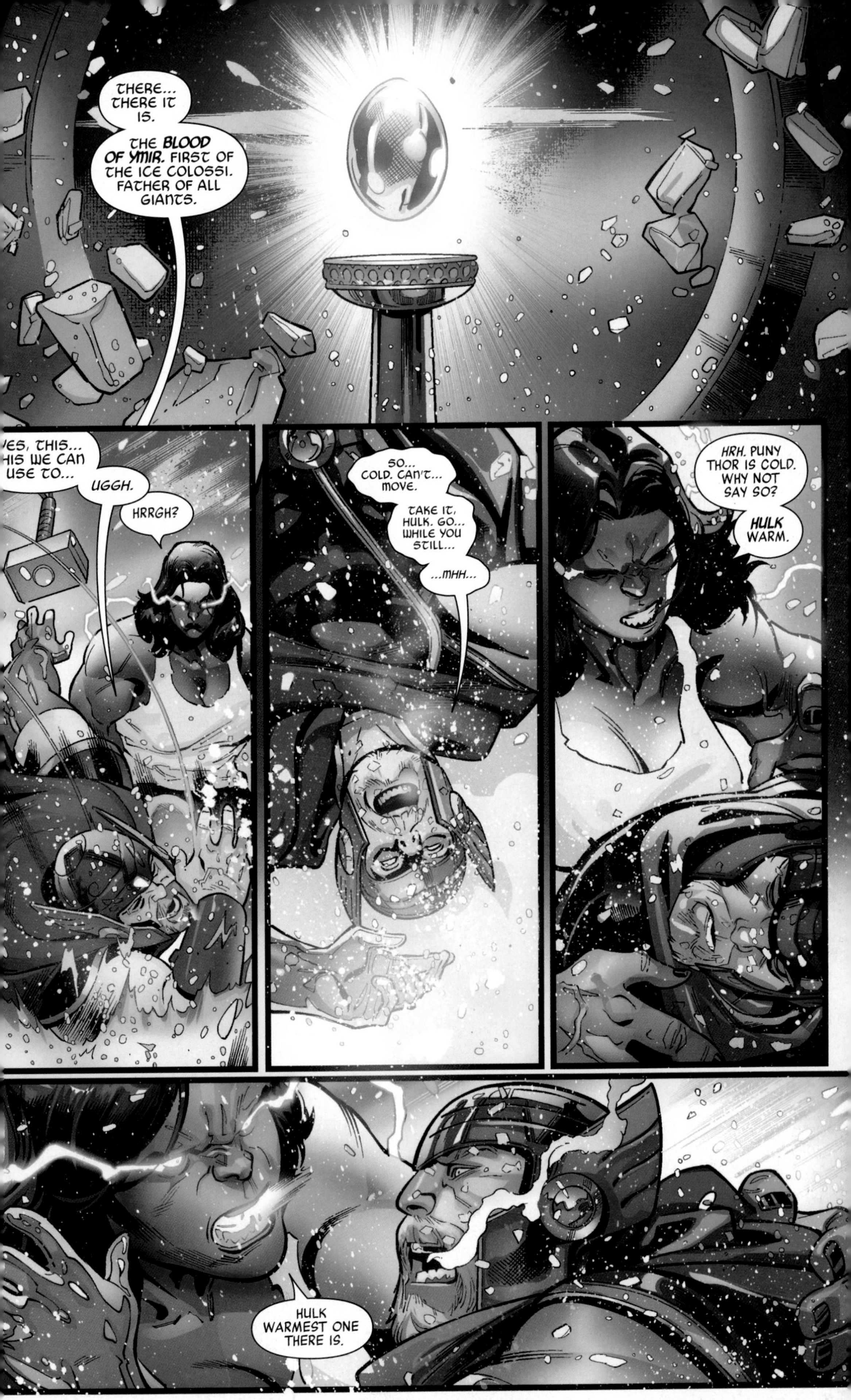
THERE... THERE IT IS.
THE **BLOOD OF YMIR.** FIRST OF THE ICE COLOSSI. FATHER OF ALL GIANTS.
YES, THIS... THIS WE CAN USE TO...
UGGH.
HRRGH?
SO... COLD. CAN'T... MOVE.
TAKE IT, HULK. GO... WHILE YOU STILL...
...MHH...
HRH. PUNY THOR IS COLD. WHY NOT SAY SO?
HULK WARM.
HULK WARMEST ONE THERE IS.

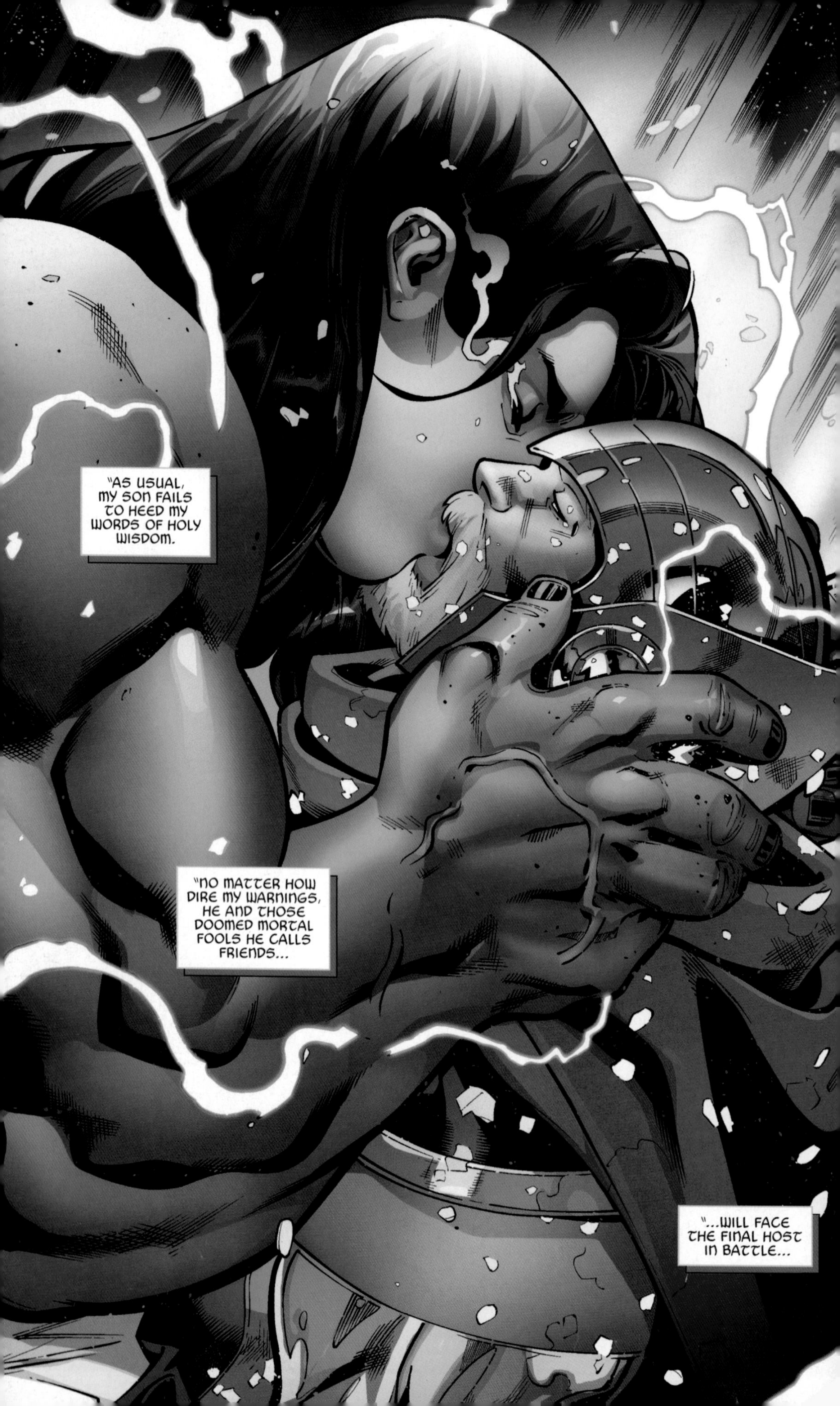
"AS USUAL, MY SON FAILS TO HEED MY WORDS OF HOLY WISDOM.
"NO MATTER HOW DIRE MY WARNINGS, HE AND THOSE DOOMED MORTAL FOOLS HE CALLS FRIENDS...
"...WILL FACE THE FINAL HOST IN BATTLE...

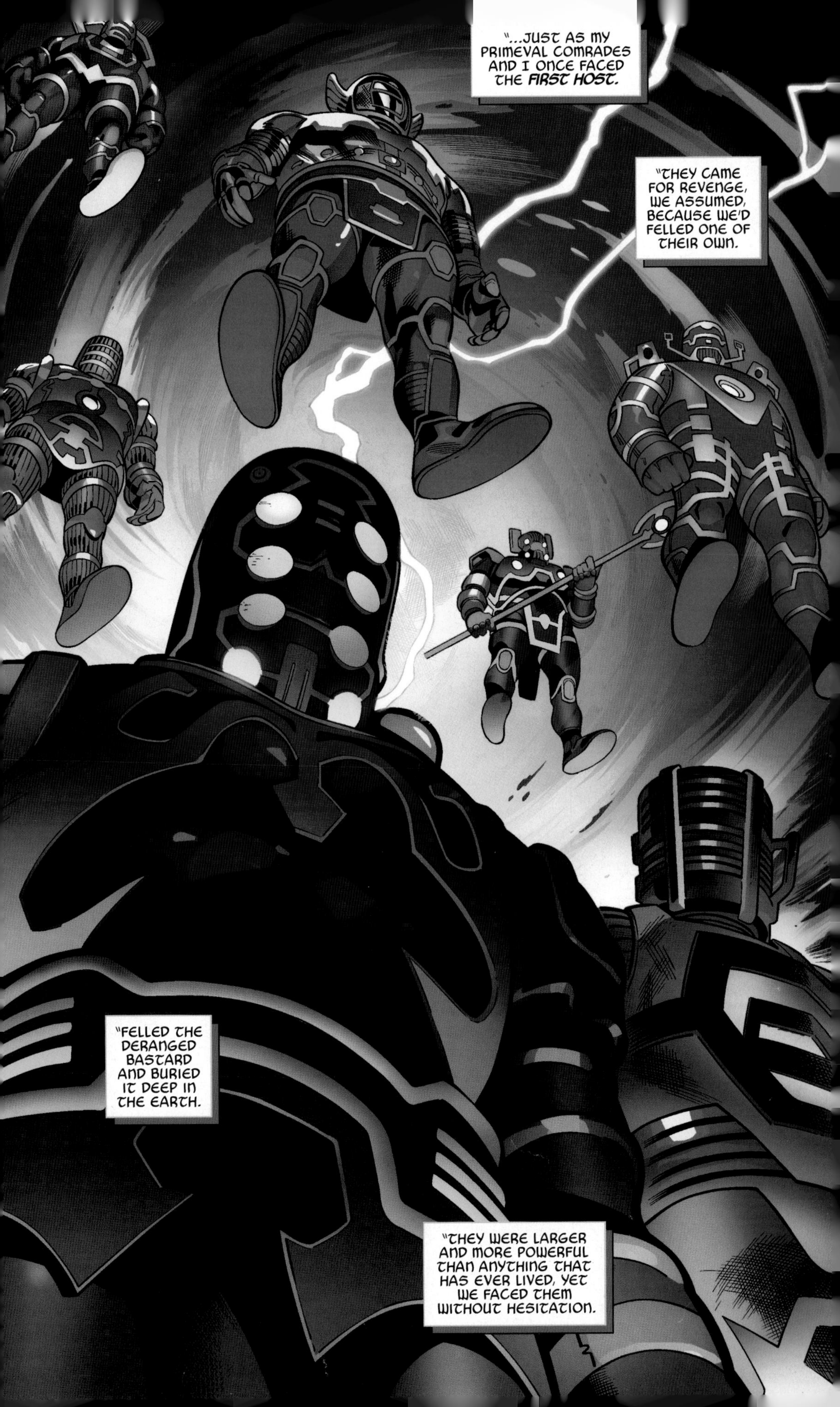
"...JUST AS MY PRIMEVAL COMRADES AND I ONCE FACED THE *FIRST HOST*.
"THEY CAME FOR REVENGE, WE ASSUMED, BECAUSE WE'D FELLED ONE OF THEIR OWN.
"FELLED THE DERANGED BASTARD AND BURIED IT DEEP IN THE EARTH.
"THEY WERE LARGER AND MORE POWERFUL THAN ANYTHING THAT HAS EVER LIVED, YET WE FACED THEM WITHOUT HESITATION.

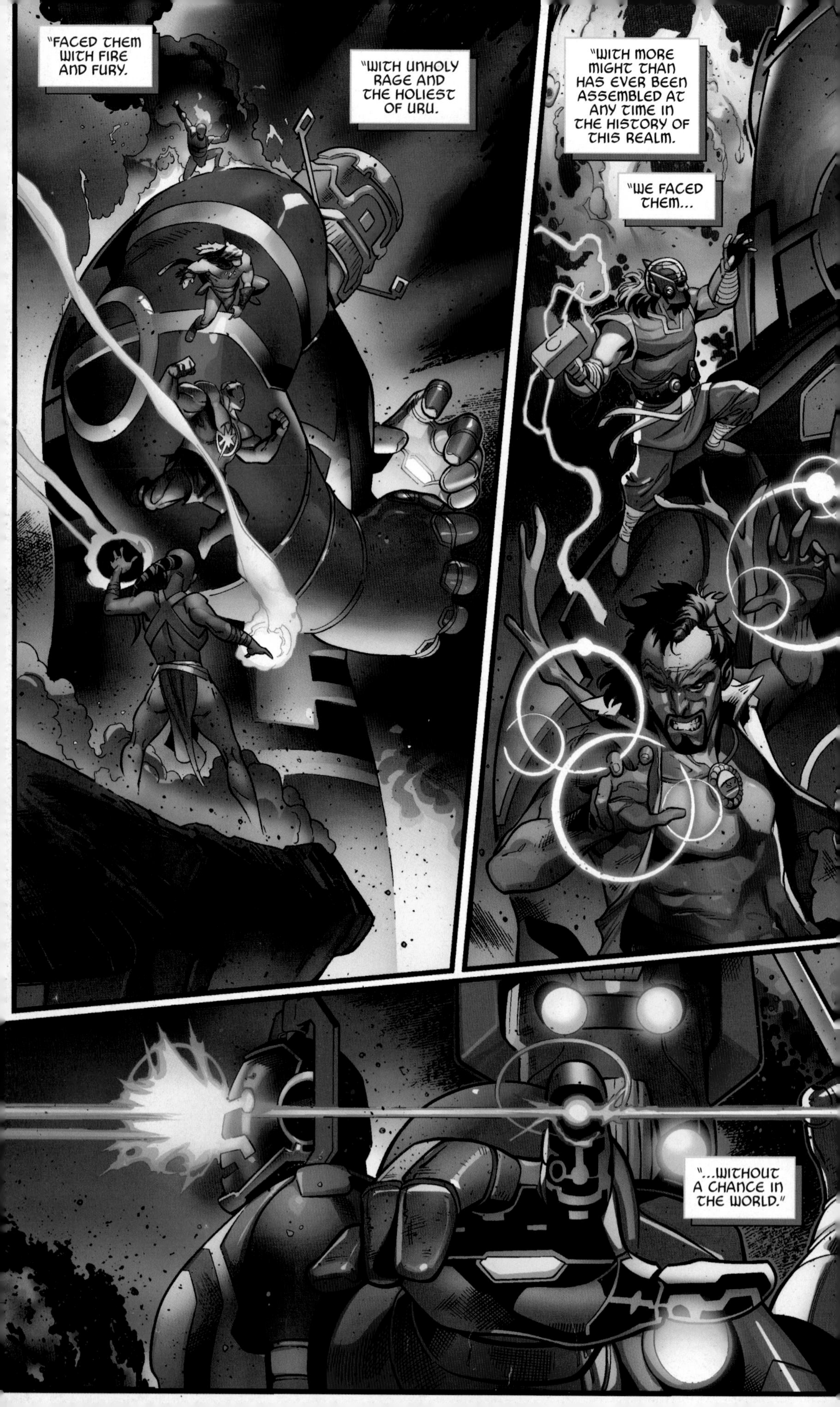
"FACED THEM WITH FIRE AND FURY.
"WITH UNHOLY RAGE AND THE HOLIEST OF URU.
"WITH MORE MIGHT THAN HAS EVER BEEN ASSEMBLED AT ANY TIME IN THE HISTORY OF THIS REALM.
"WE FACED THEM...
"...WITHOUT A CHANCE IN THE WORLD."

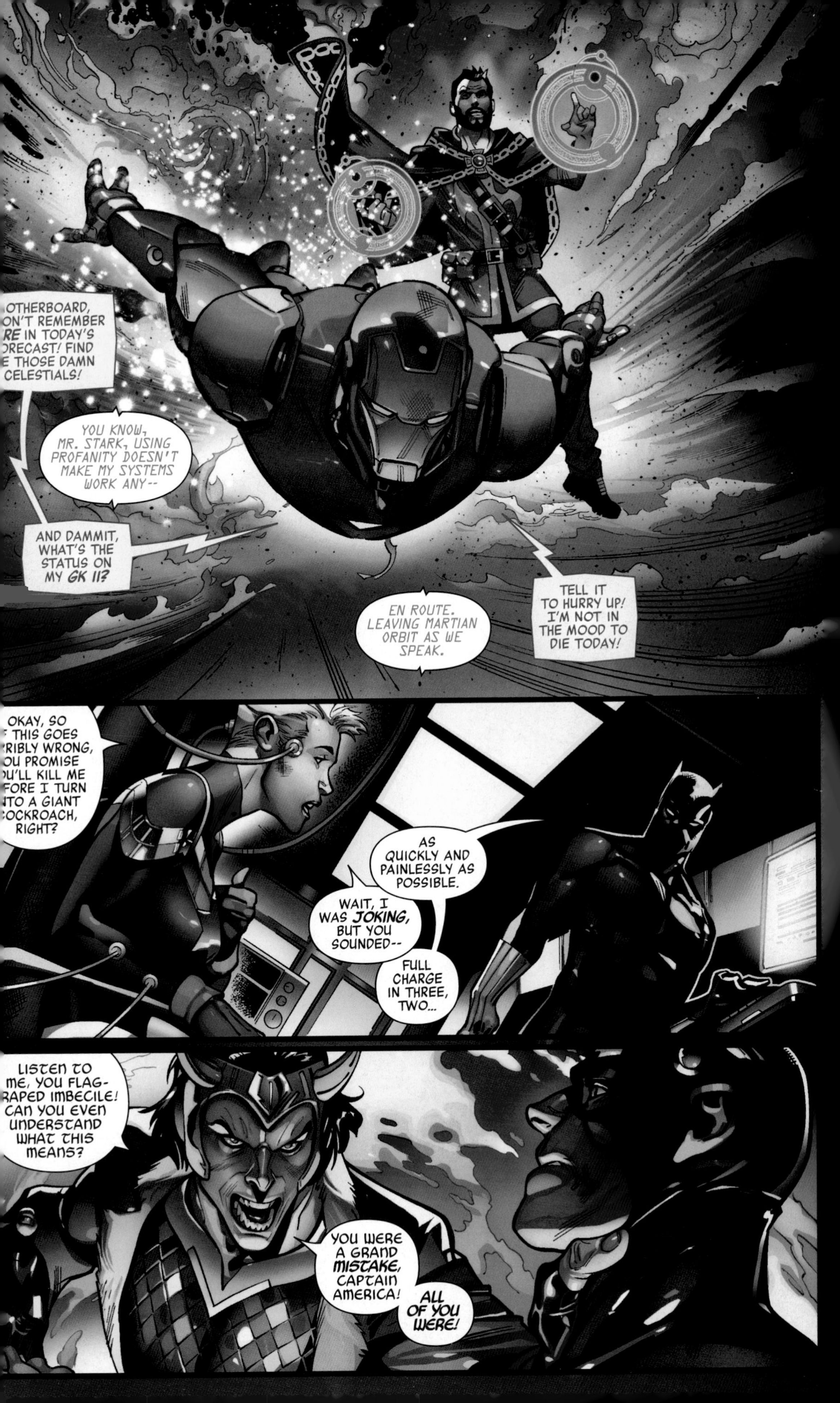

OTHERBOARD, ON'T REMEMBER RE IN TODAY'S ORECAST! FIND E THOSE DAMN CELESTIALS!
YOU KNOW, MR. STARK, USING PROFANITY DOESN'T MAKE MY SYSTEMS WORK ANY--
AND DAMMIT, WHAT'S THE STATUS ON MY GK II?
EN ROUTE. LEAVING MARTIAN ORBIT AS WE SPEAK.
TELL IT TO HURRY UP! I'M NOT IN THE MOOD TO DIE TODAY!
OKAY, SO F THIS GOES RIBLY WRONG, OU PROMISE OU'LL KILL ME FORE I TURN NTO A GIANT COCKROACH, RIGHT?
AS QUICKLY AND PAINLESSLY AS POSSIBLE.
WAIT, I WAS JOKING, BUT YOU SOUNDED--
FULL CHARGE IN THREE, TWO...
LISTEN TO ME, YOU FLAG-RAPED IMBECILE! CAN YOU EVEN UNDERSTAND WHAT THIS MEANS?
YOU WERE A GRAND MISTAKE, CAPTAIN AMERICA!
ALL OF YOU WERE!

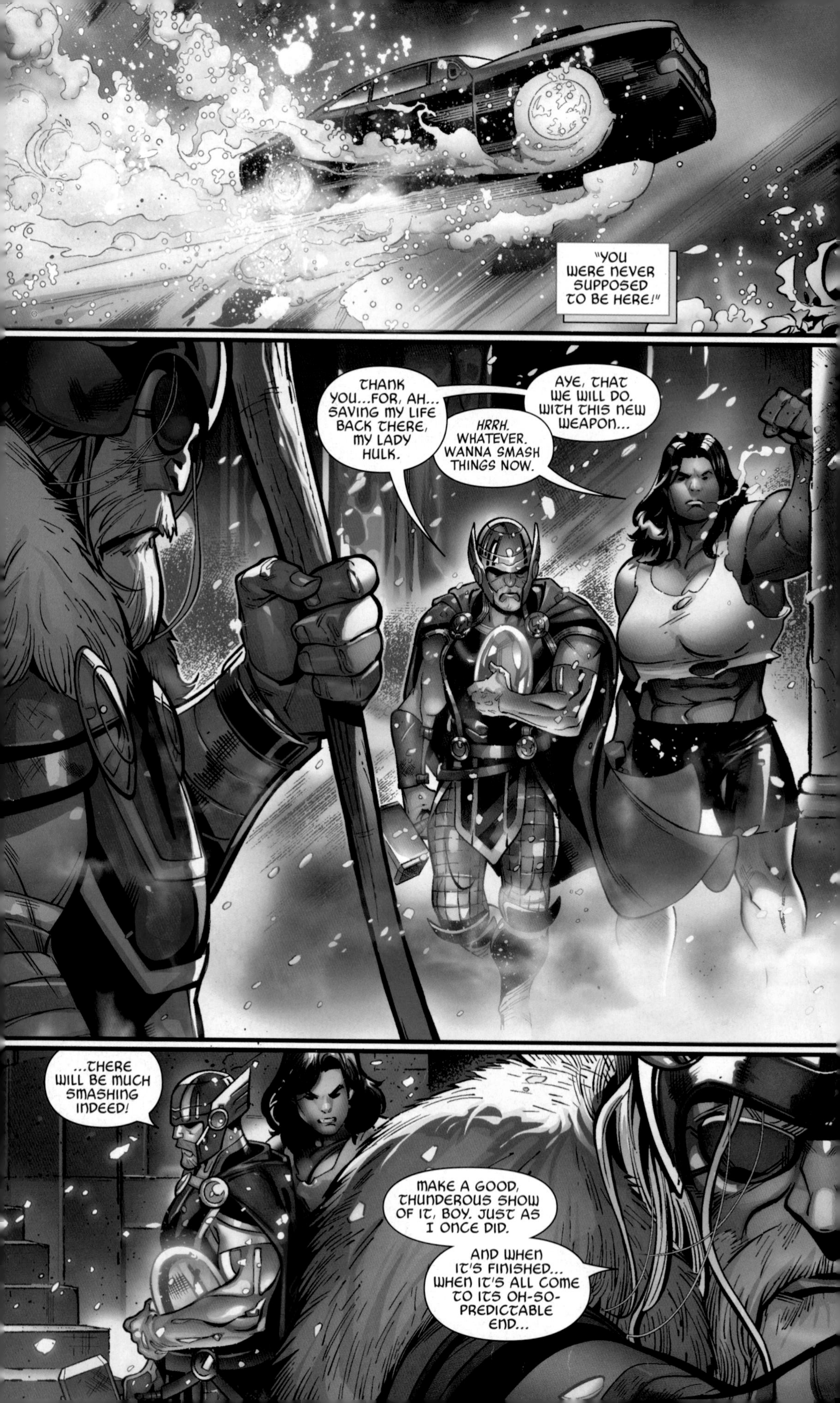
"YOU WERE NEVER SUPPOSED TO BE HERE!"
THANK YOU...FOR, AH... SAVING MY LIFE BACK THERE, MY LADY HULK.
HRRH. WHATEVER. WANNA SMASH THINGS NOW.
AYE, THAT WE WILL DO. WITH THIS NEW WEAPON...
...THERE WILL BE MUCH SMASHING INDEED!
MAKE A GOOD, THUNDEROUS SHOW OF IT, BOY. JUST AS I ONCE DID.
AND WHEN IT'S FINISHED... WHEN IT'S ALL COME TO ITS OH-SO-PREDICTABLE END...

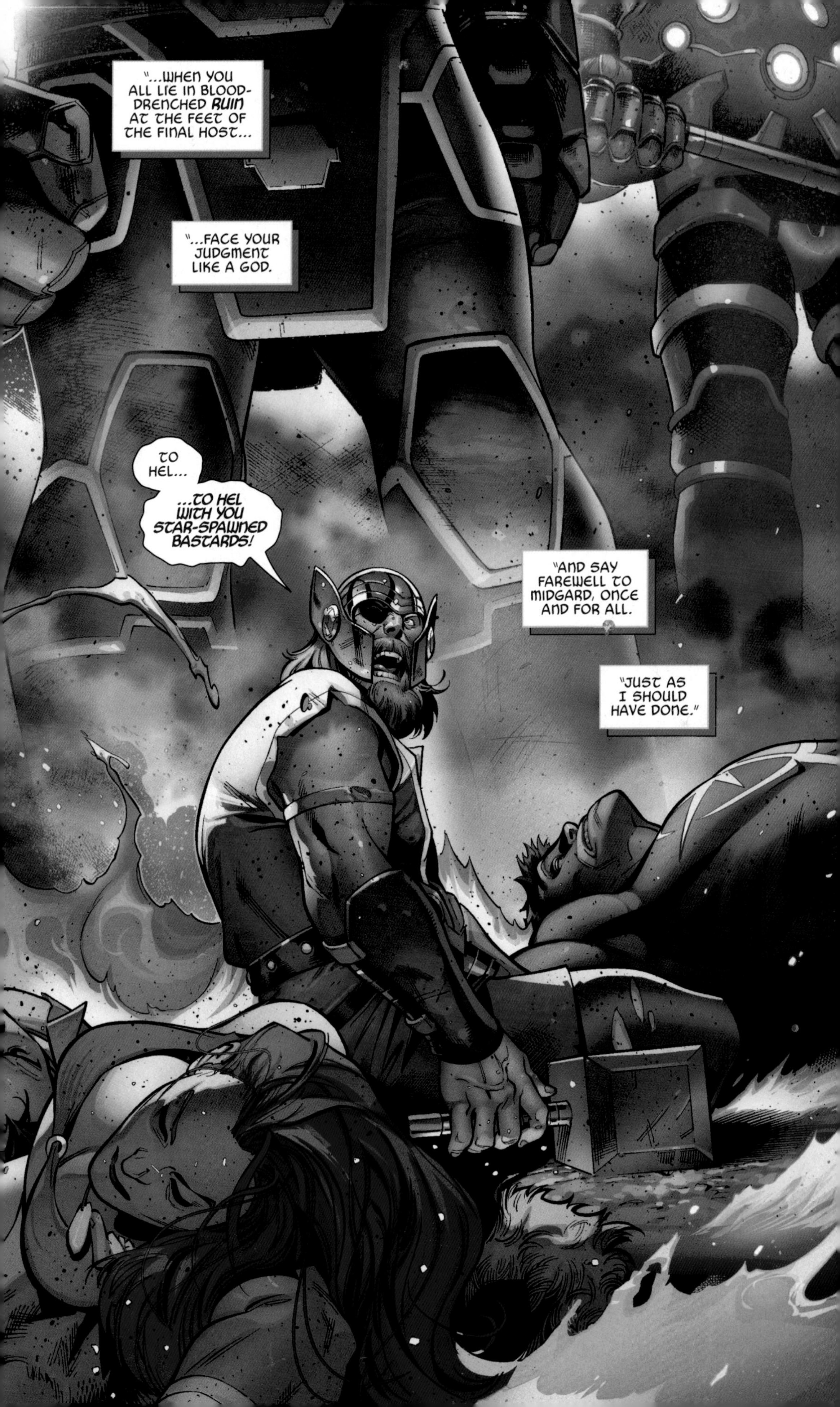
"...WHEN YOU ALL LIE IN BLOOD-DRENCHED RUIN AT THE FEET OF THE FINAL HOST...
"...FACE YOUR JUDGMENT LIKE A GOD.
TO HEL...
...TO HEL WITH YOU STAR-SPAWNED BASTARDS!
"AND SAY FAREWELL TO MIDGARD, ONCE AND FOR ALL.
"JUST AS I SHOULD HAVE DONE."

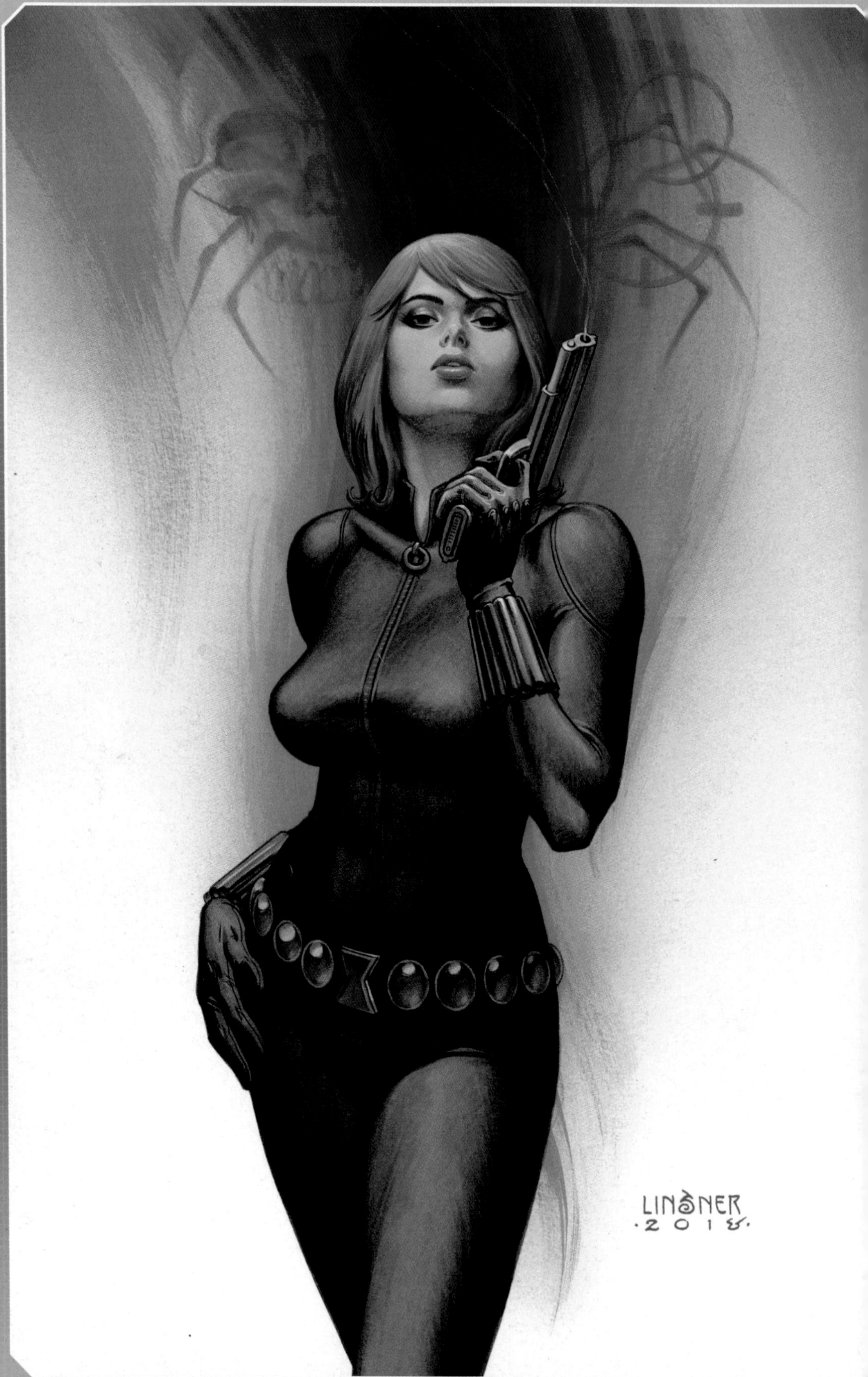
LINSNER
·2018·

JOSEPH MICHAEL LINSNER
1 VARIANT COVER

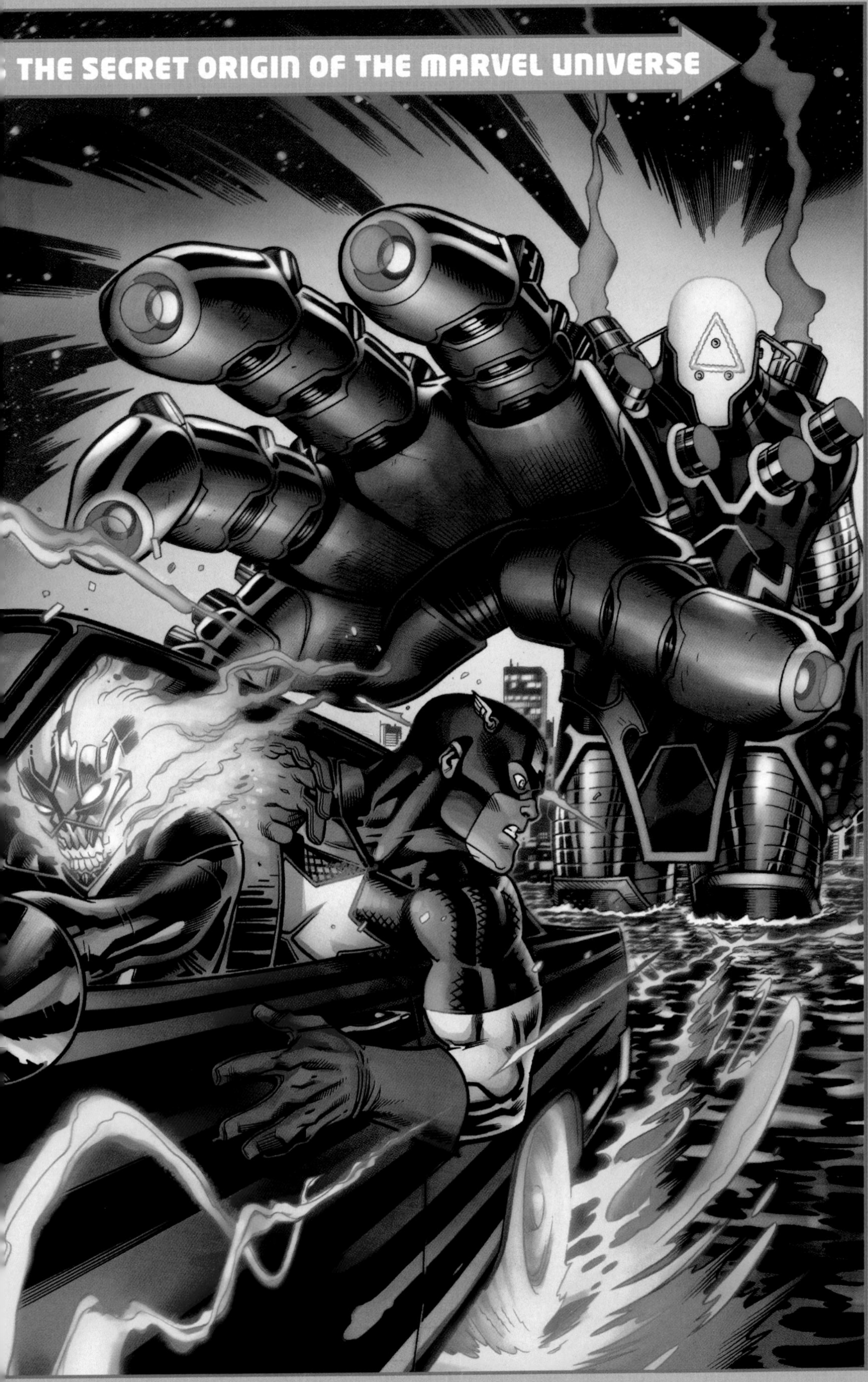
THE SECRET ORIGIN OF THE MARVEL UNIVERSE

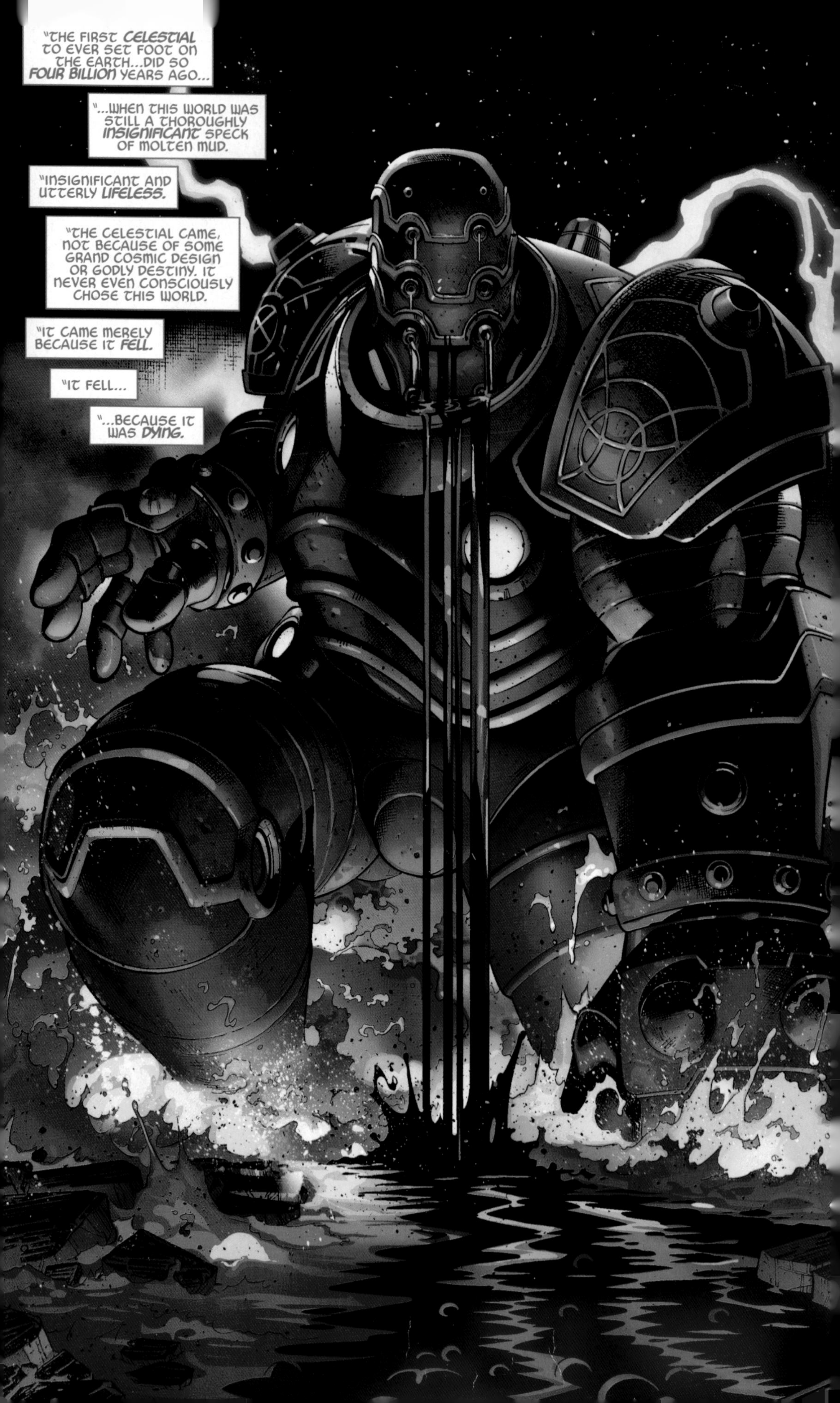
"THE FIRST CELESTIAL TO EVER SET FOOT ON THE EARTH...DID SO FOUR BILLION YEARS AGO...
"...WHEN THIS WORLD WAS STILL A THOROUGHLY INSIGNIFICANT SPECK OF MOLTEN MUD.
"INSIGNIFICANT AND UTTERLY LIFELESS.
"THE CELESTIAL CAME, NOT BECAUSE OF SOME GRAND COSMIC DESIGN OR GODLY DESTINY. IT NEVER EVEN CONSCIOUSLY CHOSE THIS WORLD.
"IT CAME MERELY BECAUSE IT FELL.
"IT FELL...
"...BECAUSE IT WAS DYING.

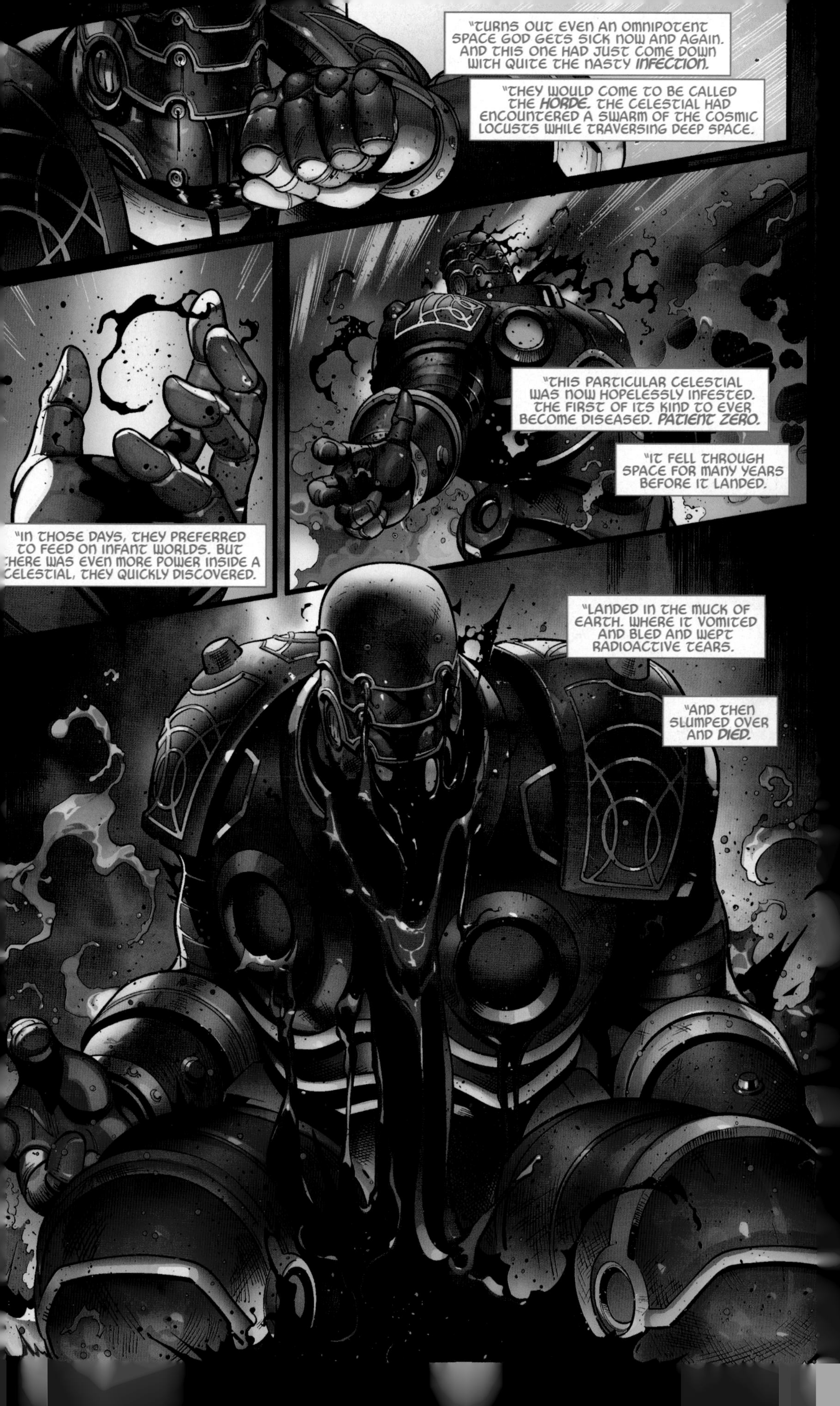
"TURNS OUT EVEN AN OMNIPOTENT SPACE GOD GETS SICK NOW AND AGAIN. AND THIS ONE HAD JUST COME DOWN WITH QUITE THE NASTY *INFECTION.*
"THEY WOULD COME TO BE CALLED THE *HORDE.* THE CELESTIAL HAD ENCOUNTERED A SWARM OF THE COSMIC LOCUSTS WHILE TRAVERSING DEEP SPACE.
"IN THOSE DAYS, THEY PREFERRED TO FEED ON INFANT WORLDS. BUT THERE WAS EVEN MORE POWER INSIDE A CELESTIAL, THEY QUICKLY DISCOVERED.
"THIS PARTICULAR CELESTIAL WAS NOW HOPELESSLY INFESTED. THE FIRST OF ITS KIND TO EVER BECOME DISEASED. *PATIENT ZERO.*
"IT FELL THROUGH SPACE FOR MANY YEARS BEFORE IT LANDED.
"LANDED IN THE MUCK OF EARTH. WHERE IT VOMITED AND BLED AND WEPT RADIOACTIVE TEARS.
"AND THEN SLUMPED OVER AND *DIED.*

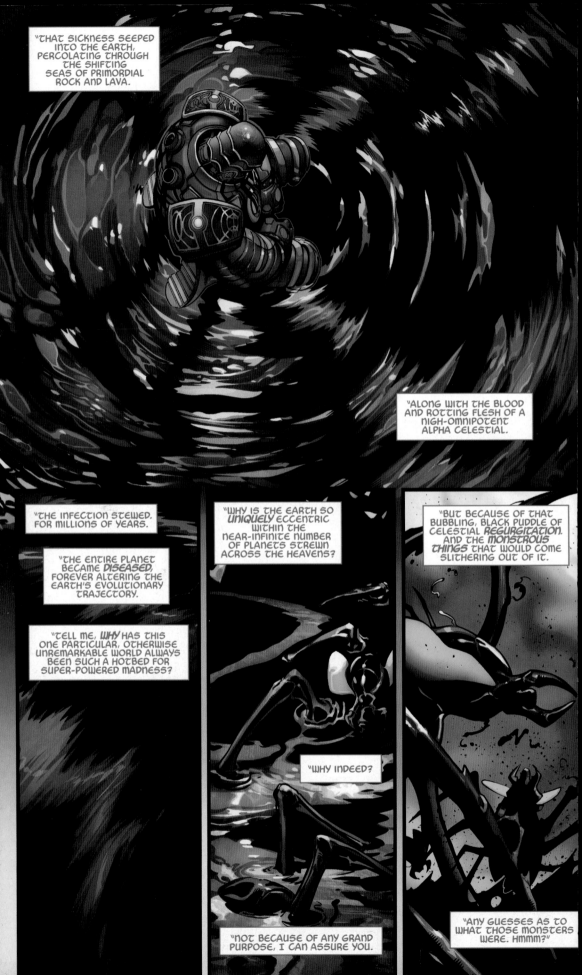

"THAT SICKNESS SEEPED INTO THE EARTH, PERCOLATING THROUGH THE SHIFTING SEAS OF PRIMORDIAL ROCK AND LAVA.

"ALONG WITH THE BLOOD AND ROTTING FLESH OF A NIGH-OMNIPOTENT ALPHA CELESTIAL.

"THE INFECTION STEWED. FOR MILLIONS OF YEARS.

"THE ENTIRE PLANET BECAME DISEASED, FOREVER ALTERING THE EARTH'S EVOLUTIONARY TRAJECTORY.

"TELL ME, WHY HAS THIS ONE PARTICULAR, OTHERWISE UNREMARKABLE WORLD ALWAYS BEEN SUCH A HOTBED FOR SUPER-POWERED MADNESS?

"WHY IS THE EARTH SO UNIQUELY ECCENTRIC WITHIN THE NEAR-INFINITE NUMBER OF PLANETS STREWN ACROSS THE HEAVENS?

"WHY INDEED?

"BUT BECAUSE OF THAT BUBBLING, BLACK PUDDLE OF CELESTIAL REGURGITATION. AND THE MONSTROUS THINGS THAT WOULD COME SLITHERING OUT OF IT.

"NOT BECAUSE OF ANY GRAND PURPOSE, I CAN ASSURE YOU.

"ANY GUESSES AS TO WHAT THOSE MONSTERS WERE. HMMM?"

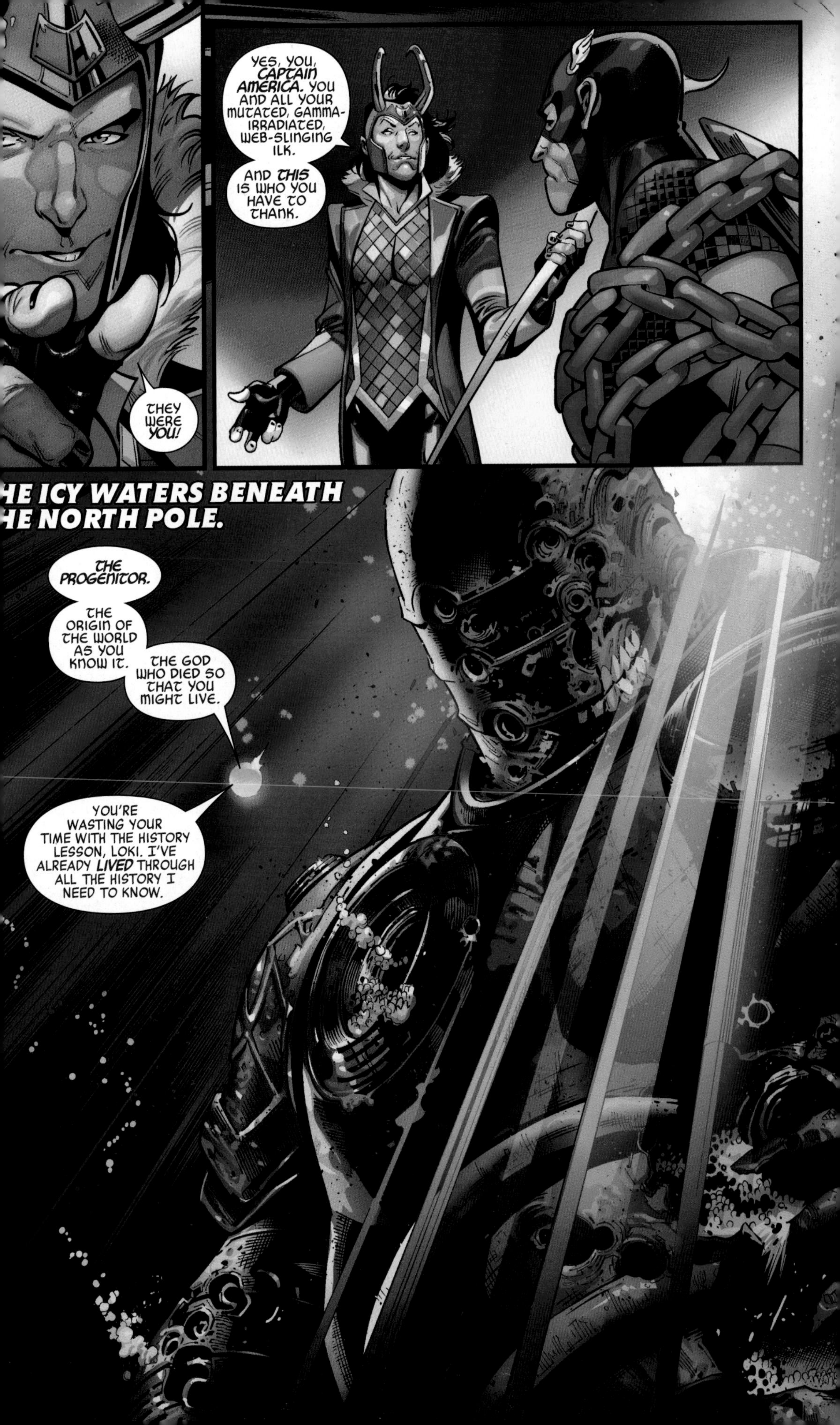
YES, YOU, CAPTAIN AMERICA. YOU AND ALL YOUR MUTATED, GAMMA-IRRADIATED, WEB-SLINGING ILK.
AND THIS IS WHO YOU HAVE TO THANK.
THEY WERE YOU!
HE ICY WATERS BENEATH HE NORTH POLE.
THE PROGENITOR.
THE ORIGIN OF THE WORLD AS YOU KNOW IT.
THE GOD WHO DIED SO THAT YOU MIGHT LIVE.
YOU'RE WASTING YOUR TIME WITH THE HISTORY LESSON, LOKI. I'VE ALREADY LIVED THROUGH ALL THE HISTORY I NEED TO KNOW.

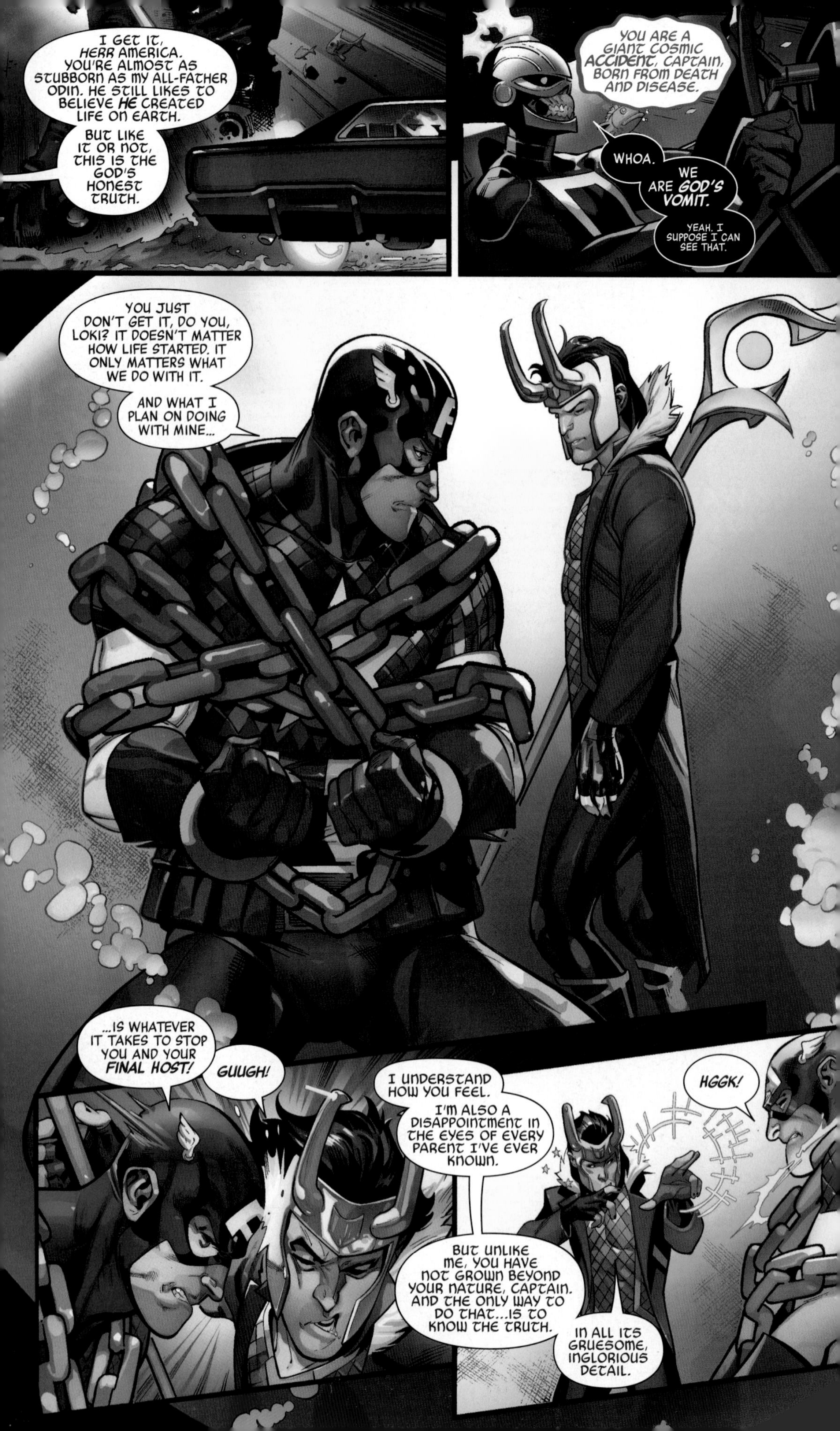
I GET IT, HERR AMERICA. YOU'RE ALMOST AS STUBBORN AS MY ALL-FATHER ODIN. HE STILL LIKES TO BELIEVE HE CREATED LIFE ON EARTH.
BUT LIKE IT OR NOT, THIS IS THE GOD'S HONEST TRUTH.
YOU ARE A GIANT COSMIC ACCIDENT, CAPTAIN, BORN FROM DEATH AND DISEASE.
WHOA.
WE ARE GOD'S VOMIT.
YEAH. I SUPPOSE I CAN SEE THAT.
YOU JUST DON'T GET IT, DO YOU, LOKI? IT DOESN'T MATTER HOW LIFE STARTED. IT ONLY MATTERS WHAT WE DO WITH IT.
AND WHAT I PLAN ON DOING WITH MINE...
...IS WHATEVER IT TAKES TO STOP YOU AND YOUR FINAL HOST!
GUUGH!
I UNDERSTAND HOW YOU FEEL.
I'M ALSO A DISAPPOINTMENT IN THE EYES OF EVERY PARENT I'VE EVER KNOWN.
BUT UNLIKE ME, YOU HAVE NOT GROWN BEYOND YOUR NATURE, CAPTAIN. AND THE ONLY WAY TO DO THAT...IS TO KNOW THE TRUTH.
IN ALL ITS GRUESOME, INGLORIOUS DETAIL.
HGGK!

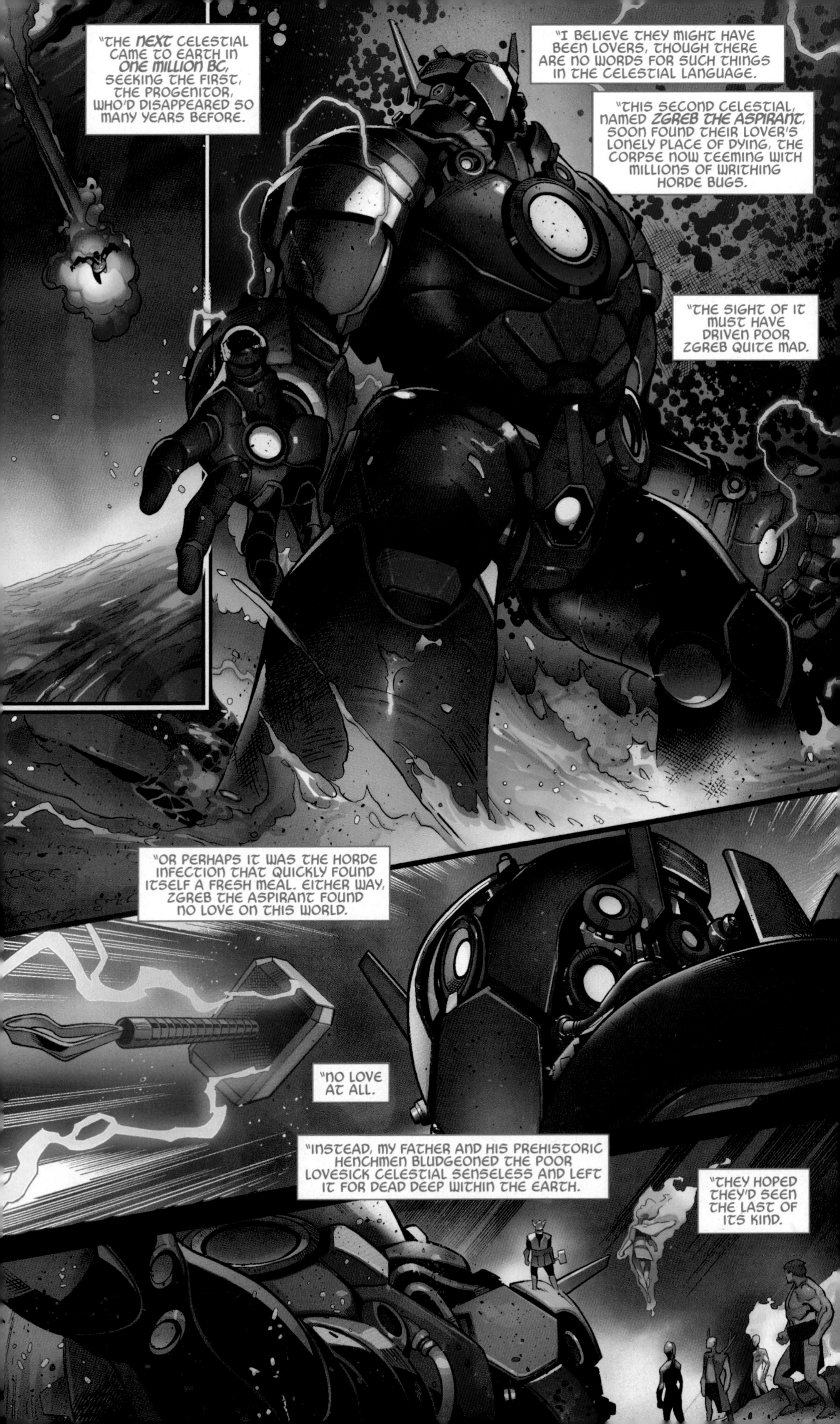
"THE NEXT CELESTIAL CAME TO EARTH IN ONE MILLION BC, SEEKING THE FIRST, THE PROGENITOR, WHO'D DISAPPEARED SO MANY YEARS BEFORE.
"I BELIEVE THEY MIGHT HAVE BEEN LOVERS, THOUGH THERE ARE NO WORDS FOR SUCH THINGS IN THE CELESTIAL LANGUAGE.
"THIS SECOND CELESTIAL, NAMED ZGREB THE ASPIRANT, SOON FOUND THEIR LOVER'S LONELY PLACE OF DYING, THE CORPSE NOW TEEMING WITH MILLIONS OF WRITHING HORDE BUGS.
"THE SIGHT OF IT MUST HAVE DRIVEN POOR ZGREB QUITE MAD.
"OR PERHAPS IT WAS THE HORDE INFECTION THAT QUICKLY FOUND ITSELF A FRESH MEAL. EITHER WAY, ZGREB THE ASPIRANT FOUND NO LOVE ON THIS WORLD.
"NO LOVE AT ALL.
"INSTEAD, MY FATHER AND HIS PREHISTORIC HENCHMEN BLUDGEONED THE POOR LOVESICK CELESTIAL SENSELESS AND LEFT IT FOR DEAD DEEP WITHIN THE EARTH.
"THEY HOPED THEY'D SEEN THE LAST OF ITS KIND.

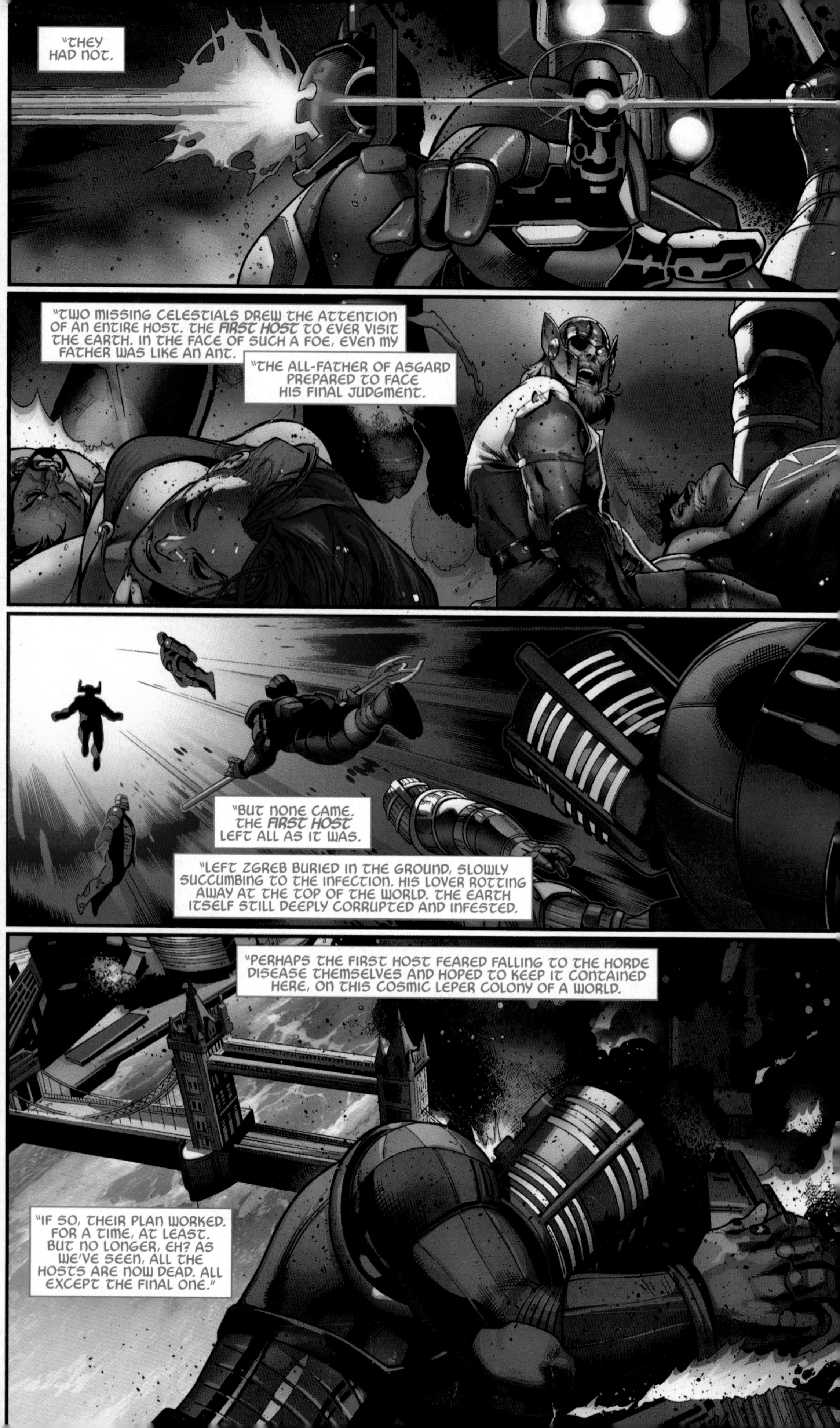
"THEY HAD NOT.
"TWO MISSING CELESTIALS DREW THE ATTENTION OF AN ENTIRE HOST. THE FIRST HOST TO EVER VISIT THE EARTH. IN THE FACE OF SUCH A FOE, EVEN MY FATHER WAS LIKE AN ANT.
"THE ALL-FATHER OF ASGARD PREPARED TO FACE HIS FINAL JUDGMENT.
"BUT NONE CAME. THE FIRST HOST LEFT ALL AS IT WAS.
"LEFT ZGREB BURIED IN THE GROUND, SLOWLY SUCCUMBING TO THE INFECTION. HIS LOVER ROTTING AWAY AT THE TOP OF THE WORLD. THE EARTH ITSELF STILL DEEPLY CORRUPTED AND INFESTED.
"PERHAPS THE FIRST HOST FEARED FALLING TO THE HORDE DISEASE THEMSELVES AND HOPED TO KEEP IT CONTAINED HERE, ON THIS COSMIC LEPER COLONY OF A WORLD.
"IF SO, THEIR PLAN WORKED. FOR A TIME, AT LEAST. BUT NO LONGER, EH? AS WE'VE SEEN, ALL THE HOSTS ARE NOW DEAD. ALL EXCEPT THE FINAL ONE."

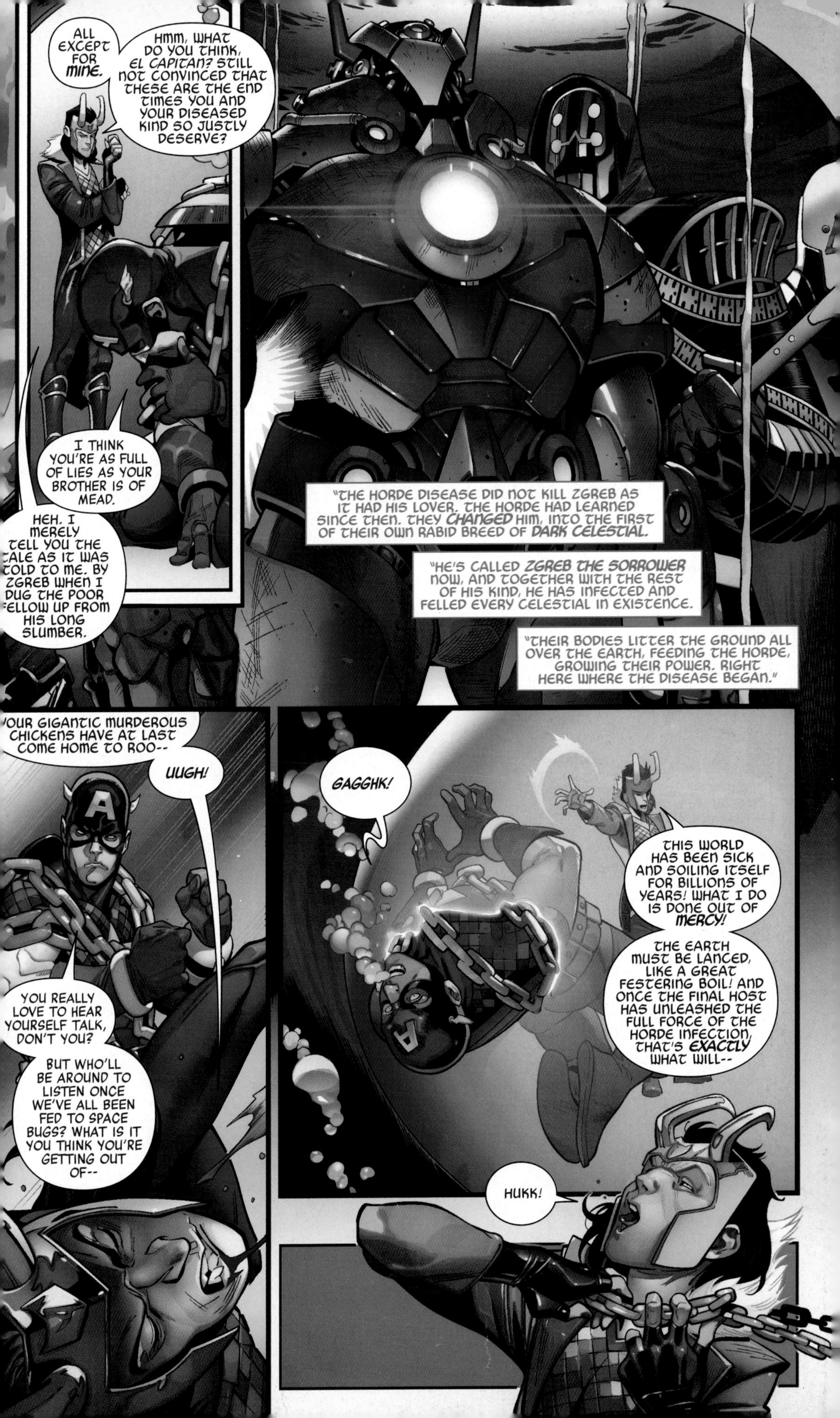
ALL EXCEPT FOR *MINE.*
HMM, WHAT DO YOU THINK, *EL CAPITAN?* STILL NOT CONVINCED THAT THESE ARE THE END TIMES YOU AND YOUR DISEASED KIND SO JUSTLY DESERVE?
I THINK YOU'RE AS FULL OF LIES AS YOUR BROTHER IS OF MEAD.
HEH. I MERELY TELL YOU THE TALE AS IT WAS TOLD TO ME. BY ZGREB WHEN I DUG THE POOR FELLOW UP FROM HIS LONG SLUMBER.
"THE HORDE DISEASE DID NOT KILL ZGREB AS IT HAD HIS LOVER. THE HORDE HAD LEARNED SINCE THEN. THEY *CHANGED* HIM, INTO THE FIRST OF THEIR OWN RABID BREED OF *DARK CELESTIAL.*
"HE'S CALLED *ZGREB THE SORROWER* NOW, AND TOGETHER WITH THE REST OF HIS KIND, HE HAS INFECTED AND FELLED EVERY CELESTIAL IN EXISTENCE.
"THEIR BODIES LITTER THE GROUND ALL OVER THE EARTH, FEEDING THE HORDE, GROWING THEIR POWER. RIGHT HERE WHERE THE DISEASE BEGAN."
YOUR GIGANTIC MURDEROUS CHICKENS HAVE AT LAST COME HOME TO ROO--
UUGH!
GAGGHK!
THIS WORLD HAS BEEN SICK AND SOILING ITSELF FOR BILLIONS OF YEARS! WHAT I DO IS DONE OUT OF *MERCY!*
THE EARTH MUST BE LANCED, LIKE A GREAT FESTERING BOIL! AND ONCE THE FINAL HOST HAS UNLEASHED THE FULL FORCE OF THE HORDE INFECTION, THAT'S *EXACTLY* WHAT WILL--
YOU REALLY LOVE TO HEAR YOURSELF TALK, DON'T YOU?
BUT WHO'LL BE AROUND TO LISTEN ONCE WE'VE ALL BEEN FED TO SPACE BUGS? WHAT IS IT YOU THINK YOU'RE GETTING OUT OF--
HUKK!

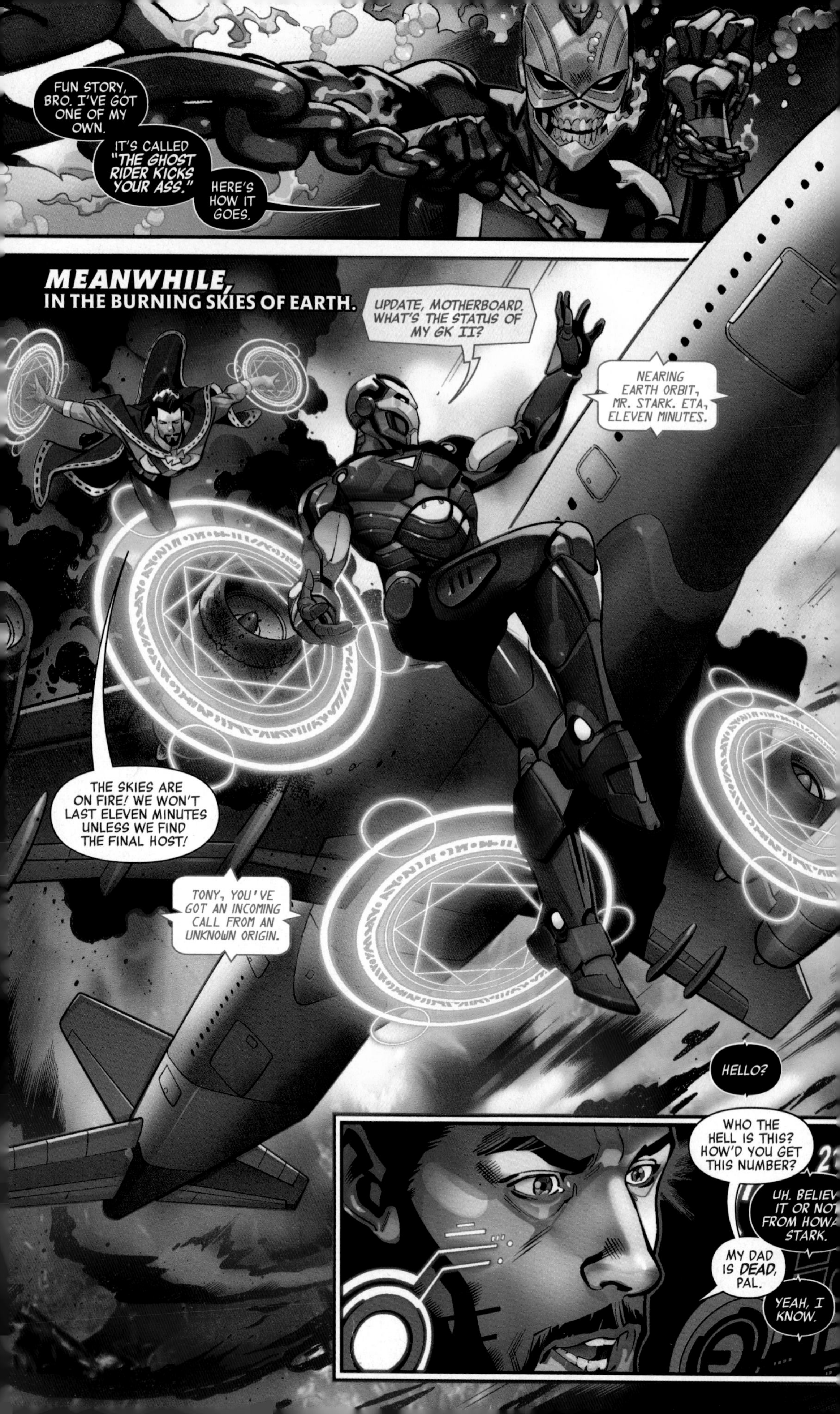
FUN STORY, BRO. I'VE GOT ONE OF MY OWN.
IT'S CALLED "THE GHOST RIDER KICKS YOUR ASS."
HERE'S HOW IT GOES.
MEANWHILE, IN THE BURNING SKIES OF EARTH.
UPDATE, MOTHERBOARD. WHAT'S THE STATUS OF MY GK II?
NEARING EARTH ORBIT, MR. STARK. ETA, ELEVEN MINUTES.
THE SKIES ARE ON FIRE! WE WON'T LAST ELEVEN MINUTES UNLESS WE FIND THE FINAL HOST!
TONY, YOU'VE GOT AN INCOMING CALL FROM AN UNKNOWN ORIGIN.
HELLO?
WHO THE HELL IS THIS? HOW'D YOU GET THIS NUMBER?
UH. BELIEV IT OR NOT FROM HOWA STARK.
MY DAD IS DEAD, PAL.
YEAH, I KNOW.

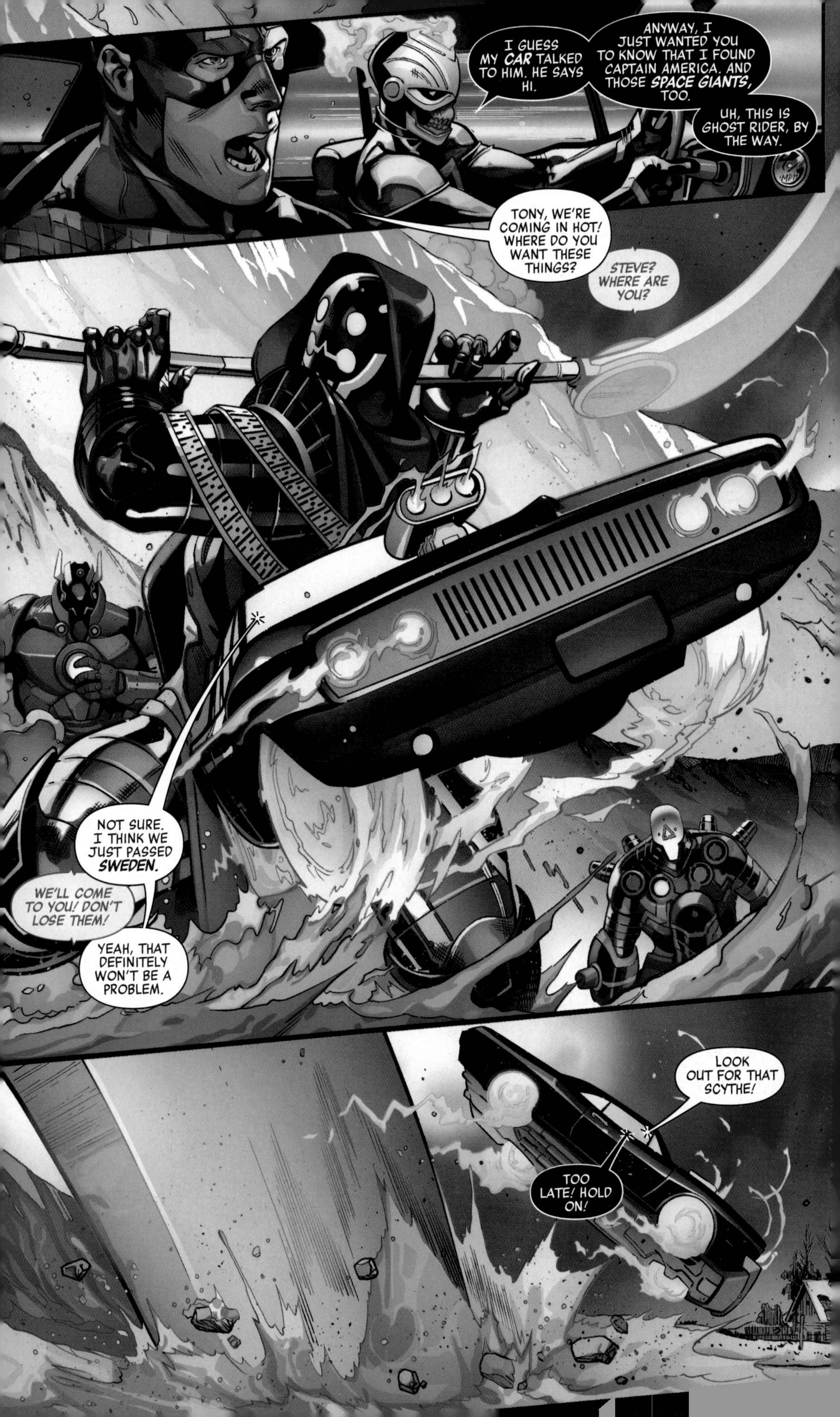
I GUESS MY CAR TALKED TO HIM. HE SAYS HI.
ANYWAY, I JUST WANTED YOU TO KNOW THAT I FOUND CAPTAIN AMERICA. AND THOSE SPACE GIANTS, TOO.
UH, THIS IS GHOST RIDER, BY THE WAY.
TONY, WE'RE COMING IN HOT! WHERE DO YOU WANT THESE THINGS?
STEVE? WHERE ARE YOU?
NOT SURE. I THINK WE JUST PASSED SWEDEN.
WE'LL COME TO YOU! DON'T LOSE THEM!
YEAH, THAT DEFINITELY WON'T BE A PROBLEM.
LOOK OUT FOR THAT SCYTHE!
TOO LATE! HOLD ON!

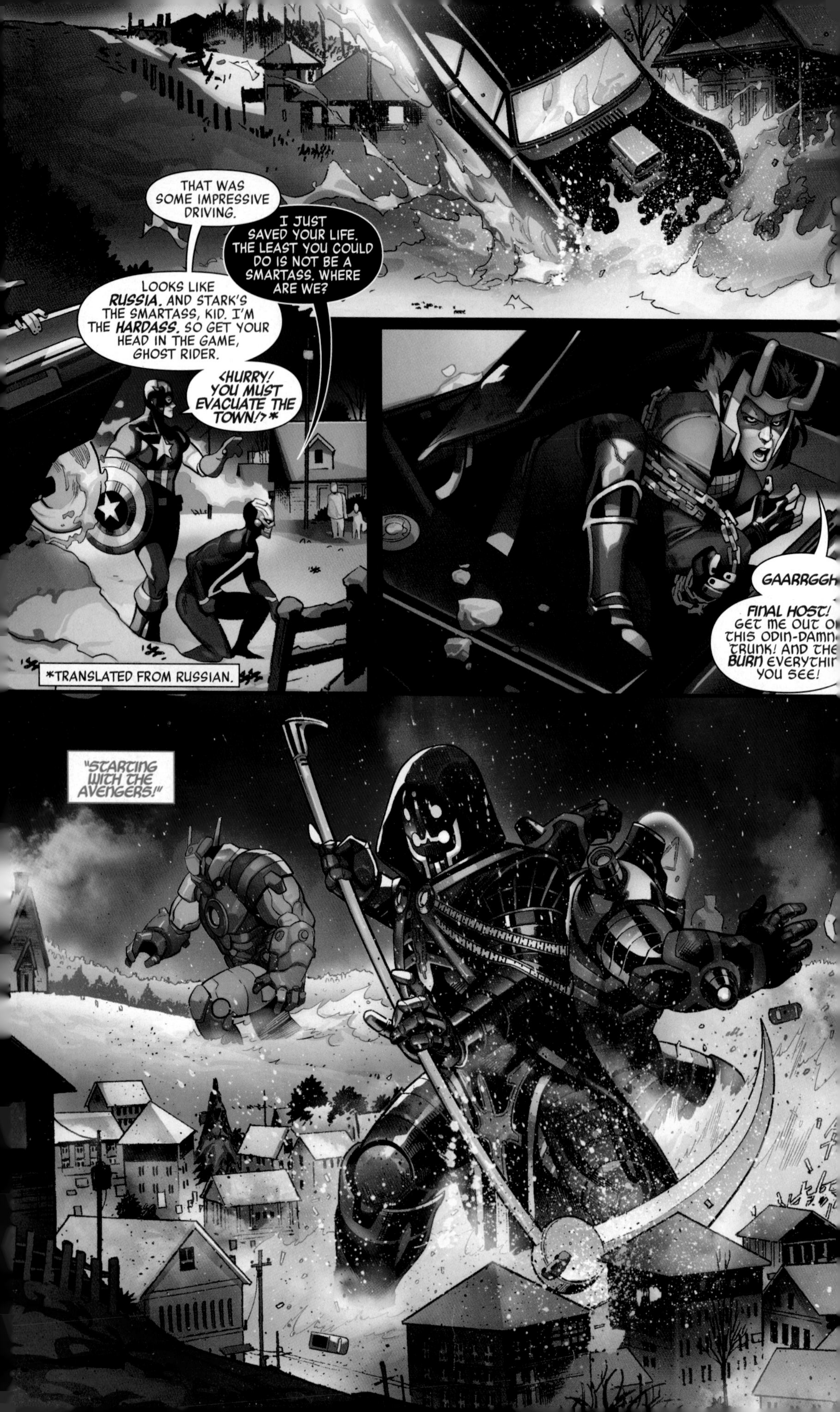
THAT WAS SOME IMPRESSIVE DRIVING.
I JUST SAVED YOUR LIFE. THE LEAST YOU COULD DO IS NOT BE A SMARTASS. WHERE ARE WE?
LOOKS LIKE RUSSIA. AND STARK'S THE SMARTASS, KID. I'M THE HARDASS. SO GET YOUR HEAD IN THE GAME, GHOST RIDER.
<HURRY! YOU MUST EVACUATE THE TOWN!>*
*TRANSLATED FROM RUSSIAN.
GAARRGGH
FINAL HOST! GET ME OUT O THIS ODIN-DAMN TRUNK! AND THE BURN EVERYTHI YOU SEE!
"STARTING WITH THE AVENGERS!"

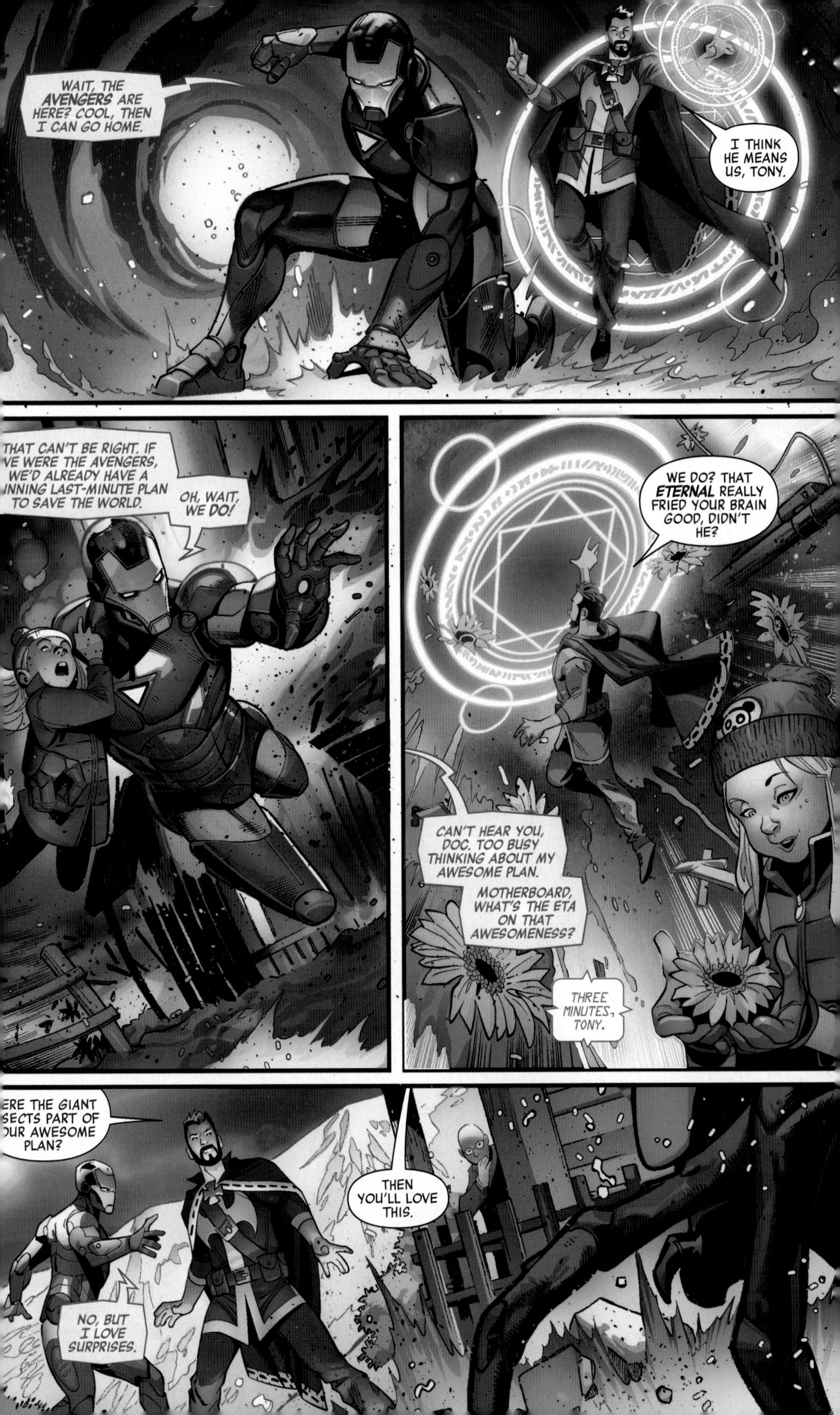

WAIT, THE AVENGERS ARE HERE? COOL, THEN I CAN GO HOME.
I THINK HE MEANS US, TONY.
THAT CAN'T BE RIGHT. IF WE WERE THE AVENGERS, WE'D ALREADY HAVE A WINNING LAST-MINUTE PLAN TO SAVE THE WORLD.
OH, WAIT, WE DO!
WE DO? THAT ETERNAL REALLY FRIED YOUR BRAIN GOOD, DIDN'T HE?
CAN'T HEAR YOU, DOC. TOO BUSY THINKING ABOUT MY AWESOME PLAN.
MOTHERBOARD, WHAT'S THE ETA ON THAT AWESOMENESS?
THREE MINUTES, TONY.
ERE THE GIANT SECTS PART OF OUR AWESOME PLAN?
NO, BUT I LOVE SURPRISES.
THEN YOU'LL LOVE THIS.

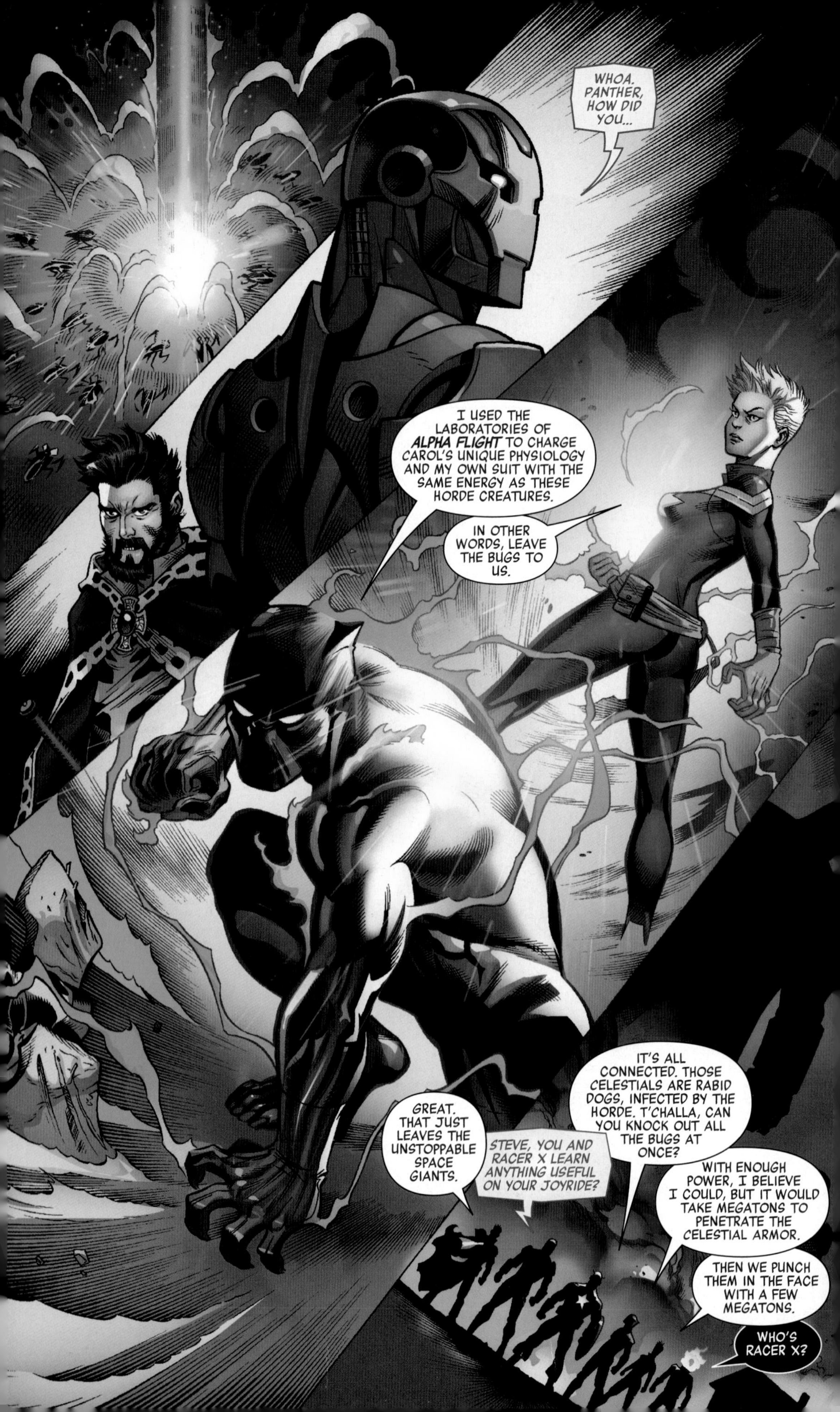
WHOA. PANTHER, HOW DID YOU...
I USED THE LABORATORIES OF ALPHA FLIGHT TO CHARGE CAROL'S UNIQUE PHYSIOLOGY AND MY OWN SUIT WITH THE SAME ENERGY AS THESE HORDE CREATURES.
IN OTHER WORDS, LEAVE THE BUGS TO US.
GREAT. THAT JUST LEAVES THE UNSTOPPABLE SPACE GIANTS.
STEVE, YOU AND RACER X LEARN ANYTHING USEFUL ON YOUR JOYRIDE?
IT'S ALL CONNECTED. THOSE CELESTIALS ARE RABID DOGS, INFECTED BY THE HORDE. T'CHALLA, CAN YOU KNOCK OUT ALL THE BUGS AT ONCE?
WITH ENOUGH POWER, I BELIEVE I COULD, BUT IT WOULD TAKE MEGATONS TO PENETRATE THE CELESTIAL ARMOR.
THEN WE PUNCH THEM IN THE FACE WITH A FEW MEGATONS.
WHO'S RACER X?

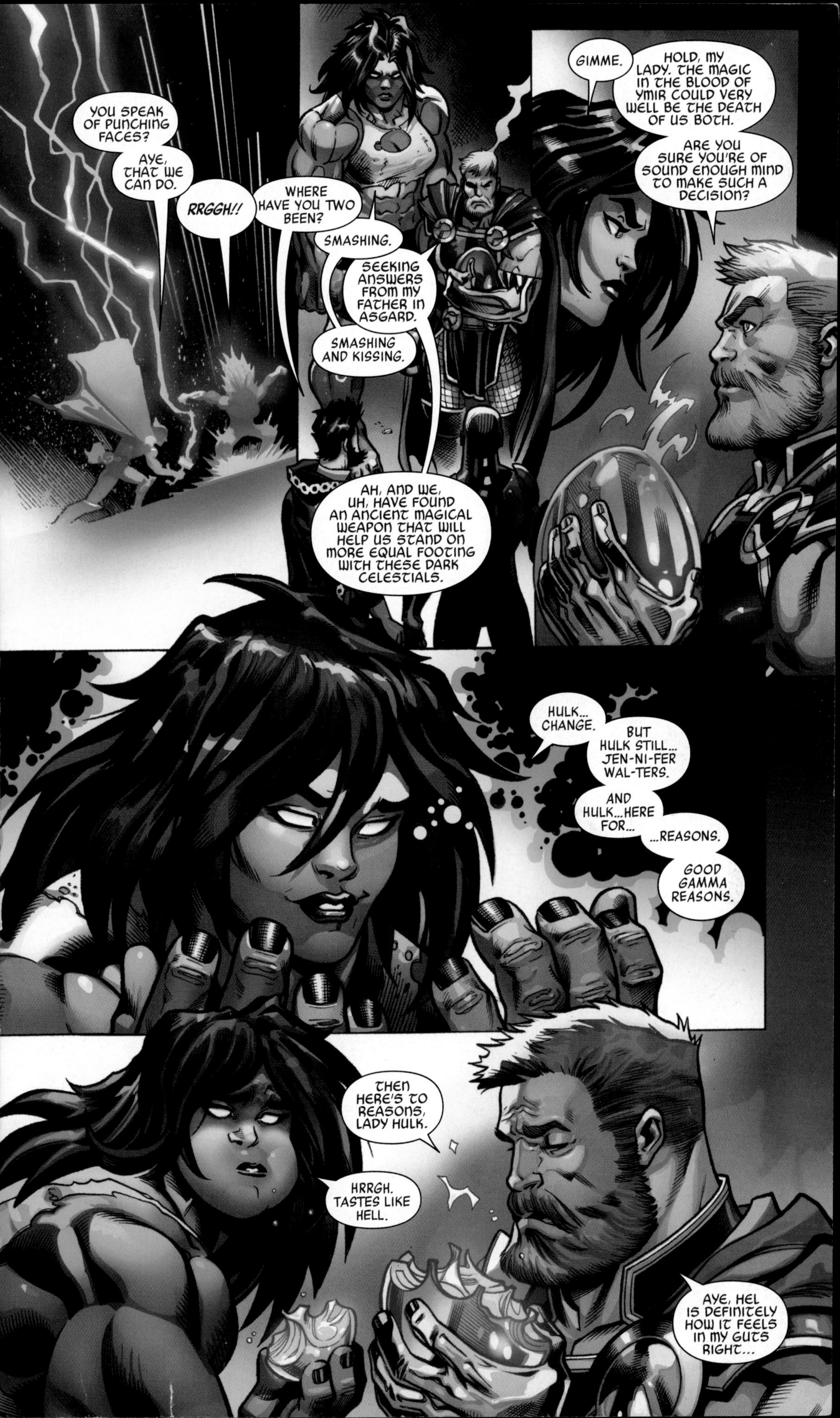
YOU SPEAK OF PUNCHING FACES?
AYE, THAT WE CAN DO.
RRGGH!!
WHERE HAVE YOU TWO BEEN?
SMASHING.
SEEKING ANSWERS FROM MY FATHER IN ASGARD.
SMASHING AND KISSING.
AH, AND WE, UH, HAVE FOUND AN ANCIENT MAGICAL WEAPON THAT WILL HELP US STAND ON MORE EQUAL FOOTING WITH THESE DARK CELESTIALS.
GIMME.
HOLD, MY LADY. THE MAGIC IN THE BLOOD OF YMIR COULD VERY WELL BE THE DEATH OF US BOTH.
ARE YOU SURE YOU'RE OF SOUND ENOUGH MIND TO MAKE SUCH A DECISION?
HULK... CHANGE.
BUT HULK STILL... JEN-NI-FER WAL-TERS.
AND HULK...HERE FOR...
...REASONS.
GOOD GAMMA REASONS.
THEN HERE'S TO REASONS, LADY HULK.
HRRGH. TASTES LIKE HELL.
AYE, HEL IS DEFINITELY HOW IT FEELS IN MY GUTS RIGHT...

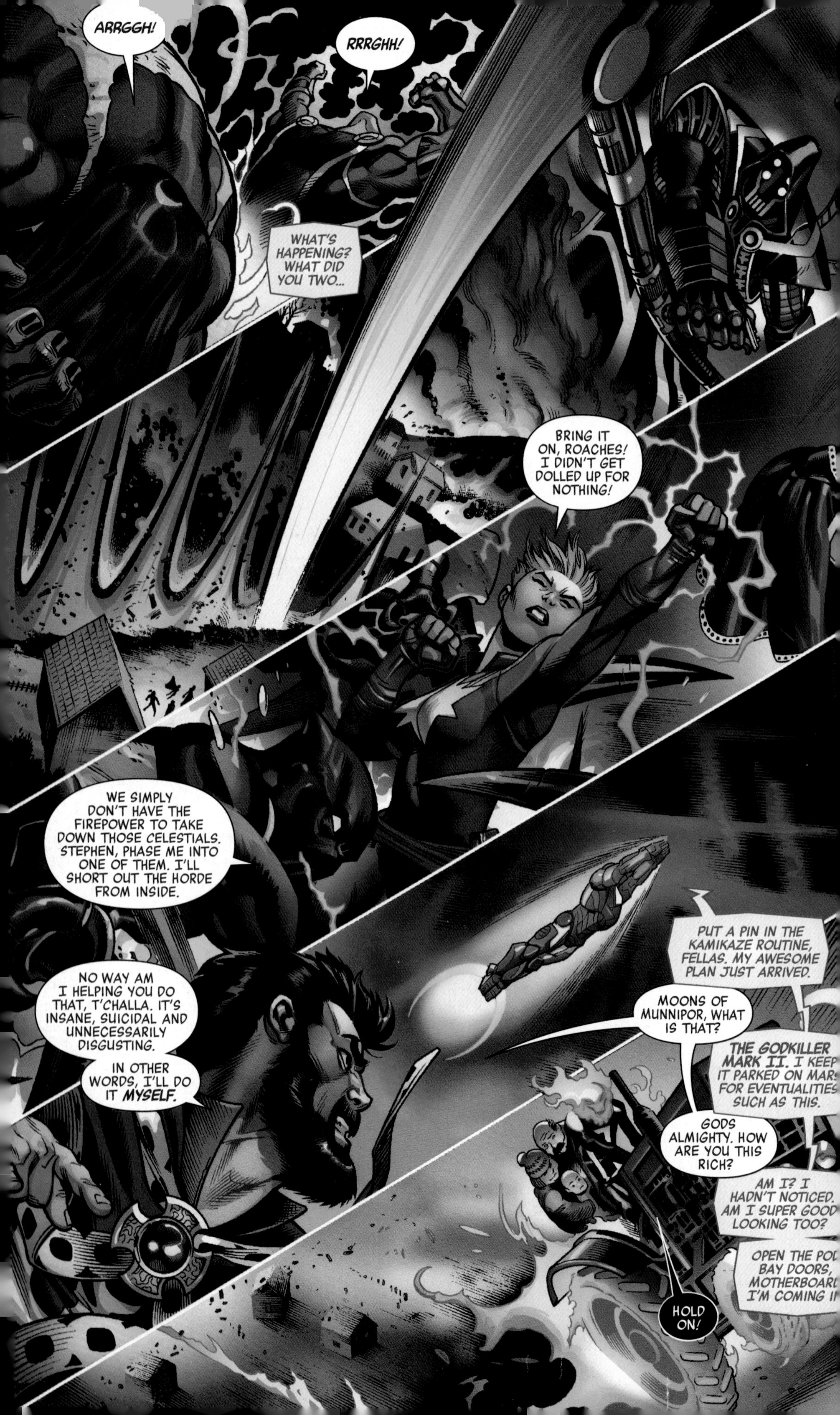
ARRGGH!
RRRGHH!
WHAT'S HAPPENING? WHAT DID YOU TWO...
BRING IT ON, ROACHES! I DIDN'T GET DOLLED UP FOR NOTHING!
WE SIMPLY DON'T HAVE THE FIREPOWER TO TAKE DOWN THOSE CELESTIALS. STEPHEN, PHASE ME INTO ONE OF THEM. I'LL SHORT OUT THE HORDE FROM INSIDE.
NO WAY AM I HELPING YOU DO THAT, T'CHALLA. IT'S INSANE, SUICIDAL AND UNNECESSARILY DISGUSTING.
IN OTHER WORDS, I'LL DO IT MYSELF.
PUT A PIN IN THE KAMIKAZE ROUTINE, FELLAS. MY AWESOME PLAN JUST ARRIVED.
MOONS OF MUNNIPOR, WHAT IS THAT?
THE GODKILLER MARK II. I KEEP IT PARKED ON MARS FOR EVENTUALITIES SUCH AS THIS.
GODS ALMIGHTY. HOW ARE YOU THIS RICH?
AM I? I HADN'T NOTICED. AM I SUPER GOOD LOOKING TOO?
OPEN THE POD BAY DOORS, MOTHERBOARD. I'M COMING IN
HOLD ON!

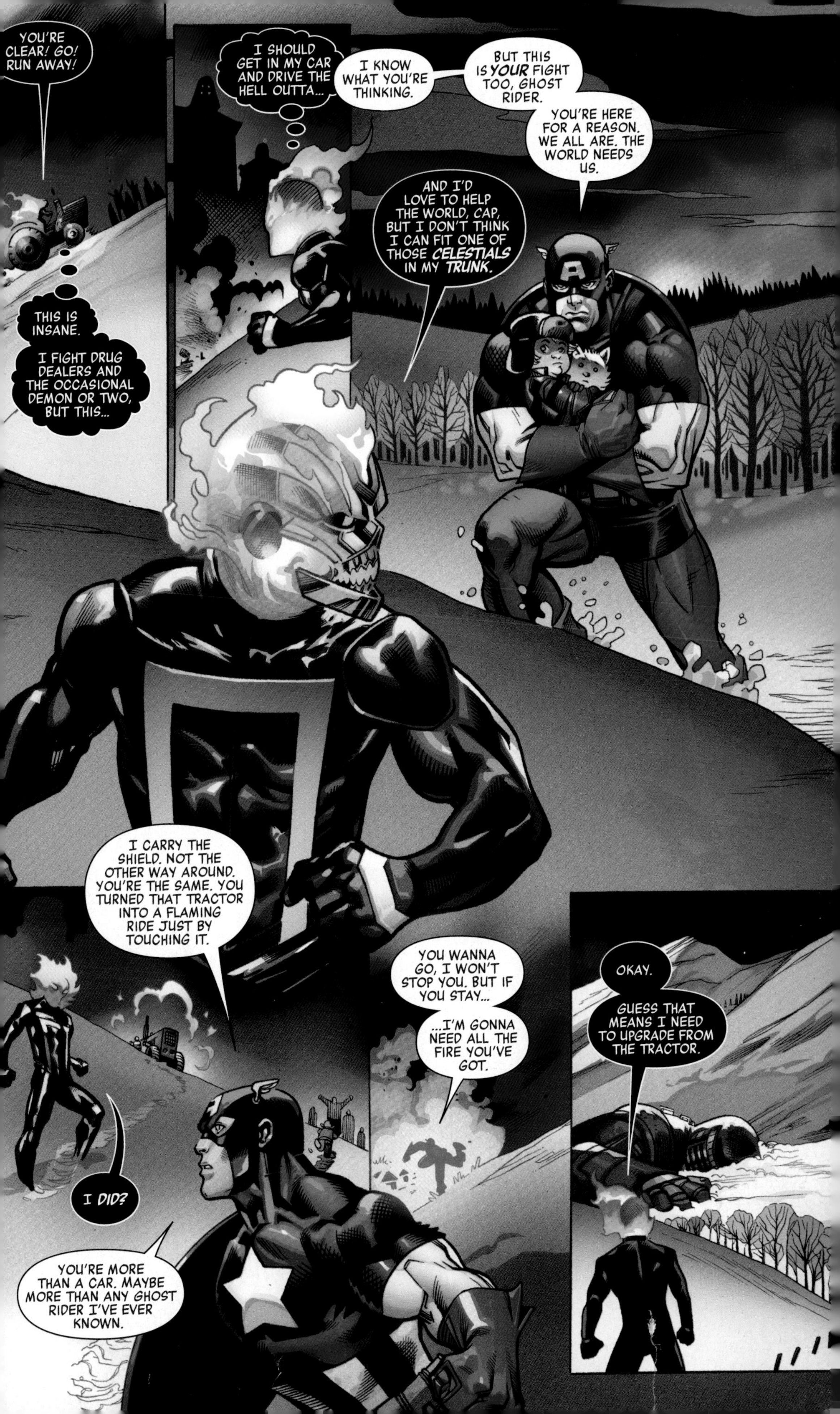
YOU'RE CLEAR! GO! RUN AWAY!
THIS IS INSANE.
I FIGHT DRUG DEALERS AND THE OCCASIONAL DEMON OR TWO, BUT THIS...
I SHOULD GET IN MY CAR AND DRIVE THE HELL OUTTA...
I KNOW WHAT YOU'RE THINKING.
BUT THIS IS YOUR FIGHT TOO, GHOST RIDER.
YOU'RE HERE FOR A REASON. WE ALL ARE. THE WORLD NEEDS US.
AND I'D LOVE TO HELP THE WORLD, CAP, BUT I DON'T THINK I CAN FIT ONE OF THOSE CELESTIALS IN MY TRUNK.
I CARRY THE SHIELD. NOT THE OTHER WAY AROUND. YOU'RE THE SAME. YOU TURNED THAT TRACTOR INTO A FLAMING RIDE JUST BY TOUCHING IT.
I DID?
YOU'RE MORE THAN A CAR. MAYBE MORE THAN ANY GHOST RIDER I'VE EVER KNOWN.
YOU WANNA GO, I WON'T STOP YOU. BUT IF YOU STAY...
...I'M GONNA NEED ALL THE FIRE YOU'VE GOT.
OKAY.
GUESS THAT MEANS I NEED TO UPGRADE FROM THE TRACTOR.

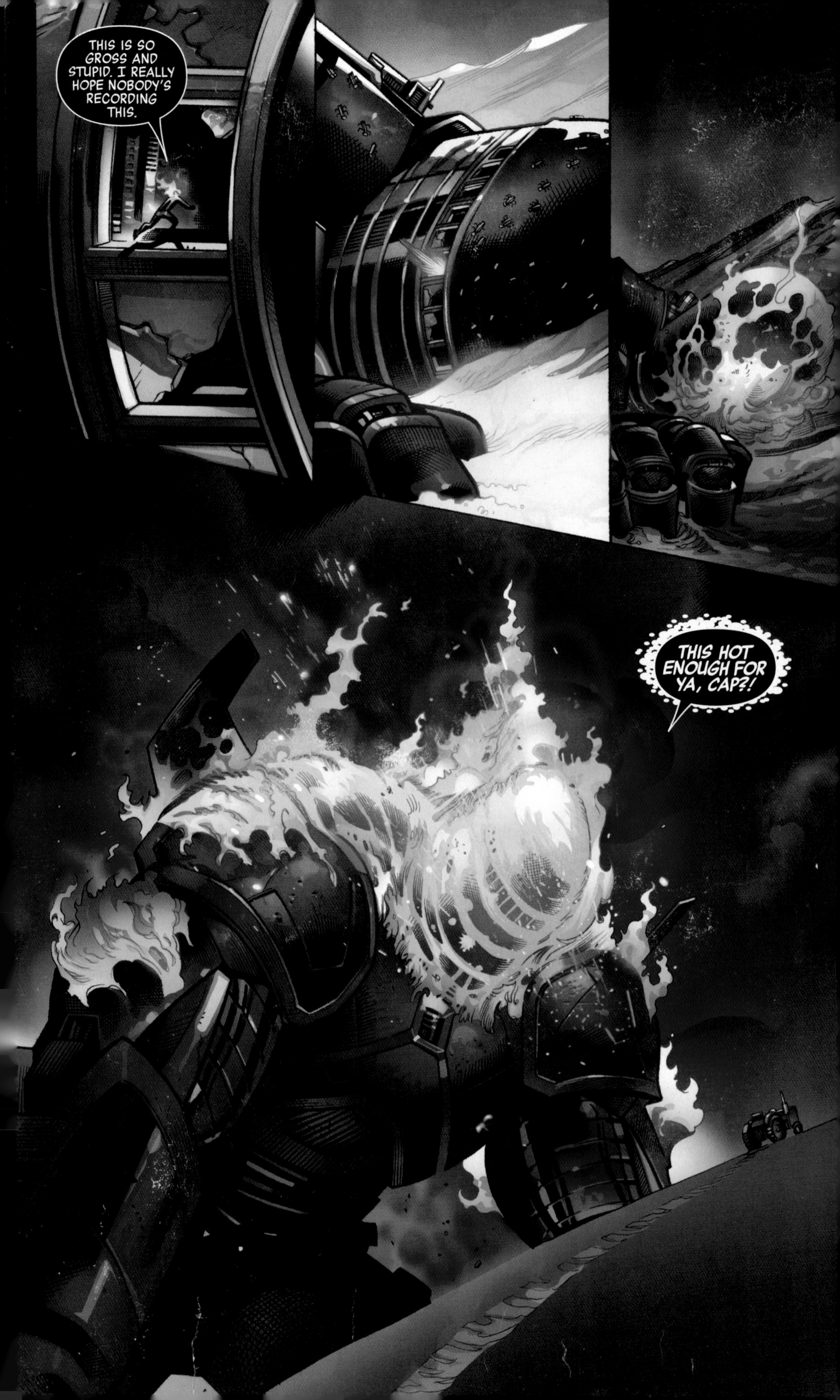
THIS IS SO GROSS AND STUPID. I REALLY HOPE NOBODY'S RECORDING THIS.
THIS HOT ENOUGH FOR YA, CAP?!

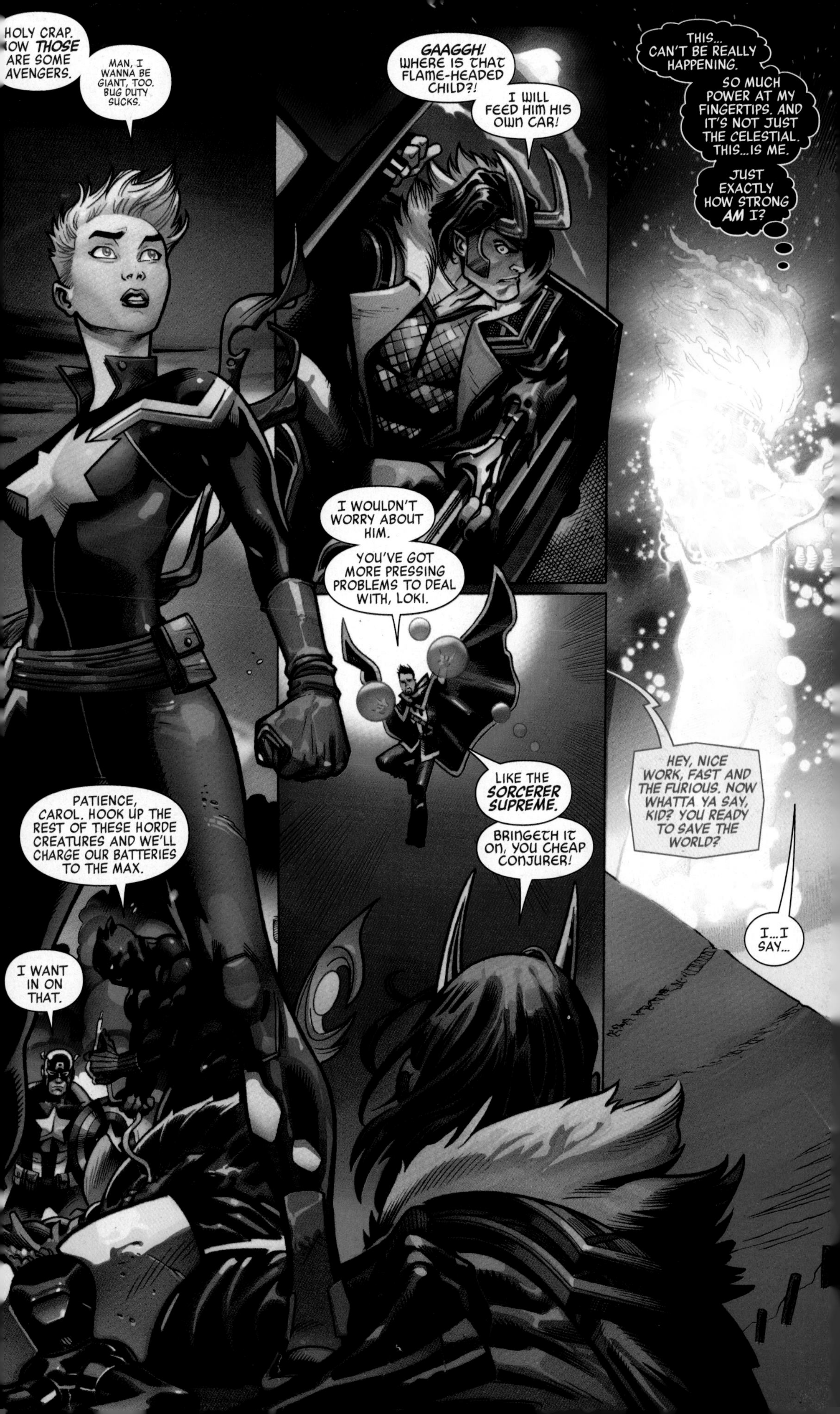
HOLY CRAP. NOW THOSE ARE SOME AVENGERS.
MAN, I WANNA BE GIANT, TOO. BUG DUTY SUCKS.
GAAGGH! WHERE IS THAT FLAME-HEADED CHILD?!
I WILL FEED HIM HIS OWN CAR!
THIS... CAN'T BE REALLY HAPPENING.
SO MUCH POWER AT MY FINGERTIPS. AND IT'S NOT JUST THE CELESTIAL. THIS...IS ME.
JUST EXACTLY HOW STRONG AM I?
I WOULDN'T WORRY ABOUT HIM.
YOU'VE GOT MORE PRESSING PROBLEMS TO DEAL WITH, LOKI.
LIKE THE SORCERER SUPREME.
BRINGETH IT ON, YOU CHEAP CONJURER!
PATIENCE, CAROL. HOOK UP THE REST OF THESE HORDE CREATURES AND WE'LL CHARGE OUR BATTERIES TO THE MAX.
I WANT IN ON THAT.
HEY, NICE WORK, FAST AND THE FURIOUS. NOW WHATTA YA SAY, KID? YOU READY TO SAVE THE WORLD?
I...I SAY...

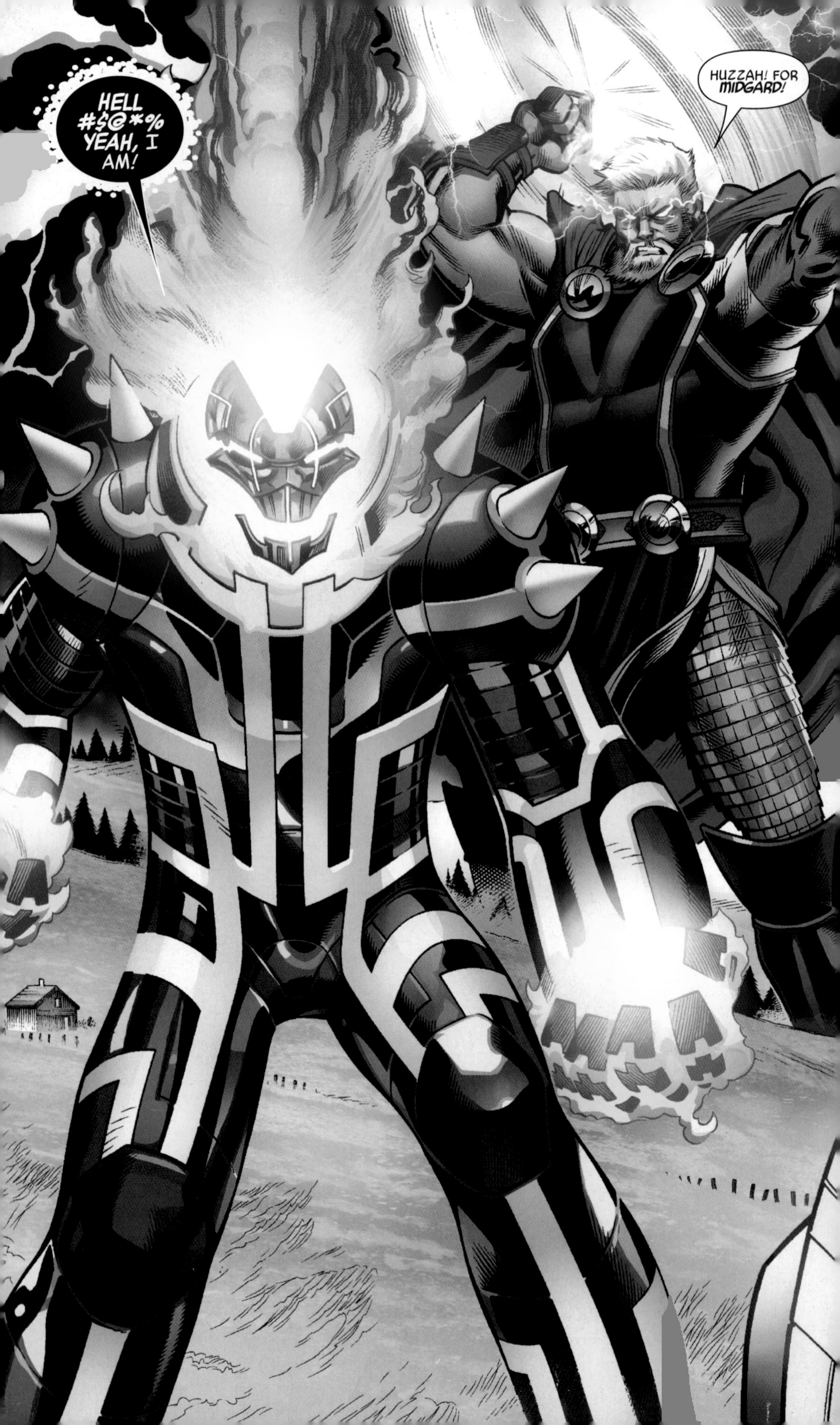
HUZZAH! FOR MIDGARD!
HELL #$@*% YEAH, I AM!

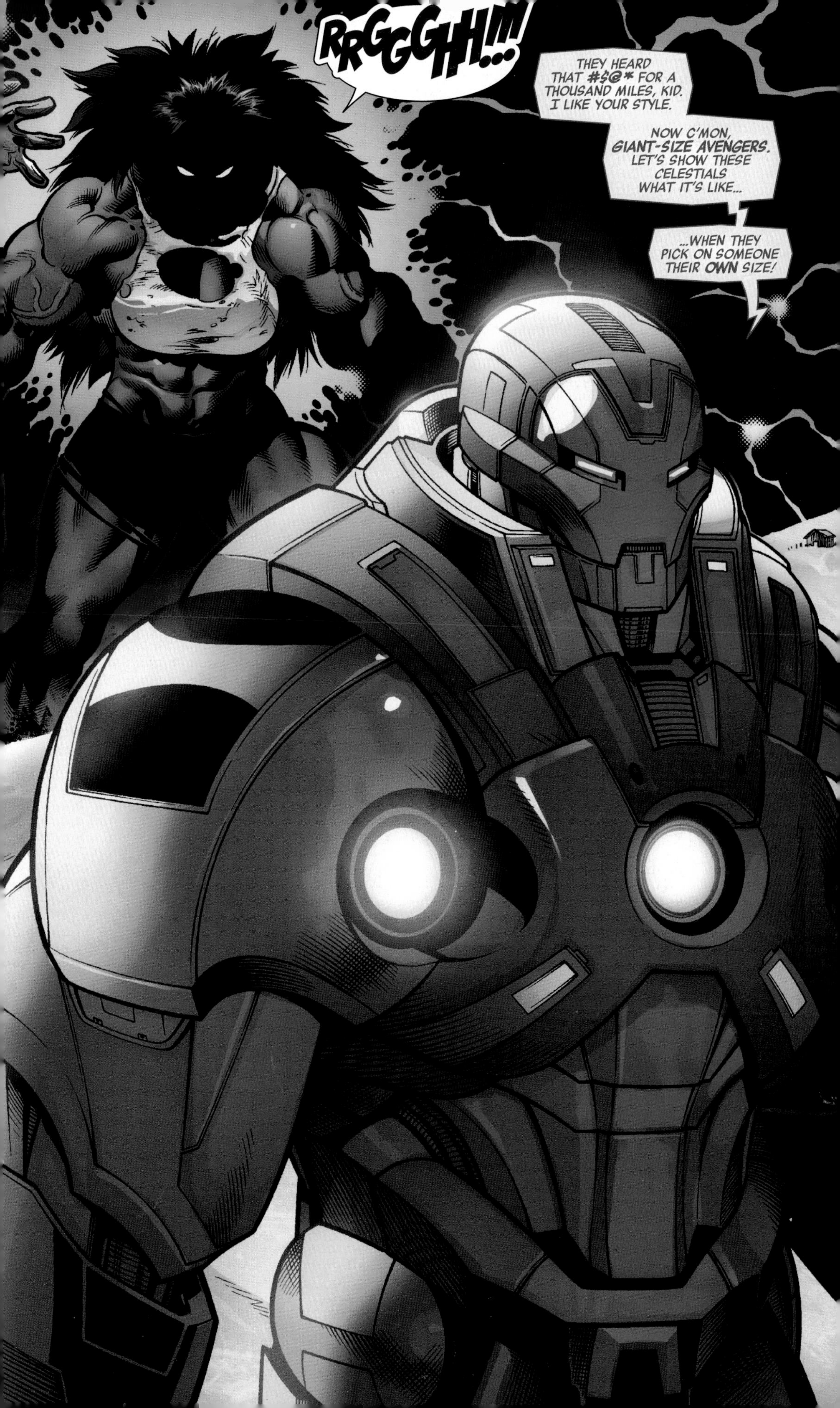

RRGGGHH!!!...
THEY HEARD THAT #$@* FOR A THOUSAND MILES, KID. I LIKE YOUR STYLE.
NOW C'MON, GIANT-SIZE AVENGERS. LET'S SHOW THESE CELESTIALS WHAT IT'S LIKE...
...WHEN THEY PICK ON SOMEONE THEIR OWN SIZE!

6 PLANET OF PATHOGENS

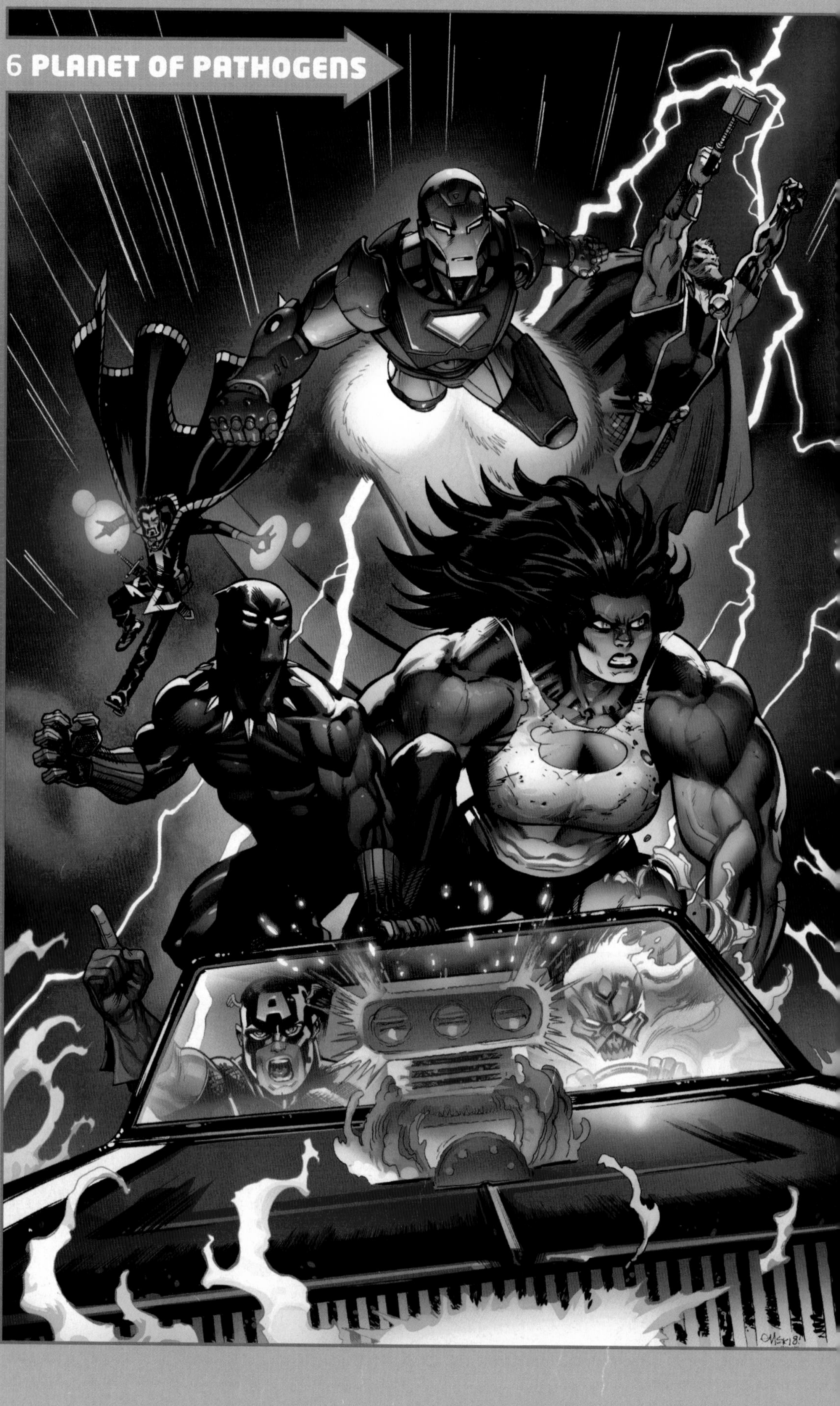

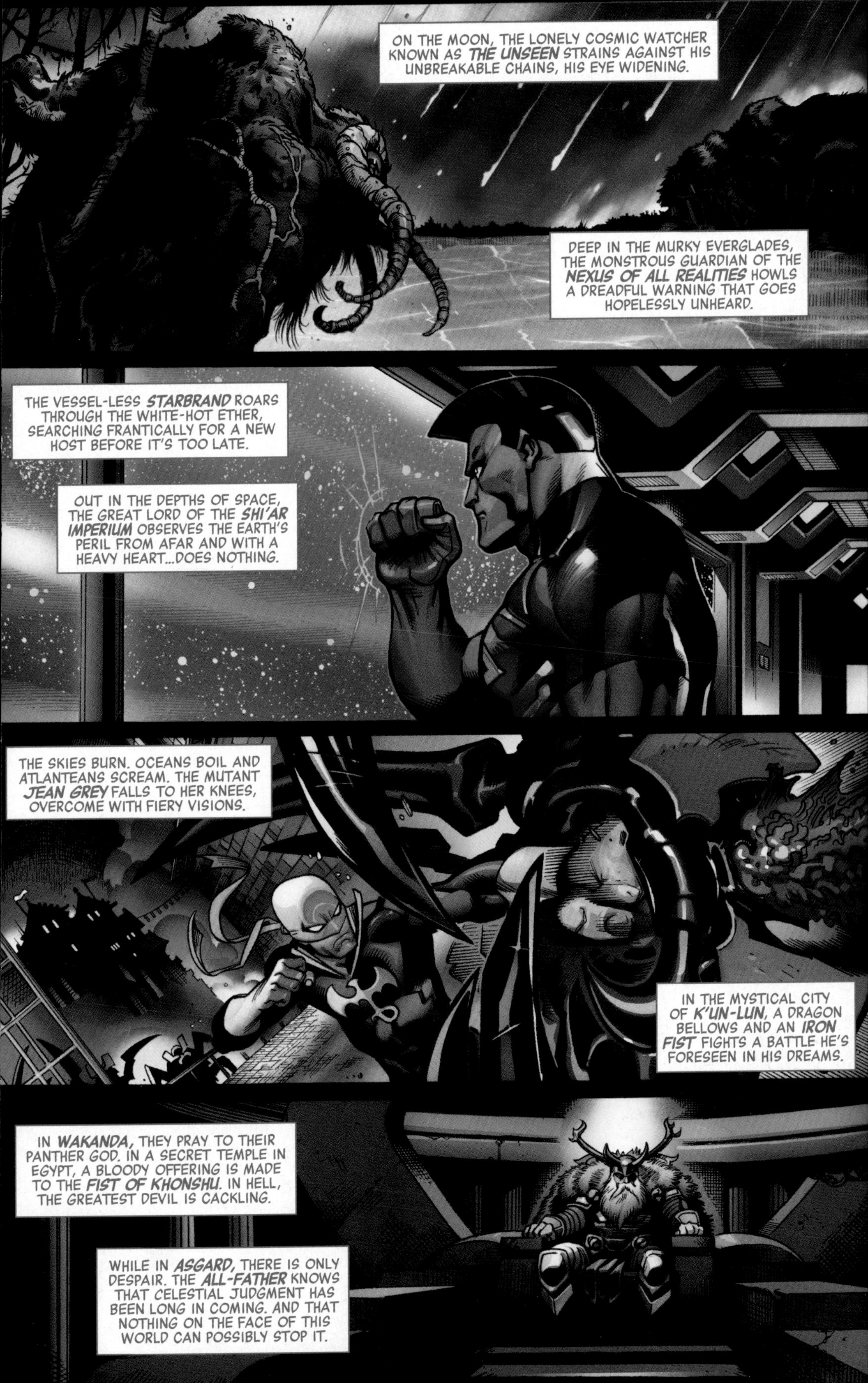
ON THE MOON, THE LONELY COSMIC WATCHER KNOWN AS THE UNSEEN STRAINS AGAINST HIS UNBREAKABLE CHAINS, HIS EYE WIDENING.
DEEP IN THE MURKY EVERGLADES, THE MONSTROUS GUARDIAN OF THE NEXUS OF ALL REALITIES HOWLS A DREADFUL WARNING THAT GOES HOPELESSLY UNHEARD.
THE VESSEL-LESS STARBRAND ROARS THROUGH THE WHITE-HOT ETHER, SEARCHING FRANTICALLY FOR A NEW HOST BEFORE IT'S TOO LATE.
OUT IN THE DEPTHS OF SPACE, THE GREAT LORD OF THE SHI'AR IMPERIUM OBSERVES THE EARTH'S PERIL FROM AFAR AND WITH A HEAVY HEART...DOES NOTHING.
THE SKIES BURN. OCEANS BOIL AND ATLANTEANS SCREAM. THE MUTANT JEAN GREY FALLS TO HER KNEES, OVERCOME WITH FIERY VISIONS.
IN THE MYSTICAL CITY OF K'UN-LUN, A DRAGON BELLOWS AND AN IRON FIST FIGHTS A BATTLE HE'S FORESEEN IN HIS DREAMS.
IN WAKANDA, THEY PRAY TO THEIR PANTHER GOD. IN A SECRET TEMPLE IN EGYPT, A BLOODY OFFERING IS MADE TO THE FIST OF KHONSHU. IN HELL, THE GREATEST DEVIL IS CACKLING.
WHILE IN ASGARD, THERE IS ONLY DESPAIR. THE ALL-FATHER KNOWS THAT CELESTIAL JUDGMENT HAS BEEN LONG IN COMING. AND THAT NOTHING ON THE FACE OF THIS WORLD CAN POSSIBLY STOP IT.

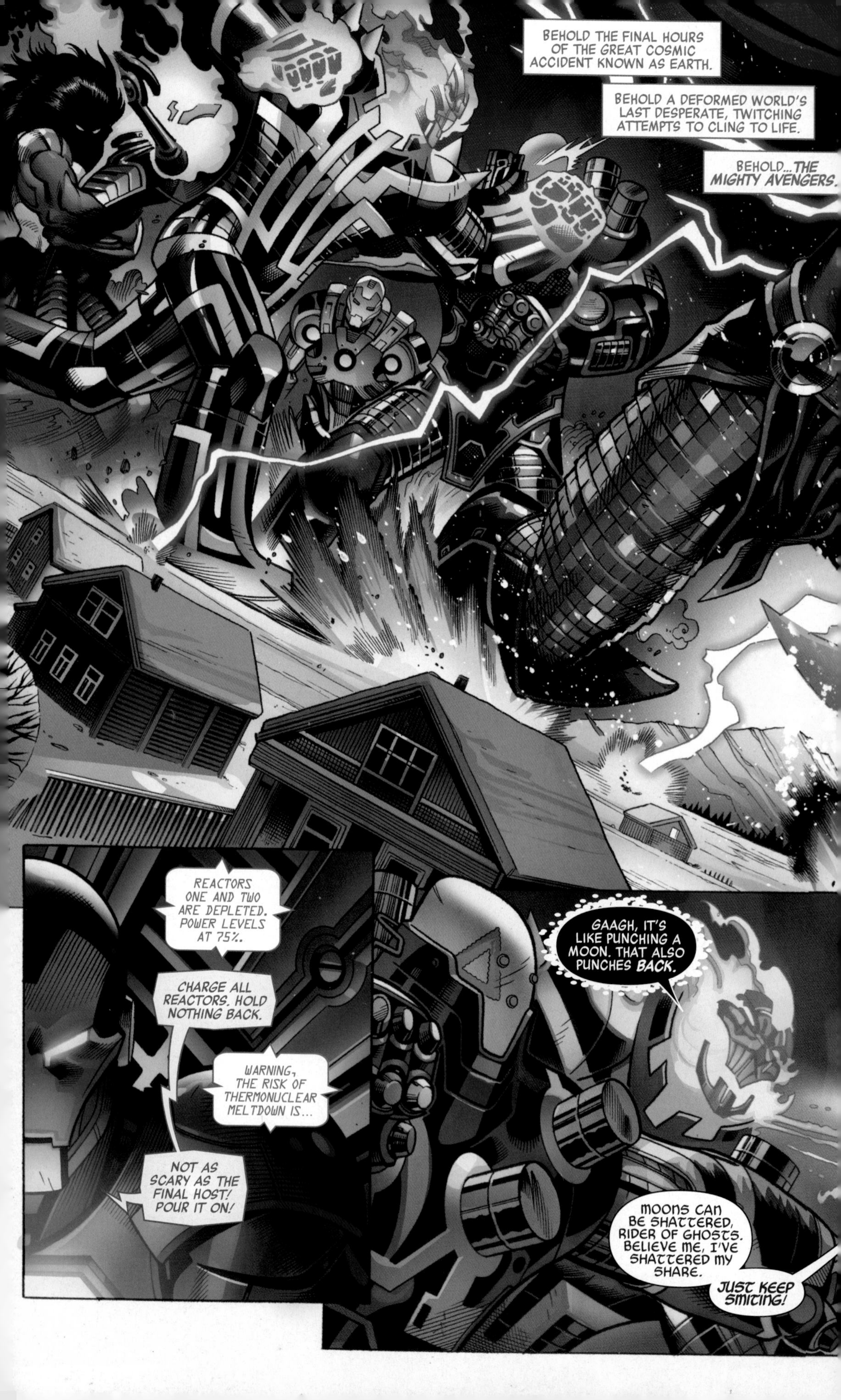
BEHOLD THE FINAL HOURS OF THE GREAT COSMIC ACCIDENT KNOWN AS EARTH.
BEHOLD A DEFORMED WORLD'S LAST DESPERATE, TWITCHING ATTEMPTS TO CLING TO LIFE.
BEHOLD... THE MIGHTY AVENGERS.
REACTORS ONE AND TWO ARE DEPLETED. POWER LEVELS AT 75%.
CHARGE ALL REACTORS. HOLD NOTHING BACK.
WARNING, THE RISK OF THERMONUCLEAR MELTDOWN IS...
NOT AS SCARY AS THE FINAL HOST! POUR IT ON!
GAAGH, IT'S LIKE PUNCHING A MOON. THAT ALSO PUNCHES BACK.
MOONS CAN BE SHATTERED, RIDER OF GHOSTS. BELIEVE ME, I'VE SHATTERED MY SHARE.
JUST KEEP SMITING!

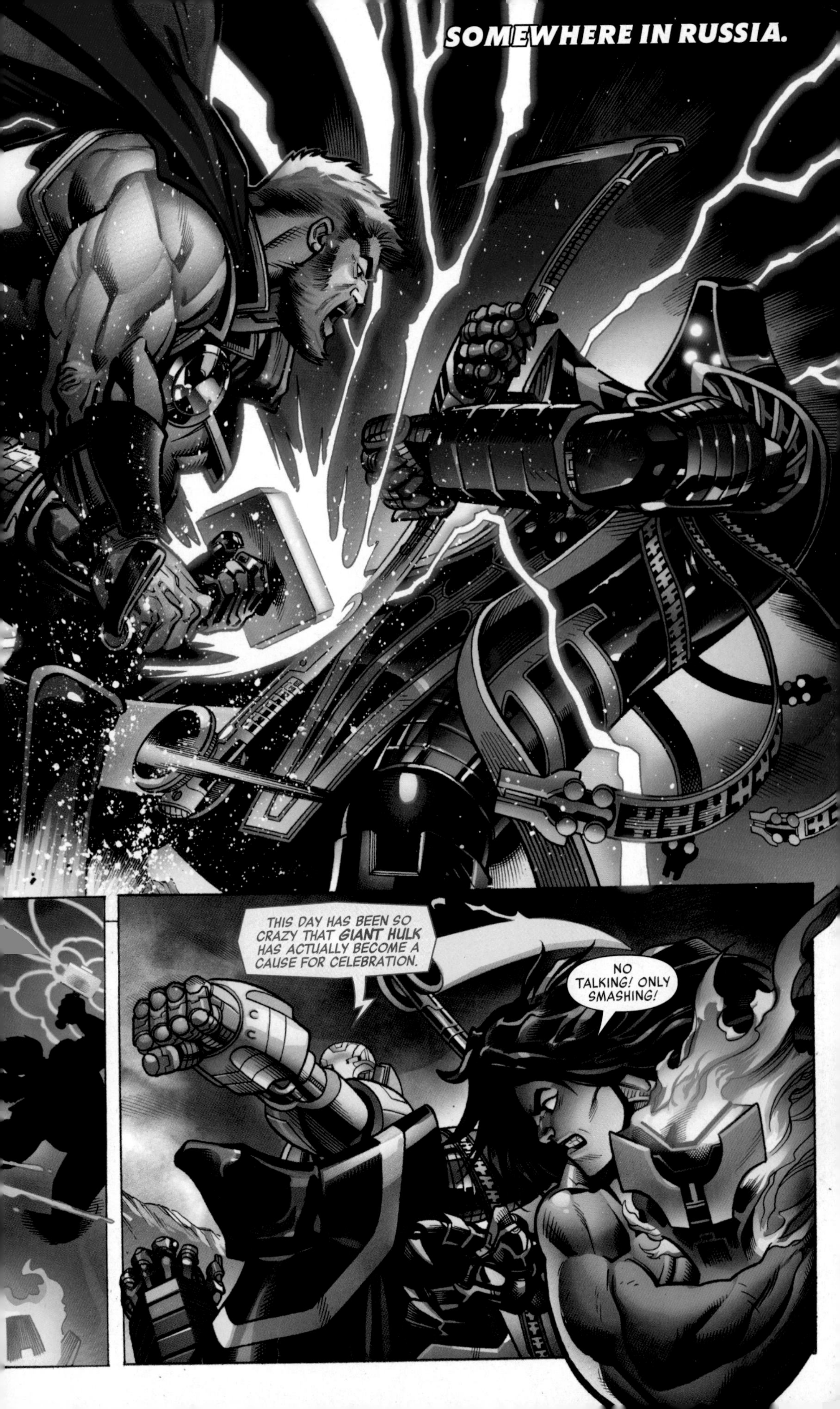
SOMEWHERE IN RUSSIA.
THIS DAY HAS BEEN SO CRAZY THAT GIANT HULK HAS ACTUALLY BECOME A CAUSE FOR CELEBRATION.
NO TALKING! ONLY SMASHING!

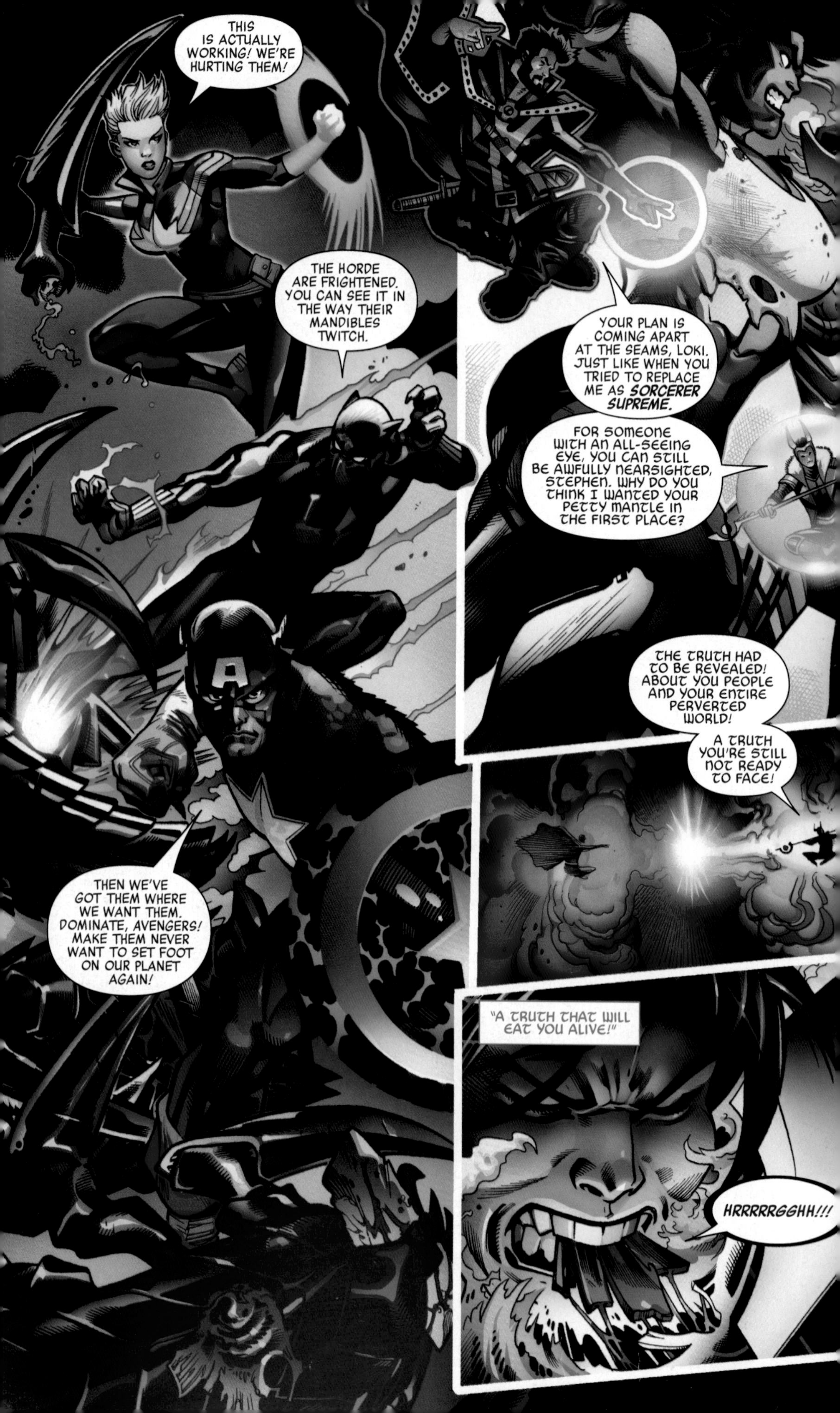

THIS IS ACTUALLY WORKING! WE'RE HURTING THEM!
THE HORDE ARE FRIGHTENED. YOU CAN SEE IT IN THE WAY THEIR MANDIBLES TWITCH.
THEN WE'VE GOT THEM WHERE WE WANT THEM. DOMINATE, AVENGERS! MAKE THEM NEVER WANT TO SET FOOT ON OUR PLANET AGAIN!
YOUR PLAN IS COMING APART AT THE SEAMS, LOKI. JUST LIKE WHEN YOU TRIED TO REPLACE ME AS SORCERER SUPREME.
FOR SOMEONE WITH AN ALL-SEEING EYE, YOU CAN STILL BE AWFULLY NEARSIGHTED, STEPHEN. WHY DO YOU THINK I WANTED YOUR PETTY MANTLE IN THE FIRST PLACE?
THE TRUTH HAD TO BE REVEALED! ABOUT YOU PEOPLE AND YOUR ENTIRE PERVERTED WORLD!
A TRUTH YOU'RE STILL NOT READY TO FACE!
"A TRUTH THAT WILL EAT YOU ALIVE!"
HRRRRRGGHH!!!

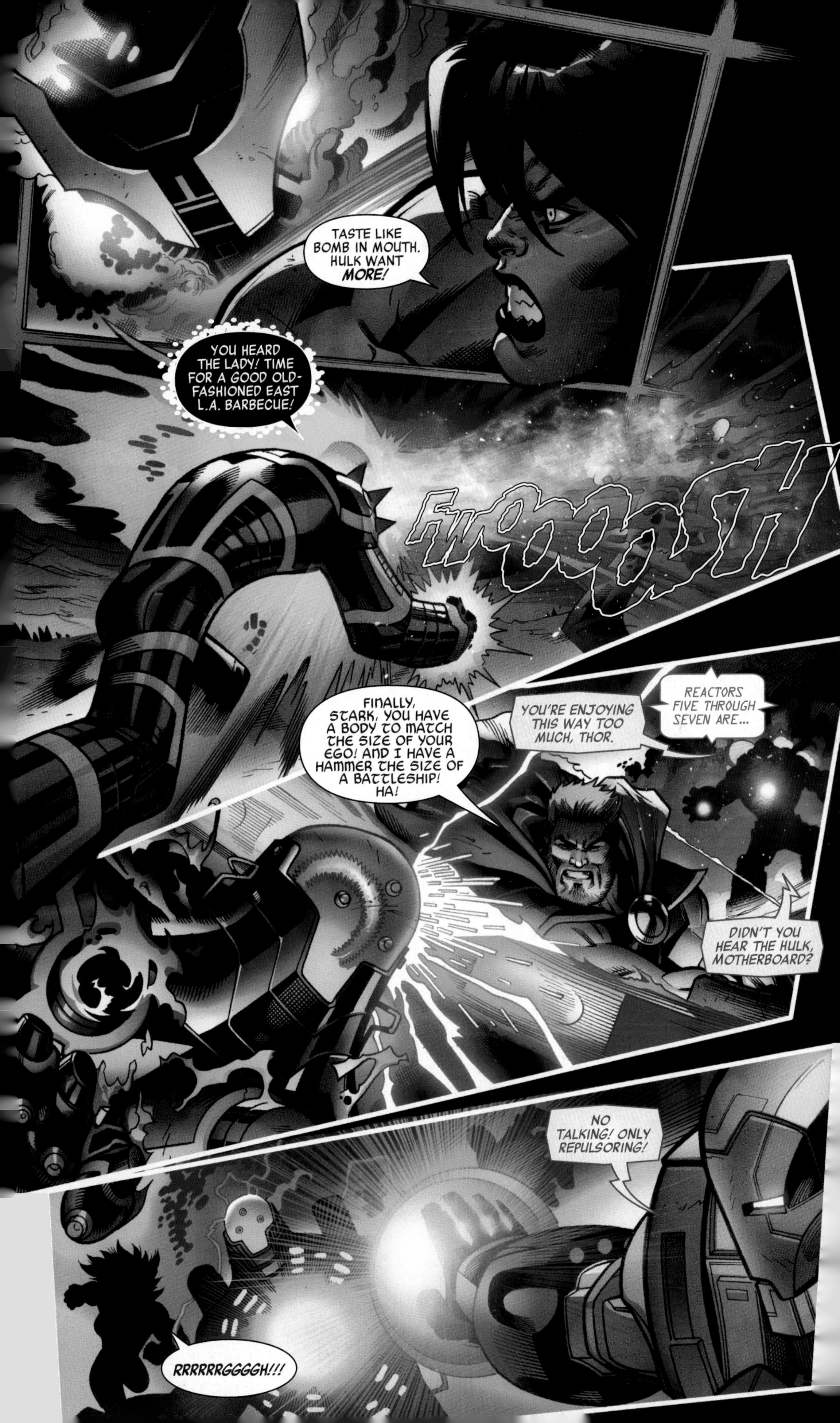

TASTE LIKE BOMB IN MOUTH. HULK WANT MORE!
YOU HEARD THE LADY! TIME FOR A GOOD OLD-FASHIONED EAST L.A. BARBECUE!
FWOOOOSH
FINALLY, STARK, YOU HAVE A BODY TO MATCH THE SIZE OF YOUR EGO! AND I HAVE A HAMMER THE SIZE OF A BATTLESHIP! HA!
YOU'RE ENJOYING THIS WAY TOO MUCH, THOR.
REACTORS FIVE THROUGH SEVEN ARE...
DIDN'T YOU HEAR THE HULK, MOTHERBOARD?
NO TALKING! ONLY REPULSORING!
RRRRRRGGGGH!!!

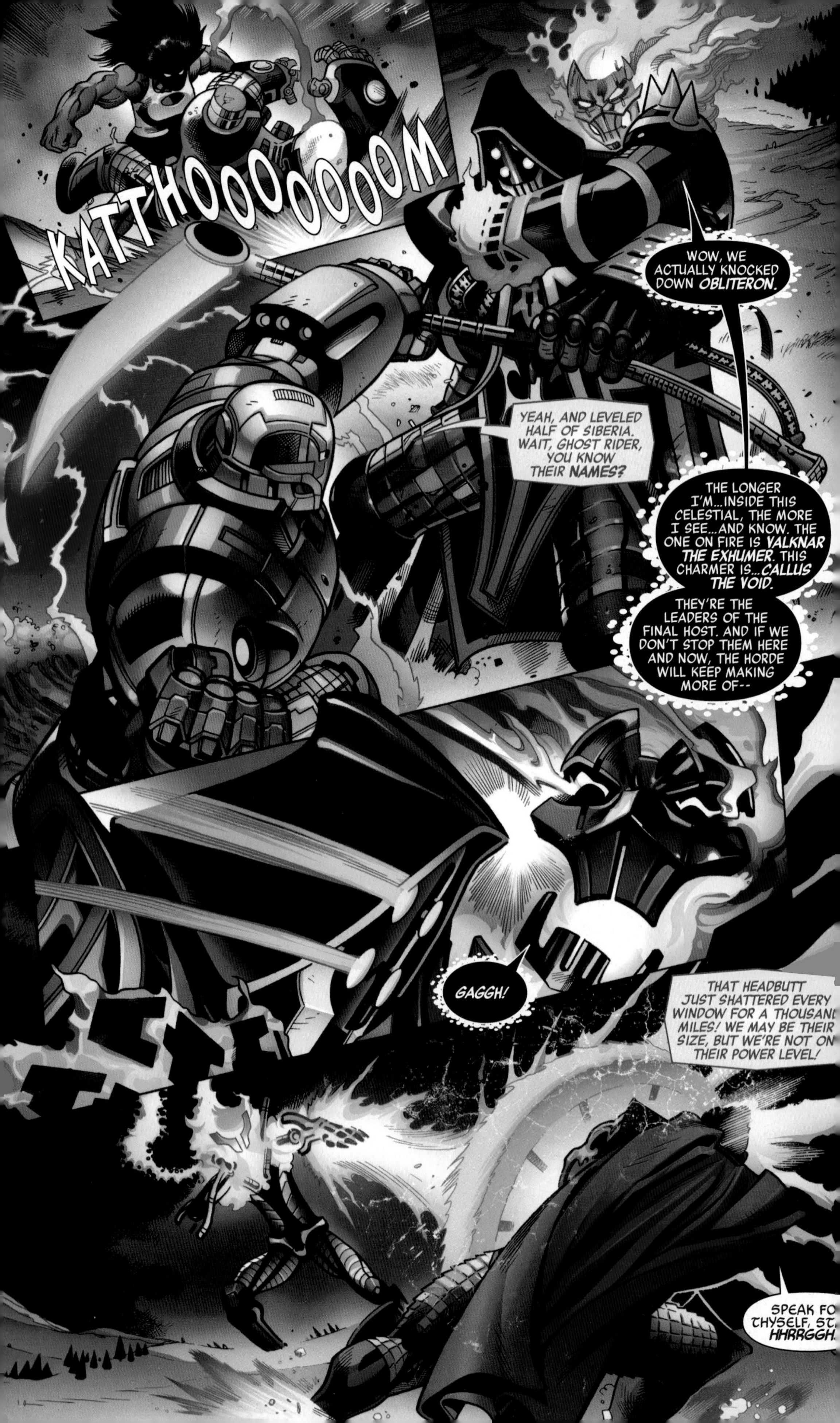
KATTHOOOOOOOM
WOW, WE ACTUALLY KNOCKED DOWN OBLITERON.
YEAH, AND LEVELED HALF OF SIBERIA. WAIT, GHOST RIDER, YOU KNOW THEIR NAMES?
THE LONGER I'M...INSIDE THIS CELESTIAL, THE MORE I SEE...AND KNOW. THE ONE ON FIRE IS VALKNAR THE EXHUMER. THIS CHARMER IS...CALLUS THE VOID.
THEY'RE THE LEADERS OF THE FINAL HOST. AND IF WE DON'T STOP THEM HERE AND NOW, THE HORDE WILL KEEP MAKING MORE OF--
GAGGH!
THAT HEADBUTT JUST SHATTERED EVERY WINDOW FOR A THOUSAN MILES! WE MAY BE THEIR SIZE, BUT WE'RE NOT ON THEIR POWER LEVEL!
SPEAK FO THYSELF, ST HHRRGGH

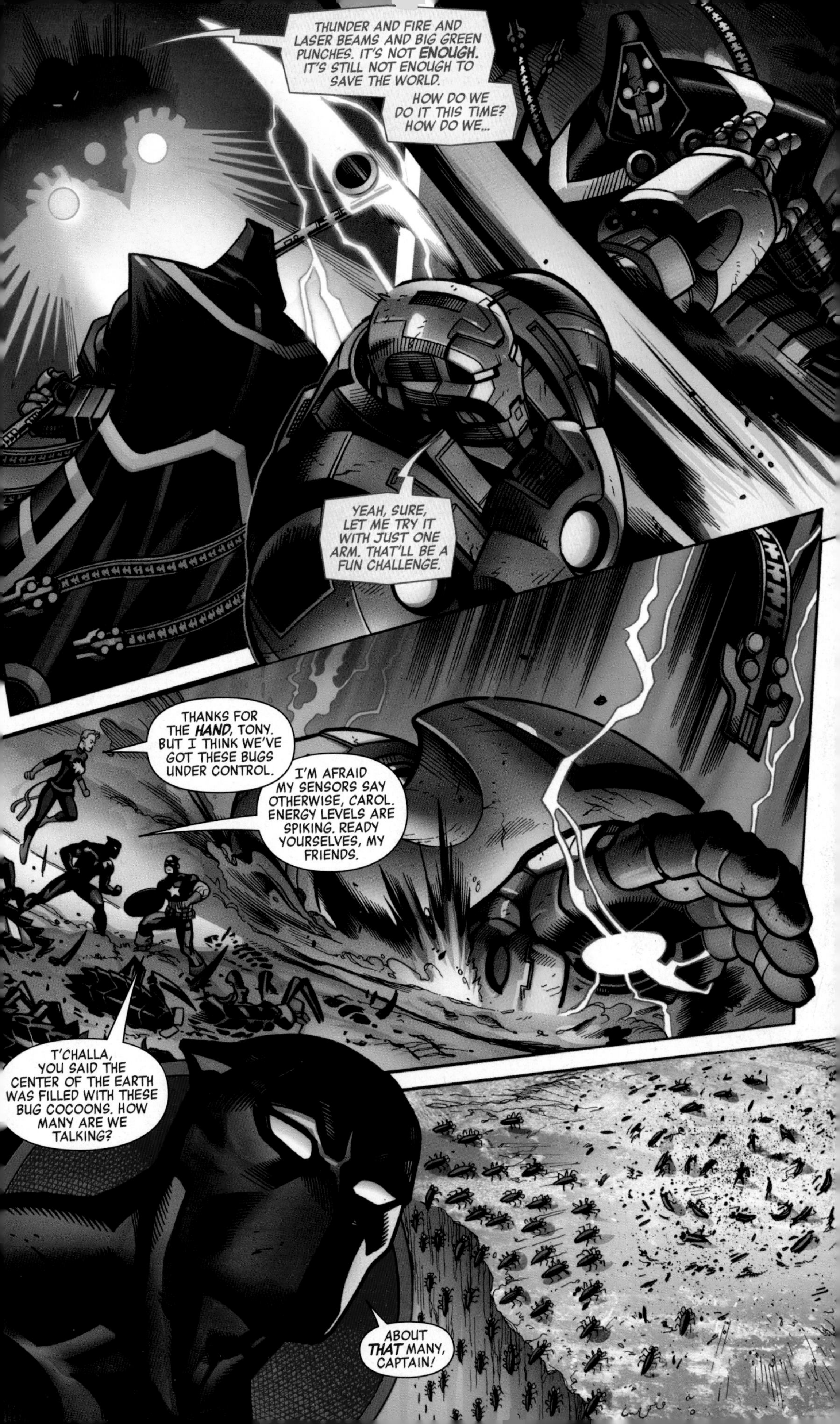
THUNDER AND FIRE AND LASER BEAMS AND BIG GREEN PUNCHES. IT'S NOT **ENOUGH.** IT'S STILL NOT ENOUGH TO SAVE THE WORLD.
HOW DO WE DO IT THIS TIME? HOW DO WE...
YEAH, SURE, LET ME TRY IT WITH JUST ONE ARM. THAT'LL BE A FUN CHALLENGE.
THANKS FOR THE ***HAND***, TONY. BUT I THINK WE'VE GOT THESE BUGS UNDER CONTROL.
I'M AFRAID MY SENSORS SAY OTHERWISE, CAROL. ENERGY LEVELS ARE SPIKING. READY YOURSELVES, MY FRIENDS.
T'CHALLA, YOU SAID THE CENTER OF THE EARTH WAS FILLED WITH THESE BUG COCOONS. HOW MANY ARE WE TALKING?
ABOUT ***THAT*** MANY, CAPTAIN!

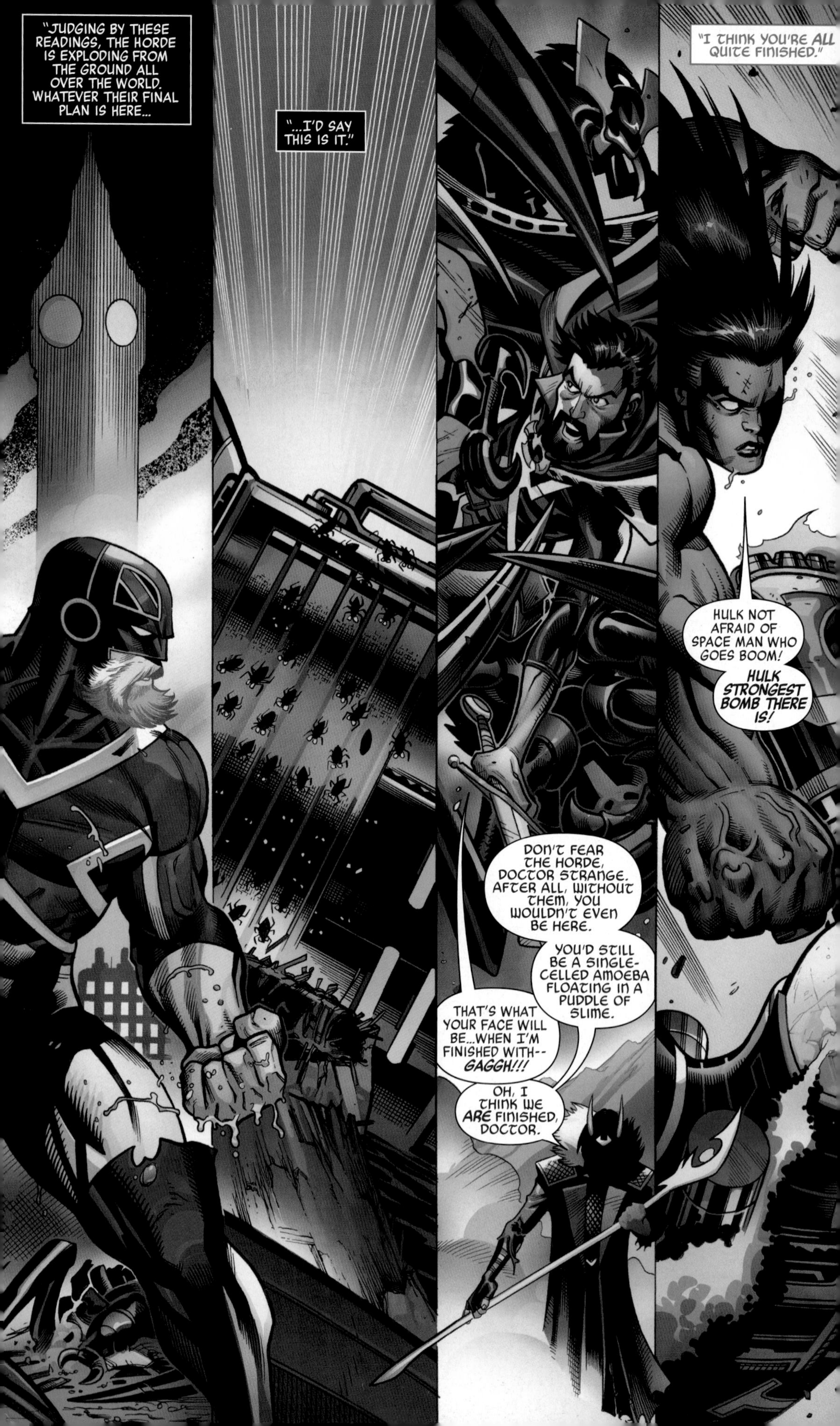
"JUDGING BY THESE READINGS, THE HORDE IS EXPLODING FROM THE GROUND ALL OVER THE WORLD. WHATEVER THEIR FINAL PLAN IS HERE...
"...I'D SAY THIS IS IT."
DON'T FEAR THE HORDE, DOCTOR STRANGE. AFTER ALL, WITHOUT THEM, YOU WOULDN'T EVEN BE HERE.
YOU'D STILL BE A SINGLE-CELLED AMOEBA FLOATING IN A PUDDLE OF SLIME.
THAT'S WHAT YOUR FACE WILL BE...WHEN I'M FINISHED WITH-- GAGGH!!!
OH, I THINK WE ARE FINISHED, DOCTOR.
"I THINK YOU'RE ALL QUITE FINISHED."
HULK NOT AFRAID OF SPACE MAN WHO GOES BOOM!
HULK STRONGEST BOMB THERE IS!

BOOOOM
HE VOMITS FLAMING BUGS! GAGGH, I CAN'T... I CAN'T DEAL WITH THIS!
GUARDIAN OF THE NEXUS OF ALL REALITIES IS HOWLING. BLOODY OFFERING BEING MADE TO THE FIST OF KHONSHU. THE STARBRAND ROARING.
EYES WATCHING FROM BEYOND THE RAW VOID BETWEEN DIMENSIONS. NIGHT AND NUCLEAR DECAY AND ALL THE COLORS OF RAGE. I SEE...EVERYTHING NOW. I...
I THINK MY BRAIN IS BURNING.
TO HELL WITH IT. I'LL FLY THIS GUY INTO SPACE AND BLOW THE WHOLE SUIT.
DON'T BE A FOOL, TONY!
I'M NOT, STEVE. I'M BEING AN AVENGER. IF WE TAKE OUT ONE, MAYBE THE OTHERS WILL TURN TAIL AND...
HEY, WHOA, WHAT'S...

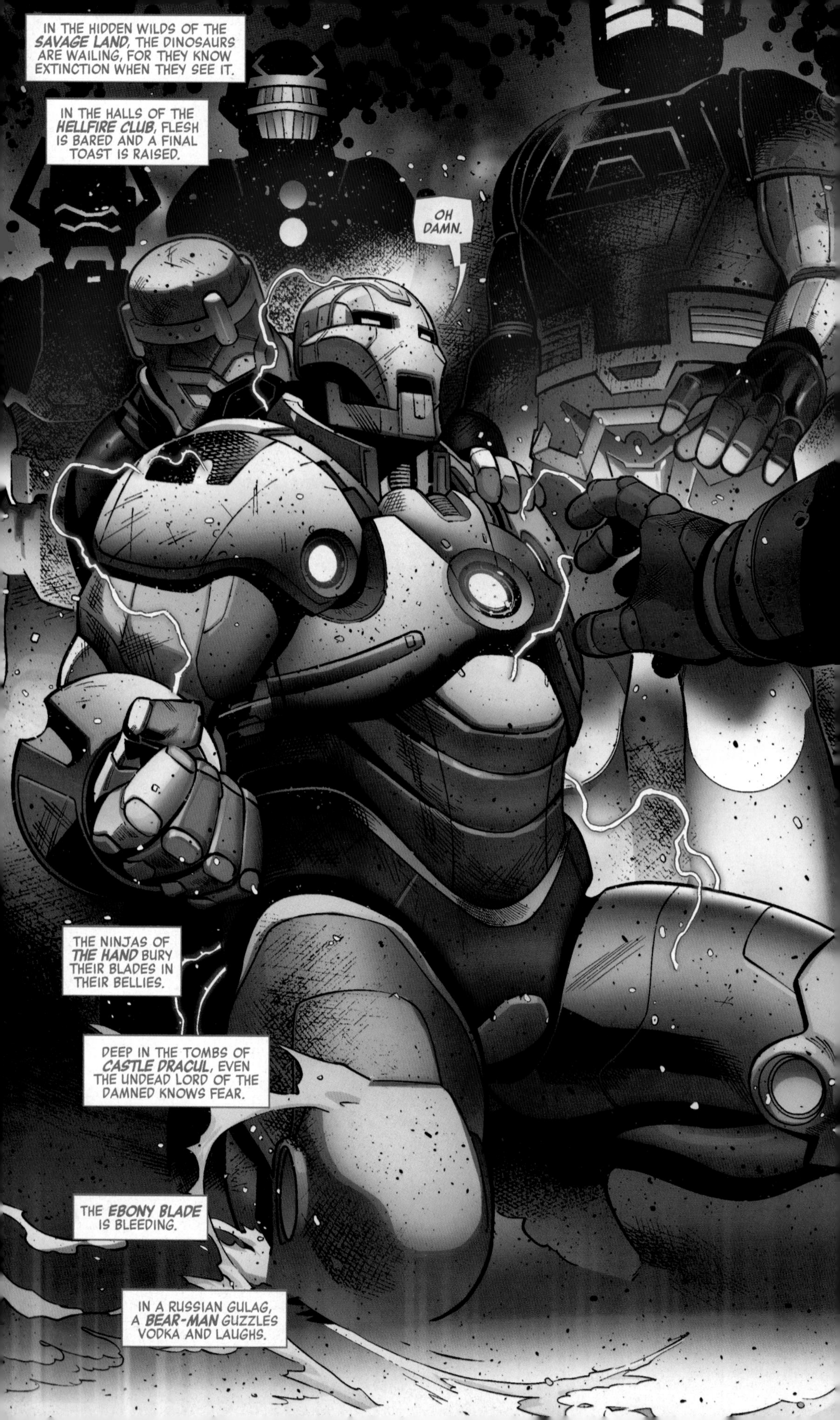
IN THE HIDDEN WILDS OF THE SAVAGE LAND, THE DINOSAURS ARE WAILING, FOR THEY KNOW EXTINCTION WHEN THEY SEE IT.
IN THE HALLS OF THE HELLFIRE CLUB, FLESH IS BARED AND A FINAL TOAST IS RAISED.
OH DAMN.
THE NINJAS OF THE HAND BURY THEIR BLADES IN THEIR BELLIES.
DEEP IN THE TOMBS OF CASTLE DRACUL, EVEN THE UNDEAD LORD OF THE DAMNED KNOWS FEAR.
THE EBONY BLADE IS BLEEDING.
IN A RUSSIAN GULAG, A BEAR-MAN GUZZLES VODKA AND LAUGHS.

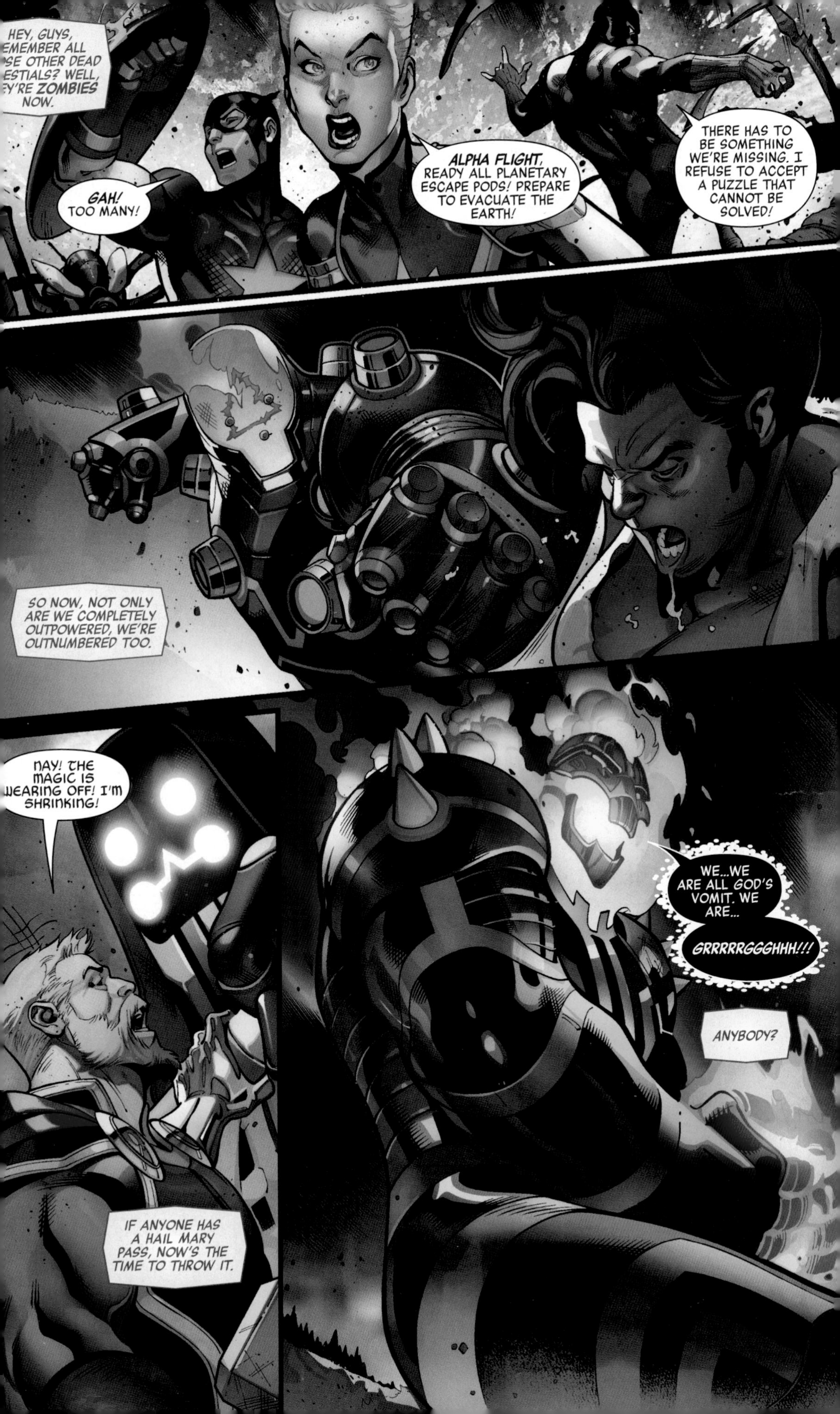
HEY, GUYS, EMEMBER ALL SE OTHER DEAD ESTIALS? WELL, EY'RE ZOMBIES NOW.
GAH! TOO MANY!
ALPHA FLIGHT, READY ALL PLANETARY ESCAPE PODS! PREPARE TO EVACUATE THE EARTH!
THERE HAS TO BE SOMETHING WE'RE MISSING. I REFUSE TO ACCEPT A PUZZLE THAT CANNOT BE SOLVED!
SO NOW, NOT ONLY ARE WE COMPLETELY OUTPOWERED, WE'RE OUTNUMBERED TOO.
NAY! THE MAGIC IS WEARING OFF! I'M SHRINKING!
WE...WE ARE ALL GOD'S VOMIT. WE ARE...
GRRRRRGGGHHH!!!
ANYBODY?
IF ANYONE HAS A HAIL MARY PASS, NOW'S THE TIME TO THROW IT.

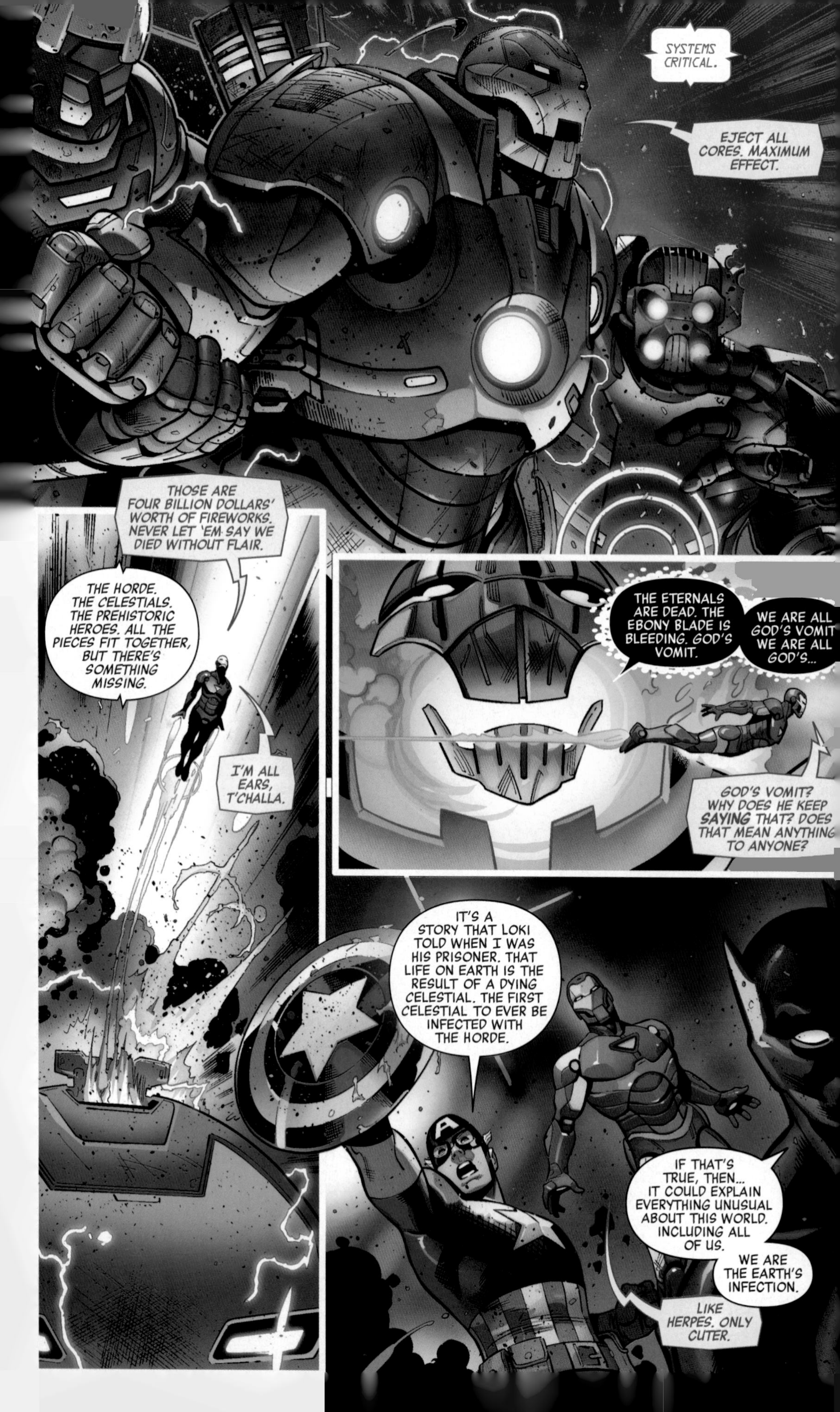
SYSTEMS CRITICAL.
EJECT ALL CORES. MAXIMUM EFFECT.
THOSE ARE FOUR BILLION DOLLARS' WORTH OF FIREWORKS. NEVER LET 'EM SAY WE DIED WITHOUT FLAIR.
THE HORDE. THE CELESTIALS. THE PREHISTORIC HEROES. ALL THE PIECES FIT TOGETHER, BUT THERE'S SOMETHING MISSING.
I'M ALL EARS, T'CHALLA.
THE ETERNALS ARE DEAD. THE EBONY BLADE IS BLEEDING. GOD'S VOMIT.
WE ARE ALL GOD'S VOMIT WE ARE ALL GOD'S...
GOD'S VOMIT? WHY DOES HE KEEP SAYING THAT? DOES THAT MEAN ANYTHING TO ANYONE?
IT'S A STORY THAT LOKI TOLD WHEN I WAS HIS PRISONER. THAT LIFE ON EARTH IS THE RESULT OF A DYING CELESTIAL. THE FIRST CELESTIAL TO EVER BE INFECTED WITH THE HORDE.
IF THAT'S TRUE, THEN... IT COULD EXPLAIN EVERYTHING UNUSUAL ABOUT THIS WORLD. INCLUDING ALL OF US.
WE ARE THE EARTH'S INFECTION.
LIKE HERPES. ONLY CUTER.

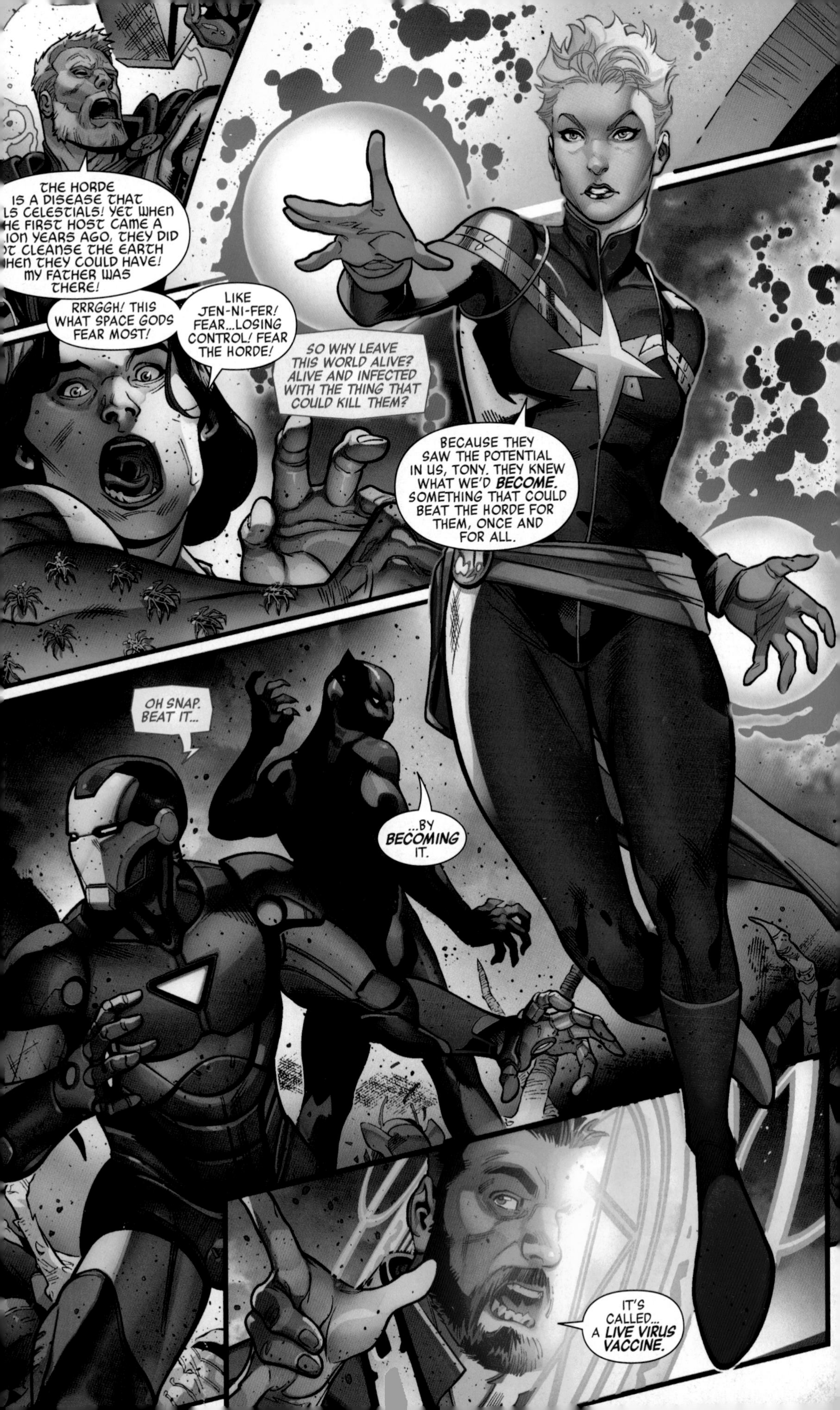
THE HORDE IS A DISEASE THAT LS CELESTIALS! YET WHEN HE FIRST HOST CAME A ION YEARS AGO, THEY DID T CLEANSE THE EARTH HEN THEY COULD HAVE! MY FATHER WAS THERE!
RRRGGH! THIS WHAT SPACE GODS FEAR MOST!
LIKE JEN-NI-FER! FEAR...LOSING CONTROL! FEAR THE HORDE!
SO WHY LEAVE THIS WORLD ALIVE? ALIVE AND INFECTED WITH THE THING THAT COULD KILL THEM?
BECAUSE THEY SAW THE POTENTIAL IN US, TONY. THEY KNEW WHAT WE'D BECOME. SOMETHING THAT COULD BEAT THE HORDE FOR THEM, ONCE AND FOR ALL.
OH SNAP. BEAT IT...
...BY BECOMING IT.
IT'S CALLED... A LIVE VIRUS VACCINE.

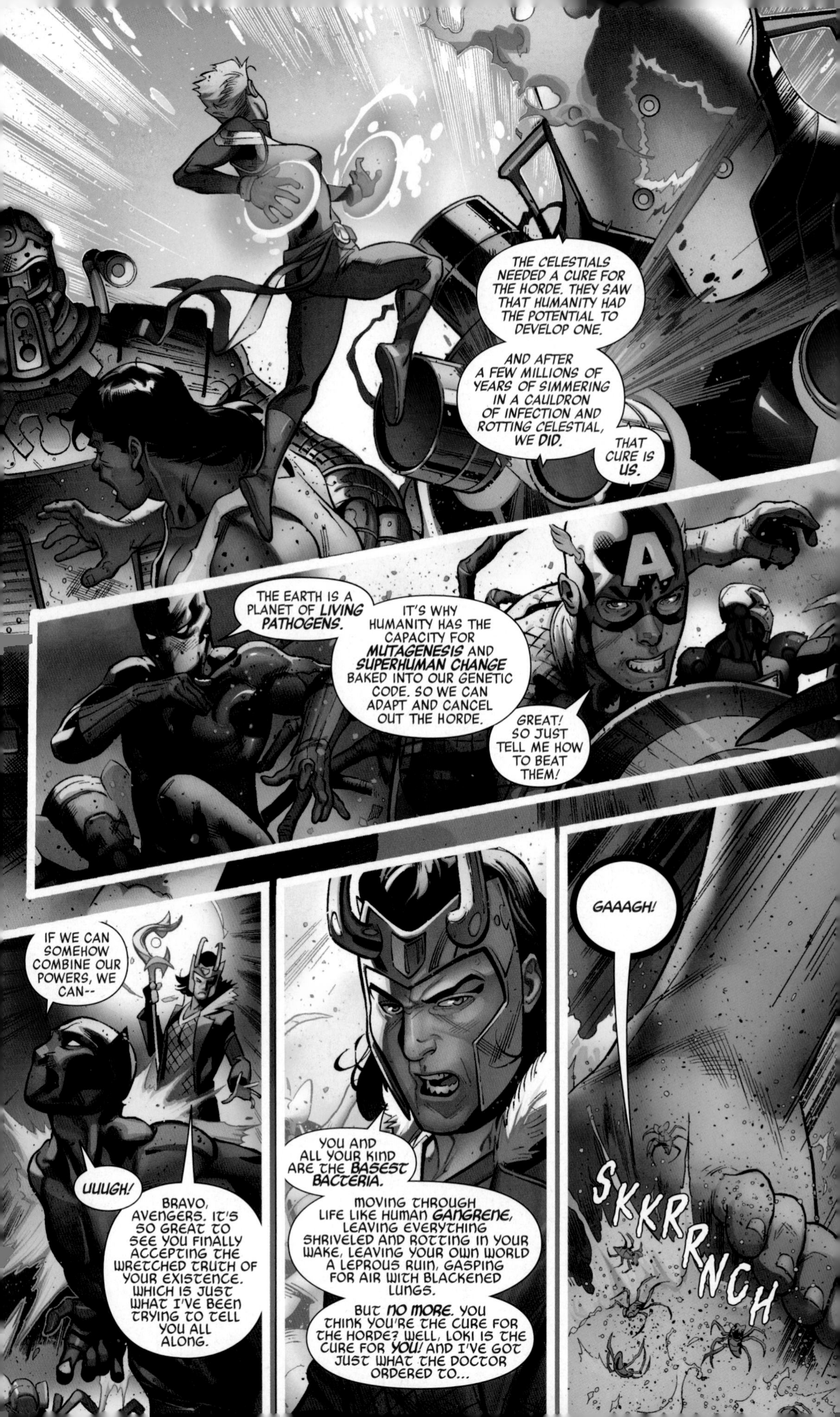
THE CELESTIALS NEEDED A CURE FOR THE HORDE. THEY SAW THAT HUMANITY HAD THE POTENTIAL TO DEVELOP ONE.
AND AFTER A FEW MILLIONS OF YEARS OF SIMMERING IN A CAULDRON OF INFECTION AND ROTTING CELESTIAL, WE DID.
THAT CURE IS US.
THE EARTH IS A PLANET OF LIVING PATHOGENS.
IT'S WHY HUMANITY HAS THE CAPACITY FOR MUTAGENESIS AND SUPERHUMAN CHANGE BAKED INTO OUR GENETIC CODE. SO WE CAN ADAPT AND CANCEL OUT THE HORDE.
GREAT! SO JUST TELL ME HOW TO BEAT THEM!
IF WE CAN SOMEHOW COMBINE OUR POWERS, WE CAN--
UUUGH!
BRAVO, AVENGERS. IT'S SO GREAT TO SEE YOU FINALLY ACCEPTING THE WRETCHED TRUTH OF YOUR EXISTENCE. WHICH IS JUST WHAT I'VE BEEN TRYING TO TELL YOU ALL ALONG.
YOU AND ALL YOUR KIND ARE THE BASEST BACTERIA.
MOVING THROUGH LIFE LIKE HUMAN GANGRENE, LEAVING EVERYTHING SHRIVELED AND ROTTING IN YOUR WAKE, LEAVING YOUR OWN WORLD A LEPROUS RUIN, GASPING FOR AIR WITH BLACKENED LUNGS.
BUT NO MORE. YOU THINK YOU'RE THE CURE FOR THE HORDE? WELL, LOKI IS THE CURE FOR YOU! AND I'VE GOT JUST WHAT THE DOCTOR ORDERED TO...
GAAAGH!
SKKRRNCH

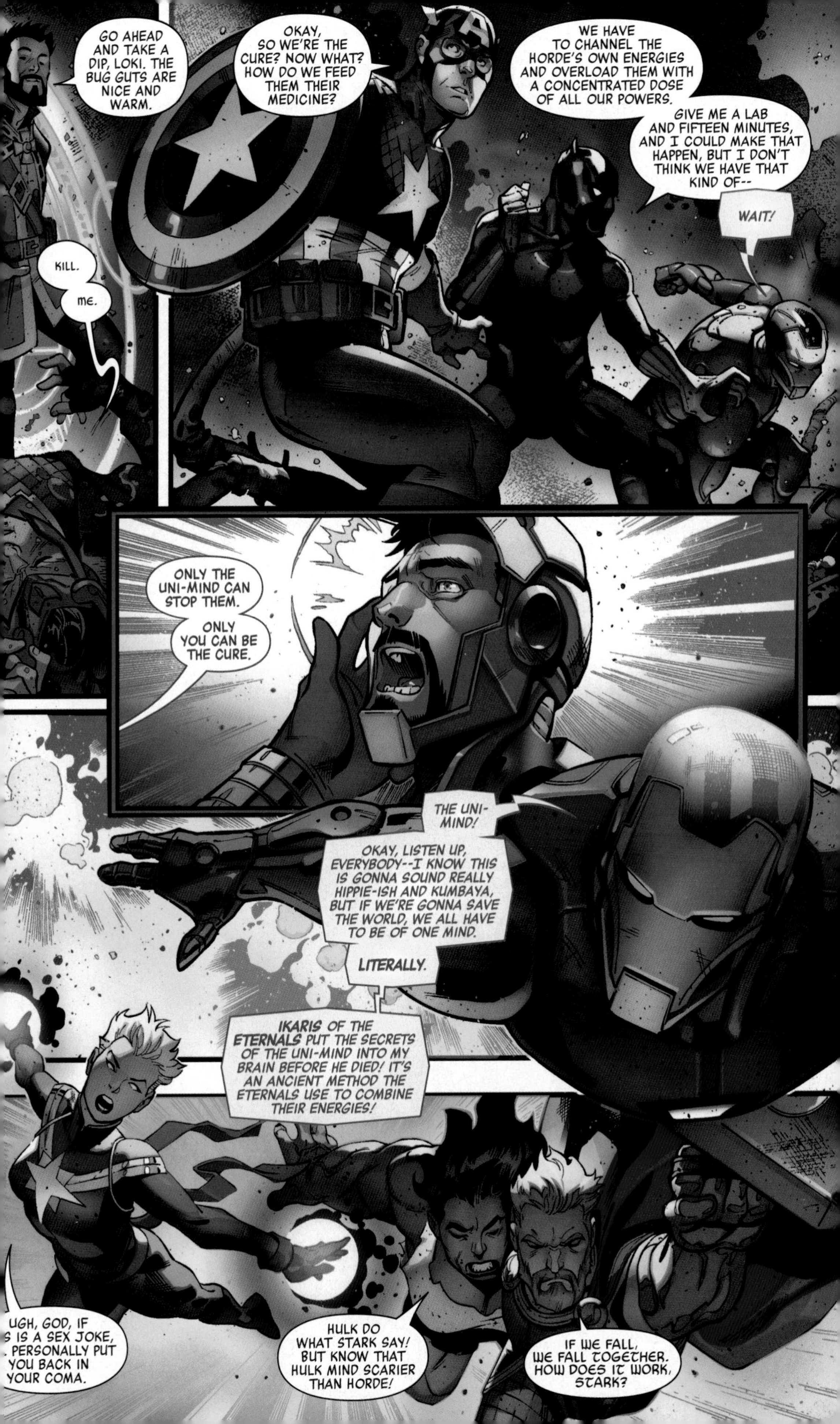
GO AHEAD AND TAKE A DIP, LOKI. THE BUG GUTS ARE NICE AND WARM.
OKAY, SO WE'RE THE CURE? NOW WHAT? HOW DO WE FEED THEM THEIR MEDICINE?
WE HAVE TO CHANNEL THE HORDE'S OWN ENERGIES AND OVERLOAD THEM WITH A CONCENTRATED DOSE OF ALL OUR POWERS.
GIVE ME A LAB AND FIFTEEN MINUTES, AND I COULD MAKE THAT HAPPEN, BUT I DON'T THINK WE HAVE THAT KIND OF--
WAIT!
KILL.
ME.
ONLY THE UNI-MIND CAN STOP THEM.
ONLY YOU CAN BE THE CURE.
THE UNI-MIND!
OKAY, LISTEN UP, EVERYBODY--I KNOW THIS IS GONNA SOUND REALLY HIPPIE-ISH AND KUMBAYA, BUT IF WE'RE GONNA SAVE THE WORLD, WE ALL HAVE TO BE OF ONE MIND.
LITERALLY.
IKARIS OF THE ETERNALS PUT THE SECRETS OF THE UNI-MIND INTO MY BRAIN BEFORE HE DIED! IT'S AN ANCIENT METHOD THE ETERNALS USE TO COMBINE THEIR ENERGIES!
UGH, GOD, IF S IS A SEX JOKE, . PERSONALLY PUT YOU BACK IN YOUR COMA.
HULK DO WHAT STARK SAY! BUT KNOW THAT HULK MIND SCARIER THAN HORDE!
IF WE FALL, WE FALL TOGETHER. HOW DOES IT WORK, STARK?

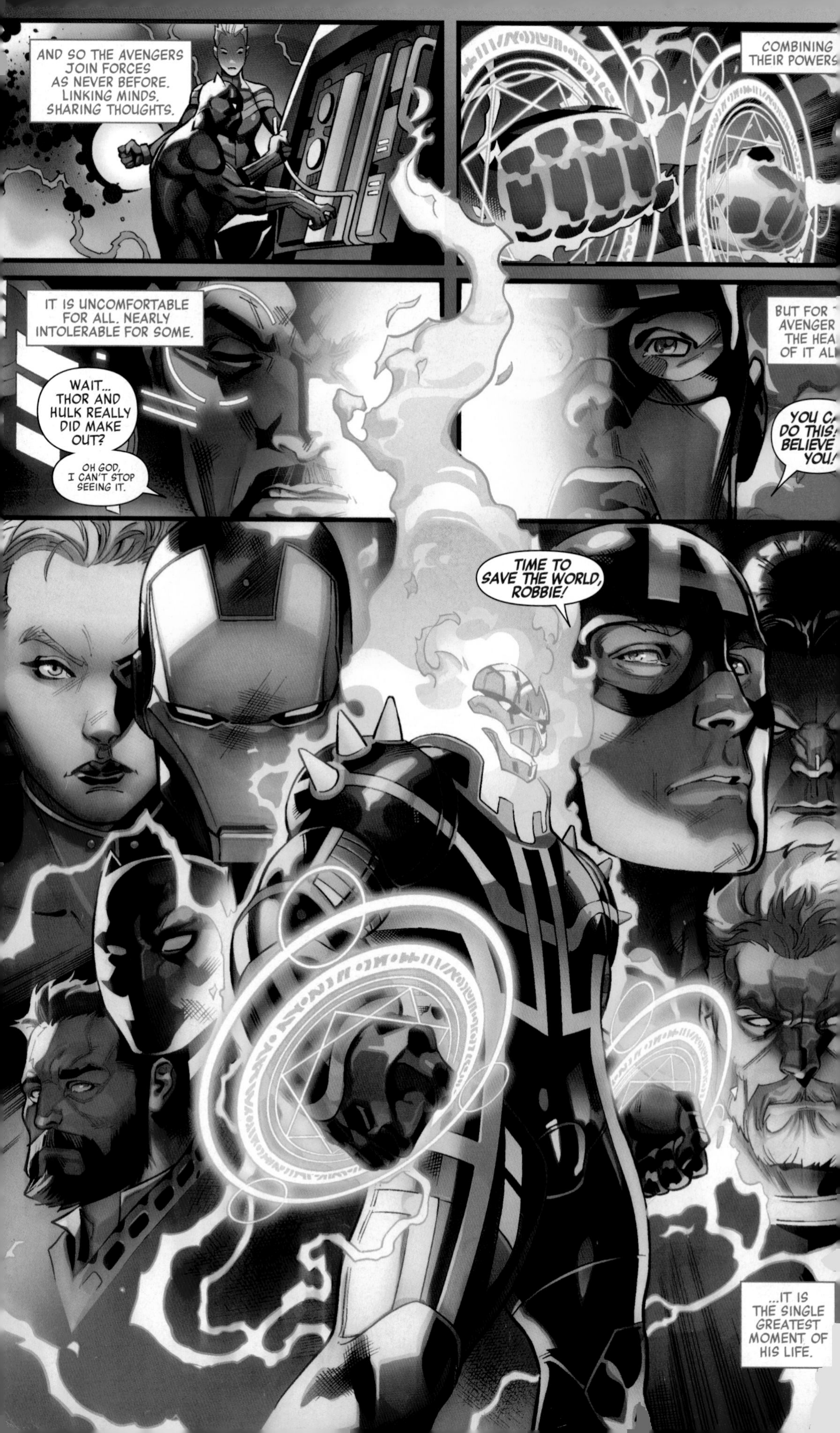
AND SO THE AVENGERS JOIN FORCES AS NEVER BEFORE. LINKING MINDS. SHARING THOUGHTS.
COMBINING THEIR POWERS
IT IS UNCOMFORTABLE FOR ALL. NEARLY INTOLERABLE FOR SOME.
WAIT... THOR AND HULK REALLY DID MAKE OUT?
OH GOD, I CAN'T STOP SEEING IT.
TIME TO SAVE THE WORLD, ROBBIE!
...IT IS THE SINGLE GREATEST MOMENT OF HIS LIFE.

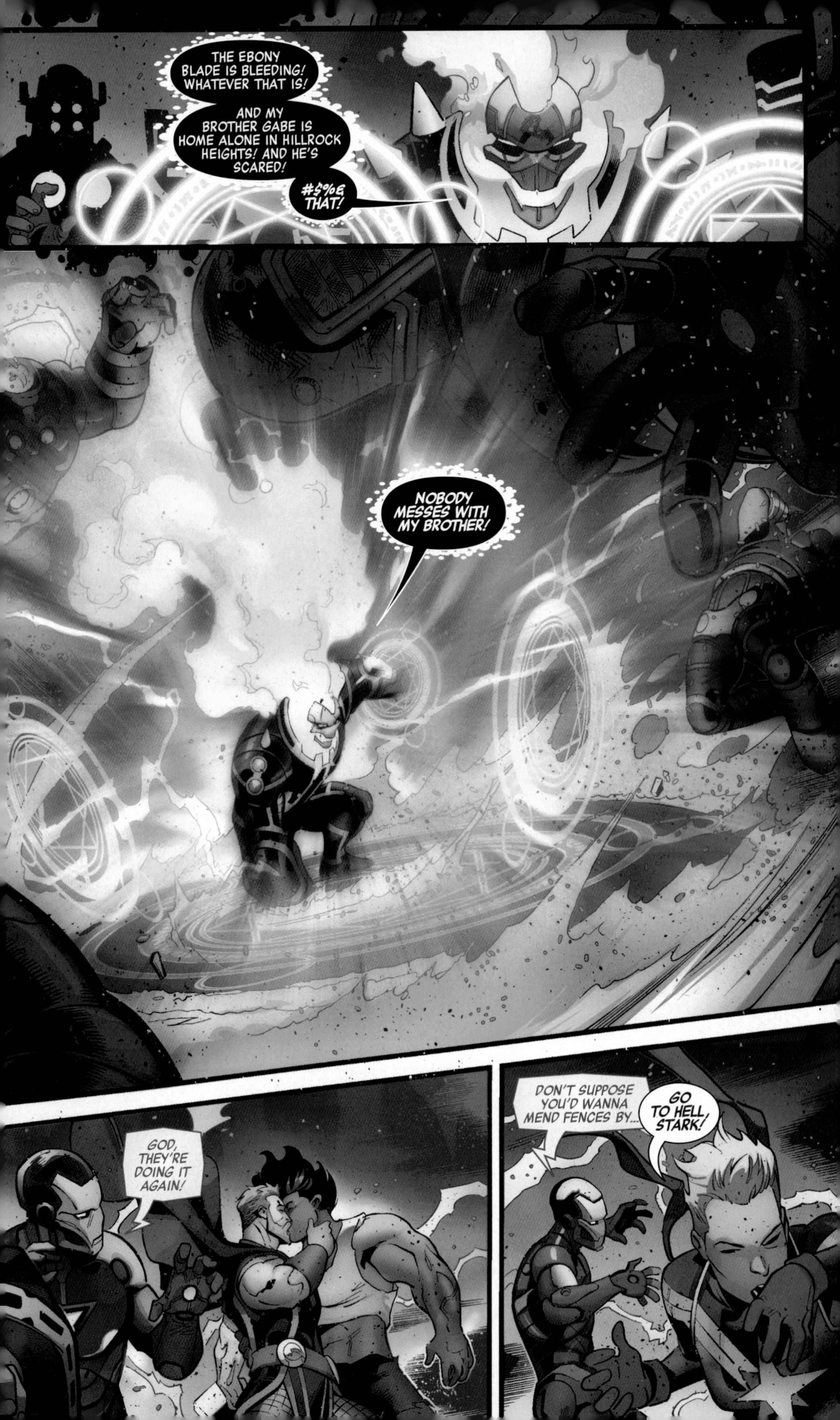
THE EBONY BLADE IS BLEEDING! WHATEVER THAT IS!
AND MY BROTHER GABE IS HOME ALONE IN HILLROCK HEIGHTS! AND HE'S SCARED!
#$%€ THAT!
NOBODY MESSES WITH MY BROTHER!
GOD, THEY'RE DOING IT AGAIN!
DON'T SUPPOSE YOU'D WANNA MEND FENCES BY...
GO TO HELL, STARK!

HA! THAT ACTUALLY WORKED! UNI-MIND FOR THE WIN!

TODAY YOU ALL SHARED THE MIND OF A GOD. YOU ARE WELCOME.

HULK WANT PUKE OUT OWN BRAIN.

UUUGH. I GOT SPAT OUT BY A CELESTIAL.

YOU DID GREAT, GHOST KID. THE HORDE IS DORMANT.

NOT ALL OF IT.

THE BUGS INSIDE THE FINAL HOST ARE TOO FIRMLY ENTRENCHED. THEY'LL HAVE TO BE PULLED OUT BY THE ROOTS.

THIS FIGHT ISN'T OVER.

FOR THIS GUY IT IS.

GOOD LORD, STEPHEN. HOW DO YOU ALWAYS MANAGE TO END UP WITH THE MOST DISGUSTING PART OF THE BATTLE?

IT'S A GIFT.

ALSO, MAGIC IS NINE-TENTHS GROSS THINGS.

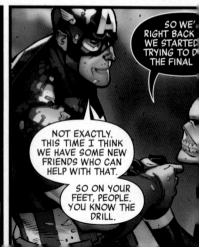

SO WE' RIGHT BACK WE STARTED TRYING TO D THE FINAL

NOT EXACTLY. THIS TIME I THINK WE HAVE SOME NEW FRIENDS WHO CAN HELP WITH THAT.

SO ON YOUR FEET, PEOPLE. YOU KNOW THE DRILL.

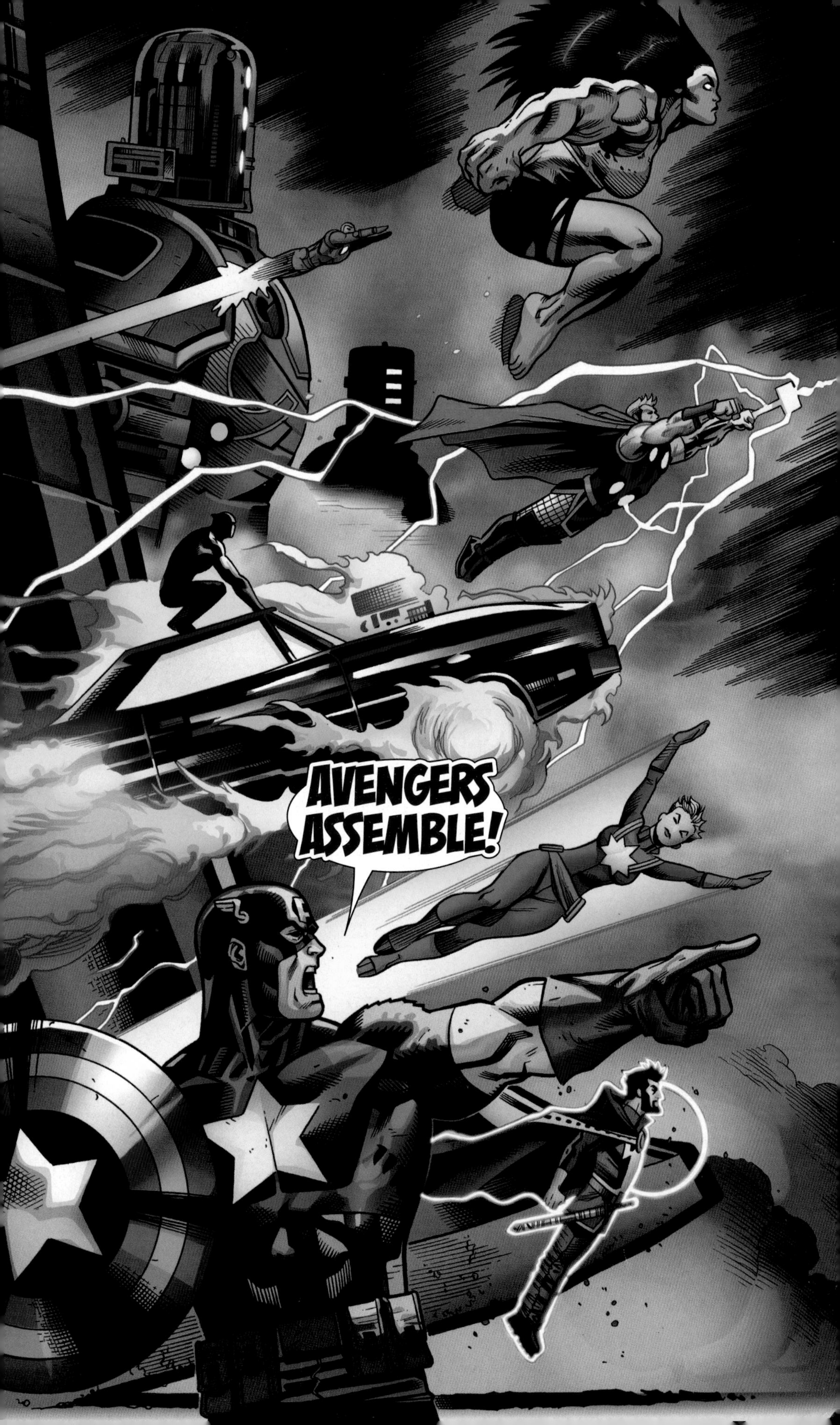
AVENGERS ASSEMBLE!

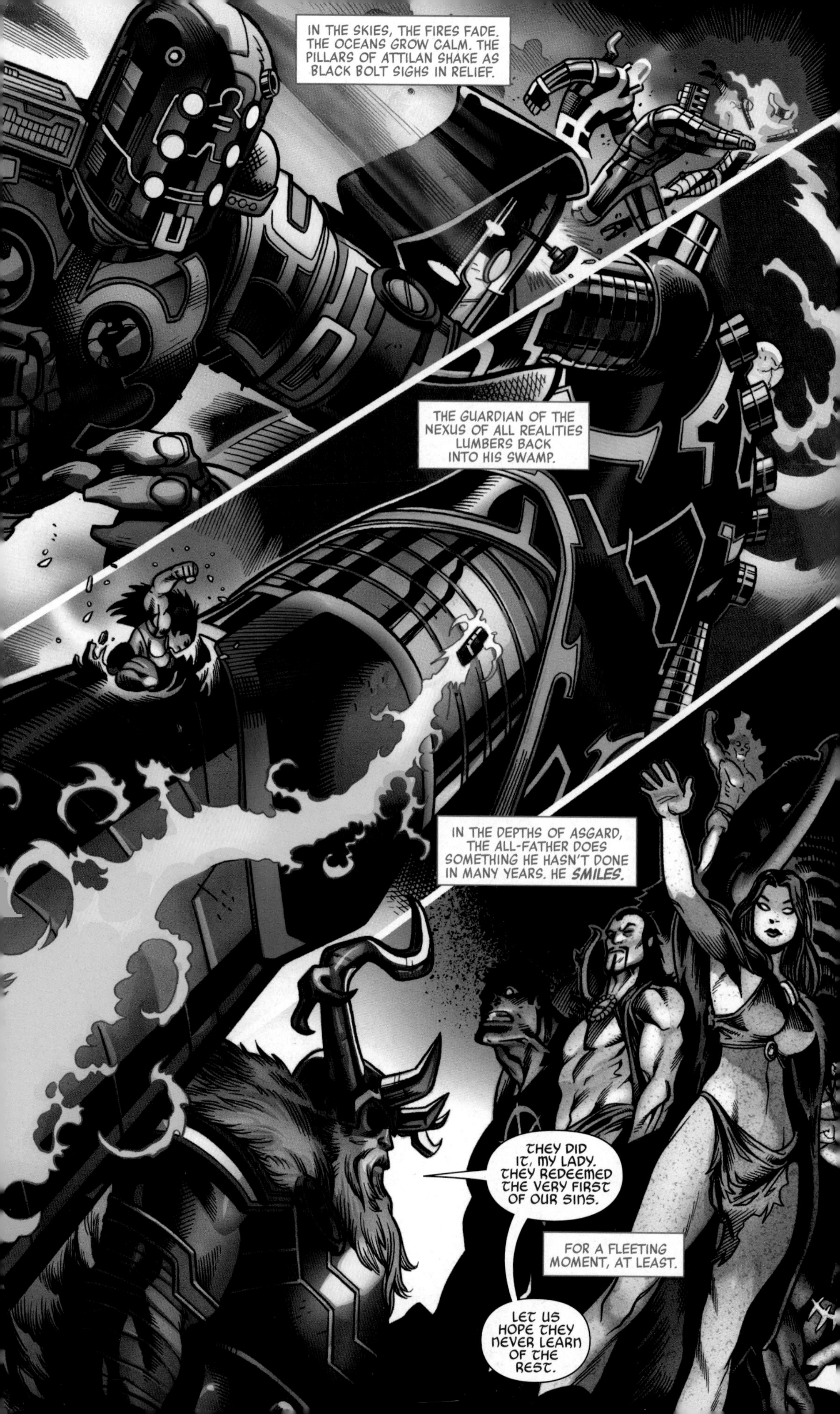
IN THE SKIES, THE FIRES FADE. THE OCEANS GROW CALM. THE PILLARS OF ATTILAN SHAKE AS BLACK BOLT SIGHS IN RELIEF.
THE GUARDIAN OF THE NEXUS OF ALL REALITIES LUMBERS BACK INTO HIS SWAMP.
IN THE DEPTHS OF ASGARD, THE ALL-FATHER DOES SOMETHING HE HASN'T DONE IN MANY YEARS. HE *SMILES.*
THEY DID IT, MY LADY. THEY REDEEMED THE VERY FIRST OF OUR SINS.
FOR A FLEETING MOMENT, AT LEAST.
LET US HOPE THEY NEVER LEARN OF THE REST.

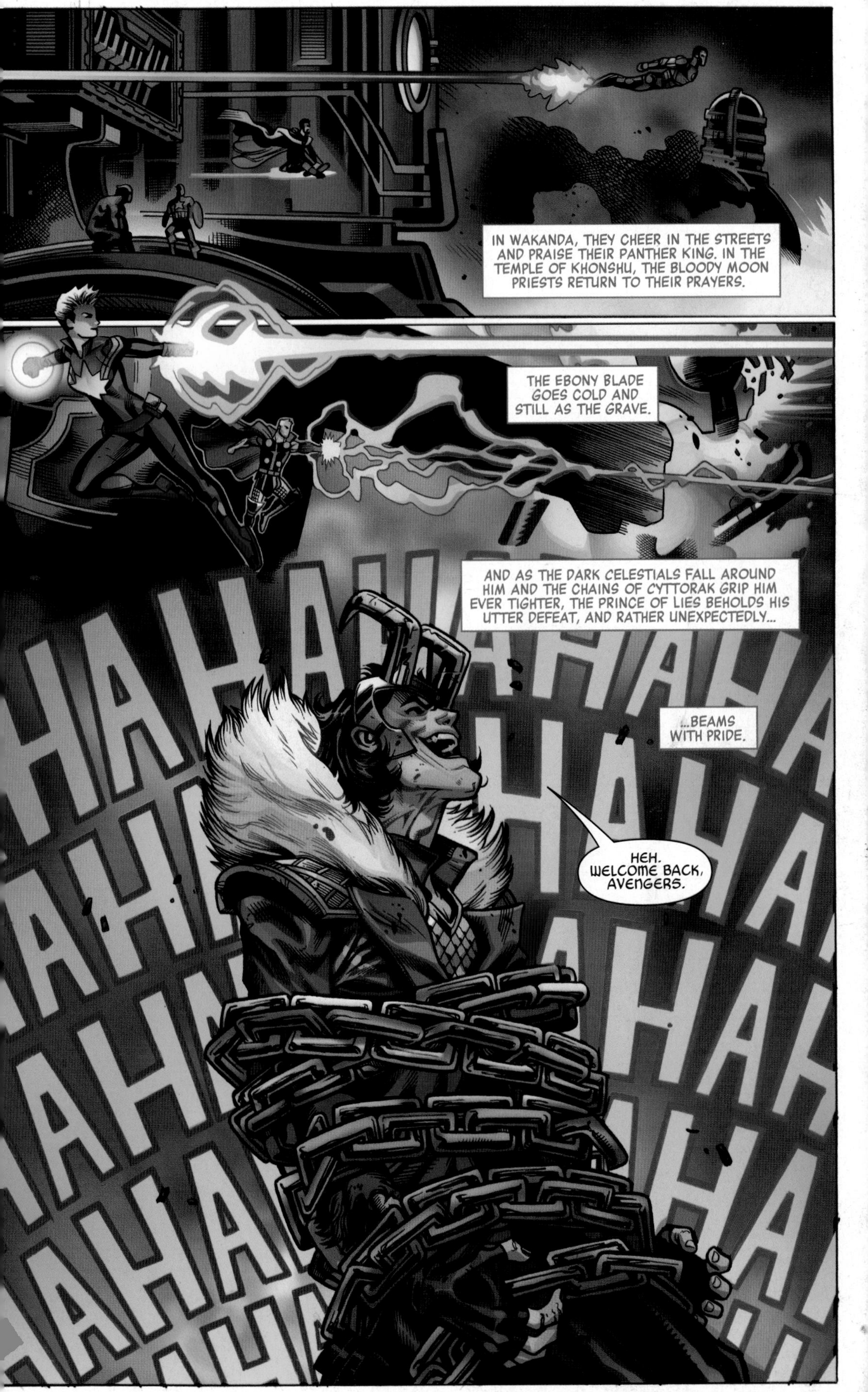
IN WAKANDA, THEY CHEER IN THE STREETS AND PRAISE THEIR PANTHER KING. IN THE TEMPLE OF KHONSHU, THE BLOODY MOON PRIESTS RETURN TO THEIR PRAYERS.
THE EBONY BLADE GOES COLD AND STILL AS THE GRAVE.
AND AS THE DARK CELESTIALS FALL AROUND HIM AND THE CHAINS OF CYTTORAK GRIP HIM EVER TIGHTER, THE PRINCE OF LIES BEHOLDS HIS UTTER DEFEAT, AND RATHER UNEXPECTEDLY...
...BEAMS WITH PRIDE.
HEH. WELCOME BACK, AVENGERS.
HAHAHAHAHA

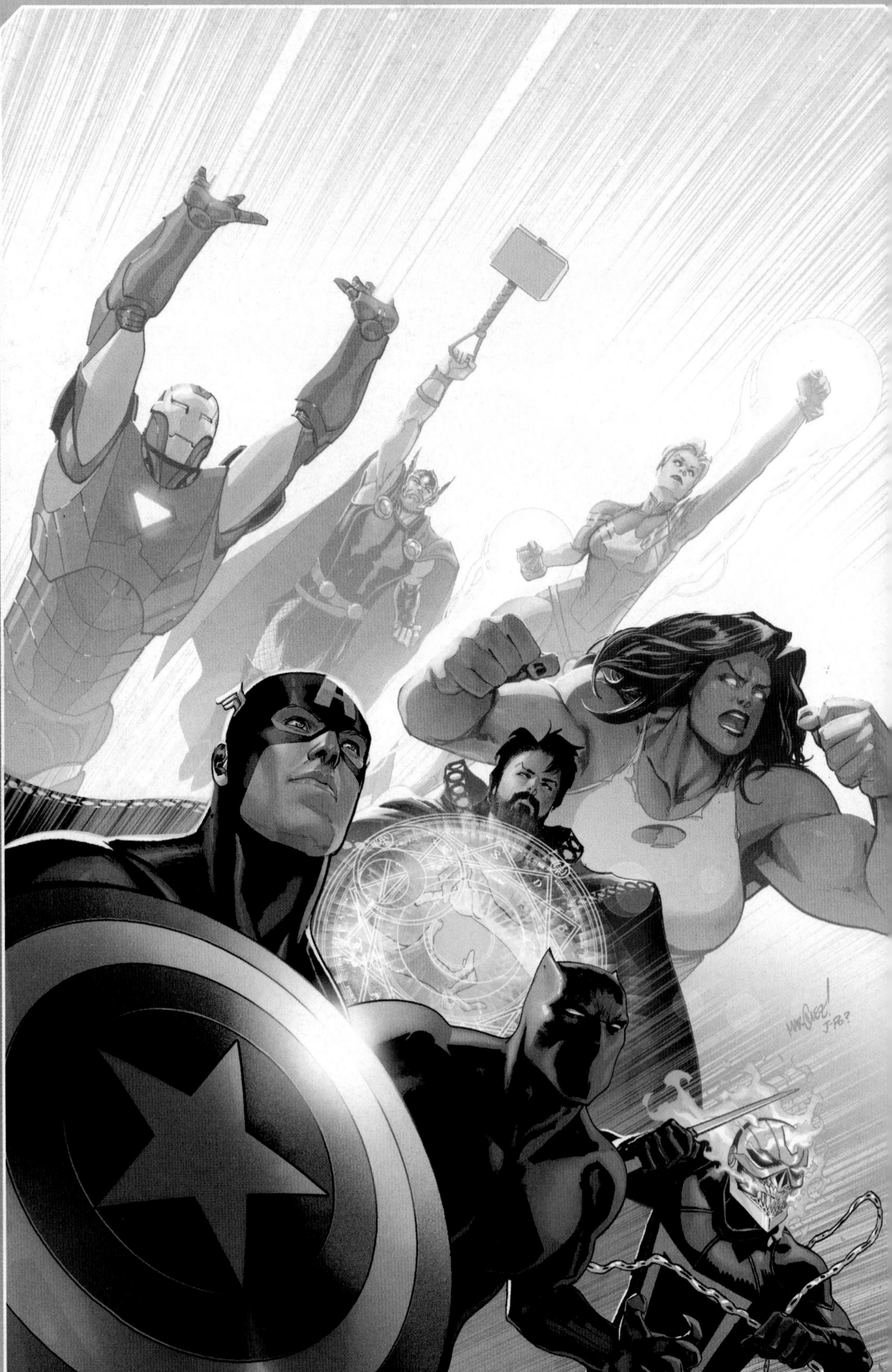
MARQUEZ!
J-P0?

DAVID MARQUEZ & JUSTIN PONSOR
2 VARIANT COVER

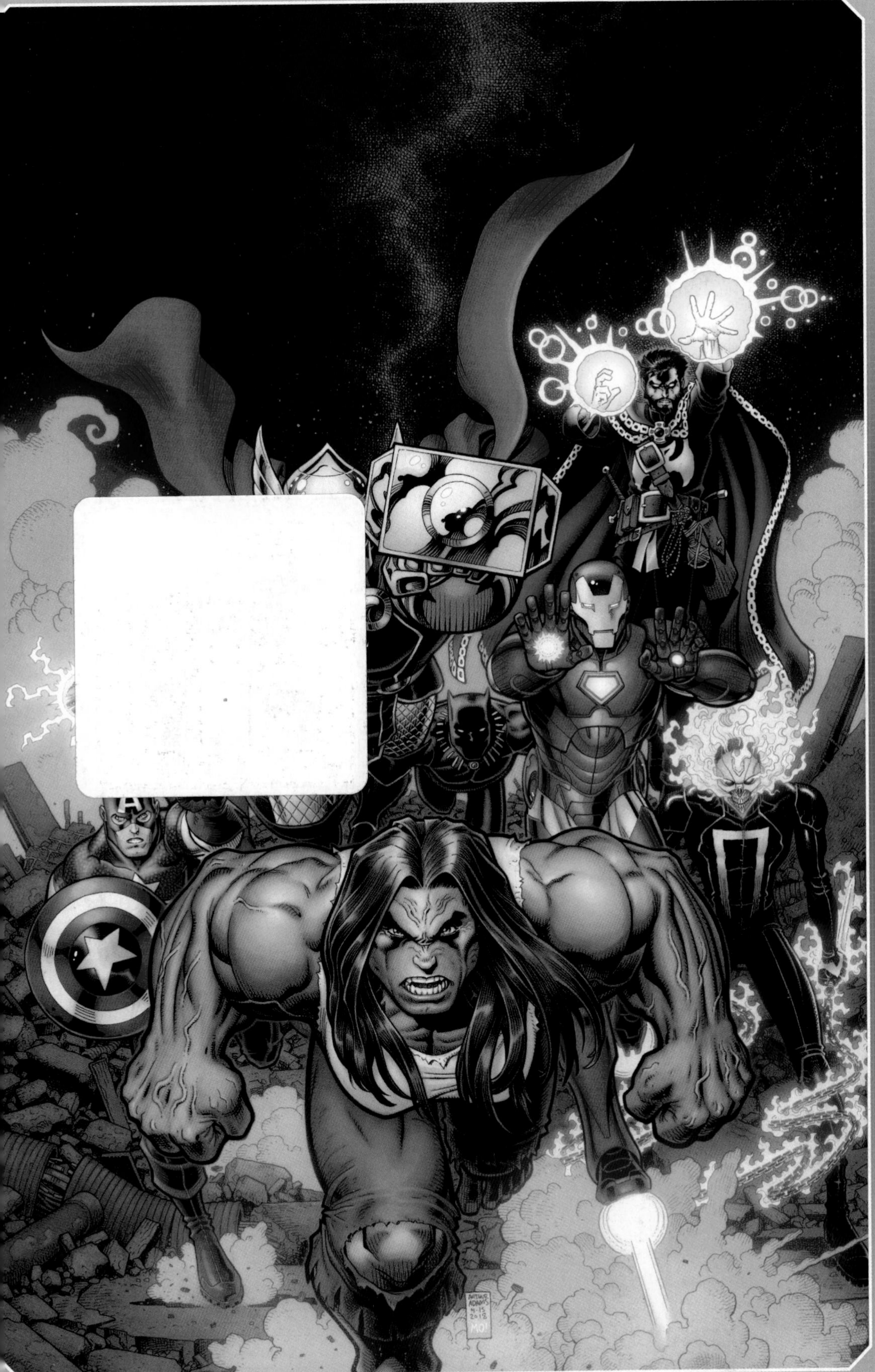

ARTHUR ADAMS & MORRY HOLLOWELL
3 VARIANT COVER

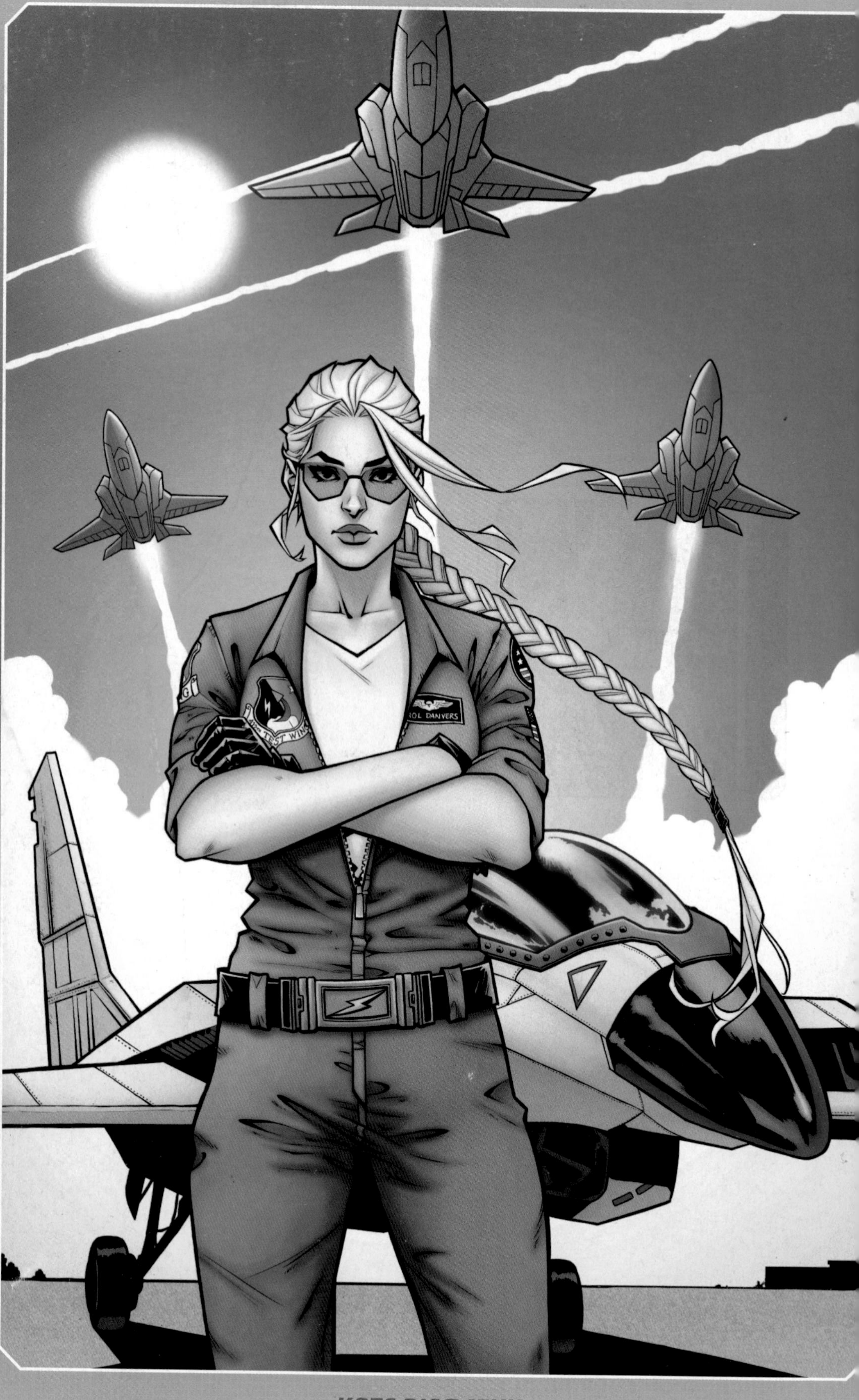

KATE NIEMCZYK
4 CAROL DANVERS 50TH ANNIVERSARY VARIANT COVER